Salesforce1 Platform API Services Guide

Version 1
November 2013

Salesforce1 Platform API Services Guide

Written by Pavi Sandhu, Quinton Wall, Diana Widjaja, and Daniel Yu with contributions by Michael
Alderete, Gavin Austin, Mysti Berry, Jody Bleyle, Caitlin Cronkhite, Leah Cutter, Adam Dennis, Andre
Dorr, Jeff Fitzgerald, Katia Hage, Dave Jacowitz, Mario Korf, Mark Leonard, Ian Livingstone, Terry
Martin, Dale McCrory, Jon Mountjoy, Mike Mullen, Ian Murdock, Ali Sadat, Kim Shain, Jennifer Shipma
Dianne Siebold, Jon Varese, Richard Whitley, and Ben Yoskovitz.

Table of Contents

Preface

Transformation often appears to happen overnight. A blast of creativity out of the clear blue sky that changes everything in the blink of an eye. Almost overnight the era of desktops, and rooms full of servers ended. The cloud transformed everything. Customers were free to innovate again. And now, in the middle of the social and mobile revolution, this transformation has happened again.

But true transformation only occurs when individuals or organizations take their experiences and learnings and apply them to a new medium or focus. Further, every great technical transformation—the automobile, the television, the Macintosh, the iPhone, the cloud, social networking, wearable devices, to name a few— put the customer first. How could the customer benefit from this technology? How would it change their work or personal lives? That customer-centric passion drives all great transformations. The Salesforce1 Platform is such a transformation.

For over 14 years salesforce.com has been a customer company. Our apps, including Sales Cloud, Service Cloud, Marketing Cloud, and Chatter have won numerous awards and proven the potential of multi-tenancy, the cloud, and the fundamental importance of trust. Our apps help our customers grow their business.

Every customer is unique. They have unique needs that require technology that supports these needs. Behind every app is an incredible, powerful platform for business users, sales people, marketers, ISVs, and developers to customize, extend, and create entirely new apps faster than ever. The platform has always been a customer platform. Customers could innovate and create their own apps.

Salesforce1 takes this customer platform and transforms it for today's most demanding customers and businesses, and does it mobile-first. Salesforce1 isn't a re-invention. It's a transformation of the same platform that over 100,000 customers trust to run roughly 500,000 apps, which perform more than a billion transactions a day.

So what is Salesforce1? Perhaps surprisingly, it started as a philosophy. Since its earliest days, salesforce.com has focused on delivering incredible customer experience by providing a great product without the need to install complicated software, or manage expensive hardware. To achieve this goal, salesforce.com leveraged the cloud to deliver enterprise apps via the browser. The user experience, and for the most part, engineering effort, was driven by this simple notion. Priority was given to how a customer would point, click, and interact from their desktop or laptop. Over the years, API integrations–systems connecting to Salesforce–have steadily grown to roughly half of the transactions performed on the platform on a daily basis. Salesforce became a system of innovation, allowing customer to create new apps and processes atop existing back office and legacy systems.

The incredible adoption of mobile devices in both our personal and professional lives changed everything. The browser is no longer the lingua franca for how users interact with systems and apps. Customers spend more time on mobile phones and tablets that ever before. They work in micro-moments checking email between meetings, scanning news feeds while waiting in the line for lunch, doing banking on the train, or tapping a button to request a cab that instantly knows who they are, and where they're located. This fundamental re-imagining of how customers work and live required a transformation in how salesforce.com–its apps, services, platform, and culture–delivered the benefits our customers need to be successful in today's business. The culmination of this transformation, and the philosophy of mobile and API-first is Salesforce1.

Transformation often appears to happen overnight, and for our customers, for you, we sincerely hope you see it this way. Salesforce1 is your platform. And, from everyone at salesforce.com, we hope you love it.

About this Book

This book provides a comprehensive tour of all the APIs in the Salesforce1 Platform. It's organized into the following parts.

- **Introduction** — overview of the Salesforce1 Platform and its key components: Force.com, Heroku, and ExactTarget Fuel
- **Force.com** — APIs and development tools for Force.com
- **Collaboration** — Chatter REST API and GoInstant API
- **Mobile** — Mobile SDK, including all the developer tools for HTML5, iOS, and Android
- **Marketing Cloud** — APIs for ExactTarget, Radian6, and Pardot
- **Service Cloud** — APIs for Desk.com, Live Agent, Open CTI, and the Console Integration Toolkit

After reading this book, you'll have a solid understanding of the features of the Salesforce1 Platform. Once you're ready to start development, consult the documentation for each individual API for technical details and reference information.

INTRODUCTION

Chapter 1

Introducing the Salesforce1 Platform

Mobile has become the new normal for staying connected in both our personal and professional lives. We follow friends, update status feeds, check in to local businesses, collaborate with colleagues, email suppliers, and much more, all increasingly performed on the go. The successful businesses of the future must embrace this mobile-first world, and the freedom mobile provides to get things done regardless of where you are and what you are doing.

However, until now, mobile apps in the enterprise have often lagged behind their desktop equivalent in functionality, and adoption despite the explosive trend in consumer mobile apps. IT departments have typically not had the expertise in house, and must allocate precious technical resources to keep pace with the demands of the current backlog of projects. When they have delivered custom mobile apps, development cycles have been long, complicated, expensive, and failed to engage the user in the same way today's leading consumer-based apps have.

Salesforce1 solves the problem of lack of mobile specialists and lagging innovation with a revolutionary approach to app development for the social and mobile-first world. It delivers breakthrough productivity for all users by putting the customer—employees, partners, consumers, and devices—at the center of everything, and making every employee a mobile developer. The result is an insanely fast, hyper-connected mobile solution with the potential to be as disruptive as Software as a Service. It's time to build the future today!

The Salesforce1 Platform gives organizations the freedom to innovate. Designed for scale, it provides open APIs for extensibility and integration as well as powerful developer tools; there's no limit to what developers can build. The Salesforce1 Platform's flexible development models enable every administrator or developer to create custom apps with a unique, yet familiar, mobile user experience and powered by mobile back-end services.

Features of Salesforce1

Salesforce1 is a mobile app development platform for everyone. It allows incredible freedom for ISVs, developers, administrators, and every user to innovate. This revolutionary approach to unlocking mobile app development for organizations is built for today's needs: mobile, and social solutions, delivered in days, and weeks! Apps, driven by metadata, intelligently provide context to the user experience, delivering information based mobile device features: responsive design, address fields are plotted on maps, and phone numbers can be dialed with a simple tap, feed-centric workflows, and much more.

Business users and adminstrators can develop apps with clicks, not code, complete with powerful workflows rules, approval processes, databases, and dynamic interfaces user interfaces. Unlike other solutions where business users often created independent applications that IT had little visibility over security, or reliability, Salesforce1 provides administrators the tools with centrally manage and govern apps without limiting the businesses need to innovate.

Designed for massive scale, open APIs for extensibilty and integration, and powerful developer tools, there is no limit to what developers and ISVs can build on the platform. Salesforce1's flexibile development models enable every user to create custom apps backed by mobile backend services and a unique, yet familar, mobile user experience. ISVs developing on Salesforce1 can develop apps that take advantange of advanced packaged and version management controls, complete enterprise marketplace capabilities with the AppExchange, the world's enterprise app market, and feed-first discovery of their apps within the Salesforce1 platform.

The Salesforce1 Platform brings together Force.com, Heroku, and ExactTarget Fuel into one incredibly powerful family of social, mobile, and cloud services—all built API first. Salesforce1 delivers the following capabilities.

Social Data

The ability to share, follow, collaborate, and take business actions directly on data within Salesforce1 is at the core of the platform. Users can follow records and data with a single tap. They can be notified of changes in real-time, and collaborate directly within the record feed. This feed-based approach to working lets users can focus on what's most important to them.

By treating data as social and as an important participant in business, Salesforce1 allows data to share updates, trigger workflows, and be part of the collaboration process with workers, teams, partners, and customers. The result is an unparalleled opportunity to create new business apps and processes for business productivity.

Declarative and Programmatic Development

IT departments have struggled to keep pace with the level of change required for businesses to remain competitive. Too often, IT is resource-constrained because they must manage existing on-premise systems while at the same time recruit and retain professional developers, especially those with mobile application development experience.

Salesforce1 solves the problem of speed to delivery by providing intuitive drag-and-drop tools for storing and working with data, defining cloud-based logic with workflows, creating approval processes and formulas, and creating mobile-ready apps.

Professional developers can use the most popular open-source languages, tools, and standards to build completely custom apps and user interfaces. Unlike other platforms, Salesforce1 delivers a unique experience where developers and administrators create apps on the same platform eliminating the effort required to build complicated integration solutions.

Action-Based App Model

Salesforce1 puts the customer at the center of the development process. Rather than require complicated development cycles, apps can be declared through actions: create an order, set a delivery date, select a route, and so on. Administrators can define default values for actions to streamline apps down to the click of a mouse or swipe of the finger.

Actions defined via the desktop are instantly available in context-sensitive menus on mobile devices. And, for developers building integrations with Salesforce1, actions are automatically enabled with RESTful endpoints capable of accepting either XML or JSON data envelopes.

Connect to Everything with Open APIs

Salesforce provides the connectivity and flexibility to create apps that connect to everything using efficient and scalable APIs that perform over 1.3 billion transactions a day. Every object or data entity is instantly REST-enabled.

Our APIs include access to bulk APIs for data loading, social APIs for ubiquitous collaboration anywhere, cutting-edge streaming APIs to support push notification integrations, and metadata APIs that describe every aspect of your app and business such as permissions, data access policies, field types, and user experience.

To date, developers have built more than 500,000 apps on the platform. These apps connect to existing back-end systems, cloud platforms including Google, Facebook, and Twitter, and, in ever-increasing numbers, consumer devices such as fridges, cars, vending machines, and much more.

Trusted Identity

Today's IT landscape consists of on-premises systems, internal processes, cloud providers, social networks, and mobile devices. The ability to have a single, simple identity to span these technology and business silos is a fundamental ingredient for business success and velocity for change. With over 7 billion logins a year, Salesforce1 provides a trusted identity hub that reaches beyond perimeter-based identity management solutions and leverages the social data and multi-tenant core of the platform.

Organizations can build solutions that leverage standards such as:

- SAML and delegated authentication to authenticate with on-premises systems
- OAuth for connecting to social and cloud platforms
- Connected app policies for app providers to connect to Salesforce as a trusted identity provider

Further, Salesforce1 supports easy-to-use, centralized policy-management tools for controlling record visibility across organizational units and disparate systems regardless of location.

Key Business Use Cases

The Salesforce1 Platform is designed to deliver a customer benefit behind every app. It is API and mobile first, where every aspect can be extended, and customized by every user regardless of whether they work within lines of business, IT, or looking to build an entire company and product. And every app is instantly mobile.

From an engineering perspective, Salesforce1 as a philosophy means:

- Every new feature must be designed for mobile first, and have an API for developers.
- User interfaces should be responsive and change dynamically depending on whether the app is running on a smartphone, tablet, or laptop.
- The user experience should change depending on device features. Address fields should leverage geo-location and provide maps, nearby information, and context. You should be able to click on a phone number to make a call.
- Apps should be personal. Your identity should drive the user interface by interacting with calendars, personal preferences, and usage history.
- The entire platform should grow with your needs, constantly delivering customer benefit for every app, and every action.

Salesforce1 is a transformation, not a re-invention. We have invested years of effort in to provide exactly what you expect from Salesforce—scale, trust, no software or hardware, and painless upgrades. If you're an existing customer with data, applications, custom logic or user interfaces built on Salesforce, this investment is now instantly mobile-aware. Tomorrow's leading businesses are those companies that get to the future first. Customers should not spend months or years building mobile apps. Salesforce1 delivers this mobile-first future now.

Salesforce1 is an enabler for business success. Developing with the Salesforce1 Platform is about delivering apps that customers benefit from. The following sections describe the most common scenarios customers request to deliver the apps their employees, customers, and partners will love. Each scenario describes intended customer benefits, a high level depiction of app architecture, and references to the recommended APIs and design strategies for success. Readers should use this section by starting with the question "What benefit to my customer/end user will this app provide, and how do I build it?"

Customize Existing Salesforce Apps and Make Them Mobile

Motivation

Many current Salesforce customers have existing apps and processes developed in Salesforce1. Salesforce1 may be used to access all of this information instantly–no development required.

Strategy

Salesforce app development typically falls into two categories: those created with declarative tools that use the traditional Salesforce web interface, and those created with custom user interfaces and programmatic technologies, including Apex and Visualforce. Salesforce1 supports the rendering of both types of apps on mobile devices. However, depending on the level of user interface customization, developers may be required to modify Visualforce and Apex pages for optimal user experience. Specific attention should be given to complicated Visualforce pages designed for heavy data manipulation, or graphic-intensive activity. Mobile web page development requires optimizing data traffic and the user interface to make it intuitive for users on smaller screen sizes.

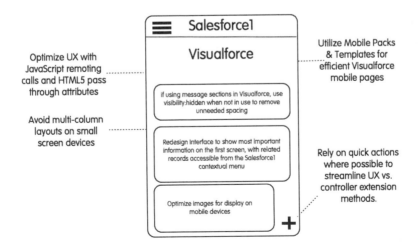

Getting Started

Start by performing an inventory of custom apps, listing out Visualforce pages, and any business processes that take multiple steps/pages to complete. Identify potential candidates for optimization ranked by most frequently used. If there are opportunities to eliminate steps by creating custom actions, prioritize these first.

Next, look for performance optimizations that do no require significant re-coding. Modern browsers such as Safari, Firefox, and Chrome include tools where developers can view the relative size and duration of http requests for pages. Example quick change candidates may be large image file size, and modifying pages to use server-side view state (new in Winter '14), and non-optimized Javascript libraries (look for Javascript libraries ending with '-min' for compressed versions).

Orchestrate Relevant and Targeted Multi-Channel Marketing Campaigns

Motivation

Your customers are inundated with messages of all types—email in the inbox, printed material in the mailbox, billboards on highways, SMS and push messages on mobile devices. To be effective, your marketing campaigns have to stand out, to be highly-targeted and relevant. Highly-targeted, relevant communication is as much a technology problem as it is a marketer's dilemma—the most successful marketing campaigns involve highly sophisticated interactions across multiple channels driven by data from multiple data sources tied to precise audience segments, delivering just the right message at just the right moment.

Strategy

Customers interact with your business through dozens of sources: web, mobile, social networks, and much more. In order to effectively target customers it is critical to be able to synchronize data between systems using a flexible data model and integration strategies without complicated, multi-month IT projects. Just as bad as long, complicated projects are rushed implementations that miss key customer touchpoints.

Successful campaigns rely on targeted, relevant messages. How relevant a message is to a customer relies on the ability to analyze the information obtained through the customer touchpoints. Analysis of this customer information ensures that marketers are able to deliver just the right message at just the right moment.

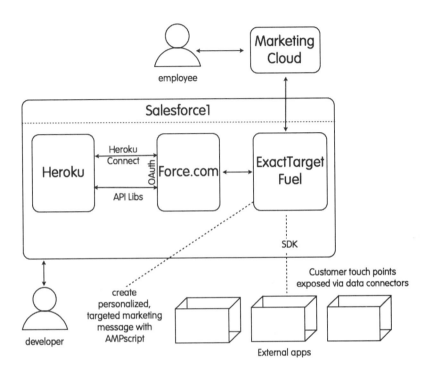

Getting Started

Developers will typically use ExactTarget Fuel to build integrated campaigns. ExactTarget Fuel provides developer SDKs for exposing customer touchpoints as integrations, and configure them via the App Center. Developers famiar with the Connected App model in Force.com should find the ExactTarget App Center very similar: apps which have been authorized and configured to connect with the Salesforce1 Platform.

Create Seamless Interaction Between Customer and Employee Facing Apps

Motivation

Customers engage with your products and brands via social networks, web-sites, and mobile apps. However, many organizations have disconnected systems for customer facing and employee facing apps. The result is complicated integration processes at best, and poor customer experience at worst.

Strategy

Salesforce1 provides easy integration between all aspects of the platform to ensure that organizations have a complete view of their customer. Heroku is designed for consumer scale, and supports the most current development languages used today's most popular apps and websites including Paper, Apple's 2012 app of the year. Force.com is designed for employee apps and working with business data. ExactTarget offers the ability to send targeted messages and marketing campaigns to users. Seamless customer interaction touches all aspects of these products. The Salesforce1 Platform delivers this functionality in an optimized experience for developers, business users, and customers.

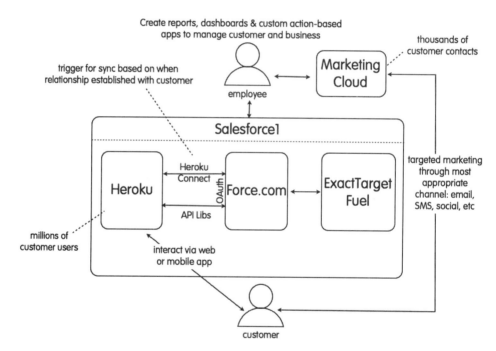

Developers building customer-facing apps should develop their apps on Heroku and configure Heroku Connect, or use language specific open source libraries for API level integration. Typical integrations use an integration user account established in Force.com that manages customer details as contact records rather than a one-to-one mapping of consumer profiles to Force.com accounts. The decoupled approach lets consumer and employee apps scale independently.

With integration users and customer contact strategies established, developers and business users should identify what information should be synchronized between Heroku and Force.com. The driving factor in determining the right data and triggers for synchronization is when a 'relationship' is formed between the customer and businesses product. For example, typical consumer apps display generic information on their web or mobile app until a user registers or expresses interest in a particular product or service. As soon as this relationship is established, customer companies begin to build a customer profile around the user: what are their interests, how can we send targeted marketing messages, keep track of customer contacts such as service tickets, social network interactions, and analysis of trends across all customers to better determine business priorities.

Getting Started

Start with the customer experience. Create a list of relationship touchpoints which can be used to define which data to sync between systems and when. Once established, development teams can work independently on apps for customer and employee-facing needs using the right technology, and scale required (Heroku apps are typically architected in a stateless usage model for consumer scale, whilst Force.com apps are typically architected based on users), and feedback loops established to maintain, or grow the relationship. With the touchpoints and apps created, business users should create reports based on this customer information. From these reports marketers can easily create targeted campaigns using ExactTarget.

Enable Employees to Access Corporate Data from Anywhere

Motivation

The majority of organizations have considerable investment in existing backend systems and custom applications. These systems often perform current functions well, but are difficult and costly to create new apps, especially for mobile. Salesforce1 provides open APIs to connect to existing systems and customer applications allowing customers to create an agile layer for innovation.

Strategy

Existing systems are either located behind corporate firewalls, or in cloud providers. Traditional approaches of integration, such as ETL (Extract, Transform, Load) solve access to data problems, but can create duplicated data silos. Where possible, determine systems of record, often existing systems that are no longer used for new application development, and connect them to Salesforce using the most efficient Salesforce1 API based on the integration requirements. For example, avoid polling-based solutions due to the heavy computational overhead and complex try-retry logic, and utilize the Streaming API instead.

Wherever possible, maintain user identity from the source of data entry (typically Salesforce1 for new app development) to destination (system of record). Begin to create external identifiers to maintain data integrity between systems with Salesforce1 as the source of new app innovation. Expose business process actions in existing systems as service end that can be executed from Salesforce1 actions, and actionable from mobile apps. Utilize the strategies for identity management defined in the section below called "Evolve Identity and Data Security Beyond the Perimeter."

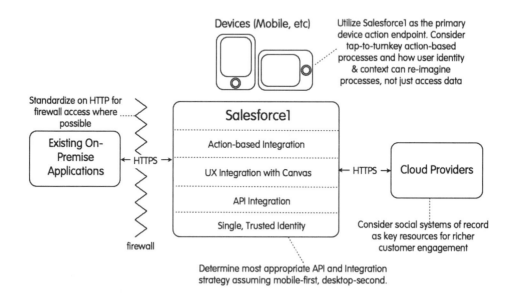

Getting Started

Start with the business need, not the need for data access alone. Clearly identitying the business need will expose opportunities for determining whether a system of record-based approach is correct, a data migration exercise will unlock future innovation and retire legacy systems, or what the most efficient Salesforce1 API is most appropriate, for eample, Bulk API for data loading, Streaming API for pub-sub models, and action-based integration for tap-to-turnkey business processes that can span system boundaries. Developers should become familiar with triggers, custom Apex REST, External IDs for data modeling, and Canvas-based publisher actions.

Analyze Real-Time Data From Connected Devices

Motivation

The Internet of things is a term used to describe the next wave of smart devices connected to the Internet. Today, the most prevalent of these devices are mobile phones and tablets. We are beginning to see cars, vending machines, and much more sharing information back to businesses on customer usage, and habits. The future of business lies in considering that behind every device is a customer. The result is the need to connect everything back to your business and analyze this data for exception customer service.

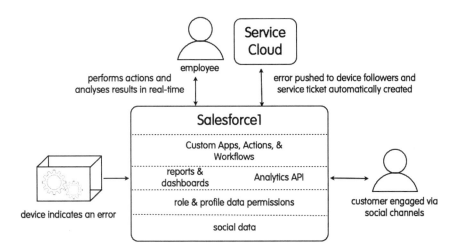

Strategy

Connected device strategies are evolving incredibly rapidly. Salesforce1 provides robust reporting and dashboard functionality including Analytics APIs for aggregating this data, and representing it on mobile devices for users to make information decisions in real-time.

Organizations looking to capitalize on connected devices and tie them to customer services goals, should focus on how to work effectively with this data, and communicate back with their customer.

Getting Started

Connected devices typically require system integrators who are specialists in connecting physical devices to the internet. Once connected, app developers should focus on what information retrieved from the devices is important for customer service requirements. Perhaps it's the analysis of heat sensors, or an indication on every time a fridge door is opened, or when a truck's speed falls below a certain threshold.

With data points identified, reports and dashboards should be created to identify trends, and analyze usage with key workflows, and actions implemented to support immediate customer escalations.

Create Mobile Apps that Drive Employee Productivity

Getting Started

Without the ability to deliver timely and accurate business information where the customer needs it, adoption of any system will fail. Apps must not only deliver this information, but make it relevant, contextual, and easy to work with.

Motivation

Today's business environment requires data to be available on mobile devices. However, enterprise mobile app strategies often fail due to trying to replicate existing systems on a mobile phone or tablet. How users access, and interact with data on a smart device is different. Data must be delivered in context of where the user is both geographically (as identified through geo-enabled devices) and organizationally (as identified through which record a user is working with).

Feed-centric discovery, integration with social networks, and action-based workflows offer app developers the ability to deliver the most important information at the right time to users on mobile devices, who, with a tap or a swipe can perform actions immediately.

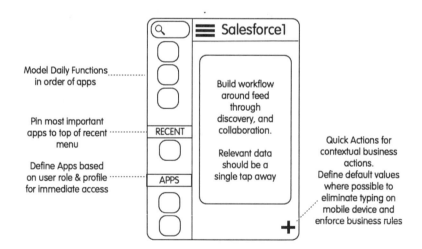

Strategy

Start by defining actions on records and identity areas where default values may be set on the users behalf. The goal is to eliminate the requirement to enter data that can be obtained by contextual information. Typical examples may include geo-location, date, username, and associated record information such as a contact details, account name etc.

Once actions are defined, study user activities on an a daily basis, and create apps which can be configured to appear in the Salesforce1 left-hand menu for single tab access.

Evolve Identity and Data Security Beyond the Perimeter

Getting Started

Modern identity management solutions must support more than traditional perimeter based authentication, and offer a single, simple, and trusted way to manage authentication and authorization of on premise systems, cloud-based offerings, and, ever increasingly social and mobile applications.

Motivation

Salesforce1 can be used to connect to on-premise systems using standards such as SAML and Delegated Authentication offering organizations an flexible way of leveraging existing identity stores, and extending them to the cloud. For cloud-based, and custom mobile apps, oAuth2 has become the leading mechanism for securely authenticting and authorizing apps. Salesforce1 provides a robust ConnectedApp model which allows adminstrators to declaratively define permissions on an app-by-app basis.

Combined with the powerful roles and profile capabilities with Salesforce1, administrators can control which records are accessible to what users, or groups or users, regardless of whether that user is connecting using on-premise authentication tokens, or via a connected app running on a mobile device on the other side of the world.

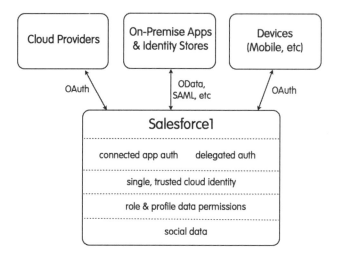

Strategy

Start with the data that your apps needs. Define what this data is, where it comes from, and who has access. With a clear understanding of data requirements, map out where users identity comes from. Does the organization have an existing ActiveDirectory implementation, is single sign-on important, and are external apps going to be connecting to Salesforce1?

Chapter 2

Overview of Force.com

Force.com, a core component of the Salesforce1 Platform, is designed to help create custom apps in minutes. Administrators and users can build apps using intuitive drag and drop tools, a powerful workflow and approval engine, and much more. Developers and ISVs can build apps using programmatic tools, open APIs, and the leading languages and frameworks.

Force.com provides APIs that can be used for developing integration and data access applications, adding application logic to your organization's data, creating custom user interfaces or integrating existing application UI in your organizations, and developing applications that use Salesforce social and collaboration functionality. Because there are no servers or software to buy or manage, you can focus solely on building apps that include built-in social and mobile functionality, business processes, reporting, and search. Your apps run on a secure, proven service that scales, tunes, and backs up data automatically.

For integration and data access, Force.com provides:

- SOAP API: A SOAP-based API for accessing your Salesforce data.
- REST API: A REST-based API for accessing your Salesforce data.
- Metadata API: An API used for managing and migrating organization metadata.
- Bulk API: A REST-based API for asynchronously loading or querying very large sets of data.
- Streaming API: A push technology API for efficiently managing notifications of organization data changes.
- Salesforce Object Query Language (SOQL): A query language used to form complex queries, used in many of the Salesforce APIs.
- Salesforce Object Search Language (SOSL): A search language used to form complex data searches, used in many of the Salesforce APIs.
- Tooling API: A REST and SOAP-based API used for creating custom Salesforce development tools.

- Analytics API: A REST-based API used for running and accessing report data in Salesforce.

For application logic, Force.com provides:

- Apex: An object-oriented programming language that lets you add business logic, triggers, and more to you organization's data.

For user interface development and integration, Force.com provides:

- Visualforce: A tag-based markup language used for building applications and custom interfaces in Salesforce.
- Force.com Canvas: A set of tools and frameworks used to integrate your existing web applications directly in Salesforce.

Resources

Search on the Salesforce Developer's Network at `http://developer.salesforce.com/docs` for comprehensive documentation on all aspects of Force.com.

Chapter 3

Overview of Heroku

Heroku, a core component of the Salesforce1 Platform, empowers your business to build, deliver and manage all of your customer-facing apps. You can use the Salesforce1 APIs to bring deep customer insight into your applications, integrate and extend your core business systems, and connect your business to customers, end-to-end. Heroku is the ideal place to run these applications.

This chapter covers how to use Heroku to build, deploy, and scale your customer-facing apps, leveraging Salesforce1 APIs on the backend and Heroku's suite of powerful developer tools and cutting-edge cloud services for better and faster application delivery.

Apps are the new channel to reach customers, letting companies create contextual, interactive experiences that can reach today's mobile, social and connected customers - wherever they are, on any device. In addition to leveraging robust APIs, core business systems, and rich customer data, today's companies need to deliver customer-facing apps and new features quickly, optimize for mobile and connected devices, and efficiently scale out to meet traffic spikes and accommodate new users.

Here are some examples of apps that bring together Salesforce1 APIs and Heroku's application delivery platform to deliver engaging, customized experiences to users.

- **Customer Engagement** — These apps connect company to customer through engaging app experiences. Some of the successful customer engagement apps deployed on the Heroku platform include: marketing campaigns around major events and product launches, viral campaigns, acquisition and loyalty campaigns, consumer purchase flows, social apps, content platforms, and innovative connected device apps. These apps can help companies reach new markets, achieving broader and deeper reach into new customer bases and demographics.
- **Consumer Mobile** — In order to remain competitive, today's companies must be able to extend their brand, services and products across across the many screens of today's connected consumer. Mobile apps enable relevant engagement regardless of location and across all of

your customers' mobile devices - or their connected products, gaming consoles, TV sets and even their cars. These apps can build brand loyalty, bridge the brick & mortar experience to allow customers to browse and buy on any device, access important data, and receive notifications or interact and socialize with the company on-the-go. These apps can also power self-service experiences ranging from e-commerce to business interactions like making appointments, checking order statuses, and more.

- **Force.com + Heroku** — These apps connect a company to customers through the rich customer data stored within the Sales Cloud. Integrated with intelligent data, companies are able to build deeply customized, contextual customer applications, automate business processes, capture data, and tie everything back to core business systems.

About Heroku

Heroku is designed from the ground up for developer productivity, focused on removing the pains of managing infrastructure and operations, so you and your team can focus on delivering amazing apps to customers. Heroku provides instant deployment, streamlined workflows, a marketplace of fully-managed cloud services, and built-in best practices for application development - all from a single, scalable, reliable platform for hosting and managing your apps.

Heroku provides the essential tools and building blocks for your applications, including:

- Support for Ruby, Node.js, Java, and Python so your development team can be productive immediately with languages they already know.
- A robust, on-demand Add-ons marketplace of fully managed services you can add and scale in a single command, including services for monitoring, logging, persistence, caching, mail delivery. Add-ons give you the power to easily provision and consume top technologies including Redis, MongoDB, PubNub, Mailgun, Hadoop, and more, without needing to manage the underlying infrastructure.
- Mobile backend services for essential mobile app infrastructure, including push notifications, data synchronization, and in-app purchases.
- Heroku Postgres, a SQL database-as-a-service that lets you focus on your data with continuous protection, automated health checks, simple configuration, easy set-up of read-only replicas, and powerful querying features.

More than an infrastructure provider, Heroku is a developer productivity platform designed from the ground-up to maximize developer productivity and application maintainability at every stage of the lifecycle, featuring:

- An efficient, safe workflow that lets you deploy with git and easily create staging, development, and production environments for fast and continuous delivery.
- A simple, powerful model for scaling your app up as your grow.
- Easy, intuitive interfaces and tools — including a powerful command line interface and streamlined dashboard
- Built-in collaboration for more efficient work across your team, extended team, and third-party partners, such as application development shops.

- Centralized billing and management for all of your apps.

Key Features of Heroku

This section provides a tour of the essential features and core concepts of Heroku, and how to leverage them in your applications. It covers running and deployment, the Add-ons marketplace, Heroku Postgres, and workflow and collaboration on the platform.

Deploy, Run, and Scale

Getting started on Heroku is easy — simply sign up for an account and install our Toolbelt, your get-started package which installs the Heroku CLI and other essential tools. On Heroku, you can write apps in the languages you know – we support standard Ruby, Node.js, Python, and Java. When your app is ready to deploy, use git to push your code to Heroku. Heroku will fetch and compile app dependencies, binaries and assets, apply the configuration you've specified, and execute its processes. Your app will be up and running immediately, and accessible from any browser or device on a unique URL. Of course, when you're ready to launch, you can easily apply a custom domain. We take care of provisioning, operations, security, and upgrades so you can focus on your app instead of managing the infrastructure.

Heroku uses a simple, powerful process model to support fast, efficient and tunable scale. "Dynos" are the basic unit of scale on Heroku. A dyno is a lightweight, virtualized container running a single user-specified command. Dynos run web, worker, queue, and other processes needed to power your app. Dynos can be scaled up independently and on-demand as you grow - through the Heroku CLI, or through the Heroku dashboard, our web-based UI.

An app may consist of one or many dynos, depending on the memory and concurrency requirements of the app. Heroku offers two dyno sizes:

- 1x dynos are the default on Heroku, and each provides 512MB of memory and 1x CPU share.
- 2x dynos offer double the memory and CPU share of 1x dynos, for a total of 1024 MB of memory and 2x CPU share. 2x dynos are ideal for memory-intensive applications or those that require enhanced concurrency.

Because your application can be scaled on a per-dyno basis and new resources are provisioned to your app within seconds, you have a great deal of flexibility and control over your app. For example, if you need to accommodate more web traffic and you simply scale up the number of web dynos - Heroku will take care of routing so you can just add more dynos without additional operations overhead.

Add-Ons

Sure, you can can scale dynos up and down on demand in response to events like peak hours, a viral event, growth in users or addition of new features. But what if you want to try an auto-scaling service, or hook in top monitoring systems so you can better anticipate and respond to increased demand on your app?

In addition to providing on-demand, highly scalable infrastructure for running your core app infrastructure, Heroku also makes it easy to extend your app with best-of-breed technologies from our Add-ons marketplace. The marketplace features over 100 fully managed cloud services, operated by experts in their field and integrated directly into Heroku.

Add-ons are fully managed third-party services by top providers, integrated into Heroku so they can be easily added, scaled, and consumed by your application. Add-ons can be added through one command, and come in a variety of plans of various price points in order to accommodate apps of all sizes - from small demo-apps and sample projects to large scale production applications. Many of these add-ons specifically provide services required for launched and growing apps, such as monitoring, persistence, logging, and caching. Here are some examples.

- Persistence — Persisting, managing, and scaling state is one of the primary concerns of a production application. The Heroku Add-ons marketplace provides a variety of data storage solutions so you can easily integrate the type of data store that best meets you needs. Add-ons span relational, non-relational and graph databases, as well as analytics solutions including Postgres, MongoDB, Neo4j, Hadoop, and others.
- Caching — Caching is critical for web and mobile performance, significantly improving the response time and user experience of your app. Caching add-ons include MemCachier, which lets you add memcache to your production app; IronCache, which supports the memcache protocol; and Cachely, which is a rack middleware for Ruby on Rails apps.
- Monitoring — Monitoring provides peace-of-mind, problem detection, and visibility into key indicators over time. Heroku's Add-on marketplace offers New Relic, one of our most popular Add-ons, which will automatically create a private New Relic account and configure access to your apps so you can get up and running quickly. Node.js developers can look to Nodetime for performance profiling and monitoring. For those who want to customize their dashboards, Librato is quick to set up and consumes data right from your application logs.
- Logging — Logs provide the foundation for trend analysis, error inspection, performance tuning, and other processes critical for running production apps. Heroku routes and collates real-time logs from each part of your app, including running processes, system components, API events, and even Add-ons themselves. We offer several Add-ons which consume your log stream and provide higher-order services such as persistence, search, alerts, and integration with other services - including Papertrail, Logentries, Loggly, and Flydata.
- Other — Add-ons include services to provide core engagement features to your customers, including services for email delivery, telephony services, push notifications, video encoders, payments, and more. Our full selection includes Add-ons from providers including StatusPage, Zencoder, PandaStream, Blitz, Pusher, PubNub, Urban Airship, and many more.

Heroku Postgres

Heroku Postgres is Heroku's database-as-a-service product, allowing you to easily provision and scale a Postgres database for your Heroku application. Heroku Postgres offers a number of features, including continuous protection, automated health care checks, "followers" so you can easily set up read-only replicas of your database, and simple configuration for a variety of languages, command line tools and application frameworks. You can also use the Heroku Postgres "fork" feature to create a perfect, byte-for-byte clone of your database for use in testing, load experiments, safely trying new schema migrations, and more.

We know that the data stored in Heroku Postgres isn't only important for your application to access. The app and user data it holds is incredibly valuable to your core business - and people need to access it. To this end, Heroku Postgres makes it easy to access, query, and share your data across your company. Dataclips, available on all Heroku Postgres production and starter databases, let you run SQL queries against your data and share the results in an easy, visual way with your team members.

Dataclips can be downloaded or shared via URLs, are downloadable and exportable in many formats, and are executed via a read-only transaction so your data stays safe. This makes it easy to safely and easily capture and share the data that drives your business.

Workflow

In addition to providing the core infrastructure needed to run your app, Heroku also provides a number of features to ensure you can set up fast, efficient developer workflows for maximum productivity and faster time to market. Using Heroku's application fork feature, you can easily set up a natural, standardized workflow with homogenous staging, development and production environments - providing a safe way to develop code, test it, then promote it to production when you are ready. Further, continuous integration Add-ons in the Heroku Add-ons marketplace, including Travis CI and CircleCI, can improve your development workflow even further.

Collaboration

Collaboration is integral to developer productivity. Customer-facing apps are often the product of extended application development teams that may include product managers, engineering managers, remote employees, and application development agencies and consultants. To support the often complex and changing composition and velocity of app teams, Heroku makes it easy to add collaborators to your application so you can work together. Collaborators can immediately access your application, push code, and pull down and merge changes. If you need to revoke permissions down the road, it's easy to do that too. Collaboration is built into every part of Heroku - you can view and manage all collaborators from the Heroku Dashboard, and Heroku's comprehensive logging system tracks collaborators so you can easily see a full history of actions on your apps - especially useful for drilling down into specific events like releases.

Visibility and App Management

For today's businesses, visibility and app management is critical to ensure efficient business operations and app delivery. Heroku provides centralized invoicing and management for all of your application resources — from dynos to Add-ons, all in a single interface.

When you sign into Heroku from your browser, you're in the Heroku Dashboard. Dashboard is a personalized, interactive command center for all of your apps on Heroku. It provides simple visibility and management for app status, activity, resources, Add-ons, collaborators, and other critical aspects of your app. You can also use it to manage all information about your Heroku account – from SSH keys to past invoices. You can even use Dashboard to run a production check on your app. Production check runs a series of tests on your app that we recommend for maintaining and monitoring availability – such as appropriate DNS configuration, dyno redundancy, and app and log monitoring.

Finally, we would be remiss to discuss visibility on Heroku without talking about Heroku logging in more depth. Logs tell the story of your app - a continuous, living stream of events, changes and behaviors. Logs let you rapidly identify and act on critical events, debug issues in your code, and analyze trends to make better decisions over time.

Heroku brings simplicity and order back to logging. Heroku automatically collates and routes logs from every part of your app into a single channel, providing truly comprehensive, extensible, app-centric logging. Your log stream comes with rich command line functionality, is easy to plug into other services, and handles the heavy lifting of log management for you. Logplex collects underlying events from the Heroku platform, API logs with administrative actions performed by you and your collaborators, and output from within your app, app server, installed libraries, and any backing services that have been configured to publish to your stream. The result is a full story of your application — logs from every piece of Heroku, each component of your app, all of its processes, and all changes made to it by you or your teammates.

Trusted, Open Platform

Heroku is a part of Salesforce1, the #1 enterprise cloud computing platform trusted by 100k+ customers. Over 4 million apps have been deployed on Heroku. And Heroku is open, built on open source components. Heroku buildpacks — the scripts that prepare your code for execution on Heroku — are all open source, extensible, and supported on other cloud platforms for maximum portability. Heroku supports standard tools and languages including git, standard versions of all major languages, and standard implementations of Postgres, WebHooks, and other open source technologies. Heroku also offers a platform API, allowing third party developers to automate, extend and combine the Heroku platform with other services in a programmatic, self-service way — building 3rd party businesses and services like continuous integration tools, mobile apps for managing your Heroku apps, and more.

Heroku Quick Start

In this section, we'll walk through how to get started deploying your first app on Heroku. For illustration's sake, we'll use a Ruby app as an example - however, the process for deploying applications in all of Heroku's supported languages - Ruby, Python, Node.js, and Java - is similar, even though some small differences due to the norms and structure of the language might be present. Visit https://devcenter.heroku.com/quickstart for more language-specific details.

Step 1: Sign up

First, go to Heroku.com and click "sign up" to get your free Heroku account. Along with your free account, you'll receive some free dyno hours to get you started.

Step 2: Install the Heroku Toolbelt

The Heroku Toolbelt contains the Heroku client, a command-line tool for creating and managing Heroku apps; Foreman, an easy option for running your apps locally; and Git, the revision control system needed for pushing applications to Heroku.

The Heroku Toolbelt offers packages for Mac OS X, Windows, and Debian/Ubuntu in addition to a stand-alone package.

Step 3: Log In from Your Command Line

After installing the Toolbelt, you'll have access to the `heroku` command from your command shell.

Authenticate using the email address and password you used when creating your Heroku account. If you have previously uploaded a key to Heroku, we assume you'll keep using it and don't prompt you about creating a new one during login.

Press enter at the prompt to upload your existing ssh key or create a new one, used for pushing code later on.

```
$ heroku login
Enter your Heroku credentials.
Email: adam@example.com
Password:
Could not find an existing public key.
Would you like to generate one? [Yn]
Generating new SSH public key.
Uploading ssh public key /Users/adam/.ssh/id_rsa.pub
```

If you would prefer to create and upload a new key after login, simply run `heroku keys:add`.

Step 4: Prepare your App for Deployment

Now you're ready to deploy your app on Heroku! (If you don't have an existing app, we have "Hello World!" examples available in our online Dev Center for you to try.)

Heroku detects that your app is written in Ruby by the presence of a Gemfile. For Java, Heroku looks for a pom.xml file; requirements.txt for Python, and package.json for Node.js.

When getting ready to deploy an app to Heroku, there are a few things you must do to prepare: declare dependencies, declare process types, test your app locally, and commit your code to git.

First, you must declare dependencies, making sure not to list any system-level dependencies. Test your app locally to make sure that all gems your app depends on are present in the Gemfile - and don't forget to specify the version of Ruby you use (Heroku supports Ruby 2.0 by default, but all apps should specify a version for consistency).

Next, you need to declare process types in a Procfile - a text file in the root of your application to explicitly declare what command should be executed to start a dyno. This may include web, worker, or other processes. For this example, we'll start a web dyno.

```
web: bundle exec ruby web.rb -p $PORT
```

This declares a single process type - web - and the command needed to run it. The name "web" is important here. It declares that this process type will be attached to the HTTP routing stack of Heroku, and receive web traffic when deployed.

At this point, you can should try running your app locally using Foreman, a command-line tool for running Procfile-backed apps. Foreman got installed along with the Heroku Toolbelt.

Simply run `foreman start` and your app will boot up on port 5000 for you to check out.

Finally, you'll want to commit your app files to a local git repository.

```
$ git init
$ git add
$ git commit -m "init"
```

Step 5: Deploy

Now you're ready to deploy your application to Heroku - the hard work is over.

First, create the app on Heroku using the heroku create command.

```
$ heroku create
Creating blazing-galaxy-997... done, stack is cedar
http://blazing-galaxy-997.herokuapp.com/ |
git@heroku.com:blazing-galaxy-997.git
Git remote heroku added
```

Then, deploy your app with git using the git push heroku master command.

```
$ git push heroku master
Counting objects: 6, done.
Delta compression using up to 4 threads.
Compressing objects: 100% (5/5), done.
Writing objects: 100% (6/6), 660 bytes, done.
Total 6 (delta 0), reused 0 (delta 0)

-----> Ruby/Rack app detected
-----> Using Ruby version: ruby-2.0.0
-----> Installing dependencies using Bundler version 1.3.2
       Running: bundle install --without development:test --path
vendor/bundle --binstubs vendor/bundle/bin --deployment
       Fetching gem metadata from https://rubygems.org/..........
       Fetching gem metadata from https://rubygems.org/..
       Installing rack (1.2.2)
       Installing tilt (1.3)
       Installing sinatra (1.1.0)
       Using bundler (1.3.2)
     Your bundle is complete! It was installed into ./vendor/bundle

       Cleaning up the bundler cache.
-----> Discovering process types
       Procfile declares types     -> web
       Default types for Ruby/Rack -> console, rake
-----> Compiled slug size: 25.1MB
-----> Launching... done, v3
       http://blazing-galaxy-997.herokuapp.com deployed to Heroku

To git@heroku.com:blazing-galaxy-997.git
 * [new branch]      master -> master
```

You'll be able to view your app in a web browser, or test it with curl, at
http://blazing-galaxy-997.herokuapp.com.

Congratulations, you've deployed your first app on Heroku!

Step 6: Using the CLI

The Heroku CLI can be used to manipulate your app, letting you view the consolidated logs,
scale the application, or even add Add-on services.

If you need to scale up web traffic, simply tell Heroku to dial up the number of web dynos.

```
$ heroku ps:scale web=2
Scaling web dynos... done, now running 2
```

Check to see how many dynos are running.

```
$ heroku ps
git:master
=== web (1X): `bundle exec ruby web.rb -p $PORT`
```

```
web.1: up 2013/10/15 11:28:17 (~ 5m ago)
web.2: up 2013/10/15 11:33:24 (~ 1s ago)
```

View the consolidated log stream, tailing it to see all new log events as they come in.

```
$ heroku logs --tail
2013-10-15T10:24:25.602652+00:00 app[web.1]: Started GET
"/articles/getting-started-with-nodejs" for 84.32.143.141 at
2013-10-15 10:24:25 +0000
2013-10-15T10:24:25.885004+00:00 heroku[router]: at=info method=GET
 path=/assets/public/feed-icon-sprite.png host=devcenter.heroku.com
 request_id=fd511f6195f52e8e58f58cccbc07109c fwd="77.252.246.255"
 dyno=web.12 connect=0ms service=15ms status=200 bytes=4867
2013-10-15T10:24:26.563176+00:00 heroku[web.1]: source=web.1
 dyno=heroku.12227120.90edce79-b91e-403e-be3f-2f2ba11aa5af
 sample#load_avg_1m=0.00 sample#load_avg_5m=0.00
 sample#load_avg_15m=0.00
...
```

Want to persist logs and send alerts on critical events? Add one of our many logging Add-ons, like Papertrail.

```
$ heroku addons:add papertrail
Adding papertrail on blazing-galaxy-997... done, v6 (free)
Use `heroku addons:docs papertrail` to view documentation.
```

Want to set up a more efficient and productive developer workflow? Heroku lets you fork entire apps so you can easily set up homogenous staging environments.

```
$ heroku fork staging-galaxy
Creating fork blazing-galaxy-997... done
Copying slug... done
Copying config vars... done
Fork complete, view it at http://staging-galaxy.herokuapp.com/
```

Now you can deploy a new branch of your source to this new application.

```
$ heroku git:remote -a staging-galaxy -r staging
                              git:master
Git remote staging added
$ git push staging newbranch:master
```

Ready to launch with a custom domain? It's easy to do once you've set up your DNS and CNAME.

```
$ heroku domains:add www.mydomain.com
Adding www.mydomain.com to blazing-galaxy-997... done
```

Heroku separates configuration from code, making it easy to change values that may affect your app, such as secret keys.

```
$ heroku config:set SECRET_KEY=2342434434343433555422
Setting config vars and restarting blazing-galaxy-997….done, v8
```

Want to drill down into your release history to get more information on your velocity, latest changes or to troubleshoot problems? There's a command for that too.

```
$ heroku releases
=== demo-for-james Releases
v6   Add SECRET_KEY config                          jon@heroku.com
        2013/10/15 12:00:10 (~ 59s ago)
v5   Add papertrail:choklad add-on     jon@heroku.com
2013/10/15 11:26:59 (~ 34m ago)
v4   Deploy 9579f23                    jon@heroku.com
2013/10/15 10:23:32 (~ 1h ago)
v3   Deploy 0eb78aa                    jon@heroku.com
2013/10/15 10:21:33 (~ 1h ago)
v2   Enable Logplex                    heroku@herokumanager.com
2013/10/15 09:58:21 (~ 2h ago)
v1   Initial release                   heroku@herokumanager.com
2013/10/15 09:58:20 (~ 2h ago)
```

Rollback to a previous release in order to fix a problem.

```
$ heroku rollback v6
Rolling back blazing-galaxy-997... done, v6
 !    Warning: rollback affects code and config vars; it doesn't add
 or remove addons. To undo, run: heroku rollback v7
```

Best Practices for Consuming Salesforce1 APIs from Heroku

Let's say you want to build an application to extend the functionality of your Salesforce organization. You can use OAuth to authenticate your app with the platform, and allow users to authenticate using their Salesforce credentials so it can take actions on their behalf. For detailed instructions on setting up OAuth credentials, refer to the earlier section on defining remote access applications. Here, we discuss safely managing OAuth on Heroku.

One security best practice that Heroku enforces for application development is separating configuration information (such as credentials) from code. Doing this prevents sensitive information such as passwords from unnecessarily proliferating in source-code repos and development computers. It also lets you independently manage configuration for different deployments of your app (for example, staging and production), a model that scales up smoothly as the app naturally expands into more deploys over its lifetime.

For this reason, Heroku stores configuration - like your OAuth consumer key and consumer secret - in config vars, keeping your keys out of your code. Heroku manifests these config vars as environment variables to the application. These environment variables are persistent – they will remain in place across deploys and app restarts – so unless you need to change values, you only need to set them once.

Here's an example of how to manage your app's OAuth credentials for authenticating with Salesforce:

First, set the config for the OAuth consumer key and secret.

```
$ heroku config:set
OAUTH_ID=3MRG81KcPoNINVBJSoQsNCD.HHDdbugPsNXwwyFbgb47KWa_ABc
Adding config vars and restarting myapp... done, v12
OAUTH_ID: 3MRG81KcPoNINVBJSoQsNCD.HHDdbugPsNXwwyFbgb47KWa_ABc
$ heroku config:set OAUTH_SECRET=5678471853609579511
Adding config vars and restarting myapp... done, v13
OAUTH_SECRET: 5678471853609579511
```

Then you can retrieve, unset, or change the config at any time through the command line.

```
$ heroku config:get OAUTH_ID
3MRG81KcPoNINVBJSoQsNCD.HHDdbugPsNXwwyFbgb47KWa_ABc

$ heroku config:unset OAUTH_ID
Unsetting OAUTH_ID and restarting myapp... done, v14
```

Once you've set your consumer key and consumer secret in your app's config vars on Heroku, your app will be able to implement OAuth logic and perform the OAuth authentication flow against the appropriate Salesforce authorization endpoint. Simply access the config vars from within your app just as you would any other environment variable.

Resources

Use the following resources to get more information about Heroku.

- Heroku Dev Center: https://devcenter.heroku.com
- Getting Started with Heroku:
  https://devcenter.heroku.com/articles/quickstart
- Heroku Reference: https://devcenter.heroku.com/categories/reference

## Chapter 4

Overview of ExactTarget

ExactTarget Fuel, a core component of the Salesforce1 Platform, powers multi-channel marketing programs for many of the world's top brands. The foundation of the ExactTarget Marketing Cloud, Fuel is open to third-party development, enabling you to build upon, extend, and integrate with ExactTarget's industry-leading digital marketing products.

Fuel is an integrated collection of technologies and includes:

- **APIs** — our comprehensive APIs are the foundation of our platform, enabling developers to automate email campaigns, seamlessly integrate marketing, analytics, and other business software, and build Marketing Cloud applications. Fuel provides both REST and SOAP APIs to support cloud and enterprise development needs. The REST APIs offer cross-channel integration capabilities using easy to use JSON payloads.

- **SDKs** — the Fuel SDKs (Software Development Kits) enable developers to integrate with ExactTarget using native platform and language constructs. Fuel SDKs are currently available for Java, .NET, PHP, Python, and Ruby. SDKs are the preferred method of starting any development initiative using the Fuel platform. If an SDK is not provided for your language of choice, you can program directly against our Fuel APIs.

- **Fuel UX** — Fuel UX is the user interface toolkit used by the ExactTarget Marketing Cloud and ExactTarget's Marketing Cloud apps. Based on leading open-source JavaScript technologies, Fuel UX makes it easy to build apps that deeply integrate with the ExactTarget Marketing Cloud.

- **Fuel Cloud Editor** — the Fuel Cloud Editor is an easy-to-use, highly configurable content editor that can be easily embedded in both ExactTarget Marketing Cloud and stand-alone applications. Part of Fuel UX, the Fuel Cloud Editor can be extended using Gears, typed content that can be dragged and dropped onto the editor canvas to quickly and easily build rich, dynamic messages.

What can you do with Fuel? If you're a customer, you can use Fuel to automate entire marketing campaigns, customize the ExactTarget application to your exact needs, or integrate ExactTarget with a variety of marketing, analytics, and other business software. If you're a partner, you can use Fuel to build or extend marketing applications and take those applications to market with ExactTarget via one of our platform-related partner programs.

The next section explains the fundamental concepts behind successful customer touchpoints: permission, personalization and data, and describes the opportunity developers have to use technology to reach individual customers.

Customer Touchpoints for Developers

Every email sent, every message delivered and every notification has something in common: they all touch people—people who are customers, either existing or prospective. The email, message or notification may be as simple as letting someone know their credit card has expired, or it may be as complex as but one component of a multi-channel marketing campaign designed to sell an automobile.

In both cases, the email, message or notification should be thought of as a touchpoint, an opportunity to influence your customers and prospects. Unfortunately, these opportunities are often lost when there is a rush to get a new system online or when utilizing existing infrastructure to save time and effort. The ExactTarget Marketing Cloud helps marketers take maximum advantage of customer touchpoints. By using Fuel, developers can get in on the action and help your company create even more relevant and effective touchpoints.

This section discusses the keys to maximizing the impact of each customer touchpoint from a developer's perspective. Those keys revolve around permission, personalization, and maximizing the value of each interaction.

Boring == Static || (Cool == Relevant && Relevant == Successful)

Customers are inundated with messages of all types—emails in the inbox, printed material in the mailbox, billboards on highways, SMS messages on phones, ads on social networks, tweets and Facebook friend requests and on and on and on. Marketers know that to be effective they have to make these messages relevant just to get noticed.

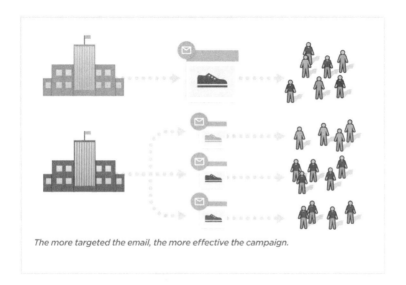

The more targeted the email, the more effective the campaign.

Relevant communication is as much a technology problem as it is a marketer's dilemma—the most relevant, successful marketing campaigns involve highly sophisticated integrations with multiple data sources tied to precise audience segments who receive personalized messages at exactly the right moment. As such, marketers routinely require technical help to accomplish their goals, giving developers the opportunity to innovate alongside them.

To help marketers build more relevant communications, Fuel enables large amounts of data to be synchronized across multiple systems through a flexible data model and multiple integration methods. This data from multiple sources can be used at the time of customer communication using AMPscript—the Marketing Cloud's scripting language for messaging—to create unique messages for each customer. For example, we can create a data extension (more on data extensions later) that maps zip codes to city names and use that mapping dynamically in our communications via the following AMPscript.

```
%%=Lookup("PostalCode","City","PostalCode",postalcode)=%%
```

Every Event Improves Relevancy

Event-driven architectures are critical for scaling real-time systems and applications—especially as we enter the era of the Internet of Things. Each event, whether generated by a server, a web browser or a mobile application, represents an opportunity to interact with a customer or provide insight into that customer through his or her response to that event—insight that can be used to make later interactions more relevant and timely.

What could a marketer using the Marketing Cloud do with additional insight on customer interactions? A customer event (such as a "Contact Us" confirmation) may directly lead to a specific message on a specific channel delivered through the Marketing Cloud. Or a customer event (like a "Purchase" event) may just need to be passed into the Marketing Cloud Interactions engine so a marketer can decide how valuable it and what messages to deliver (if any) for the event.

An example of a cross-channel event-based communication engine is a password reminder system that delivers reminders via email or SMS. Fuel enables this type of engine to scale to millions of messages a day.

A cross-channel scenario where the Marketing Cloud is sending password reminders through multiple channels.

A movie rental system may want to deliver confirmations to customers and start a chain of communication with the customer asking them for a movie review and to rent other movies. Using a Fuel API to inform the Marketing Cloud Interactions engine that a customer has rented a movie may trigger a number of other events or wait states in the system, all designed to take that customer along the next desired step of the customer journey. This represents a collaboration between technology and marketing to pull off a sophisticated chain of events geared toward adding value to your organization's relationship with individual customers and respecting their privacy.

The ExactTarget Marketing Cloud is capable of taking raw events from systems interacting with customers and managing the entire customer lifecycle.

Permission, Permission, Permission

If you're not careful about how you manage your customer touchpoints, your email could be considered unsolicited commercial email—a.k.a. spam.

In the United States, CAN-SPAM is a law passed in 2003 that mandates the addition of an unsubscribe mechanism to all emails and requires the sender to comply with customer opt-out requests within ten days. Many other countries have similar laws in place to protect consumers.

CAN-SPAM draws a distinction between *commercial* email, email which is designed to advertise or promote a commercial product or service, and *transactional* email, email which is triggered as the result of an event or contains information about a specific transaction (e.g., password reset emails, purchase confirmation emails, etc.).

A common mistake companies make is sending commercial email to a list of email addresses that have been either accumulated over time or purchased. If that list is old or has a large number of subscribers who flag your message as spam because it is not relevant to them, your ability to send email successfully in the future will be impeded by a negative reputation applied to your sending IP address.

The key to successfully managing your customer touchpoints is permission. The ExactTarget Marketing Cloud helps you manage the complexity of permission by persisting communication preferences associated with customers (for example, whether they have opted in or opted out to a particular communication) and allowing message sends to be specified as commercial or transactional. If the type of send is commercial, ExactTarget will validate your email content for opt-out links to ensure that subscribers have a way to express their desire to opt-in or opt-out of future communications as required by CAN-SPAM.

The Technology Is About The Customer

For all the possibilities for technology and marketing to intersect using the Marketing Cloud, the focus is always about innovating on behalf of customers and how they relate to your business or organization. Fuel enables you to innovate in critical ways to gain and retain customers or build systems that help others do the same thing.

The technologies exposed through Fuel, in conjunction with Marketing Cloud applications, enable developers to innovate and add value to their organization at the individual customer level. The technologies exposed reach out to customers and are accessible by marketers, allowing Fuel to be a conduit for business growth and innovation.

Resources

Use the following resources to get more information about ExactTarget.

- Code@ExactTarget Developer Community: https://code.exacttarget.com
- Code@ExactTarget App Center: https://code.exacttarget.com/appcenter
- Fuel APIs: https://code.exacttarget.com/api
- Fuel SDKs: https://code.exacttarget.com/sdks
- Fuel Cloud Editor: https://code.exacttarget.com/cloudeditor
- Fuel UX: https://code.exacttarget.com/fuelux
- ExactTarget AppExchange Developer Documentation: https://code.exacttarget.com/appexchange

FORCE.COM

Chapter 5

Authentication

Force.com APIs use authentication to securely access Salesforce user information.

Before using any Force.com API that accesses user data, use OAuth to authenticate as the desired user. Successful authentication provides an access token that is used to make authenticated Force.com API calls.

To authenticate using OAuth, you'll need to:

- Set up a remote access application definition in Salesforce.
- Determine the correct OAuth endpoint to use.
- Authenticate the user via one of several different OAuth 2.0 authentication flows. An OAuth authentication flow defines a series of steps used to coordinate the authentication process between your application and Salesforce. Supported OAuth flows include:

  ◊ Web server flow, where the server can securely protect the consumer secret.
  ◊ User-agent flow, used by applications that cannot securely store the consumer secret.
  ◊ Username-password flow, where the application has direct access to user credentials.

Defining Connected Apps

To authenticate using OAuth, you must define a connected app in Salesforce.

A *remote access application* is an application external to Salesforce that uses the OAuth protocol to verify both the Salesforce user and the external application. A remote access application is implemented as a "connected app" in the Salesforce Help. When you develop a new external application that needs to authenticate with Salesforce, you need to define a new connected app that informs Salesforce of this new authentication entry point.

Use the following steps to create a new connected app.

1. From Setup, click **Create** > **Apps** and click **New**.
2. Enter the name of your application.
3. Enter the contact email information, as well as any other information appropriate for your application.
4. Select **Enable OAuth Settings**.
5. Enter a `Callback URL`. Depending on which OAuth flow you use, this is typically the URL that a user's browser is redirected to after successful authentication. As this URL is used for some OAuth flows to pass an access token, the URL must use secure HTTP (HTTPS) or a custom URI scheme.
6. Add all supported OAuth scopes to **Selected OAuth Scopes**. These scopes refer to permissions given by the user running the connected app.
7. Enter a URL for `Info URL`. This is where the user can go for more information about your application.
8. Click **Save**. The `Consumer Key` is created and displayed, and the `Consumer Secret` is created (click the link to reveal it).

Once you define a remote access application, you use the consumer key and consumer secret to authenticate your application. See the Salesforce online help for more information about connected apps.

Understanding OAuth Endpoints

OAuth endpoints are the URLs you use to make OAuth authentication requests to Salesforce.

You need to use the correct Salesforce OAuth endpoint when issuing authentication requests in your application. The primary OAuth endpoints are:

- For authorization: `https://login.salesforce.com/services/oauth2/authorize`
- For token requests: `https://login.salesforce.com/services/oauth2/token`
- For revoking OAuth tokens:
  `https://login.salesforce.com/services/oauth2/revoke`

All endpoints require secure HTTP (HTTPS). Each OAuth flow defines which endpoints you need to use and what request data you need to provide.

If you're verifying authentication on a sandbox organization, use "test.salesforce.com" instead of "login.salesforce.com" in all the OAuth endpoints listed above.

Understanding the Web Server OAuth Authentication Flow

The Web server authentication flow is used by applications that are hosted on a secure server. A critical aspect of the Web server flow is that the server must be able to protect the consumer secret.

In this flow, the client application requests the authorization server to redirect the user to another web server or resource that authorizes the user and sends the application an authorization code. The application uses the authorization code to request an access token. The following shows the steps for this flow.

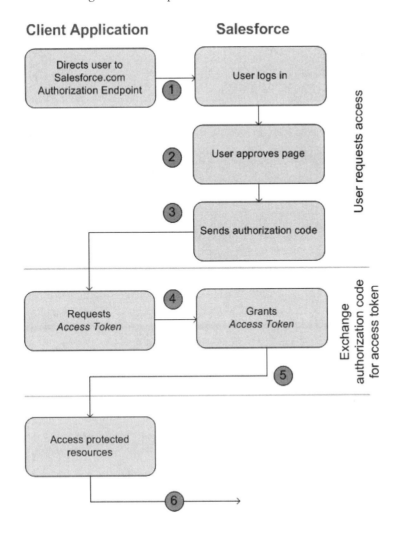

1. The application redirects the user to the appropriate Salesforce authorization endpoint, such as `https://login.salesforce.com/services/oauth2/authorize`. The following parameters are required:

Parameter	Description
`response_type`	Must be `code` for this authentication flow.
`client_id`	The `Consumer Key` from the remote access application definition.
`redirect_url`	The `Callback URL` from the remote access application definition.

The following parameters are optional:

Parameter	Description
`display`	Changes the login page's display type. Valid values are: • `page`—Full-page authorization screen. This is the default value if none is specified. • `popup`—Compact dialog optimized for modern Web browser popup windows. • `touch`—Mobile-optimized dialog designed for modern smartphones such as Android and iPhone. • `mobile`—Mobile optimized dialog designed for smartphones such as BlackBerry OS 5 that don't support touch screens.
`immediate`	Determines whether the user should be prompted for login and approval. Values are either `true` or `false`. Default is `false`. • If set to `true`, and if the user is currently logged in and has previously

Parameter	Description
	approved the application, the approval step is skipped. • If set to `true` and the user is not logged in or has not previously approved the application, the session is immediately terminated with the `immediate_unsuccessful` error code.
state	Specifies any additional URL-encoded state data to be returned in the callback URL after approval.
scope	Specifies what data your application can access. See "Scope Parameter Values" in the online help for more information.

An example authorization URL might look something like the following:

```
https://login.salesforce.com/services/oauth2/authorize?response_type=code
&client_id=3MVG9lKcPoNINVBIPJjdw1J9LLM82HnFVVX19KY1uA5mu0QqEWhqKpoW3svG3X
HrXDiCQjK1mdgAvhCscA9GE&redirect_uri=https%3A%2F%2Fwww.mysite.com%2F
code_callback.jsp&state=mystate
```

2. The user logs into Salesforce with their credentials. The user is interacting with the authorization endpoint directly, so the application never sees the user's credentials. After successfully logging in, the user is asked to authorize the application. Note that if the user has already authorized the application, this step is skipped.

3. Once Salesforce confirms that the client application is authorized, the end-user's Web browser is redirected to the callback URL specified by the `redirect_uri` parameter. Salesforce appends authorization information to the redirect URL with the following values:

Parameters	Description
code	Authorization code the consumer must use to obtain the access and refresh tokens.
state	The state value that was passed in as part of the initial request, if applicable.

An example callback URL with authorization information might look something like:

```
https://www.mysite.com/authcode_callback?code=aWekysIEeqM9PiT
hEfmOCnr6MoLIfwWyRJcqOqHdF8f9INokharAS09ia7UNP6RiVScerfhc4w%3D%3D
```

4. The application extracts the authorization code and passes it in a request to Salesforce for an access token. This request is a POST request sent to the appropriate Salesforce token request endpoint, such as `https://login.salesforce.com/services/oauth2/token`. The following parameters are required:

Parameter	Description
grant_type	Value must be `authorization_code` for this flow.
client_id	The `Consumer Key` from the remote access application definition.
client_secret	The `Consumer Secret` from the remote access application definition.
redirect_uri	The `Callback URL` from the remote access application definition.
code	Authorization code the consumer must use to obtain the access and refresh tokens.

The following parameter is optional:

Parameter	Description
format	Expected return format. The default is `json`. Values are: • `urlencoded` • `json` • `xml` The return format can also be specified in the header of the request using one of the following: • `Accept: application/x-www-form-urlencoded`

Parameter	Description
	• `Accept: application/json` • `Accept: application/xml`

An example access token POST request might look something like:

```
POST /services/oauth2/token HTTP/1.1
Host: login.salesforce.com
grant_type=authorization_code&code=aPrxsmIEeqM9PiQroGEWx1UiMQd95_5JUZ
VEhsOFhS8EVvbfYBBJli2W5fn3zbo.8hojaNW_1g%3D%3D&client_id=3MVG9lKcPoNI
NVBIPJjdw1J9LLM82HnFVVX19KY1uA5mu0QqEWhqKpoW3svG3XHrXDiCQjK1mdgAvhCs
cA9GE&client_secret=1955279925675241571&
redirect_uri=https%3A%2F%2Fwww.mysite.com%2Fcode_callback.jsp
```

5. If this request is successful, the server returns a response body that contains the following:

Parameters	Description
`access_token`	Access token that acts as a session ID that the application uses for making requests. This token should be protected as though it were user credentials.
`refresh_token`	Token that can be used in the future to obtain new access tokens. ⚠ **Warning:** This value is a secret. You should treat it like the user's password and use appropriate measures to protect it.
`instance_url`	Identifies the Salesforce instance to which API calls should be sent.
`id`	Identity URL that can be used to both identify the user as well as query for more information about the user. Can be used in an HTTP request to get more information about the end user.
`issued_at`	When the signature was created, represented as the number of seconds

Parameters	Description
	since the Unix epoch (00:00:00 UTC on 1 January 1970).
signature	Base64-encoded HMAC-SHA256 signature signed with the consumer's private key containing the concatenated ID and issued_at value. The signature can be used to verify that the identity URL wasn't modified because it was sent by the server.

An example JSON response body might look something like:

```
{"id":"https://login.salesforce.com/id/00Dx0000000BV7z/005x00000012Q9P",
"issued_at":"1278448101416",
"refresh_token":"5Aep8614iLM.Dq661ePDmPEgaAW9Oh_L3JKkDpB4xReb54_
pZebnUGOh6Sb4KUVDpNtWEofWM39yg==",
"instance_url":"https://na1.salesforce.com",
"signature":"CMJ4l+CCaPQiKjoOEwEig9H4wqhpuLSk4J2urAe+fVg=",
"access_token":"00Dx0000000BV7z!AR8AQPOjITN80ESEsj5EbaZTFGOR
NBaT1cyWk7TrqoDjoNIWQ2ME_sTZzBjfmOE6zMHq6y8PIW4eWze9JksNEkWUl.Cju7m4"}
```

6. The application uses the provided access token and refresh token to access protected user data.

Understanding the User-Agent OAuth Authentication Flow

The user-agent authentication flow is used by client applications (consumers) residing in the user's device. This could be implemented in a browser using a scripting language such as JavaScript, or from a mobile device or a desktop application. These consumers cannot keep the client secret confidential.

In this flow, the client application requests the authorization server to redirect the user to another Web server or resource which is capable of extracting the access token and passing it back to the application. The following shows the steps for this flow.

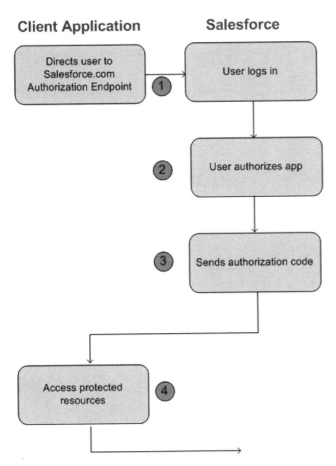

1. The application redirects the user to the appropriate Salesforce authorization endpoint, such as `https://login.salesforce.com/services/oauth2/authorize`. The following parameters are required:

Parameter	Description
response_type	Must be token for this authentication flow
client_id	The Consumer Key from the remote access application definition.
redirect_url	The Callback URL from the remote access application definition.

The following parameters are optional:

Parameter	Description
display	Changes the login page's display type. Valid values are: • page—Full-page authorization screen. This is the default value if none is specified. • popup—Compact dialog optimized for modern Web browser popup windows. • touch—Mobile-optimized dialog designed for modern smartphones such as Android and iPhone. • mobile—Mobile optimized dialog designed for smartphones such as BlackBerry OS 5 that don't support touch screens.
scope	Specifies what data your application can access. See "Scope Parameter Values" in the online help for more information.
state	Specifies any additional URL-encoded state data to be returned in the callback URL after approval.

An example authorization URL might look something like the following:

```
https://login.salesforce.com/services/oauth2/authorize?response_type=token&
client_id=3MVG9lKcPoNINVBIPJjdw1J9LLJbP_pqwoJYyuisjQhr_LLurNDv7AgQvDTZwCoZuD
ZrXcPCmBv4o.8ds.5iE&redirect_uri=https%3A%2F%2Fwww.mysite.com%2Fuser_callback.jsp&
state=mystate
```

2. The user logs into Salesforce with their credentials. The user interacts with the authorization endpoint directly, so the application never sees the user's credentials.

3. Once authorization is granted, the authorization endpoint redirects the user to the redirect URL. This URL is defined in the remote access application created for the application. Salesforce appends access token information to the redirect URL with the following values:

Parameters	Description
access_token	Access token that acts as a session ID that the application uses for making requests. This token should be protected as though it were user credentials.
expires_in	Amount of time the access token is valid, in seconds.
refresh_token	Token that can be used in the future to obtain new access tokens. ⚠ **Warning:** This value is a secret. You should treat it like the user's password and use appropriate measures to protect it. The refresh token is only returned if the redirect URI is https://login.salesforce.com/services/oauth2/success or used with a custom protocol that is not HTTPS.
state	The state value that was passed in as part of the initial request, if applicable.
instance_url	Identifies the Salesforce instance to which API calls should be sent.
id	Identity URL that can be used to both identify the user as well as query for more information about the user. Can be used in an HTTP request to get more information about the end user.
issued_at	When the signature was created, represented as the number of seconds since the Unix epoch (00:00:00 UTC on 1 January 1970).
signature	Base64-encoded HMAC-SHA256 signature signed with the consumer's private key containing the concatenated ID and issued_at value. The

Parameters	Description
	`signature` can be used to verify that the identity URL wasn't modified because it was sent by the server.

An example callback URL with access information appended after the hash sign (#) might look something like:

```
https://www.mysite.com/user_callback.jsp#access_token=00Dx0000000BV7z%21AR8
AQBM8J_xr9kLqmZIRyQxZgLcM4HVi41aGtWOqW3JCzf5xdTGGGSoVim8FfJkZEqxbjaFbberKGk
8v8AnYrvChG4qJbQo8&refresh_token=5Aep8614iLM.Dq661ePDmPEgaAW9Oh_L3JKkDpB4xR
eb54_pZfVtildPEk8aimw4Hr9ne7VXXVSIQ%3D%3D&expires_in=7200&state=mystate
```

4. The application uses the provided access token and refresh token to access protected user data.

Keep the following considerations in mind when using the user-agent OAuth flow:

- Because the access token is encoded into the redirection URI, it might be exposed to the end-user and other applications residing on the computer or device. If you're authenticating using JavaScript, call `window.location.replace();` to remove the callback from the browser's history.

Understanding the Username-Password OAuth Authentication Flow

The username-password authentication flow can be used to authenticate when the consumer already has the user's credentials.

In this flow, the user's credentials are used by the application to request an access token as shown in the following steps.

 Warning: This OAuth authentication flow involves passing the user's credentials back and forth. Use this authentication flow only when necessary. No refresh token will be issued.

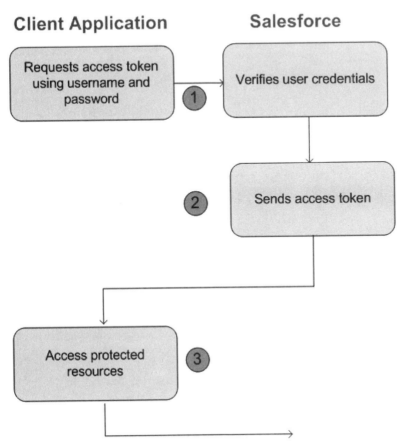

1. The application uses the user's username and password to request an access token. This is done via an out-of-band POST request to the appropriate Salesforce token request endpoint, such as `https://login.salesforce.com/services/oauth2/token`. The following request fields are required:

Parameter	Description
grant_type	Must be `password` for this authentication flow.
client_id	The `Consumer Key` from the remote access application definition.
client_secret	The `Consumer Secret` from the remote access application definition.
username	End-user's username.

Parameter	Description
password	End-user's password.
	Note: You must append the user's security token to their password A security token is an automatically-generated key from Salesforce. For example, if a user's password is mypassword, and their security token is XXXXXXXXXX, then the value provided for this parmeter must be mypasswordXXXXXXXXXX. For more information on security tokens see "Resetting Your Security Token" in the online help.

An example request body might look something like the following:

```
grant_type=password&client_id=3MVG91KcPoNINVBIPJjdw1J9LLM82Hn
FVVX19KY1uA5mu0QqEWhqKpoW3svG3XHrXDiCQjK1mdgAvhCscA9GE&client_secret=
1955279925675241571&username=testuser%40salesforce.com&password=mypassword123456
```

2. Salesforce verifies the user credentials, and if successful, sends a response to the application with the access token. This response contains the following values:

Parameters	Description
access_token	Access token that acts as a session ID that the application uses for making requests. This token should be protected as though it were user credentials.
instance_url	Identifies the Salesforce instance to which API calls should be sent.
id	Identity URL that can be used to both identify the user as well as query for more information about the user. Can be used in an HTTP request to get more information about the end user.

Parameters	Description
issued_at	When the signature was created, represented as the number of seconds since the Unix epoch (00:00:00 UTC on 1 January 1970).
signature	Base64-encoded HMAC-SHA256 signature signed with the consumer's private key containing the concatenated ID and issued_at value. The signature can be used to verify that the identity URL wasn't modified because it was sent by the server.

An example response body might look something like:

```
{"id":"https://login.salesforce.com/id/00Dx0000000BV7z/005x00000012Q9P",
"issued_at":"1278448832702","instance_url":"https://na1.salesforce.com",
"signature":"0CmxinZir53Yex7nE0TD+zMpvIWYGb/bdJh6XfOH6EQ=","access_token":
"00Dx0000000BV7z!AR8AQAxo9UfVkh8AlV0Gomt9Czx9LjHnSSpwBMnbRcgKFmxOtvxjTrKW1
9ye6PE3Ds1eQz3z8jr3W7_VbWmEu4Q8TVGSTHxs"}
```

3. The application uses the provided access token to access protected user data.

Keep the following considerations in mind when using the user-agent OAuth flow:

• Since the user is never redirected to login at Salesforce in this flow, the user can't directly authorize the application, so no refresh tokens can be used. If your application requires refresh tokens, you should consider using the Web server or user-agent OAuth flow.

Understanding the OAuth Refresh Token Process

The Web server OAuth authentication flow and user-agent flow both provide a refresh token that can be used to obtain a new access token.

Access tokens have a limited lifetime specified by the session timeout in Salesforce. If an application uses an expired access token, a "Session expired or invalid" error is returned. If the application is using the Web server or user-agent OAuth authentication flows, a refresh token may be provided during authorization that can be used to get a new access token.

The client application obtains a new access token by sending a POST request to the token request endpoint with the following request parameters:

Parameters	Description
grant_type	Value must be `refresh_token`.
refresh_token	The refresh token the client application already received.
client_id	The `Consumer Key` from the remote access application definition.
client_secret	The `Consumer Secret` from the remote access application definition. This parameter is optional.
format	Expected return format. The default is `json`. Values are: • `urlencoded` • `json` • `xml` The return format can also be specified in the header of the request using one of the following: • `Accept: application/x-www-form-urlencoded` • `Accept: application/json` • `Accept: application/xml` This parameter is optional.

An example refresh token POST request might look something like:

```
POST /services/oauth2/token HTTP/1.1
Host: https://login.salesforce.com/
grant_type=refresh_token&client_id=3MVG9lKcPoNINVBIPJjdw1J9LLM82HnFVVX19KY1uA5mu0
QqEWhqKpoW3svG3XHrXDiCQjK1mdgAvhCscA9GE&client_secret=1955279925675241571
&refresh_token=your token here
```

Once Salesforce verifies the refresh token request, it sends a response to the application with the following response body parameters:

Parameters	Description
access_token	Access token that acts as a session ID that the application uses for making requests. This

Parameters	Description
	token should be protected as though it were user credentials.
instance_url	Identifies the Salesforce instance to which API calls should be sent.
id	Identity URL that can be used to both identify the user as well as query for more information about the user. Can be used in an HTTP request to get more information about the end user.
issued_at	When the signature was created, represented as the number of seconds since the Unix epoch (00:00:00 UTC on 1 January 1970).
signature	Base64-encoded HMAC-SHA256 signature signed with the consumer's private key containing the concatenated ID and issued_at value. The signature can be used to verify that the identity URL wasn't modified because it was sent by the server.

An example JSON response body might look something like:

```
{
"id":"https://login.salesforce.com/id/00Dx0000000BV7z/005x00000012Q9P",
"issued_at":"1278448384422","instance_url":"https://na1.salesforce.com",
"signature":"SSSbLO/gBhmmyNUvN18ODBDFYHzakxOMgqYtu+hDPsc=",
"access_token":"00Dx0000000BV7z!AR8AQP0jITN80ESEsj5EbaZTFG0RNBaT1cyWk7T
rqoDjoNIWQ2ME_sTZzBjfmOE6zMHq6y8PIW4eWze9JksNEkWUl.Cju7m4"}
```

Keep in mind the following considerations when using the refresh token OAuth process:

- The session timeout for an access token can be configured in Salesforce from Setup by clicking **Security Controls** > **Session Settings**.
- If the application uses the username-password OAuth authentication flow, no refresh token is issued, as the user cannot authorize the application in this flow. If the access token expires, the application using username-password OAuth flow must re-authenticate the user.

## Chapter 6

SOAP API

SOAP API lets you integrate Force.com applications that can create, retrieve, update or delete records managed by Salesforce, using any development environment that supports Web services.

When to Use SOAP API

SOAP API provides a powerful, convenient, and simple SOAP-based Web services interface for interacting with Salesforce. You can use SOAP API to create, retrieve, update, or delete records. You can also use SOAP API to perform searches and much more. Use SOAP API in any language that supports Web services.

For example, you can use SOAP API to integrate Salesforce with your organization's ERP and finance systems, deliver real-time sales and support information to company portals, and populate critical business systems with customer information.

Supported Editions and Platforms

To use SOAP API, your organization must use Enterprise Edition, Performance Edition, Unlimited Edition, or Developer Edition. If you are an existing Salesforce customer and want to upgrade to Enterprise, Unlimited, or Performance Edition, contact your account representative.

Quick Start

Use this topic to create a sample application in your development environment.

Note: Before you begin building an integration or other client application:

- Install your development platform according to its product documentation.

- Read through all the steps before beginning this quick start. You may also wish to review the rest of this document to familiarize yourself with terms and concepts.

Step 1: Obtain a Salesforce Developer Edition Organization

If you are not already a member of the Force.com developer community, go to `http://developer.force.com/join` and follow the instructions for signing up for a Developer Edition organization. Even if you already have Enterprise Edition, Unlimited Edition, or Performance Edition, use Developer Edition for developing, staging, and testing your solutions against sample data to protect your organization's live data. This is especially true for applications that insert, update, or delete data (as opposed to simply reading data).

If you already have a Developer Edition organization, verify that you have the "API Enabled" permission. This permission is enabled by default, but may have been changed by an administrator. For more information, see the help in the Salesforce user interface.

Step 2: Generate or Obtain the Web Service WSDL

To access the Force.com Web service, you need a Web Service Description Language (WSDL) file. The WSDL file defines the Web service that is available to you. Your development platform uses this WSDL to generate an API to access the Force.com Web service it defines. You can either obtain the WSDL file from your organization's Salesforce administrator or you can generate it yourself if you have access to the WSDL download page in the Salesforce user interface. You can navigate to the most recent WSDL for your organization from Setup by clicking **Develop > API**.

For more information about WSDL, see `http://www.w3.org/TR/wsdl`.

Generating the WSDL File for Your Organization

Any user with the "Modify All Data" permission can download the Web Services Description Language (WSDL) file to integrate and extend Salesforce using the API. (The System Administrator profile has this permission.)

The WSDL file is dynamically generated based on which type of WSDL file (enterprise or partner) you download. The generated WSDL defines all of the API calls, objects (including standard and custom objects), and fields that are available for API access for your organization.

To generate the WSDL file for your organization:

1. Log in to your Enterprise, Unlimited, Performance, or Developer Edition Salesforce account. You must log in as an administrator or as a user who has the "Modify All Data" permission. Logins are checked to ensure they are from a known IP address. For more information, see "Setting Login Restrictions" in the Salesforce online help.
2. From Setup, click **Develop** > **API** to display the WSDL download page.
3. Download the appropriate WSDL:

   • If you are downloading an enterprise WSDL and you have managed packages installed in your organization, click **Generate Enterprise WSDL**. Salesforce prompts you to select the version of each installed package to include in the generated WSDL.
   • Otherwise, right-click the link for the appropriate WSDL document to save it to a local directory. In the right-click menu, Internet Explorer users can choose **Save Target As**, while Mozilla Firefox users can choose **Save Link As**.

Step 3: Import the WSDL File Into Your Development Platform

Once you have the WSDL file, you need to import it into your development platform so that your development environment can generate the necessary objects for use in building client Web service applications in that environment. This section provides sample instructions for WSC and Microsoft Visual Studio. For instructions about other development platforms, see your platform's product documentation.

Note: The process for importing WSDL files is identical for the enterprise and partner WSDL files.

Instructions for Java Environments (WSC)

Java environments access the API through Java objects that serve as proxies for their server-side counterparts. Before using the API, you must first generate these objects from your organization's WSDL file.

Each SOAP client has its own tool for this process. For WSC, use the `wsdlc` utility.

Note: Before you run `wsdlc`, you must have the WSC JAR file installed on your system and referenced in your classpath.

The basic syntax for `wsdlc` is:

```
java -classpath pathToJAR/wsc-22.jar com.sforce.ws.tools.wsdlc
pathToWsdl/WsdlFilename pathToOutputJar/OutputJarFilename
```

This command generates an output jar file based on the specified WSDL file. After the output jar file is created, reference it along with the wsc jar file (for example, wsc-22.jar) in your Java program to create a client application.

Instructions for Microsoft Visual Studio

Visual Studio languages access the API through objects that serve as proxies for their server-side counterparts. Before using the API, you must first generate these objects from your organization's WSDL file.

Once you have the proxy classes for the server-side objects, you need to ensure that you specify whether you have set any values on non-string fields. For more information, see Implementation Considerations.

Visual Studio provides two approaches for importing your WSDL file and generating an XML Web service client: an IDE-based approach and a command line approach. This walkthrough describes how to import your WSDL file through the IDE.

Note: Before you begin, the first step is to create a new application or open an existing application in Visual Studio. In addition, you need to have generated the WSDL file, as described in Generating the WSDL File for Your Organization.

An XML Web service client is any component or application that references and uses an XML Web service. This does not necessarily need to be a client-based application. In fact, in many cases, your XML Web service clients might be other Web applications, such as Web Forms or even other XML Web services. When accessing XML Web services in managed code, a proxy class and the .NET Framework handle all of the infrastructure coding.

To access an XML Web service from managed code:

1. Name your project `Walkthrough` or change the `using` directive in the following sample to `your_project_name.web_reference_name`. Then, add a Web reference to your project for the XML Web service that you want to access. The Web reference creates a proxy class with methods that serve as proxies for each exposed method of the XML Web service.
2. Add the namespace for the Web reference.
3. Create an instance of the proxy class and then access the methods of that class as you would the methods of any other class.

To add a Web reference:

Note: These steps may be different depending on the version of Visual Studio that you're using. For more information, see "Adding and Removing Web References" in the Visual Studio documentation.

1. On the Project menu, choose **Add Web Reference.**

2. In the URL box of the Add Web Reference dialog box, type the URL to obtain the service description of the XML Web service you want to access, such as:

```
c:\WSDLFiles\enterprise.wsdl
```

3. Click **Go** to retrieve information about the XML Web service.
4. In the Web reference name box, rename the Web reference to `sforce`, which is the name you will use for this Web reference.
5. Click **Add Reference** to add a Web reference for the target XML Web service.
6. Visual Studio retrieves the service description and generates a proxy class to interface between your application and the XML Web service.

 Note: If you are using Visual Basic .Net 1.1 and the enterprise WSDL, you will need to modify the generated Web service client to overcome a bug in Visual Studio's client generation utility. The API exposes two objects (Case and Event) whose names conflict with Visual Basic keywords. When the classes that represent these objects are created, Visual Studio wraps the class names with brackets (`[Case]` and `[Event]`). This is the method by which you can reuse keywords.

Unfortunately, in the definition of the `SObject` class, Visual Studio does not wrap Case and Event to class references in the `System.Xml.Serialization.XmlIncludeAttribute` that are part of the `SObject` definition. To work around this problem in Visual Studio, you need to edit the `XmlIncludeAttribute` settings for Case and Event as shown below. This does not apply to C# and only applies when using the enterprise version of the WSDL.

```
System.Xml.Serialization.XmlIncludeAttribute(GetType([Event])),

System.Xml.Serialization.XmlIncludeAttribute(GetType([Case])),
```

Step 4: Walk Through the Sample Code

Once you have imported your WSDL file, you can begin building client applications that use the API. Use the following samples to create a basic client application. Comments embedded in the sample explain each section of code.

Java Sample Code

This section walks through a sample Java client application that uses the WSC SOAP client. The purpose of this sample application is to show the required steps for logging into the login server and to demonstrate the invocation and subsequent handling of several API calls.

To run this sample, you must pass the authentication endpoint URL as an argument for your program. You can obtain this URL from the WSDL file. This sample application performs the following main tasks:

1. Prompts the user for their Salesforce username and password.
2. Calls login() to log in to the single login server and, if the login succeeds, retrieves user information and writes it to the console along with session information.
3. Calls describeGlobal() to retrieve a list of all available objects for the organization's data. The describeGlobal method determines the objects that are available to the logged in user. This call should not be made more than once per session, since the data returned from the call is not likely to change frequently. The DescribeGlobalResult is echoed to the console.
4. Calls describeSObjects() to retrieve metadata (field list and object properties) for a specified object. The describeSObject method illustrates the type of metadata information that can be obtained for each object available to the user. The sample client application executes a describeSObjects() call on the object that the user specifies and then echoes the returned metadata information to the console. Object metadata information includes permissions, field types and lengths, and available values for picklist fields and types for referenceTo fields.
5. Calls query(), passing a simple query string ("SELECT FirstName, LastName FROM Contact"), and iterating through the returned QueryResult.
6. Calls logout() to the log the user out.

The following sample code uses try/catch blocks to handle exceptions that might be thrown by the API calls.

```
package com.example.samples;

import java.io.BufferedReader;
import java.io.FileNotFoundException;
import java.io.InputStreamReader;
import java.io.IOException;
import com.sforce.soap.enterprise.DeleteResult;
import com.sforce.soap.enterprise.DescribeGlobalResult;
import com.sforce.soap.enterprise.DescribeGlobalSObjectResult;
import com.sforce.soap.enterprise.DescribeSObjectResult;
import com.sforce.soap.enterprise.EnterpriseConnection;
import com.sforce.soap.enterprise.Error;
import com.sforce.soap.enterprise.Field;
import com.sforce.soap.enterprise.FieldType;
import com.sforce.soap.enterprise.GetUserInfoResult;
import com.sforce.soap.enterprise.LoginResult;
import com.sforce.soap.enterprise.PicklistEntry;
import com.sforce.soap.enterprise.QueryResult;
import com.sforce.soap.enterprise.SaveResult;
import com.sforce.soap.enterprise.sobject.Account;
import com.sforce.soap.enterprise.sobject.Contact;
import com.sforce.soap.enterprise.sobject.SObject;
```

```java
import com.sforce.ws.ConnectorConfig;
import com.sforce.ws.ConnectionException;

public class QuickstartApiSample {

    private static BufferedReader reader = new BufferedReader(
        new InputStreamReader(System.in));

    EnterpriseConnection connection;
    String authEndPoint = "";

    public static void main(String[] args) {
        if (args.length < 1) {
            System.out.println("Usage: com.example.samples."
                    + "QuickstartApiSamples <AuthEndPoint>");

            System.exit(-1);
        }

        QuickstartApiSample sample = new QuickstartApiSample(args[0]);

        sample.run();
    }

    public void run() {
        // Make a login call
        if (login()) {
            // Do a describe global
            describeGlobalSample();

            // Describe an object
            describeSObjectsSample();

            // Retrieve some data using a query
            querySample();

            // Log out
            logout();
        }
    }

    // Constructor
    public QuickstartApiSample(String authEndPoint) {
        this.authEndPoint = authEndPoint;
    }

    private String getUserInput(String prompt) {
        String result = "";
        try {
            System.out.print(prompt);
            result = reader.readLine();
        } catch (IOException ioe) {
            ioe.printStackTrace();
        }

        return result;
    }
```

```java
    private boolean login() {
        boolean success = false;
        String username = getUserInput("Enter username: ");
        String password = getUserInput("Enter password: ");

        try {
            ConnectorConfig config = new ConnectorConfig();
            config.setUsername(username);
            config.setPassword(password);

            System.out.println("AuthEndPoint: " + authEndPoint);
            config.setAuthEndpoint(authEndPoint);

            connection = new EnterpriseConnection(config);
            printUserInfo(config);

            success = true;
        } catch (ConnectionException ce) {
            ce.printStackTrace();
        }

        return success;
    }

    private void printUserInfo(ConnectorConfig config) {
        try {
            GetUserInfoResult userInfo = connection.getUserInfo();

            System.out.println("\nLogging in ...\n");
            System.out.println("UserID: " + userInfo.getUserId());
            System.out.println("User Full Name: " +
userInfo.getUserFullName());
            System.out.println("User Email: " + userInfo.getUserEmail());

            System.out.println();
            System.out.println("SessionID: " + config.getSessionId());
            System.out.println("Auth End Point: " +
config.getAuthEndpoint());
            System.out
                .println("Service End Point: " +
config.getServiceEndpoint());
            System.out.println();
        } catch (ConnectionException ce) {
            ce.printStackTrace();
        }
    }

    private void logout() {
        try {
            connection.logout();
            System.out.println("Logged out.");
        } catch (ConnectionException ce) {
            ce.printStackTrace();
        }
    }
```

```
    /**
     * To determine the objects that are available to the logged-in
user, the
     * sample client application executes a describeGlobal call, which
 returns
     * all of the objects that are visible to the logged-in user. This
 call
     * should not be made more than once per session, as the data
returned from
     * the call likely does not change frequently. The
DescribeGlobalResult is
     * simply echoed to the console.
     */
    private void describeGlobalSample() {
        try {
            // describeGlobal() returns an array of object results that

            // includes the object names that are available to the
logged-in user.
            DescribeGlobalResult dgr = connection.describeGlobal();

            System.out.println("\nDescribe Global Results:\n");
            // Loop through the array echoing the object names to the
console
            for (int i = 0; i < dgr.getSobjects().length; i++) {
                System.out.println(dgr.getSobjects()[i].getName());
            }
        } catch (ConnectionException ce) {
            ce.printStackTrace();
        }
    }

    /**
     * The following method illustrates the type of metadata
information that can
     * be obtained for each object available to the user. The sample
client
     * application executes a describeSObject call on a given object
and then
     * echoes the returned metadata information to the console. Object
metadata
     * information includes permissions, field types and length and
available
     * values for picklist fields and types for referenceTo fields.
     */
    private void describeSObjectsSample() {
        String objectToDescribe = getUserInput("\nType the name of the
object to "
                + "describe (try Account): ");

        try {
            // Call describeSObjects() passing in an array with one
object type
            // name
            DescribeSObjectResult[] dsrArray = connection
                .describeSObjects(new String[] { objectToDescribe });
```

```java
                 // Since we described only one sObject, we should have only

                 // one element in the DescribeSObjectResult array.
                 DescribeSObjectResult dsr = dsrArray[0];

                 // First, get some object properties
                 System.out.println("\n\nObject Name: " + dsr.getName());

                 if (dsr.getCustom())
                     System.out.println("Custom Object");
                 if (dsr.getLabel() != null)
                     System.out.println("Label: " + dsr.getLabel());

                 // Get the permissions on the object

                 if (dsr.getCreateable())
                     System.out.println("Createable");
                 if (dsr.getDeletable())
                     System.out.println("Deleteable");
                 if (dsr.getQueryable())
                     System.out.println("Queryable");
                 if (dsr.getReplicateable())
                     System.out.println("Replicateable");
                 if (dsr.getRetrieveable())
                     System.out.println("Retrieveable");
                 if (dsr.getSearchable())
                     System.out.println("Searchable");
                 if (dsr.getUndeletable())
                     System.out.println("Undeleteable");
                 if (dsr.getUpdateable())
                     System.out.println("Updateable");

           System.out.println("Number of fields: " +
dsr.getFields().length);

                 // Now, retrieve metadata for each field
           for (int i = 0; i < dsr.getFields().length; i++) {
                 // Get the field
                 Field field = dsr.getFields()[i];

                 // Write some field properties
                 System.out.println("Field name: " + field.getName());
          System.out.println("\tField Label: " + field.getLabel());


                 // This next property indicates that this
                 // field is searched when using
                 // the name search group in SOSL
                 if (field.getNameField())
                     System.out.println("\tThis is a name field.");

                 if (field.getRestrictedPicklist())
                     System.out.println("This is a RESTRICTED picklist
field.");

                 System.out.println("\tType is: " + field.getType());
```

```
            if (field.getLength() > 0)
               System.out.println("\tLength: " + field.getLength());


            if (field.getScale() > 0)
               System.out.println("\tScale: " + field.getScale());

            if (field.getPrecision() > 0)
                System.out.println("\tPrecision: " +
field.getPrecision());

            if (field.getDigits() > 0)
               System.out.println("\tDigits: " + field.getDigits());


            if (field.getCustom())
               System.out.println("\tThis is a custom field.");

            // Write the permissions of this field
            if (field.getNillable())
               System.out.println("\tCan be nulled.");
            if (field.getCreateable())
               System.out.println("\tCreateable");
            if (field.getFilterable())
               System.out.println("\tFilterable");
            if (field.getUpdateable())
               System.out.println("\tUpdateable");

            // If this is a picklist field, show the picklist values

            if (field.getType().equals(FieldType.picklist)) {
               System.out.println("\t\tPicklist values: ");
               PicklistEntry[] picklistValues =
field.getPicklistValues();

               for (int j = 0; j < field.getPicklistValues().length;
  j++) {
                   System.out.println("\t\tValue: "
                       + picklistValues[j].getValue());
               }
            }

            // If this is a foreign key field (reference),
            // show the values
            if (field.getType().equals(FieldType.reference)) {
               System.out.println("\tCan reference these objects:");

               for (int j = 0; j < field.getReferenceTo().length;
j++) {
                   System.out.println("\t\t" +
field.getReferenceTo()[j]);
               }
            }
            System.out.println("");
         }
      } catch (ConnectionException ce) {
```

```
            ce.printStackTrace();
        }
    }

    private void querySample() {
        String soqlQuery = "SELECT FirstName, LastName FROM Contact";
        try {
            QueryResult qr = connection.query(soqlQuery);
            boolean done = false;

            if (qr.getSize() > 0) {
                System.out.println("\nLogged-in user can see "
                        + qr.getRecords().length + " contact records.");

                while (!done) {
                    System.out.println("");
                    SObject[] records = qr.getRecords();
                    for (int i = 0; i < records.length; ++i) {
                        Contact con = (Contact) records[i];
                        String fName = con.getFirstName();
                        String lName = con.getLastName();

                        if (fName == null) {
                            System.out.println("Contact " + (i + 1) + ": "
    + lName);
                        } else {
                            System.out.println("Contact " + (i + 1) + ": "
    + fName
                                    + " " + lName);
                        }
                    }

                    if (qr.isDone()) {
                        done = true;
                    } else {
                        qr = connection.queryMore(qr.getQueryLocator());
                    }
                }
            } else {
                System.out.println("No records found.");
            }
        } catch (ConnectionException ce) {
            ce.printStackTrace();
        }
    }
}
```

C# Sample Code

This section walks through a sample C# client application. The purpose of this sample application is to show the required steps for logging in and to demonstrate the invocation and subsequent handling of several API calls.

This sample application performs the following main tasks:

1. Prompts the user for their Salesforce username and password.
2. Calls `login()` to log in to the single login server and, if the login succeeds:

   - Sets the returned `sessionId` into the session header, which is required for session authentication on subsequent API calls.
   - Resets the Force.com endpoint to the returned `serverUrl`, which is the target of subsequent API calls.

     All client applications that access the API must complete the tasks in this step before attempting any subsequent API calls.

   - Retrieves user information and writes it to the console along with session information.

3. Calls `describeGlobal()` to retrieve a list of all available objects for the organization's data. The `describeGlobal` method determines the objects that are available to the logged in user. This call should not be made more than once per session, since the data returned from the call is not likely to change frequently. The DescribeGlobalResult is echoed to the console.
4. Calls `describeSObjects()` to retrieve metadata (field list and object properties) for a specified object. The `describeSObject` method illustrates the type of metadata information that can be obtained for each object available to the user. The sample client application executes a `describeSObjects()` call on the object that the user specifies and then echoes the returned metadata information to the console. Object metadata information includes permissions, field types and lengths, and available values for picklist fields and types for `referenceTo` fields.
5. Calls `query()`, passing a simple query string (`"SELECT FirstName, LastName FROM Contact"`), and iterating through the returned QueryResult.
6. Calls `logout()` to the log the user out.

The following sample code uses try/catch blocks to handle exceptions that might be thrown by the API calls.

The following code begins the sample C# client application.

```
using System;
using System.Collections.Generic;
using System.Linq;
using System.Text;
using System.Web.Services.Protocols;
using Walkthrough.sforce;

namespace Walkthrough
{

    class QuickstartApiSample
```

```
    {
        private SforceService binding;

        [STAThread]
        static void Main(string[] args)
        {
            QuickstartApiSample sample = new QuickstartApiSample();
            sample.run();
        }

        public void run()
        {
            // Make a login call
            if (login())
            {
                // Do a describe global
                describeGlobalSample();

                // Describe an account object
                describeSObjectsSample();

                // Retrieve some data using a query
                querySample();

                // Log out
                logout();
            }
        }

        private bool login()
        {
            Console.Write("Enter username: ");
            string username = Console.ReadLine();
            Console.Write("Enter password: ");
            string password = Console.ReadLine();

            // Create a service object
            binding = new SforceService();

            // Timeout after a minute
            binding.Timeout = 60000;

            // Try logging in
            LoginResult lr;
            try
            {

                Console.WriteLine("\nLogging in...\n");
                lr = binding.login(username, password);
            }

            // ApiFault is a proxy stub generated from the WSDL contract
when
            // the web service was imported
            catch (SoapException e)
            {
                // Write the fault code to the console
```

```
            Console.WriteLine(e.Code);

            // Write the fault message to the console
            Console.WriteLine("An unexpected error has occurred: "
+ e.Message);

            // Write the stack trace to the console
            Console.WriteLine(e.StackTrace);

            // Return False to indicate that the login was not
successful
            return false;
        }


        // Check if the password has expired
        if (lr.passwordExpired)
        {
            Console.WriteLine("An error has occurred. Your password
 has expired.");
            return false;
        }


        /** Once the client application has logged in successfully,
 it will use
         * the results of the login call to reset the endpoint of
the service
         * to the virtual server instance that is servicing your
organization
         */
        // Save old authentication end point URL
        String authEndPoint = binding.Url;
        // Set returned service endpoint URL
        binding.Url = lr.serverUrl;

        /** The sample client application now has an instance of
the SforceService
         * that is pointing to the correct endpoint. Next, the sample
 client
         * application sets a persistent SOAP header (to be included
 on all
         * subsequent calls that are made with SforceService) that
contains the
         * valid sessionId for our login credentials. To do this,
the sample
         * client application creates a new SessionHeader object
and persist it to
         * the SforceService. Add the session ID returned from the
 login to the
         * session header
         */
        binding.SessionHeaderValue = new SessionHeader();
        binding.SessionHeaderValue.sessionId = lr.sessionId;

        printUserInfo(lr, authEndPoint);
```

```
            // Return true to indicate that we are logged in, pointed
            // at the right URL and have our security token in place.
        return true;
    }

    private void printUserInfo(LoginResult lr, String authEP)
    {
        try
        {
            GetUserInfoResult userInfo = lr.userInfo;

            Console.WriteLine("\nLogging in ...\n");
            Console.WriteLine("UserID: " + userInfo.userId);
            Console.WriteLine("User Full Name: " +
                userInfo.userFullName);
            Console.WriteLine("User Email: " +
                userInfo.userEmail);
            Console.WriteLine();
            Console.WriteLine("SessionID: " +
                lr.sessionId);
            Console.WriteLine("Auth End Point: " +
                authEP);
            Console.WriteLine("Service End Point: " +
                lr.serverUrl);
            Console.WriteLine();
        }
        catch (SoapException e)
        {
            Console.WriteLine("An unexpected error has occurred: "
+ e.Message +
                " Stack trace: " + e.StackTrace);
        }
    }

    private void logout()
    {
        try
        {
            binding.logout();
            Console.WriteLine("Logged out.");
        }
        catch (SoapException e)
        {
            // Write the fault code to the console
            Console.WriteLine(e.Code);

            // Write the fault message to the console
            Console.WriteLine("An unexpected error has occurred: "
+ e.Message);

            // Write the stack trace to the console
            Console.WriteLine(e.StackTrace);
        }
    }
```

```
/**
 * To determine the objects that are available to the logged-in
 * user, the sample client application executes a describeGlobal
 * call, which returns all of the objects that are visible to
 * the logged-in user. This call should not be made more than
 * once per session, as the data returned from the call likely
 * does not change frequently. The DescribeGlobalResult is
 * simply echoed to the console.
 */
private void describeGlobalSample()
{
    try
    {
        // describeGlobal() returns an array of object results
that
        // includes the object names that are available to the
logged-in user.
        DescribeGlobalResult dgr = binding.describeGlobal();

        Console.WriteLine("\nDescribe Global Results:\n");
        // Loop through the array echoing the object names to
the console
        for (int i = 0; i < dgr.sobjects.Length; i++)
        {
            Console.WriteLine(dgr.sobjects[i].name);
        }
    }
    catch (SoapException e)
    {
        Console.WriteLine("An exception has occurred: " +
e.Message +
            "\nStack trace: " + e.StackTrace);
    }
}

/**
 * The following method illustrates the type of metadata
 * information that can be obtained for each object available
 * to the user. The sample client application executes a
 * describeSObject call on a given object and then echoes
 * the returned metadata information to the console. Object
 * metadata information includes permissions, field types
 * and length and available values for picklist fields
 * and types for referenceTo fields.
 */
private void describeSObjectsSample()
{
    Console.Write("\nType the name of the object to " +
        "describe (try Account): ");
    string objectType = Console.ReadLine();
    try
    {

        // Call describeSObjects() passing in an array with one
```

```
object type name
        DescribeSObjectResult[] dsrArray =
            binding.describeSObjects(new string[] { objectType
});

        // Since we described only one sObject, we should have
only
        // one element in the DescribeSObjectResult array.
        DescribeSObjectResult dsr = dsrArray[0];

        // First, get some object properties
        Console.WriteLine("\n\nObject Name: " + dsr.name);

        if (dsr.custom) Console.WriteLine("Custom Object");
        if (dsr.label != null) Console.WriteLine("Label: " +
dsr.label);

        // Get the permissions on the object
        if (dsr.createable) Console.WriteLine("Createable");
        if (dsr.deletable) Console.WriteLine("Deleteable");
        if (dsr.queryable) Console.WriteLine("Queryable");
      if (dsr.replicateable) Console.WriteLine("Replicateable");

      if (dsr.retrieveable) Console.WriteLine("Retrieveable");

        if (dsr.searchable) Console.WriteLine("Searchable");
        if (dsr.undeletable) Console.WriteLine("Undeleteable");
        if (dsr.updateable) Console.WriteLine("Updateable");

        Console.WriteLine("Number of fields: " +
dsr.fields.Length);

        // Now, retrieve metadata for each field
        for (int i = 0; i < dsr.fields.Length; i++)
        {
            // Get the field
            Field field = dsr.fields[i];

            // Write some field properties
            Console.WriteLine("Field name: " + field.name);
            Console.WriteLine("\tField Label: " + field.label);

            // This next property indicates that this
            // field is searched when using
            // the name search group in SOSL
            if (field.nameField)
                Console.WriteLine("\tThis is a name field.");

            if (field.restrictedPicklist)
                Console.WriteLine("This is a RESTRICTED picklist
field.");

            Console.WriteLine("\tType is: " +
field.type.ToString());

            if (field.length > 0)
                Console.WriteLine("\tLength: " + field.length);
```

```
            if (field.scale > 0)
                Console.WriteLine("\tScale: " + field.scale);

            if (field.precision > 0)
                Console.WriteLine("\tPrecision: " +
field.precision);

            if (field.digits > 0)
                Console.WriteLine("\tDigits: " + field.digits);

            if (field.custom)
                Console.WriteLine("\tThis is a custom field.");

            // Write the permissions of this field
            if (field.nillable) Console.WriteLine("\tCan be
nulled.");
            if (field.createable)
Console.WriteLine("\tCreateable");
            if (field.filterable)
Console.WriteLine("\tFilterable");
            if (field.updateable)
Console.WriteLine("\tUpdateable");

            // If this is a picklist field, show the picklist
values
            if (field.type.Equals(fieldType.picklist))
            {
                Console.WriteLine("\tPicklist Values");
                for (int j = 0; j < field.picklistValues.Length;
j++)
                    Console.WriteLine("\t\t" +
field.picklistValues[j].value);
            }

            // If this is a foreign key field (reference),
            // show the values
            if (field.type.Equals(fieldType.reference))
            {
             Console.WriteLine("\tCan reference these objects:");

                for (int j = 0; j < field.referenceTo.Length; j++)

                    Console.WriteLine("\t\t" + field.referenceTo[j]);

            }
            Console.WriteLine("");
        }
    }
    catch (SoapException e)
    {
        Console.WriteLine("An exception has occurred: " +
e.Message +
            "\nStack trace: " + e.StackTrace);
    }
    Console.WriteLine("Press ENTER to continue...");
    Console.ReadLine();
```

```
        }

    private void querySample()
    {
      String soqlQuery = "SELECT FirstName, LastName FROM Contact";

        try
        {
            QueryResult qr = binding.query(soqlQuery);
            bool done = false;

            if (qr.size > 0)
            {
                Console.WriteLine("Logged-in user can see "
                    + qr.records.Length + " contact records.");

                while (!done)
                {
                    Console.WriteLine("");
                    sObject[] records = qr.records;
                    for (int i = 0; i < records.Length; i++)
                    {
                        Contact con = (Contact)records[i];
                        string fName = con.FirstName;
                        string lName = con.LastName;
                        if (fName == null)
                            Console.WriteLine("Contact " + (i + 1) + ":
" + lName);
                        else
                            Console.WriteLine("Contact " + (i + 1) + ":
" + fName
                                    + " " + lName);
                    }

                    if (qr.done)
                    {
                        done = true;
                    }
                    else
                    {
                        qr = binding.queryMore(qr.queryLocator);
                    }
                }
            }
            else
            {
                Console.WriteLine("No records found.");
            }
        }
        catch (Exception ex)
        {
          Console.WriteLine("\nFailed to execute query succesfully,"
+
                "error message was: \n{0}", ex.Message);
        }
        Console.WriteLine("\nPress ENTER to continue...");
        Console.ReadLine();
```

```
        }
      }
    }
```

Best Practices

Before you build an integration application or other client application, consider the data management, use limits, and communication issues explained in this section.

User Permissions

When your client application connects to the SOAP API, it must first log in. Client applications run with the permissions and sharing of the logged-in user.

An organization's Salesforce administrator controls the availability of various features and views by configuring profiles and permission sets, and assigning users to them. To access the API (to issue calls and receive the call results), a user must be granted the "API Enabled" permission. Client applications can query or update only those objects and fields to which they have access via the permissions of the logged-in user.

If the client application logs in as a user who has access to data via a sharing rule, then the API must issue an extra query to check access. To avoid this, log in as a user with the "Modify All Data" permission.

API Usage Monitoring

You can monitor the number of SOAP API requests generated by your organization in two ways.

- Any user can see the number of API requests sent in the last 24 hours. To view the information, from Setup, click **Company Profile** > **Company Information**. Look for the "API Requests, Last 24 Hours" field in the right column.
- If a user has the "Modify All Data" permission, the user can view a report of the API requests sent for the last seven days. To view the information, click the Reports tab, scroll to the **Administrative Reports** section and click the **API Usage Last 7 Days** link. Users can sort the report by any of the fields listed in the **Summarize Information by:** drop-down list.

Query Limits

There is a limit on the number of queries that a user can execute concurrently. A user can have up to 10 query cursors open at a time. If 10 QueryLocator cursors are open when a client application, logged in as the same user, attempts to open a new one, then the oldest of the 10 cursors is released. If the client application attempts to open the released query cursor, an error results.

Multiple client applications can log in using the same `username` argument. However, this increases your risk of getting errors due to query limits.

If multiple client applications are logged in using the same user, they all share the same session. If one of the client applications calls `logout()`, it invalidates the session for all the client applications. Using a different user for each client application makes it easier to avoid these limits.

API Request Limits

To maintain optimum performance and ensure that the Force.com API is available to all of our customers, salesforce.com balances transaction loads by imposing two types of limits:

- Concurrent API Request Limits
- Total API Request Limits

When a call exceeds a request limit, an error is returned.

The following table lists the limits for various types of organizations for concurrent requests (calls) with a duration of 20 seconds or longer.

Organization Type	Limit
Developer Edition	5
Trial organizations	5
Production organizations	25
Sandbox	25

The following table lists the limits for the total API requests (calls) per 24-hour period for an organization.

Salesforce Edition	API Calls Per License Type	Minimum	Maximum
All Editions: DebuggingHeader on API testing calls for Apex specified. Valid in API version 20 and later.	N/A	1,000	1,000
Developer Edition	N/A	5,000	5,000
• Enterprise Edition	• Salesforce: 1,000	5,000	1,000,000

Salesforce Edition	API Calls Per License Type	Minimum	Maximum
• Professional Edition with API access enabled	• Force.com App Subscription: 200 • Salesforce Platform: 1,000 **Note:** This license is not available to new customers. • Force.com - One App: 200 **Note:** This license is not available to new customers. • Gold Partner: 200		
• Unlimited Edition • Performance Edition	• Salesforce: 5,000 • Force.com App Subscription: 200 • Salesforce Platform: 5,000 **Note:** This license is not available to new customers. • Force.com - One App: 200 **Note:** This license is not available to new customers. • Gold Partner: 200	5,000	Unlimited. However, at any high limit, it is likely that other limiting factors such as system load may prevent you from using your entire allocation of calls in a 24–hour period.
Sandbox	N/A	N/A	5,000,000

Limits are enforced against the aggregate of all API calls made by the organization in a 24 hour period; limits are not on a per-user basis. When an organization exceeds a limit, all users in the organization may be temporarily blocked from making additional calls. Calls will be blocked until usage for the preceding 24 hours drops below the limit.

Multiple Instances of Salesforce.com Database Servers

Salesforce.com provides many database server instances. Although organizations are generally allocated by geographic regions, an organization may be on any instance.

Content Type Requirement

In the API version 7.0 and later, all requests must contain a correct content type HTTP header, for example: `Content-Type: text/xml; charset=utf-8`. Earlier versions of the API do not enforce this requirement.

Compression

SOAP API allows the use of compression on the request and the response, using the standards defined by the HTTP 1.1 specification. This is automatically supported by some SOAP/WSDL clients, and can be manually added to others. Visit `http://wiki.developerforce.com/page/Tools` for more information on particular clients.

To indicate that the client supports compression, you should include the HTTP header "Accept-Encoding: gzip, deflate" or a similar heading. SOAP API compresses the response if the client properly specifies this header. The response includes the header "Content-Encoding: deflate" or "Content-Encoding: gzip," as appropriate. You can also compress any request by including a "Content-Encoding: deflate" or "gzip" header.

HTTP Persistent Connections

Most clients achieve better performance if they use HTTP 1.1 persistent connection to reuse the socket connection for multiple requests. Persistent connections are normally handled by your SOAP/WSDL client automatically. For more details, see the HTTP 1.1 specification at:

`http://www.w3.org/Protocols/rfc2616/rfc2616-sec8.html#sec8.1`

HTTP Chunking

Clients that use HTTP 1.1 may receive chunked responses. Chunking is normally handled by your SOAP/WSDL client automatically.

Resources

Search on the Salesforce Developer's Network at `http://developer.salesforce.com/docs` for the following resources on SOAP API.

- SOAP API Developer's Guide

- SOAP API Developer Cheat Sheet
- Salesforce Object Reference
- APIs and Integration forums

## Chapter 7

REST API

REST API provides a REST-based API for interacting with Salesforce. You can use REST API to create Force.com applications that can create, retrieve, update or delete records managed by Salesforce, using any development environment that supports Web services.

When to Use REST API

REST API provides a powerful, convenient, and simple REST-based Web services interface for interacting with Salesforce. Its advantages include ease of integration and development, and it's an excellent choice of technology for use with mobile applications and Web projects. However, if you have a large number of records to process, you may wish to use Bulk API, which is based on REST principles and optimized for large sets of data.

Supported Editions and Platforms

To use REST API, your organization must use Enterprise Edition, Performance Edition, Unlimited Edition, or Developer Edition. If you are an existing Salesforce customer and want to upgrade to Enterprise, Unlimited, or Performance Edition, contact your account representative.

Quick Start

Create a sample REST application in your development environment to see the power and flexibility of REST API

Prerequisites

Completing the prerequisites makes it easier to build and use the quick-start sample.

- Install your development platform according to its product documentation.
- Become familiar with cURL, the tool used to execute REST requests in this quick start. If you use another tool, you should be familiar enough with it to translate the example code.
- Become familiar with JavaScript Object Notation (JSON), which is used in this quick start, or be able to translate samples from JSON to the standard you use.
- Enable an SSL endpoint in your application server.
- Become familiar with OAuth 2.0, which requires some setup. We provide the steps, but it will help if you are familiar with the basic concepts and workflow.
- Read through all the steps before beginning this quick start. You may also wish to review the rest of this document to familiarize yourself with terms and concepts.

Step One: Obtain a Salesforce Developer Edition Organization

If you are not already a member of the Force.com developer community, go to `http://developer.force.com/join` and follow the instructions for signing up for a Developer Edition organization. Even if you already have Enterprise Edition, Unlimited Edition, or Performance Edition, use Developer Edition for developing, staging, and testing your solutions against sample data to protect your organization's live data. This is especially true for applications that insert, update, or delete data (as opposed to simply reading data).

If you already have a Developer Edition organization, verify that you have the "API Enabled" permission. This permission is enabled by default, but may have been changed by an administrator. For more information, see the help in the Salesforce user interface.

Step Two: Set Up Authorization

You can set up authorization using OAuth 2.0 or by passing a session ID.

 Important: If you're handling someone else's password, don't use session ID.

Partners, who wish to get an OAuth consumer Id for authentication, can contact salesforce.com

Setting Up OAuth 2.0

Setting up OAuth 2.0 requires that you take some steps within Salesforce and in other locations. If any of the steps are unfamiliar, see Understanding Authentication or the Salesforce online help. The following example uses the Web server OAuth flow.

1. In Salesforce, from Setup, click **Develop** > **Remote Access**, and click **New** to create a new remote access application if you have not already done so. The `Callback URL` you supply here is the same as your Web application's callback URL. Usually it is a servlet if you work with Java. It must be secure: `http://` does not work, only `https://`. For development environments, the callback URL is similar to `https://localhost:8443/RestTest/oauth/_callback`. When you click Save, the `Consumer Key` is created and displayed, and a `Consumer Secret` is created (click the link to reveal it).

    Note: The OAuth 2.0 specification uses "client" instead of "consumer." Salesforce supports OAuth 2.0.

   The values here correspond to the following values in the sample code in the rest of this procedure:

   - `client_id` is the `Consumer Key`
   - `client_secret` is the `Consumer Secret`
   - `redirect_uri` is the `Callback URL`.

   In your client application, redirect the user to the appropriate Salesforce authorization endpoint. On successful user login, Salesforce will call your redirect URI with an authorization code. You use the authorization code in the next step to get the access token.

2. From your Java or other client application, make a request to the appropriate Salesforce token request endpoint that passes in `grant_type`, `client_id`, `client_secret`, and `redirect_uri`. The `redirect_uri` is the URI that Salesforce sends a callback to.

```
initParams = {
    @WebInitParam(name = "clientId", value =

"3MVG91KcPoNINVBJSoQsNCD.HHDdbugPsNXwwyFbgb47KWa_PTv"),
    @WebInitParam(name = "clientSecret", value =
"56784718536095795O8"),
    @WebInitParam(name = "redirectUri", value =

"https://localhost:8443/RestTest/oauth/_callback"),
    @WebInitParam(name = "environment", value =

"https://na1.salesforce.com/services/oauth2/token")  }

HttpClient httpclient = new HttpClient();
PostMethod post = new PostMethod(environment);
post.addParameter("code",code);
post.addParameter("grant_type","authorization_code");

    /** For session ID instead of OAuth 2.0, use "grant_type",
    "password" **/
```

```
post.addParameter("client_id",clientId);
post.addParameter("client_secret",clientSecret);
post.addParameter("redirect_uri",redirectUri);
```

If the value of client_id (or consumer key) and client_secret (or consumer secret) are valid, Salesforce sends a callback to the URI specified in redirect_uri that contains a value for access_token.

3. Store the access token value as a cookie to use in all subsequent requests. For example:

```
//exception handling removed for brevity...
  //this is the post from step 2
  httpclient.executeMethod(post);
     String responseBody = post.getResponseBodyAsString();

  String accessToken = null;
  JSONObject json = null;
   try {
       json = new JSONObject(responseBody);
          accessToken = json.getString("access_token");
          issuedAt = json.getString("issued_at");
          /** Use this to validate session
           * instead of expiring on browser close.
           */

       } catch (JSONException e) {
           e.printStackTrace();
       }

        HttpServletResponse httpResponse =
 (HttpServletResponse)response;
          Cookie session = new Cookie(ACCESS_TOKEN,
accessToken);
          session.setMaxAge(-1); //cookie not persistent,
destroyed on browser exit
          httpResponse.addCookie(session);
```

This completes the authentication.

4. Once authenticated, every request must pass in the access_token value in the header. It cannot be passed as a request parameter.

```
HttpClient httpclient = new HttpClient();
   GetMethod gm = new GetMethod(serviceUrl);

   //set the token in the header
   gm.setRequestHeader("Authorization", "Bearer
"+accessToken);
   //set the SOQL as a query param
   NameValuePair[] params = new NameValuePair[1];

   /**
    * other option instead of query string, pass just the
fields you want back:
```

```
       *
https://instance_name.salesforce.com/services/data/v20.0/sobjects/Account/

       *
001D000000INjVe?fields=AccountNumber,BillingPostalCode
       */
  params[0] = new NameValuePair("q","SELECT name, title FROM
Contact LIMIT 100");
  gm.setQueryString(params);

  httpclient.executeMethod(gm);
  String responseBody = gm.getResponseBodyAsString();
      //exception handling removed for brevity
  JSONObject json = new JSONObject(responseBody);

  JSONArray results = json.getJSONArray("records");

  for(int i = 0; i < results.length(); i++)

response.getWriter().write(results.getJSONObject(i).getString("Name")+
      ",
        "+results.getJSONObject(i).getString("Title")+"\n");
```

The syntax to provide the access token in your REST requests:

```
Authorization: Bearer access_token
```

For example:

```
curl https://instance_name.salesforce.com/services/data/v20.0/ -H
'Authorization: Bearer access_token'
```

Session ID Authorization

You can use a session ID instead of an OAuth 2.0 access token if you aren't handling someone else's password:

1. Obtain a session ID, for example, a SOAP API `login()` call returns the session ID. You may also have the session ID, for example as part of the Apex current context. If you need a session ID just for testing purposes during development, you can use the username-password OAuth flow in a cURL command similar to the following:

```
curl https://login.salesforce.com/services/oauth2/token -d
"grant_type=password" -d "client_id=myclientid" -d
"client_secret=myclientsecret" -d "mylogin@salesforce.com"
    -d "password=mypassword123456"
```

You will need to provide your client id, client secret, username and password with user security token appended.

2. Use the session ID when you send a request to the resource. Substitute the ID for the `token` value. The syntax is the same:

```
Authorization: Bearer access_token
```

For example:

```
curl
https://instance_name.salesforce.com/services/data/v20.0/
-H 'Authorization: Bearer access_token'
```

Step Three: Send HTTP Requests with cURL

To interact with the Force.com REST API, you need to set up your client application (we use cURL) to construct HTTP requests.

Setting Up Your Client Application

The REST API uses HTTP GET and HTTP POST methods to send and receive JSON and XML content, so it is very simple to build client applications using the tool or the language of your choice. We use a command-line tool called cURL to simplify sending and receiving HTTP requests and responses.

cURL is pre-installed on many Linux and Mac systems. Windows users can download a version at `curl.haxx.se/`. When using HTTPS on Windows, ensure that your system meets the cURL requirements for SSL.

Sending HTTP Requests Using REST API Resources

Your HTTP requests to a REST API resource should contain the following information:

- An HTTP method (HEAD, GET, POST, PATCH, or DELETE).
- An OAuth 2.0 access token used to authenticate the request. For information on how to retrieve the token, see Quick Start on page 226.
- An HTTP ACCEPT header used to indicate the resource format (XML or JSON), or a `.json` or `.xml` extension to the URI. The default is JSON.
- The Force.com REST resource.
- Any JSON or XML files containing information needed for requests, such as updating a record with new information.

The HTTP methods are used to indicate the desired action, such as retrieving information, as well as creating, updating, and deleting records.

- HEAD is used to retrieve resource metadata.
- GET is used to retrieve information, such as basic resource summary information.

- POST is used to create a new object.
- PATCH is used to update a record.
- DELETE is used to delete a record.

To access a resource, submit an HTTP request containing a header, method, and resource name.

For example, assume you want to create an Account record using a JSON-formatted file called newaccount.json. It contains the information to be stored in the new account:

```
{
    "Name" : "test"
}
```

Using cURL on instance na1, the request would appear as follows:

```
curl https://na1.salesforce.com/services/data/v20.0/sobjects/Account/
 -H "Authorization: Bearer token -H "Content-Type: application/json"
 -d @newaccount.json"
```

The request HTTP header:

```
POST /services/data/v20.0/sobjects/Account HTTP/1.1
User-Agent: curl/7.19.7 (universal-apple-darwin10.0) libcurl/7.19.7
 OpenSSL/0.9.81 zlib/1.2.3
Host: na7.salesforce.com
Accept: */*
Content-Length: 1411
Content-Type: application/json
Authorization: Bearer XXXXXXXXXXXXXXXXXXXXXXXXXXXXXXXXXXXXXXXX
X-PrettyPrint:1
```

The response:

```
Date: Thu, 21 Oct 2010 22:16:22 GMT
Content-Length: 71
Location: /services/data/v20.0/sobjects/Account/001T000000NU96UIAT
Content-Type: application/json; charset=UTF-8 Server:
{ "id" : "001T000000NU96UIAT",
  "errors" : [ ],
  "success" : true }
```

For a list of the resources and their corresponding URIs, see Reference.

Step Four: Walk Through the Sample Code

In this section you will create a series of REST requests. cURL will be used to construct the requests, and JSON will be used as the format for all requests and responses. In each request, a base URI will be used in conjunction with the REST resource. The base URI for these examples is `https://na1.salesforce.com/services/data`. For more information, see Understanding Force.com REST Resources.

In this example, a series of REST requests will be used in the following scenario:

1. Get the Salesforce version.
2. Use the Salesforce version to get a list of the resources available.
3. Use one of the resources to get a list of the available objects.
4. Select one of the objects and get a description of its metadata.
5. Get a list of fields on that same object.
6. Execute a SOQL query to retrieve values from all `name` fields on Account records.
7. Update the Billing City for one of the Account objects.

Get the Salesforce Version

Begin by retrieving information about each available Salesforce version. To do this, submit a request for the Versions resource. In this case the request does not require authentication:

```
curl https://na1.salesforce.com/services/data/
```

The output from this request, including the response header:

```
Content-Length: 88
Content-Type: application/json;
charset=UTF-8 Server:
[
    {
        "version":"20.0",
        "url":"/services/data/v20.0",
        "label":"Winter '11"
    }
    ...
]
```

The output specifies the resources available for all valid versions (your result may include more than one value). Next, use one of these versions to discover the resources it contains.

Get a List of Resources

The next step is to retrieve a list of the resources available for Salesforce, in this example for version 20.0. To do this, submit a request for the Resources by Version:

```
curl https://na1.salesforce.com/services/data/v20.0/ -H
"Authorization: Bearer access_token" -H "X-PrettyPrint:1"
```

The output from this request is as follows:

```
{
    "sobjects" : "/services/data/v20.0/sobjects",
    "search" : "/services/data/v20.0/search",
    "query" : "/services/data/v20.0/query",
    "recent" : "/services/data/v20.0/recent"
}
```

From this output you can see that `sobjects` is one of the available resources in Salesforce version 20.0. You will be able to use this resource in the next request to retrieve the available objects.

Get a List of Available Objects

Now that you have the list of available resources, you can request a list of the available objects. To do this, submit a request for the Describe Global:

```
curl https://na1.salesforce.com/services/data/v20.0/sobjects/ -H
"Authorization: Bearer access_token" -H "X-PrettyPrint:1"
```

The output from this request is as follows:

```
Transfer-Encoding: chunked
Content-Type: application/json;
charset=UTF-8 Server:
{
 "encoding" : "UTF-8",
 "maxBatchSize" : 200,
 "sobjects" : [ {
    "name" : "Account",
    "label" : "Account",
    "custom" : false,
    "keyPrefix" : "001",
    "updateable" : true,
    "searchable" : true,
    "labelPlural" : "Accounts",
    "layoutable" : true,
    "activateable" : false,
    "urls" : { "sobject" : "/services/data/v20.0/sobjects/Account",
    "describe" : "/services/data/v20.0/sobjects/Account/describe",
    "rowTemplate" : "/services/data/v20.0/sobjects/Account/{ID}" },
    "createable" : true,
    "customSetting" : false,
    "deletable" : true,
    "deprecatedAndHidden" : false,
    "feedEnabled" : false,
    "mergeable" : true,
    "queryable" : true,
    "replicateable" : true,
    "retrieveable" : true,
    "undeletable" : true,
    "triggerable" : true },
```

```
        },
    ...
```

From this output you can see that the Account object is available. You will be able to get more information about the Account object in the next steps.

Get Basic Object Information

Now that you have identified the Account object as an available resource, you can retrieve some basic information about its metadata. To do this, submit a request for the SObject Basic Information:

```
curl https://na1.salesforce.com/services/data/v20.0/sobjects/Account/
  -H "Authorization: Bearer access_token" -H "X-PrettyPrint:1"
```

The output from this request is as follows:

```
{
    "objectDescribe" :
    {
        "name" : "Account",
        "updateable" : true,
        "label" : "Account",
        "keyPrefix" : "001",

        . . .

        "replicateable" : true,
        "retrieveable" : true,
        "undeletable" : true,
        "triggerable" : true
    },
    "recentItems" :
    [
        {
            "attributes" :
            {
                "type" : "Account",
                "url" :
"/services/data/v20.0/sobjects/Account/001D000000INjVeIAL"
            },
            "Id" : "001D000000INjVeIAL",
            "Name" : "asdasdasd"
        },

        . . .

    ]
}
```

From this output you can see some basic attributes of the Account object, such as its name and label, as well as a list of the most recently used Accounts. Since you may need more information about its fields, such as length and default values, in the next step you will retrieve more detailed information about the Account object.

Get a List of Fields

Now that you have some basic information about the Account object's metadata, you may be interested in retrieving more detailed information. To do this, submit a request for the SObject Describe:

```
curl
https://na1.salesforce.com/services/data/v20.0/sobjects/Account/describe/
 -H "Authorization: Bearer access_token" -H "X-PrettyPrint:1"
```

The output from this request is as follows:

```
{
    "name" : "Account",
    "fields" :
    [
        {
            "length" : 18,
            "name" : "Id",
            "type" : "id",
            "defaultValue" : { "value" : null },
            "updateable" : false,
            "label" : "Account ID",
            ...
        },
        ...
    ],
    "updateable" : true,
    "label" : "Account",
    ...
    "urls" :
    {
        "uiEditTemplate" : "https://na1.salesforce.com/{ID}/e",
        "sobject" : "/services/data/v20.0/sobjects/Account",
        "uiDetailTemplate" : "https://na1.soma.salesforce.com/{ID}",

        "describe" : "/services/data/v20.0/sobjects/Account/describe",

        "rowTemplate" : "/services/data/v20.0/sobjects/Account/{ID}",

        "uiNewRecord" : "https://na1.salesforce.com/001/e"
    },
    "childRelationships" :
    [
        {
            "field" : "ParentId",
            "deprecatedAndHidden" : false,
            ...
        },
        ...
    ],
```

```
    "createable" : true,
    "customSetting" : false,
    ...
}
```

From this output you can see much more detailed information about the Account object, such as its field attributes and child relationships. Now you have enough information to construct useful queries and updates for the Account objects in your organization, which you will do in the next steps.

Execute a SOQL Query

Now that you know the field names on the Account object, you can execute a SOQL query, for example, to retrieve a list of all the Account name values. To do this, submit a Query request:

```
curl
https://na1.salesforce.com/services/data/v20.0/query?q=SELECT+name+from+Account
  -H "Authorization: Bearer access_token" -H "X-PrettyPrint:1"
```

The output from this request is as follows:

```
{
    "done" : true,
    "totalSize" : 14,
    "records" :
    [
        {
            "attributes" :
            {
                "type" : "Account",
                "url" :
"/services/data/v20.0/sobjects/Account/001D000000IRFmaIAH"
            },
            "Name" : "Test 1"
        },
        {
            "attributes" :
            {
                "type" : "Account",
                "url" :
"/services/data/v20.0/sobjects/Account/001D000000IomazIAB"
            },
            "Name" : "Test 2"
        },
        ...
    ]
}
```

From this output you have a listing of the available Account names, and each name's preceding attributes include the Account IDs. In the next step you will use this information to update one of the accounts.

 Note: You can find more information about SOQL in the *Salesforce SOQL and SOSL Reference Guide*.

Update a Field on a Record

Now that you have the Account names and IDs, you can retrieve one of the accounts and update its Billing City. To do this, you will need to submit an SObject Rows request. To update the object, supply the new information about the Billing City. Create a text file called `patchaccount.json` containing the following information:

```
{
    "BillingCity" : "Fremont"
}
```

Specify this JSON file in the REST request. The cURL notation requires the −d option when specifying data. For more information, see *http://curl.haxx.se/docs/manpage.html*.

Also, specify the `PATCH` method, which is used for updating a REST resource. The following cURL command retrieves the specified Account object using its ID field, and updates its Billing City.

```
curl
https://na1.salesforce.com/services/data/v20.0/sobjects/Account/001D000000IroHJ
  -H "Authorization: Bearer access_token" -H "X-PrettyPrint:1" -H
"Content-Type: application/json" --data-binary @patchaccount.json -X
  PATCH
```

No response body is returned, just the headers:

```
HTTP/1.1 204 No Content
Server:
Content-Length: 0
```

Refresh the page on the account and you will see that the Billing Address has changed to Fremont.

Other Resources

* Search for Ruby on *developer.force.com*
* Force.com Cookbook recipe for getting started in Ruby
* Force.com REST API Board

Best Practices

Consider the best practices explained in this section.

JSON and XML Support

JSON is the default for REST API request and response bodies, however XML is also supported. You can use the HTTP ACCEPT header to specify either JSON or XML. XML serialization is similar to SOAP API. XML requests are supported in UTF-8 and UTF-16, and XML responses are provided in UTF-8.

Date and Time Formats

Date-time information in requests and responses is specified using the ISO8601 format.

Compression

REST API allows the use of compression on the request and the response, using the standards defined by the HTTP 1.1 specification. Compression is automatically supported by some clients, and can be manually added to others. For better performance, we recommend using clients that can support HTTP 1.1 compression.

Responses are compressed if the client uses a `Accept-Encoding: gzip` or `Accept-Encoding: deflate` HTTP header in a request. REST API compresses the response and includes `Accept-Encoding: gzip` or `Accept-Encoding: deflate` in the header of the response.

You can send compressed request data if you specify `Content-Encoding: gzip` or `Content-Encoding: deflate` header in your request. REST API will decompress any request content it receives if a `Content-Encoding` request header with supported compression algorithm is provided.

Resources

Search on the Salesforce Developer's Network at `http://developer.salesforce.com/docs` for the following resources on REST API.

- REST API Developer's Guide
- REST API Developer Cheat Sheet
- Salesforce Object Reference
- APIs and Integration forums

Chapter 8

Metadata API

Metadata API provides an API for interacting with the metadata of your Salesforce organization. You can use Metadata API through a file-based API that provides calls to deploy and retrieve wholesale metadata information via .zip files, or a components-based API that provides calls to create, update and delete individual metadata components.

When to Use Metadata API

Use Metadata API to retrieve, deploy, create, update, or delete customizations for your organization. The most common use is to migrate changes from a sandbox or testing organization to your production environment. Metadata API is intended for managing customizations and for building tools that can manage the metadata model, not the data itself.

The easiest way to access the functionality in Metadata API is to use the Force.com IDE or Force.com Migration Tool. These tools are built on top of Metadata API and use the standard Eclipse and Ant tools respectively to simplify the task of working with Metadata API. Built on the Eclipse platform, the Force.com IDE provides a comfortable environment for programmers familiar with integrated development environments, allowing you to code, compile, test, and deploy all from within the IDE itself. The Force.com Migration Tool is ideal if you want to use a script or a command-line utility for moving metadata between a local directory and a Salesforce organization.

Supported Editions and Platforms

Metadata API is available in Enterprise Edition, Performance Edition, Unlimited Edition, Developer Edition, or Database.com. If you are an existing Salesforce customer and want to upgrade to Enterprise, Unlimited, or Performance Edition, contact your account representative.

Quick Start

The easiest way to access the functionality in Metadata API is to use the Force.com IDE or Force.com Migration Tool. These tools are built on top of Metadata API and use the standard Eclipse and Ant tools respectively to simplify the task of working with Metadata API. Built on the Eclipse platform, the Force.com IDE provides a comfortable environment for programmers familiar with integrated development environments, allowing you to code, compile, test, and deploy all from within the IDE itself. The Force.com Migration Tool is ideal if you want to use a script or a command-line utility for moving metadata between a local directory and a Salesforce organization. For more information about the Force.com IDE or Force.com Migration Tool, see developer.force.com.

However, the underlying calls of Metadata API have been exposed for you to use directly, if you prefer to build your own client applications. This quick start gives you all the information you need to start writing applications that directly use Metadata API to manage customizations for your organization. It shows you how to get started with File-Based Development. For an example of CRUD-Based Development, see Java Sample Code for CRUD-Based Development.

Prerequisites

Make sure you complete these prerequisites before you start using Metadata API.

- Create a development environment.

    It is strongly recommended that you use a sandbox, which is an exact replica of your production organization. Enterprise, Unlimited, and Performance Editions come with a free developer sandbox. For more information, see
    `http://www.salesforce.com/platform/cloud-infrastructure/sandbox.jsp`.

    Alternatively, you can use a Developer Edition organization, which provides access to all of the features available with Enterprise Edition, but is limited by the number of users and the amount of storage space. A Developer Edition organization is not a copy of your production organization, but it provides an environment where you can build and test your solutions without affecting your organization's data. Developer Edition accounts are available for free at `http://developer.force.com/join`.

- Identify a user that has the "API Enabled" and "Modify All Data" permissions. These permissions are required to access Metadata API calls.
- Install a SOAP client. Metadata API works with current SOAP development environments, including, but not limited to, Visual Studio® .NET and the Force.com Web Service Connector (WSC).

In this document, we provide Java examples based on WSC and JDK 6 (Java Platform Standard Edition Development Kit 6). To run the samples, first download the latest force-wsc JAR file and its dependencies (dependencies are listed on the page when you select a version) from mvnrepository.com/artifact/com.force.api/force-wsc/.

 Note: Development platforms vary in their SOAP implementations. Implementation differences in certain development platforms might prevent access to some or all of the features in Metadata API.

Step 1: Generate or Obtain the Web Service WSDLs for Your Organization

To access Metadata API calls, you need a Web Service Description Language (WSDL) file. The WSDL file defines the Web service that is available to you. Your development platform uses this WSDL to generate stub code to access the Web service it defines. You can either obtain the WSDL file from your organization's Salesforce administrator, or you can generate it yourself if you have access to the WSDL download page in the Salesforce user interface. For more information about WSDL, see `http://www.w3.org/TR/wsdl`.

Before you can access Metadata API calls, you must authenticate to use the Web service using the `login()` call, which is defined in the enterprise WSDL and the partner WSDL. Therefore, you must also obtain one of these WSDLs.

Any user with the "Modify All Data" permission can download the WSDL file to integrate and extend the Salesforce platform. (The System Administrator profile has this permission.)

The sample code in Step 3: Walk Through the Java Sample Code on page 101 uses the enterprise WSDL, though the partner WSDL works equally well.

To generate the metadata and enterprise WSDL files for your organization:

1. Log in to your Salesforce account. You must log in as an administrator or as a user who has the "Modify All Data" permission.
2. From Setup, click **Develop** > **API**.
3. Click **Generate Metadata WSDL** and save the XML WSDL file to your file system.
4. Click **Generate Enterprise WSDL** and save the XML WSDL file to your file system.

Step 2: Import the WSDL Files Into Your Development Platform

Once you have the WSDL files, import them into your development platform so that your development environment can generate the necessary objects for use in building client Web service applications. This section provides sample instructions for WSC. For instructions about other development platforms, see your platform's product documentation.

 Note: The process for importing WSDL files is identical for the metadata and enterprise WSDL files.

Instructions for Java Environments (WSC)

Java environments access the API through Java objects that serve as proxies for their server-side counterparts. Before using the API, you must first generate these objects from your organization's WSDL file.

Each SOAP client has its own tool for this process. For WSC, use the `wsdlc` utility.

 Note: Before you run `wsdlc`, you must have the WSC JAR file installed on your system and referenced in your classpath. You can download the latest force-wsc JAR file and its dependencies (dependencies are listed on the page when you select a version) from mvnrepository.com/artifact/com.force.api/force-wsc/.

The basic syntax for `wsdlc` is:

```
java -classpath pathToWsc;pathToWscDependencies
com.sforce.ws.tools.wsdlc pathToWsdl/WsdlFilename
pathToOutputJar/OutputJarFilename
```

For example, on Windows:

```
java -classpath force-wsc-24.0.0.jar;js-1.7R2.jar
com.sforce.ws.tools.wsdlc metadata.wsdl metadata.jar
```

On Mac OS X and Unix, use a colon instead of a semicolon in between items in the classpath:

```
java -classpath force-wsc-24.0.0.jar:js-1.7R2.jar
com.sforce.ws.tools.wsdlc metadata.wsdl metadata.jar
```

`wsdlc` generates a JAR file and Java source code and bytecode files for use in creating client applications. Repeat this process for the enterprise WSDL to create an enterprise.JAR file.

Step 3: Walk Through the Java Sample Code

Once you have imported the WSDL files, you can begin building client applications that use Metadata API. The sample is a good starting point for writing your own code.

Before you run the sample, modify your project and the code to:

1. Include the WSC JAR, its dependencies, and the JAR files you generated from the WSDLs.

    Note: Although WSC has other dependencies, the following sample only requires Rhino (js-1.7R2.jar).

2. Update USERNAME and PASSWORD variables in the `MetadataLoginUtil.login()` method with your user name and password. If your current IP address isn't in your organization's trusted IP range, you'll need to append a security token to the password.
3. If you are using a sandbox, be sure to change the login URL.

Login Utility

Java users can use `ConnectorConfig` to connect to Enterprise, Partner, and Metadata SOAP API. `MetadataLoginUtil` creates a `ConnectorConfig` object and logs in using the Enterprise WSDL login method. Then it retrieves `sessionId` and `metadataServerUrl` to create a `ConnectorConfig` and connects to Metadata API endpoint. `ConnectorConfig` is defined in WSC.

The `MetadataLoginUtil` class abstracts the login code from the other parts of the sample, allowing portions of this code to be reused without change across different Salesforce APIs.

```java
import com.sforce.soap.enterprise.EnterpriseConnection;
import com.sforce.soap.enterprise.LoginResult;
import com.sforce.soap.metadata.MetadataConnection;
import com.sforce.ws.ConnectionException;
import com.sforce.ws.ConnectorConfig;

/**
 * Login utility.
 */
public class MetadataLoginUtil {

    public static MetadataConnection login() throws
ConnectionException {
        final String USERNAME = "user@company.com";
        // This is only a sample. Hard coding passwords in source
files is a bad practice.
```

```
            final String PASSWORD = "password";
            final String URL =
"https://login.salesforce.com/services/Soap/c/29.0";
            final LoginResult loginResult = loginToSalesforce(USERNAME,
      PASSWORD, URL);
            return createMetadataConnection(loginResult);
      }

      private static MetadataConnection createMetadataConnection(
            final LoginResult loginResult) throws ConnectionException
    {
            final ConnectorConfig config = new ConnectorConfig();
         config.setServiceEndpoint(loginResult.getMetadataServerUrl());

            config.setSessionId(loginResult.getSessionId());
            return new MetadataConnection(config);
      }

      private static LoginResult loginToSalesforce(
            final String username,
            final String password,
            final String loginUrl) throws ConnectionException {
            final ConnectorConfig config = new ConnectorConfig();
            config.setAuthEndpoint(loginUrl);
            config.setServiceEndpoint(loginUrl);
            config.setManualLogin(true);
            return (new EnterpriseConnection(config)).login(username,
      password);
      }
}
```

Java Sample Code for File-Based Development

The sample code logs in using the login utility. Then it displays a menu with retrieve, deploy, and exit.

The `retrieve()` and `deploy()` calls both operate on a .zip file named `components.zip`. The `retrieve()` call retrieves components from your organization into `components.zip`, and the `deploy()` call deploys the components in `components.zip` to your organization. If you save the sample to your computer and execute it, run the retrieve option first so that you have a `components.zip` file that you can subsequently deploy. After retrieve or deploy calls, it checks `checkStatus()` in a loop until the status value in `AsyncResult` indicates that the operation has completed.

The `retrieve()` call uses a manifest file to determine the components to retrieve from your organization. A sample `package.xml` manifest file follows. For more details on the manifest file structure, see Working with the Zip File. For this sample, the manifest file retrieves all custom objects, custom tabs, and page layouts.

```
<?xml version="1.0" encoding="UTF-8"?>
<Package xmlns="http://soap.sforce.com/2006/04/metadata">
    <types>
```

```
        <members>*</members>
        <name>CustomObject</name>
    </types>
    <types>
        <members>*</members>
        <name>CustomTab</name>
    </types>
    <types>
        <members>*</members>
        <name>Layout</name>
    </types>
    <version>29.0</version>
</Package>
```

Note the error handling code that follows each API call.

```java
import java.io.*;
import java.util.*;
import javax.xml.parsers.*;
import org.w3c.dom.*;
import org.xml.sax.SAXException;
import com.sforce.soap.metadata.*;

/**
 * Sample that logs in and shows a menu of retrieve and deploy
metadata options.
 */
public class FileBasedDeployAndRetrieve {

    private MetadataConnection metadataConnection;

    private static final String ZIP_FILE = "components.zip";

    // manifest file that controls which components get retrieved
    private static final String MANIFEST_FILE = "package.xml";

    private static final double API_VERSION = 29.0;

    // one second in milliseconds
    private static final long ONE_SECOND = 1000;

    // maximum number of attempts to deploy the zip file
    private static final int MAX_NUM_POLL_REQUESTS = 50;

    private BufferedReader reader = new BufferedReader(new
InputStreamReader(System.in));

    public static void main(String[] args) throws Exception {
        FileBasedDeployAndRetrieve sample = new
FileBasedDeployAndRetrieve();
        sample.run();
    }

    public FileBasedDeployAndRetrieve() {
    }
```

```
    private void run() throws Exception {
        this.metadataConnection = MetadataLoginUtil.login();

        // Show the options to retrieve or deploy until user exits
        String choice = getUsersChoice();
        while (choice != null && !choice.equals("99")) {
            if (choice.equals("1")) {
                retrieveZip();
            } else if (choice.equals("2")) {
                deployZip();
            } else {
                break;
            }
            // show the options again
            choice = getUsersChoice();
        }
    }

    /*
     * Utility method to present options to retrieve or deploy.
     */
    private String getUsersChoice() throws IOException {
        System.out.println(" 1: Retrieve");
        System.out.println(" 2: Deploy");
        System.out.println("99: Exit");
        System.out.println();
        System.out.print("Enter 1 to retrieve, 2 to deploy, or 99 to
exit: ");
        // wait for the user input.
        String choice = reader.readLine();
        return choice != null ? choice.trim() : "";
    }

    private void deployZip() throws Exception {
        byte zipBytes[] = readZipFile();
        DeployOptions deployOptions = new DeployOptions();
        deployOptions.setPerformRetrieve(false);
        deployOptions.setRollbackOnError(true);
        AsyncResult asyncResult = metadataConnection.deploy(zipBytes,
deployOptions);
        DeployResult result =
waitForDeployCompletion(asyncResult.getId());
        if (!result.isSuccess()) {
            printErrors(result, "Final list of failures:\n");
            throw new Exception("The files were not successfully
deployed");
        }
        System.out.println("The file " + ZIP_FILE + " was successfully
deployed\n");
    }

    /*
     * Read the zip file contents into a byte array.
     */
    private byte[] readZipFile() throws Exception {
        byte[] result = null;
        // We assume here that you have a deploy.zip file.
```

```
            // See the retrieve sample for how to retrieve a zip file.
            File zipFile = new File(ZIP_FILE);
            if (!zipFile.exists() || !zipFile.isFile()) {
                throw new Exception("Cannot find the zip file for deploy()
 on path:"
                        + zipFile.getAbsolutePath());
            }

            FileInputStream fileInputStream = new
FileInputStream(zipFile);
            try {
                ByteArrayOutputStream bos = new ByteArrayOutputStream();

                byte[] buffer = new byte[4096];
                int bytesRead = 0;
                while (-1 != (bytesRead = fileInputStream.read(buffer)))
 {
                    bos.write(buffer, 0, bytesRead);
                }

                result = bos.toByteArray();
            } finally {
                fileInputStream.close();
            }
            return result;
        }

    /*
     * Print out any errors, if any, related to the deploy.
     * @param result - DeployResult
     */
    private void printErrors(DeployResult result, String
messageHeader) {
        DeployDetails details = result.getDetails();
        StringBuilder stringBuilder = new StringBuilder();
        if (details != null) {
            DeployMessage[] componentFailures =
details.getComponentFailures();
            for (DeployMessage failure : componentFailures) {
                String loc = "(" + failure.getLineNumber() + ", " +
 failure.getColumnNumber();
                if (loc.length() == 0 &&
!failure.getFileName().equals(failure.getFullName()))
                {
                    loc = "(" + failure.getFullName() + ")";
                }
                stringBuilder.append(failure.getFileName() + loc +
":"
                    + failure.getProblem()).append('\n');
            }
            RunTestsResult rtr = details.getRunTestResult();
            if (rtr.getFailures() != null) {
                for (RunTestFailure failure : rtr.getFailures()) {
                    String n = (failure.getNamespace() == null ? ""
 :
                        (failure.getNamespace() + ".")) +
failure.getName();
```

```
                            stringBuilder.append("Test failure, method: " +
  n + "." +
                                failure.getMethodName() + " -- " +
failure.getMessage() +
                                " stack " + failure.getStackTrace() +
"\n\n");
                }
            }
            if (rtr.getCodeCoverageWarnings() != null) {
                for (CodeCoverageWarning ccw :
rtr.getCodeCoverageWarnings()) {
                    stringBuilder.append("Code coverage issue");
                    if (ccw.getName() != null) {
                        String n = (ccw.getNamespace() == null ? ""
  :
                        (ccw.getNamespace() + ".")) + ccw.getName();

                        stringBuilder.append(", class: " + n);
                    }
                    stringBuilder.append(" -- " + ccw.getMessage()
+ "\n");
                }
            }
        }
        if (stringBuilder.length() > 0) {
            stringBuilder.insert(0, messageHeader);
            System.out.println(stringBuilder.toString());
        }
    }

    private void retrieveZip() throws Exception {
        RetrieveRequest retrieveRequest = new RetrieveRequest();
        retrieveRequest.setApiVersion(API_VERSION);
        setUnpackaged(retrieveRequest);

        AsyncResult asyncResult =
metadataConnection.retrieve(retrieveRequest);
        asyncResult = waitForRetrieveCompletion(asyncResult);
        RetrieveResult result =

metadataConnection.checkRetrieveStatus(asyncResult.getId());

        // Print out any warning messages
        StringBuilder stringBuilder = new StringBuilder();
        if (result.getMessages() != null) {
            for (RetrieveMessage rm : result.getMessages()) {
                stringBuilder.append(rm.getFileName() + " - " +
rm.getProblem() + "\n");
            }
        }
        if (stringBuilder.length() > 0) {
            System.out.println("Retrieve warnings:\n" +
stringBuilder);
        }

        System.out.println("Writing results to zip file");
        File resultsFile = new File(ZIP_FILE);
```

```
        FileOutputStream os = new FileOutputStream(resultsFile);

        try {
            os.write(result.getZipFile());
        } finally {
            os.close();
        }
    }

  private DeployResult waitForDeployCompletion(String asyncResultId)
 throws Exception {
        int poll = 0;
        long waitTimeMilliSecs = ONE_SECOND;
        DeployResult deployResult;
        boolean fetchDetails;
        do {
            Thread.sleep(waitTimeMilliSecs);
            // double the wait time for the next iteration

            waitTimeMilliSecs *= 2;
            if (poll++ > MAX_NUM_POLL_REQUESTS) {
                throw new Exception(
                    "Request timed out. If this is a large set of
metadata components, " +
                    "ensure that MAX_NUM_POLL_REQUESTS is
sufficient.");
            }
            // Fetch in-progress details once for every 3 polls
            fetchDetails = (poll % 3 == 0);

            deployResult =
metadataConnection.checkDeployStatus(asyncResultId, fetchDetails);
            System.out.println("Status is: " +
deployResult.getStatus());
            if (!deployResult.isDone() && fetchDetails) {
                printErrors(deployResult, "Failures for deployment
in progress:\n");
            }
        }
        while (!deployResult.isDone());

        if (!deployResult.isSuccess() &&
deployResult.getErrorStatusCode() != null) {
            throw new Exception(deployResult.getErrorStatusCode() +
 " msg: " +
                    deployResult.getErrorMessage());
        }

        if (!fetchDetails) {
            // Get the final result with details if we didn't do it
 in the last attempt.
            deployResult =
metadataConnection.checkDeployStatus(asyncResultId, true);
        }

        return deployResult;
    }
```

```
    private AsyncResult waitForRetrieveCompletion(AsyncResult
asyncResult) throws Exception {
        int poll = 0;
        long waitTimeMilliSecs = ONE_SECOND;
        while (!asyncResult.isDone()) {
            Thread.sleep(waitTimeMilliSecs);
            // double the wait time for the next iteration

            waitTimeMilliSecs *= 2;
            if (poll++ > MAX_NUM_POLL_REQUESTS) {
                throw new Exception(
                    "Request timed out. If this is a large set of
metadata components, " +
                    "ensure that MAX_NUM_POLL_REQUESTS is
sufficient.");
            }

            asyncResult = metadataConnection.checkStatus(
                new String[]{asyncResult.getId()})[0];
            System.out.println("Status is: " +
asyncResult.getState());
        }

        if (asyncResult.getState() != AsyncRequestState.Completed)
{
            throw new Exception(asyncResult.getStatusCode() + " msg:
" +
                asyncResult.getMessage());
        }
        return asyncResult;
    }

    private void setUnpackaged(RetrieveRequest request) throws
Exception {
        // Edit the path, if necessary, if your package.xml file is
located elsewhere
        File unpackedManifest = new File(MANIFEST_FILE);
        System.out.println("Manifest file: " +
unpackedManifest.getAbsolutePath());

        if (!unpackedManifest.exists() || !unpackedManifest.isFile())
{
            throw new Exception("Should provide a valid retrieve
manifest " +
                "for unpackaged content. Looking for " +
                unpackedManifest.getAbsolutePath());
        }

        // Note that we use the fully quualified class name because
        // of a collision with the java.lang.Package class
        com.sforce.soap.metadata.Package p =
parsePackageManifest(unpackedManifest);
        request.setUnpackaged(p);
    }

    private com.sforce.soap.metadata.Package parsePackageManifest(File
```

```
 file)
            throws ParserConfigurationException, IOException,
SAXException {
        com.sforce.soap.metadata.Package packageManifest = null;
        List<PackageTypeMembers> listPackageTypes = new
ArrayList<PackageTypeMembers>();
        DocumentBuilder db =

DocumentBuilderFactory.newInstance().newDocumentBuilder();
        InputStream inputStream = new FileInputStream(file);
        Element d = db.parse(inputStream).getDocumentElement();
        for (Node c = d.getFirstChild(); c != null; c =
c.getNextSibling()) {
            if (c instanceof Element) {
                Element ce = (Element) c;
                NodeList nodeList = ce.getElementsByTagName("name");

                if (nodeList.getLength() == 0) {
                    continue;
                }
                String name = nodeList.item(0).getTextContent();
                NodeList m = ce.getElementsByTagName("members");
                List<String> members = new ArrayList<String>();
                for (int i = 0; i < m.getLength(); i++) {
                    Node mm = m.item(i);
                    members.add(mm.getTextContent());
                }
                PackageTypeMembers packageTypes = new
PackageTypeMembers();
                packageTypes.setName(name);
                packageTypes.setMembers(members.toArray(new
String[members.size()]));
                listPackageTypes.add(packageTypes);
            }
        }
        packageManifest = new com.sforce.soap.metadata.Package();
        PackageTypeMembers[] packageTypesArray =
            new PackageTypeMembers[listPackageTypes.size()];

packageManifest.setTypes(listPackageTypes.toArray(packageTypesArray));

        packageManifest.setVersion(API_VERSION + "");
        return packageManifest;
    }
}
```

Best Practices

Consider the best practices in this section.

Testing Metadata Changes

You should verify initial metadata changes in a test environment rather than directly on your production organization.

It is strongly recommended that you use a sandbox, which is an exact replica of your production organization. Enterprise, Unlimited, and Performance Editions come with a free developer sandbox. For more information, see
`http://www.salesforce.com/platform/cloud-infrastructure/sandbox.jsp`.

Alternatively, you can use a Developer Edition organization, which provides access to all of the features available with Enterprise Edition, but is limited by the number of users and the amount of storage space. A Developer Edition organization is not a copy of your production organization, but it provides an environment where you can build and test your solutions without affecting your organization's data. Developer Edition accounts are available for free at `http://developer.force.com/join`.

Other Common Metadata Issues

The most common metadata issues are detailed below:

- Retrieving custom fields on standard objects — When you use the wildcard symbol in `package.xml`, to retrieve all objects, you will not retrieve standard objects, or custom fields on standard objects. To retrieve custom fields on standard objects, you must name the component in `package.xml`.

- Profiles or permission sets and field-level security — The contents of a retrieved profile or permission set depend on the other contents of the retrieve request. For example, field-level security information for fields included in custom objects is returned at the same time as profiles or permission sets. For more information, see Profile and PermissionSet in the Metadata API Developer's Guide.

- Workflow — A `.workflow` file is a container for the individual workflow components associated with an object, including WorkflowAlert, WorkflowFieldUpdate, WorkflowOutboundMessage, WorkflowRule, and WorkflowTask. To retrieve all workflows, include the following XML in `package.xml`:

```
<types>
    <members>*</members>
    <name>Workflow</name>
</types>
```

- Retrieving or deploying components that depend on an object definition — The following metadata components are dependent on a particular object for their definition: `CustomField`, `Picklist`, `RecordType`, `Weblink`, and `ValidationRule`. This means you must dot-qualify the component name with the object name in `package.xml`, and may not use the wildcard symbol.

- Personal folders — Users' personal folders, for both reports and documents, are not exposed in Metadata API. To migrate reports or documents you must move them to a public folder.

Resources

Search on the Salesforce Developer's Network at
`http://developer.salesforce.com/docs` for the following resources on Metadata
API.

- Metadata API Developer's Guide
- Migration Tool Guide
- APIs and Integration forums

## Chapter 9

Bulk API

Bulk API provides programmatic access to allow you to efficiently load and retrieve your organization's data into Salesforce.

When to Use Bulk API

Bulk API is based on REST principles and is optimized for loading or deleting large sets of data. You can use it to query, insert, update, upsert, or delete a large number of records asynchronously by submitting batches which are processed in the background by Salesforce. Bulk API is designed to make it simple to process data from a few thousand to millions of records.

You can use Bulk API to process a set of records by creating a job that contains one or more batches. The job specifies which object is being processed and what type of action is being used (query, insert, upsert, update, or delete). A batch is a set of records sent to the server in an HTTP POST request. Each batch is processed independently by the server, not necessarily in the order it is received. Batches may be processed in parallel. It's up to the client to decide how to divide the entire data set into a suitable number of batches.

Supported Editions and Platforms

To use Bulk API, your organization must use Enterprise Edition, Performance Edition, Unlimited Edition, or Developer Edition. If you are an existing Salesforce customer and want to upgrade to Enterprise, Unlimited, or Performance Edition, contact your account representative.

Quick Start

Use the quick start sample in this section to create HTTP requests that insert new contact records using the REST-based Bulk API. The instructions progress through logging in, submitting the records, checking status, and retrieving the results.

Note: Before you begin building an integration or other client application:

- Install your development platform according to its product documentation.
- Read through all the steps before beginning this quick start. You may also wish to review the rest of this document to familiarize yourself with terms and concepts.

Setting Up a Salesforce Developer Edition Organization

First, you must obtain a Salesforce Developer Edition organization and enable Bulk API:

1. Obtain a Salesforce Developer Edition organization.

   If you're not already a member of the developer community, go to `http://developer.force.com/join` and follow the instructions for signing up for a Developer Edition account. Even if you already have an Enterprise Edition, Unlimited Edition, or Performance Edition account, it's strongly recommended that you use Developer Edition for developing, staging, and testing your solutions against sample data to protect your organization's live data. This is especially true for applications that query, insert, update, or delete data (as opposed to simply reading data).

2. Enable Bulk API.

   You must have the "API Enabled" permission. This permission is enabled in the System Administrator profile.

Setting Up Your Client Application

The Bulk API uses HTTP GET and HTTP POST methods to send and receive CSV and XML content, so it's very simple to build client applications using the tool or the language of your choice. This quick start uses a command-line tool called cURL to simplify sending and receiving HTTP requests and responses.

cURL is pre-installed on many Linux and Mac systems. Windows users can download a version at `curl.haxx.se/`. When using HTTPS on Windows, ensure that your system meets the cURL requirements for SSL.

> **Note:** cURL is an open source tool and is not supported by salesforce.com.

Escaping the Session ID or Using Single Quotes on Mac and Linux Systems

When running the cURL examples for the REST resources, you may get an error on Mac and Linux systems due to the presence of the exclamation mark special character in the session ID argument. To avoid getting this error, do one of the following:

- Escape the exclamation mark (!) special character in the session ID by inserting a backslash before it (\!) when the session ID is enclosed within double quotes. For example, the session ID string in this cURL command has the exclamation mark (!) escaped:

```
curl https://instance_name.salesforce.com/services/data/v29.0/

-H "Authorization: Bearer
00D50000000IehZ\!AQcAQH0dMHZfz972Szmpkb58urFRkgeBGsxL_QJWwYMfAbUeeG7c1E6
LYUfiDUkWe6H34r1AAwOR8B8fLEz6n04NPGRrq0FM"
```

- Enclose the session ID within single quotes. For example:

```
curl https://instance_name.salesforce.com/services/data/v29.0/

-H 'Authorization: Bearer sessionID'
```

Sending HTTP Requests with cURL

Now that you have configured cURL, you can start sending HTTP requests to the Bulk API. You send HTTP requests to a URI to perform operations with Bulk API.

The URI where you send HTTP requests has the following format:

```
Web_Services_SOAP_endpoint_instance_name/services/async/APIversion/Resource_address
```

The part after the API version (`Resource_address`) varies depending on the job or batch being processed.

The easiest way to start using the Bulk API is to enable it for processing records in Data Loader using CSV files. If you use Data Loader, you don't need craft your own HTTP requests or write your own client application. For an example of writing a client application using Java, see Sample Client Application Using Java.

Step 1: Logging In Using the SOAP API

The Bulk API doesn't provide a login operation, so you must use SOAP API to log in.

To log in to Salesforce using cURL:

1. Create a text file called login.txt containing the following text:

```
<?xml version="1.0" encoding="utf-8" ?>
<env:Envelope xmlns:xsd="http://www.w3.org/2001/XMLSchema"
    xmlns:xsi="http://www.w3.org/2001/XMLSchema-instance"
    xmlns:env="http://schemas.xmlsoap.org/soap/envelope/">
  <env:Body>
    <n1:login xmlns:n1="urn:partner.soap.sforce.com">
      <n1:username>your_username</n1:username>
      <n1:password>your_password</n1:password>
    </n1:login>
  </env:Body>
</env:Envelope>
```

2. Replace *your_username* and *your_password* with your Salesforce user name and password.

3. Using a command-line window, execute the following cURL command:

```
curl https://login.salesforce.com/services/Soap/u/29.0 -H
"Content-Type: text/xml; charset=UTF-8" -H "SOAPAction: login"
-d @login.txt
```

The Soap/u/ portion of the URI specifies the partner WSDL. You can use Soap/c/ to specify the enterprise WSDL.

4. Salesforce returns an XML response that includes <sessionId> and <serverUrl> elements. Note the values of the <sessionId> element and the first part of the host name (instance), such as na1-api, from the <serverUrl> element. Use these values in subsequent requests to the Bulk API.

Step 2: Creating a Job

Before you can load any data, you first have to create a job. The job specifies the type of object, such as Contact, that you're loading, and the operation that you're performing, such as query, insert, update, upsert, or delete. A job also grants you some control over the data load process. For example, you can abort a job that is in progress.

To create a job using cURL:

1. Create a text file called job.txt containing the following text:

```
<?xml version="1.0" encoding="UTF-8"?>
<jobInfo
xmlns="http://www.force.com/2009/06/asyncapi/dataload">
    <operation>insert</operation>
    <object>Contact</object>
    <contentType>CSV</contentType>
</jobInfo>
```

 Warning: The operation value must be all lower case. For example, you get an error if you use INSERT instead of insert.

2. Using a command-line window, execute the following cURL command:

```
curl https://instance.salesforce.com/services/async/29.0/job
-H "X-SFDC-Session: sessionId" -H "Content-Type:
application/xml; charset=UTF-8" -d @job.txt
```

instance is the portion of the <serverUrl> element and *sessionId* is the <sessionId> element that you noted in the login response.

Salesforce returns an XML response with data such as the following:

```
<?xml version="1.0" encoding="UTF-8"?>
<jobInfo
   xmlns="http://www.force.com/2009/06/asyncapi/dataload">
  <id>750x0000000005LAAQ</id>
  <operation>insert</operation>
  <object>Contact</object>
  <createdById>005x0000000wPWdAAM</createdById>
  <createdDate>2009-09-01T16:42:46.000Z</createdDate>
  <systemModstamp>2009-09-01T16:42:46.000Z</systemModstamp>
  <state>Open</state>
  <concurrencyMode>Parallel</concurrencyMode>
  <contentType>CSV</contentType>
  <numberBatchesQueued>0</numberBatchesQueued>
  <numberBatchesInProgress>0</numberBatchesInProgress>
  <numberBatchesCompleted>0</numberBatchesCompleted>
  <numberBatchesFailed>0</numberBatchesFailed>
  <numberBatchesTotal>0</numberBatchesTotal>
  <numberRecordsProcessed>0</numberRecordsProcessed>
  <numberRetries>0</numberRetries>
  <apiVersion>29.0</apiVersion>
</jobInfo>
```

3. Note the value of the job ID returned in the <id> element. Use this ID in subsequent operations.

Step 3: Adding a Batch to the Job

After creating the job, you're now ready to create a batch of contact records. You send data in batches in separate HTTP POST requests. The URI for each request is similar to the one you used when creating the job, but you append *jobId*/batch to the URI.

Format the data as either CSV or XML if you're not including binary attachments. For information about binary attachments, see Loading Binary Attachments. For information about batch size limitations, see Batch size and limits.

This example shows CSV as this is the recommended format. It's your responsibility to divide up your data set in batches that fit within the limits. In this example, we'll keep it very simple with just a few records.

To add a batch to a job:

1. Create a CSV file named data.csv with the following two records:

    ```
    FirstName,LastName,Department,Birthdate,Description
    Tom,Jones,Marketing,1940-06-07Z,"Self-described as ""the top""
     branding guru on the West Coast"
    Ian,Dury,R&D,,"World-renowned expert in fuzzy logic design.
    Influential in technology purchases."
    ```

    Note that the value for the Description field in the last row spans multiple lines, so it's wrapped in double quotes.

2. Using a command-line window, execute the following cURL command:

    ```
    curl
    https://instance.salesforce.com/services/async/29.0/job/jobId/batch
    -H "X-SFDC-Session: sessionId" -H "Content-Type: text/csv;
    charset=UTF-8" --data-binary @data.csv
    ```

    instance is the portion of the <serverUrl> element and *sessionId* is the <sessionId> element that you noted in the login response. *jobId* is the job ID that was returned when you created the job.

    Salesforce returns an XML response with data such as the following:

    ```
    <?xml version="1.0" encoding="UTF-8"?>
    <batchInfo
        xmlns="http://www.force.com/2009/06/asyncapi/dataload">
      <id>751x00000000079AAA</id>
      <jobId>750x0000000005LAAQ</jobId>
      <state>Queued</state>
      <createdDate>2009-09-01T17:44:45.000Z</createdDate>
    ```

```
    <systemModstamp>2009-09-01T17:44:45.000Z</systemModstamp>
    <numberRecordsProcessed>0</numberRecordsProcessed>
</batchInfo>
```

Salesforce does not parse the CSV content or otherwise validate the batch until later. The response only acknowledges that the batch was received.

3. Note the value of the batch ID returned in the `<id>` element. You can use this batch ID later to check the status of the batch.

Step 4: Closing the Job

When you're finished submitting batches to Salesforce, close the job. This informs Salesforce that no more batches will be submitted for the job, which, in turn, allows the monitoring page in Salesforce to return more meaningful statistics on the progress of the job.

To close a job using cURL:

1. Create a text file called `close_job.txt` containing the following text:

```
<?xml version="1.0" encoding="UTF-8"?>
<jobInfo
xmlns="http://www.force.com/2009/06/asyncapi/dataload">
    <state>Closed</state>
</jobInfo>
```

2. Using a command-line window, execute the following cURL command:

```
curl
https://instance.salesforce.com/services/async/29.0/job/jobId
-H "X-SFDC-Session: sessionId" -H "Content-Type:
application/xml; charset=UTF-8" -d @close_job.txt
```

instance is the portion of the `<serverUrl>` element and *sessionId* is the `<sessionId>` element that you noted in the login response. *jobId* is the job ID that was returned when you created the job.

This cURL command updates the job resource state from `Open` to `Closed`.

Step 5: Checking Batch Status

You can check the status of an individual batch by running the following cURL command:

```
curl
https://instance.salesforce.com/services/async/29.0/job/jobId/batch/batchId
-H "X-SFDC-Session: sessionId"
```

instance is the portion of the `<serverUrl>` element and **sessionId** is the `<sessionId>` element that you noted in the login response. **jobId** is the job ID that was returned when you created the job. **batchId** is the batch ID that was returned when you added a batch to the job.

Salesforce returns an XML response with data such as the following:

```
<?xml version="1.0" encoding="UTF-8"?>
<batchInfo
    xmlns="http://www.force.com/2009/06/asyncapi/dataload">
  <id>751x00000000079AAA</id>
  <jobId>750x0000000005LAAQ</jobId>
  <state>Completed</state>
  <createdDate>2009-09-01T17:44:45.000Z</createdDate>
  <systemModstamp>2009-09-01T17:44:45.000Z</systemModstamp>
  <numberRecordsProcessed>2</numberRecordsProcessed>
</batchInfo>
```

If Salesforce couldn't read the batch content or if the batch contained errors, such as invalid field names in the CSV header row, the batch state is `Failed`. When batch state is `Completed`, all records in the batch have been processed. However, individual records may have failed. You need to retrieve the batch result to see the status of individual records.

You don't have to check the status of each batch individually. You can check the status for all batches that are part of the job by running the following cURL command:

```
curl
https://instance.salesforce.com/services/async/29.0/job/jobId/batch
-H "X-SFDC-Session: sessionId"
```

Step 6: Retrieving Batch Results

Once a batch is `Completed`, you need to retrieve the batch result to see the status of individual records.

Retrieve the results for an individual batch by running the following cURL command:

```
curl
https://instance.salesforce.com/services/async/29.0/job/jobId/batch/batchId/result
-H "X-SFDC-Session: sessionId"
```

instance is the portion of the `<serverUrl>` element and *sessionId* is the `<sessionId>` element that you noted in the login response. *jobId* is the job ID that was returned when you created the job. *batchId* is the batch ID that was returned when you added a batch to the job.

Salesforce returns a response with data such as the following:

```
"Id","Success","Created","Error"
"003x0000004ouM4AAI","true","true",""
"003x0000004ouM5AAI","true","true",""
```

The response body is a CSV file with a row for each row in the batch request. If a record was created, the ID is contained in the row. If a record was updated, the value in the `Created` column is false. If a record failed, the `Error` column contains an error message.

Best Practices

Consider the best practices explained in this section.

General Guidelines for Data Loads

This section gives you some tips for planning your data loads for optimal processing time. Always test your data loads in a sandbox organization first. Note that the processing times may be different in a production organization.

Use Parallel Mode Whenever Possible

You get the most benefit from the Bulk API by processing batches in parallel, which is the default mode and enables faster loading of data. However, sometimes parallel processing can cause lock contention on records. The alternative is to process using serial mode. Don't process data in serial mode unless you know this would otherwise result in lock timeouts and you can't reorganize your batches to avoid the locks.

You set the processing mode at the job level. All batches in a job are processed in parallel or serial mode.

Organize Batches to Minimize Lock Contention

For example, when an AccountTeamMember record is created or updated, the account for this record is locked during the transaction. If you load many batches of AccountTeamMember records and they all contain references to the same account, they all try to lock the same account and it's likely that you'll experience a lock timeout. Sometimes, lock timeouts can be avoided by organizing data in batches. If you organize

AccountTeamMember records by `AccountId` so that all records referencing the same account are in a single batch, you minimize the risk of lock contention by multiple batches.

The Bulk API doesn't generate an error immediately when encountering a lock. It waits a few seconds for its release and, if it doesn't happen, the record is marked as failed. If there are problems acquiring locks for more than 100 records in a batch, the Bulk API places the remainder of the batch back in the queue for later processing. When the Bulk API processes the batch again later, records marked as failed are not retried. To process these records, you must submit them again in a separate batch.

If the Bulk API continues to encounter problems processing a batch, it's placed back in the queue and reprocessed up to 10 times before the batch is permanently marked as failed. Even if the batch failed, some records could have completed successfully. To get batch results to see which records, if any, were processed, see Getting Batch Results. If errors persist, create a separate job to process the data in serial mode, which ensures that only one batch is processed at a time.

Be Aware of Operations that Increase Lock Contention

The following operations are likely to cause lock contention and necessitate using serial mode:

- Creating new users
- Updating ownership for records with private sharing
- Updating user roles
- Updating territory hierarchies

If you encounter errors related to these operations, create a separate job to process the data in serial mode.

 Note: Because your data model is unique to your organization, salesforce.com can't predict exactly when you might see lock contention problems.

Minimize Number of Fields

Processing time is faster if there are fewer fields loaded for each record. Foreign key, lookup relationship, and roll-up summary fields are more likely to increase processing time. It's not always possible to reduce the number of fields in your records, but, if it is possible, loading times will improve.

Minimize Number of Workflow Actions

Workflow actions increase processing time.

Minimize Number of Triggers

You can use parallel mode with objects that have associated triggers if the triggers don't cause side-effects that interfere with other parallel transactions. However, salesforce.com doesn't recommend loading large batches for objects with complex triggers. Instead, you should rewrite the trigger logic as a batch Apex job that is executed after all the data has loaded.

Optimize Batch Size

Salesforce.com shares processing resources among all its customers. To ensure that each organization doesn't have to wait too long to process its batches, any batch that takes more than 10 minutes is suspended and returned to the queue for later processing. The best course of action is to submit batches that process in less than 10 minutes. For more information on monitoring timing for batch processing, see Monitoring a Batch.

Batch sizes should be adjusted based on processing times. Start with 5000 records and adjust the batch size based on processing time. If it takes more than five minutes to process a batch, it may be beneficial to reduce the batch size. If it takes a few seconds, the batch size should be increased. If you get a timeout error when processing a batch, split your batch into smaller batches, and try again. For more information, see Bulk API Limits.

 Note: For Bulk queries, the batch size is not applied to either the query result set, or the retrieved data size. If your bulk query is taking too long to process, you will need to filter your query statement to return less data.

Using Compression for Responses

In API version 27.0 and later, Bulk API can compress response data which reduces network traffic and improves response time.

Responses are compressed if the client makes a request using the `Accept-Encoding` header, with a value of `gzip`. Bulk API compresses the response in gzip format and sends the response to the client with a `Content-Encoding: gzip` response header. If a request is made using the `Accept-Encoding` header with a value other than `gzip`, the encoding type is ignored, and the response is not compressed.

As an example, if a Batch Results request is made with the `Accept-Encoding: gzip` header, the response looks something like:

```
HTTP/1.1 200 OK
Date: Tue, 09 Oct 2012 18:36:45 GMT
Content-Type: text/csv; charset=UTF-8
Content-Encoding: gzip
```

```
Transfer-Encoding: chunked

...compressed response body...
```

Bulk API follows the HTTP 1.1 standards for response compression. Most clients automatically support compressed responses. Visit `http://wiki.developerforce.com/page/Tools` for more information on particular clients.

Resources

Search on the Salesforce Developer's Network at `http://developer.salesforce.com/docs` for the following resources on Bulk API.

- Bulk API Developer's Guide
- Salesforce Object Reference
- APIs and Integration forums

## Chapter 10

Streaming API

Use Streaming API to receive notifications for changes to Salesforce data that match a data query you define, in a secure and scalable way.

When to Use Streaming API

Streaming API is useful when you want notifications to be pushed from the server to the client. Consider Streaming API for applications that poll frequently. Applications that have constant polling action against the Salesforce infrastructure, consuming unnecessary API call and processing time, would benefit from this API which reduces the number of requests that return no data. Streaming API is also ideal for applications that require general notification of data changes. This enables you to reduce the number of API calls and improve performance.

Streaming API events can be received by:

- Pages in the Salesforce application.
- Application servers outside of Salesforce.
- Clients outside the Salesforce application.

Streaming API uses push technology to send notification events to clients. In push technology, the server pushes out information to the client after the client has subscribed to a channel of information. In order for the client to receive the information, the client must maintain a connection to the server. Streaming API uses the Bayeux protocol and CometD, so the client-to-server connection is maintained through long polling.

Supported Editions and Platforms

To use Streaming API, your organization must use Enterprise Edition, Performance Edition, Unlimited Edition, or Developer Edition. If you are an existing Salesforce customer and want to upgrade to Enterprise, Unlimited, or Performance Edition, contact your account representative.

For Streaming API you should ensure that the "Streaming API" and "API Enabled" permissions are enabled for your organization, under Setup in **Customize** > **User Interface**.

Quick Start Using Workbench

This quick start shows you how to get started with Streaming API by using Workbench. This quick start takes you step-by-step through the process of using Streaming API to receive a notification when a record is updated.

- Prerequisites
- Step 1: Create an Object
- Step 2: Create a PushTopic
- Step 3: Subscribe to the PushTopic Channel
- Step 4: Test the PushTopic Channel

Prerequisites

You need access and appropriate permissions to complete the quick start steps.

- Access to a Developer Edition organization.

  If you are not already a member of the Force.com developer community, go to `http://developer.force.com/join` and follow the instructions for signing up for a Developer Edition organization. Even if you already have Enterprise Edition, Unlimited Edition, or Performance Edition, use Developer Edition for developing, staging, and testing your solutions against sample data to protect your organization's live data. This is especially true for applications that insert, update, or delete data (as opposed to simply reading data).

- The "API Enabled" permission must be enabled for your Developer Edition organization. This permission is enabled by default, but may have been changed by an administrator.
- The "Streaming API" permission must be enabled.

   Note: To verify that the "API Enabled" and "Streaming API" permissions are enabled in your organization, from Setup, click **Customize** > **User Interface**.

- The logged-in user must have "Read" permission on the PushTopic standard object to receive notifications.
- The logged-in user must have "Create" permission on the PushTopic standard object to create and manage PushTopic records.

• The logged-in user must have "Author Apex" permissions to create a PushTopic by using the Developer Console.

Step 1: Create an Object

The first step is to create an InvoiceStatement object. After you create a PushTopic and subscribe to it, you'll get notifications when an InvoiceStatement record is created, updated, deleted, or undeleted. You'll create the object with the user interface.

1. From Setup, click **Create** > **Objects**.
2. Click **New Custom Object** and fill in the custom object definition.

   • In the **Label field**, type `Invoice Statement`.
   • In the **Plural Label** field, type `Invoice Statements`.
   • Select **Starts with vowel sound**.
   • In the **Record Name** field , type `Invoice Number`.
   • In the **Data Type** field , select `Auto Number`.
   • In the **Display Format** field, type `INV-{0000}`.
   • In the **Starting Number** field, type `1`.

3. Click **Save**.
4. Add a Status field.

   a. Scroll down to the Custom Fields & Relationships related list and click **New**.
   b. For Data Type, select `Picklist` and click **Next**.
   c. In the Field Label field, type `Status`.
   d. Type the following picklist values in the box provided, with each entry on its own line.

   ```
   Open
   Closed
   Negotiating
   Pending
   ```

   e. Select the checkbox for **Use first value as default value**.
   f. Click **Next**.
   g. For field-level security, select `Read Only` and then click **Next**.
   h. Click **Save & New** to save this field and create a new one.

5. Now create an optional Description field.

   a. In the Data Type field, select `Text Area` and click **Next**.
   b. In the Field Label and Field Name fields, enter `Description`.
   c. Click **Next**, accept the defaults, and click **Next** again.

d. Click **Save** to go the detail page for the Invoice Statement object.

Your InvoiceStatement object should now have two custom fields.

Step 2: Create a PushTopic

Use the Developer Console to create the PushTopic record that contains a SOQL query. Event notifications are generated for updates that match the query. Alternatively, you can also use Workbench to create a PushTopic.

1. Select **Your Name** > **Developer Console**.
2. Click **Debug** > **Open Execute Anonymous Window**.
3. In the Enter Apex Code window, paste in the following Apex code, and click **Execute**.

```
PushTopic pushTopic = new PushTopic();
pushTopic.Name = 'InvoiceStatementUpdates';
pushTopic.Query = 'SELECT Id, Name, Status__c, Description__c
  FROM Invoice_Statement__c';
pushTopic.ApiVersion = 29.0;
pushTopic.NotifyForOperationCreate = true;
pushTopic.NotifyForOperationUpdate = true;
pushTopic.NotifyForOperationUndelete = true;
pushTopic.NotifyForOperationDelete = true;
pushTopic.NotifyForFields = 'Referenced';
insert pushTopic;
```

 Note: If your organization has a namespace prefix defined, then you'll need to preface the custom object and field names with that namespace when you define the PushTopic query. For example, SELECT Id, Name, **namespace**__Status__c, **namespace**__Description__c FROM **namespace**__Invoice_Statement__c.

Because NotifyForOperationCreate, NotifyForOperationUpdate, NotifyForOperationDelete and NotifyForOperationUndelete are set to true, Streaming API evaluates records that are created, updated, deleted, or undeleted and generates a notification if the record matches the PushTopic query. Because NotifyForFields is set to Referenced, Streaming API will use fields in both the SELECT clause and the WHERE clause to generate a notification. Whenever the fields Name, Status__c, or Description__c are updated, a notification will be generated on this channel. For more information about NotifyForOperationCreate, NotifyForOperationUpdate, NotifyForOperationDelete, NotifyForOperationUndelete, and NotifyForFields, see Event Notification Rules.

Note: In API version 28.0 and earlier, notifications are only generated when records are created or updated. The `NotifyForOperationCreate`, `NotifyForOperationUpdate`, `NotifyForOperationDelete`, and `NotifyForOperationUndelete` fields are unavailable and the `NotifyForOperations` enum field is used instead to set which record events generate a notification. For more information see PushTopic.

Step 3: Subscribe to the PushTopic Channel

In this step, you'll subscribe to the channel you created with the PushTopic record in the previous step.

 Important: Workbench is a free, open source, community-supported tool (see the Help page in Workbench). Salesforce.com provides a hosted instance of Workbench for demonstration purposes only—salesforce.com recommends that you do not use this hosted instance of Workbench to access data in a production database. If you want to use Workbench for your production database, you can download, host, and configure it using your own resources.

You can download Workbench from *http://code.google.com/p/forceworkbench/downloads/list.*

1. In your browser, navigate to `http://workbench.developerforce.com`.
2. For Environment, select **Production**.
3. For API Version, select 29.0.
4. Accept the terms of service and click **Login with Salesforce**.
5. Once you successfully establish a connection to your database, you land on the Select page.
6. Click **queries** > **Streaming Push Topics**.
7. In the Push Topic field, select **InvoiceStatementUpdates**.
8. Click **Subscribe**.

   You'll see the connection and response information and a response like "Subscribed to /topic/InvoiceStatementUpdates."

Keep this browser window open and make sure the connection doesn't time out. You'll be able to see the event notifications triggered by the InvoiceStatement record you create in the next step.

Step 4: Test the PushTopic Channel

Make sure the browser that you used in Step 3: Subscribe to the PushTopic Channel stays open and the connection doesn't time out. You'll view event notifications in this browser.

The final step is to test the PushTopic channel by creating a new InvoiceStatement record in Workbench and viewing the event notification.

1. In a new browser window, open an instance of Workbench and log in using the same username by following the steps in Step 3: Subscribe to the PushTopic Channel.

     Note: If the user that makes an update to a record and the user that's subscribed to the channel don't share records, then the subscribed user won't receive the notification. For example, if the sharing model for the organization is private.

2. Click **data > Insert**.
3. For Object Type, select **Invoice_Statement__c**. Ensure that the **Single Record** field is selected, and click **Next**.
4. Type in a value for the **Description__c** field.
5. Click **Confirm Insert**.
6. Switch over to your Streaming Push Topics browser window. You'll see a notification that the invoice statement was created. The notification returns the Id, Status__c, and Description__c fields that you defined in the SELECT statement of your PushTopic query. The message looks something like this:

```
{
  "channel": "/topic/InvoiceStatementUpdates",
  "data": {
    "event": {
      "type": "created",
      "createdDate": "2011-11-14T17:33:45.000+0000"
    },
    "sobject": {
      "Name": "INV-0004",
      "Id": "a00D0000008oLi8IAE",
      "Description__c": "Test invoice statement",
      "Status__c": "Open"
    }
  }
}
```

Best Practices

Consider the best practices explained in this section.

Clients and Timeouts

Streaming API imposes three timeouts, as supported in the Bayeux protocol.

Socket timeout: 110 seconds

> A client receives events (JSON-formatted HTTP responses) while it waits on a connection. If no events are generated and the client is still waiting, the connection times out after 110 seconds and the server closes the connection. Clients should reconnect before two minutes to avoid the connection timeout.

Reconnect timeout: 40 seconds

> After receiving the events, a client needs to reconnect to receive the next set of events. If the reconnection doesn't happen within 40 seconds, the server expires the subscription and the connection is closed. If this happens, the client must start again and handshake, subscribe, and connect.

Each Streaming API client logs into an instance and maintains a session. When the client handshakes, connects, or subscribes, the session timeout is restarted. A client session times out if the client doesn't reconnect to the server within 40 seconds after receiving a response (an event, subscribe result, and so on).

If there's no activity on that session, then the organization timeout goes into effect and closes the session.

Clients and Cookies for Streaming API

The client you create to work with the Streaming API must obey the standard cookie protocol with the server. The client must accept and send the appropriate cookies for the domain and URI path, for example `https://`***`instance_name`***`.salesforce.com/cometd`.

Streaming API requirements on clients:

- The `"Content-Type: application/json"` header is required on all calls to the `cometd` servlet if the content of the post is JSON.
- A header containing the Salesforce session ID or OAuth token is required. For example, `Authorization: Bearer sessionId`.

- The client must accept and send back all appropriate cookies for the domain and URI path. Clients must obey the standard cookie protocol with the server.
- The subscribe response and other responses might contain the following fields. These fields aren't contained in the CometD specification.

    ◊ `EventType` contains either `created` or `updated`.

    ◊ `CreatedDate` contains the event's creation date.

Supported Browsers

Streaming API supports the following browsers:

- Internet Explorer 8 and greater
- Firefox 4 and greater

We recommend using the latest version of your browser with the most recent security updates and fixes applied. For regions that must use Internet Explorer 6 or 7, salesforce.com has confirmed that these browsers will work with Streaming API using jQuery 1.5.1 and CometD 2.2.0.

HTTPS Recommended

Streaming API follows the preference set by your administrator for your organization. By default this is HTTPS. To protect the security of your data, we recommend you use HTTPS.

Debugging Streaming API Applications

You must be able to see all of the requests and responses in order to debug Streaming API applications. Because Streaming API applications are stateful, you need to use a proxy tool to debug your application. Use a tool that can report the contents of all requests and results, such as Burp Proxy, Fiddler, or Firebug.

The most common errors include:

- Browser and JavaScript issues
- Sending requests out of sequence
- Malformed requests that don't follow the Bayeux protocol
- Authorization issues
- Network or firewall issues with long-lived connections

Using these tools, you can look at the requests, headers, body of the post, as well as the results. If you must contact us for help, be sure to copy and save these elements to assist in troubleshooting.

The first step for any debugging process is to follow the instructions in the Quick Start Using Workbench, Example: Interactive Visualforce Page, Example: Visualforce Page, or Example: Java Client and verify that you can implement the samples provided. The next step is to use your debug tool to help isolate the symptoms and cause of any problems.

402 Error

You may sometimes receive an error notification that contains "402::Uknown client" and looks something like this:

```
Thu Mar 29 06:08:08 PDT 2012 [CHANNEL:META_CONNECT]:
{"id":"78","error":"402::Unknown
client","successful":false,"advice":{"interval":500,"reconnect":"handshake"}
```

This can be caused by various conditions including when your client connection times out. If you see this error, you should reconnect to the server with a handshake. For more information about client timeouts and Streaming API limits, see

Clients and Timeouts and Streaming API Limits.

Monitoring Events Usage

The number of events that can be generated in a 24–hour period depends on your type of organization. For more information, see Streaming API Limits. You can monitor Streaming API events usage on the Company Information page.

•   From Setup, click **Company Profile** > **Company Information**.

If you refresh the Company Information page, the Streaming API Events value may fluctuate slightly. Regardless of these small fluctuations, your limits are being assessed accurately.

Notification Message Order

Changes to data in your organization happen in a sequential manner. However, the order in which you receive event notification messages in Streaming API isn't guaranteed. On the client side, you can use `createdDate` to order the notification messages returned in a channel. The value of `createdDate` is a UTC date/time value that indicates when the event occurred.

This code shows multiple messages, one generated by the creation of a record and one generated by the update of a record.

```
{
  "channel": "/topic/InvoiceStatementUpdates",
  "clientId": "1g177wgjj14omtdo3rcl0hjhm4w",
  "data": {
    "event": {
      "type": "updated",
      "createdDate": "2013-05-10T18:16:19.000+0000"
    },
    "sobject": {
      "Name": "INV-0002",
      "test_ds__Status__c": "Negotiating",
      "test_ds__Description__c": "Update to invoice statement #2",
      "Id": "a00D0000008pvxcIAA"
    }
  }
}

{
  "channel": "/topic/InvoiceStatementUpdates",
  "clientId": "1g177wgjj14omtdo3rcl0hjhm4w",
  "data": {
    "event": {
      "type": "created",
      "createdDate": "2013-05-10T18:15:11.000+0000"
    },
    "sobject": {
      "Name": "INV-0003",
      "test_ds__Status__c": "Open",
      "test_ds__Description__c": "New invoice statement #1",
      "Id": "a00D0000008pvzdIAA"
    }
  }
}
```

Resources

Search on the Salesforce Developer's Network at
`http://developer.salesforce.com/docs` for the following resources on Streaming API.

- Streaming API Developer's Guide
- SOQL and SOSL Reference Guide
- APIs and Integration forums

Chapter 11

Data.com API

Data.com API includes Data.com Search API and Data.com Match API.

Data.com Search API is a REST and APEX API-based interface that searches the Data.com database for contacts and companies, and returns information for the fields you've specified. The API is available to customers who have purchased Data.com Prospector.

Data.com Match API is a REST API-based interface that provides a matching service (or algorithm) to match contact and company information with the latest Data.com data. The API is available to customers who have purchased Data.com Clean.

 Note: Data.com API is currently available through a pilot program. For information on enabling this API for your organization, contact salesforce.com. Any unreleased services or features referenced in this or other press releases or public statements are not currently available and may not be delivered on time or at all. Customers who purchase our services should make their purchase decisions based upon features that are currently available.

When to Use Data.com API

Data.com Prospector and Data.com Clean already provide advanced searching and matching capabilities through Data.com. Use Data.com Search API and Data.com Match API to extend capabilities that Data.com Prospector and Data.com Clean don't provide. Data.com API gives you a powerful, convenient, and simple interface for interacting with Salesforce.

Supported Editions and Platforms

To use Data.com API, your organization must use Enterprise Edition, Performance Edition, Unlimited Edition, or Developer Edition. Your organization must also purchase Data.com Prospector to use Data.com Search API, or Data.com Clean to use Data.com Match API.

Contact your account representative to upgrade your edition of Salesforce, or to purchase Data.com Prospector or Data.com Clean.

Data.com Search API

Data.com Search API is a REST and APEX API-based interface that searches the Data.com database for contacts and companies, and returns information for the fields you've specified. The API is available to customers who have purchased Data.com Prospector.

The Data.com Search API has two resources:

DatacloudContact

> Returns search results from Contacts in the Data.com database.

DatacloudCompany

> Returns search results from Companies in the Data.com database.

DatacloudContact SOQL Request

Use an SOQL request to search the Data.com database for contacts.

Request

```
SELECT ContactId,LastName,FirstName,Title,State,City,CompanyName
FROM DatacloudContact
WHERE CompanyName LIKE 'Cisco' AND State = 'CA'
ORDER BY LastName
LIMIT 15
OFFSET 2000
```

- SELECT — indicates the fields returned from the query
- FROM — indicated the object being queried
- WHERE — filters the query results on the specified criteria
- AND — a logical operator used to combine search criteria within the WHERE filter
- ORDER BY — sorts the results by the specified criteria
- LIMIT — specifies the number of results that are displayed per page. A LIMIT of 50 displays 50 records for each page of the results.
- OFFSET — specifies at which record the results start to display. An offset of 100 would start displaying results from the one hundred and first (101) record.

Fields

Field	Properties	Type	Description	Since Version
City	filterable, sortable	String	The name of the city where the company is located.	29.0
CompanyId	filterable	String	Unique numerical identifier for the company.	29.0
Company Name	filterable, sortable	String	The name of the company.	29.0
ContactId	filterable	String	The unique numeric identifier for this contact.	29.0
Country	filterable, sortable	String	A string representing the standard abbreviation for the country where the company is located.	29.0
Email	filterable	Email	A business email address for the contact.	29.0
ExternalId	filterable, sortable	String	Unique numerical identifier for the contact.	29.0
FirstName	filterable	String	The first name of the contact.	29.0
Id	filterable, sortable	Id	Unique numerical identifier for the contact.	29.0
IsInactive	none	Boolean	A true or false response. True means the record is no longer active. False indicates the contact us still valid and active.	29.0

Field	Properties	Type	Description	Since Version
IsOwned	none	Boolean	An indication whether you own this record or not. • True — indicates you own this record • False — indicates you do not own this record	29.0
LastName	filterable	String	The last name of the contact.	29.0
Phone	none	Phone	A numerical string containing the direct dial phone number for the contact	29.0
State	filterable, sortable	String	The two letter standard abbreviation for a state.	29.0
Street	none	String	A postal address for the company.	29.0
Title	filterable, sortable	String	The title for the position held by the contact.	29.0
Zip	filterable, sortable	String	A numeric postal code designation for the address	29.0

Contact Logical Operators

This table lists the fields you can use with specific logical operators to construct your SOQL query.

Field	=	!=	<	<=	>	>=	LIKE	IN	NOT IN	ORDER BY
CompanyId	√							√		
Company Name	√	√						√	√	√

Field	=	!=	<	<=	>	>=	LIKE	IN	NOT IN	ORDER BY
City	√						√	√		√
ContactId	√							√		
Country	√							√		√
Email		√					√	√		
FirstName		√					√	√		
LastName		√					√	√	√	
State	√							√		√
Title	√	√					√	√	√	√
Zip		√					√		√	√

Note: When you use `LIKE` in a query, wildcards are implicitly used in the query.

DatacloudContact SOQL Response

The response contains the fields you specified in the SELECT statement: `SELECT ContactId, LastName, FirstName, Title, State, City, CompanyName`

Obfuscated fields mask or hide critical data in both contact and company records. Once your organization purchases the record all obfuscated fields are fully visible.

Table 1: Obfuscated fields query results

	ContactId	LastName	FirstName	Title	State	City	CompanyName
1	13962651	C*****	J*****	******	CA	San Jose	Cisco Systems, Inc.

	ContactId	LastName	FirstName	Title	State	City	CompanyName
2	38724678	Cooper	David	Product Sales Specialists	CA	San Jose	Cisco Systems, Inc.
3	19266707	C*****	D*****	*****	CA	San Jose	Cisco Systems, Inc.
4	35023206	C*****	G*****	*****	CA	San Jose	Cisco Systems, Inc.

Here are the contact records after they've been purchased. Previously obfuscated fields are visible.

Table 2: Non-obfuscated fields query results

	ContactId	LastName	FirstName	Title	State	City	CompanyName
1	13962651	Cooney	Joe	Controller	CA	San Jose	Cisco Systems, Inc.
2	38724678	Cooper	David	Product Sales Specialists	CA	San Jose	Cisco Systems, Inc.
3	19266707	Cooper	David	Systems Engineer	CA	San Jose	Cisco Systems, Inc.
4	35023206	Cooper	Gary	Director Manufactur-ing Emtg	CA	San Jose	Cisco Systems, Inc.

DatacloudCompany SOQL Request

Use an SOQL request to search the Data.com database for companies.

Request

```
SELECT City,State,Street,CompanyId
FROM DatacloudCompany
WHERE Name like 'Cisco'
ORDER BY State
```

- SELECT — indicates the fields returned from the query
- FROM — indicated the object being queried
- WHERE — filters the query results on the specified criteria
- AND — a logical operator used to combine search criteria within the WHERE filter
- ORDER BY — sorts the results by the specified criteria
- LIMIT — specifies the number of results that are displayed per page. A LIMIT of 50 displays 50 records for each page of the results.
- OFFSET — specifies at which record the results start to display. An offset of 100 would start displaying results from the one hundred and first (101) record.

Fields

Field	Properties	Type	Description	Since Version
AnnualRevenue	filterable	Currency	The amount of money the company makes in one year. Annual revenue is measured in US dollars.	29.0
City	filterable, sortable	String	The name of the where the company is located.	29.0
CompanyId	filterable	String	Unique numerical identifier for the company. This is the Data.com identifier for this company	29.0
Country	filterable, sortable	String	A string representing the standard abbreviation for the country where the company is located.	29.0
DunsNumber	none	String	A randomly generated nine-digit number assigned by Dun &	29.0

Field	Properties	Type	Description	Since Version
			Bradstreet (D&B) to identify unique business establishments	
ExternalId	filterable, sortable	String	Unique numerical identifier for the company.	29.0
Fax	none	Phone	The telephone number used sending and receiving faxes.	29.0
Id	filterable, sortable	Id	Unique numerical identifier for the company.	29.0
Industry	none	String	A seven digit number that has two logical parts. The first three digits followed by four zeros identify an industry, for example 1010000 is the number for Agriculture & Mining. The last four digits indicate a sub-industry. Four zeros, 101**0000**, indicate all sub-industries.	29.0
IsInactive	none	Boolean	A true or false response. True means the record is no longer active. False indicates the contact us still valid and active.	29.0

Field	Properties	Type	Description	Since Version
IsOwned	none	Boolean	An indication whether you own this record or not. • True — indicates you or the org you are part of owns this record • False — indicates you have not purchased this record	29.0
NaicsCode	none	String	North American Industry Classification System (NAICS) codes were created to provide more details about a business's service orientation. The code descriptions are focused more on what a business does.	29.0
NaicsDesc	none	String	A description of the NAICS classification.	29.0
Name	filterable, sortable	String	The company's name.	29.0
NumberOf Employees	filterable	Integer	The total number of employees working for the company.	29.0
Ownership	none	Picklist	The type of ownership of the company: • Public • Private • Government • Other	29.0
Phone	none	Phone	A numerical string containing the direct	29.0

Field	Properties	Type	Description	Since Version
			dial phone number for the contact	
Sic	none	String	Standard Industrial Codes (SIC) is a numbering convention that indicates what type of service a business provides. It is a 4 digit value.	29.0
SicDesc	none	String	A description of the SIC classification.	29.0
Site	none	String	They type of location of the company such as "Headquarters."	29.0
State	filterable, sortable	String	The two letter standard abbreviation for a state.	29.0
Street	none	String	A postal address for the company.	29.0
TickerSymbol	none	String	The symbol the uniquely identifies companies traded on public stock exchanges.	29.0
Tradestyle	none	String	A legal name under which a company conducts business.	29.0
Website	none	String	The standard URL for the companies home page.	29.0
YearStarted	none	Sting	The year that the company was founded.	29.0
Zip	filterable, sortable	String	A numeric postal code designation for the address	29.0

Company Logical Operators

This table lists the fields you can use with specific logical operators to construct your SOQL query.

Field	=	!=	<	<=	>	>=	LIKE	IN	NOT IN	ORDER BY
AnnualRevenue	√		√	√	√	√				
City	√						√	√		√
CompanyId	√							√		
Country	√							√		√
Name	√	√					√	√	√	√
NumberOf Employees	√		√	√	√	√				
State	√							√		√
Zip	√						√		√	√

 Note: When you use LIKE in a query, wildcards are implicitly used in the query.

DatacloudCompany SOQL Response

The response contains the fields you specified in the SELECT statement: SELECT City, State, Street, NumberOfEmployees, CompanyId.

Obfuscated fields mask or hide critical data in both contact and company records. Once your organization purchases the record all obfuscated fields are fully visible.

Table 3: Obfuscated fields query result

Number	City	State	Street	NumberOf Employees	CompanyId
1	Milpitas	CA	******	******	4829908
2	Los Altos Hills	CA	******	******	8599704
3	San Bruno	CA	950 Elm Ave FL 1	520	8590022
4	San Jose	CA	******	******	4829903

Here are the company records after they've been purchased. Previously obfuscated fields are visible.

Table 4: Non-obfuscated fields query result

Number	City	State	Street	NumberOf Employees	CompanyId
1	Milpitas	CA	755 Sycamore Dr		4829908
2	Los Altos Hills	CA	11633 Rebecca Ln	1	8599704
3	San Bruno	CA	950 Elm Ave FL 1	520	8590022
4	San Jose	CA	125 Rio Robles	1	4829903

Data.com Match API

Data.com Match API is a REST API-based interface that provides a matching service (or algorithm) to match contact and company information with the latest Data.com data. The API is available to customers who have purchased Data.com Clean.

The Data.com Match API has two resources:

DatacloudContact

> Returns matched data from Contacts in the Data.com database.

DatacloudCompany

> Returns matched data from Companies in the Data.com database.

Requests and Responses

Create a request body formatted in XML or JSON to perform a POST request.

Request bodies contain one or more requests. There is a maximum request size of 30.

There are two basic parts to a request.

Entities

> Entities contain attributes. Each attribute contains elements. The Elements are the fields that you request.

Fields

> Fields contain the values that are returned with the request.

Contact POST Requests

For the best chance at matching with Data.com contact records, it's important that your Salesforce records have accurate and complete values for certain important fields. The important fields are:

- Email
- First Name
- Last Name
- Phone
- Title

Use the URL and the POST command to send a match request.

```
https://your
instance/services/data/v29/match/DatacloudMatchEngine/DatacloudContact/
```

Minimum required fields

There are no minimum field requirements; however, it is recommended that you use a standard email address when possible.

Use as many of the important fields as possible to improve match results.

JSON

The following is an example of a contact match request

```
{
    "entities": [
        {
            "attributes": {
                "type": "DatacloudContact"
            },
            "Email": "terry.martin@salesforce.com",
            "FirstName": "Terry",
            "LastName": "Martin",
            "Title": "Writer"
        },
        {
            "attributes": {
                "type": "DatacloudContact"
            },
            "Email": "asadat@salesforce.com",
            "FirstName": "Ali",
            "LastName": "Sadat"
        }
    ],
    "fields": [
        "City",
        "CompanyId",
        "CompanyName",
        "ContactId",
        "Country",
        "Email",
        "FirstName",
        "IsInactive",
        "LastName",
        "Phone",
        "State",
        "Street",
        "Title",
        "Zip"
```

```
        ]
    }
```

XML

```
<DatacloudMatchInput
xmlns:xsi="http://www.w3.org/2001/XMLSchema-instance">
<entities xsi:type="DatacloudContact">
        <email>asadat@salesforce.com</email>
        <firstName>Al</firstName>
        <Title>Director</Title>
</entities>
<entities xsi:type="DatacloudContact">
        <email>terry.martin@salesforce.com</email>
        <firstName>Terry</firstName>
 <Zip>95120</Zip>
 <Phone>650.235.8335</Phone>
</entities>
  <fields>City</fields>
  <fields>CompanyId</fields>
  <fields>CompanyName</fields>
  <fields>ContactId</fields>
  <fields>Country</fields>
  <fields>Email</fields>
  <fields>FirstName</fields>
  <fields>IsInactive</fields>
  <fields>LastName</fields>
  <fields>Phone</fields>
  <fields>State</fields>
  <fields>Street</fields>
  <fields>Title</fields>
  <fields>Zip</fields>
</DatacloudMatchInput>
```

In XML "entitites" contain elements that are attributes. The attributes for Data.com are the field names in records.

```
. . .
<entities xsi:type="DatacloudContact">
        <email>asadat@salesforce.com</email>
        <firstName>Al</firstName>
        <Title>Director</Title>
</entities>

. . .
```

The attributes or field names included in the match request are compared against records in the Data.com database.

The fields elements are a list of fields you want returned in a request.

```
. . .
    <fields>City</fields>
    <fields>CompanyId</fields>
    <fields>CompanyName</fields>

. . .
```

Fields

Include fields in the request entities to indicate which fields to match against the Data.com database. The more fields you include in the request element, the more restricted your match will be.

List the fields you want returned from the match request in a JSON `"fields":` list or in an XML `<fields>` element.

Field	Type	Description	Since Version
City	String	The name of the city where the company is located.	29.0
CompanyId	String	Unique numerical identifier for the company at which the contact works.	29.0
CompanyName	String	The name of the company at which the contact works.	29.0
ContactId	String	Unique numerical identifier for a contact.	29.0
Country	String	A string representing the standard abbreviation for the country where the contact works.	29.0
Email	String	An email address for this contact.	29.0
FirstName	String	The first name of a contact.	29.0
IsInactive	String	A true or false response. True means the record is no longer active. False indicates the contact us still valid and active.	29.0
LastName	String	The last name of a contact.	29.0

Field	Type	Description	Since Version
Phone	String	A numerical string containing the direct dial phone number for the contact.	29.0
State	String	The two letter standard abbreviation for a state.	29.0
Street	String	A postal address for the company where this contacts works.	29.0
Title	String	The job title for this contact	29.0
Zip	String	A numeric postal code designation for the address.	29.0

Contact Responses

Here is an example of a successful response body.

JSON

```
[
    {
        "errorCode": 0,
        "errorMessage": null,
        "matchRecords": [
            {
                "entity": {
                    "attributes": {
                        "type": "DatacloudContact"
                    },
                    "Street": "777 Mariners Island Blvd Ste 400",

                    "Phone": "+1.650.235.8335",
                    "CompanyName": "Salesforcecom Inc",
                    "LastName": "Martin",
                    "Country": "United States",
                    "Title": "Staff Technical Writer Jigsaw",
                    "City": "San Mateo",
                    "State": "CA",
                    "Email": "terry.martin@salesforce.com",
                    "FirstName": "Terry",
                    "ContactId": 33011763,
                    "Zip": "94404-5059",
                    "IsInactive": false
                },
                "matchDiffs": [
```

```
                              "Title"
                          ]
                  }
              ]
        },
        {
            "errorCode": 0,
            "errorMessage": null,
            "matchRecords": [
                {
                    "entity": {
                        "attributes": {
                            "type": "DatacloudContact"
                        },
                        "Street": "1 Market",
                        "Phone": "+1.415.778.3357",
                        "CompanyName": "Salesforce.com, Inc.",
                        "LastName": "Sadat",
                        "Country": "United States",
                        "Title": "Senior Director, Product Management
  - Api Platform",
                        "City": "San Francisco",
                        "State": "CA",
                        "Email": "asadat@salesforce.com",
                        "FirstName": "Ali",
                        "ContactId": 45003056,
                        "Zip": "94105-1596",
                        "IsInactive": false
                    },
                    "matchDiffs": [ ]
                }
            ]
        }
]
```

XML

```
<?xml version="1.0" encoding="UTF-8"?>
<Match xmlns:xsi="http://www.w3.org/2001/XMLSchema-instance">
  <MatchResult>
    <errorCode>0</errorCode>
    <errorMessage xsi:nil="true"/>
    <matchRecords>
      <entity type="DatacloudContact">
          <Id xsi:nil="true"/>
          <Street>1 Market</Street>
          <Phone>+1.415.778.3357</Phone>
          <CompanyId>159110</CompanyId>
          <CompanyName>Salesforce.com, Inc.</CompanyName>
          <LastName>Sadat</LastName>
          <Country>United States</Country>
          <Title>Senior Director, Product Management - Api
Platform</Title>
          <City>San Francisco</City>
```

```
                    <State>CA</State>
                    <Email>asadat@salesforce.com</Email>
                    <FirstName>Ali</FirstName>
                    <ContactId>45003056</ContactId>
                    <IsInactive>false</IsInactive>
                    <Zip>94105-1596</Zip>
                </entity>
            <matchDiffs>Title</matchDiffs>
            <matchDiffs>FirstName</matchDiffs>
        </matchRecords>
    </MatchResult>
    <MatchResult>
        <errorCode>0</errorCode>
        <errorMessage xsi:nil="true"/>
        <matchRecords>
            <entity type="DatacloudContact">
                <Id xsi:nil="true"/>
                <Street>777 Mariners Island Blvd Ste 400</Street>
                <Phone>+1.650.235.8335</Phone>
                <CompanyId>4827433</CompanyId>
                <CompanyName>Salesforcecom Inc</CompanyName>
                <LastName>Martin</LastName>
                <Country>United States</Country>
                <Title>Staff Technical Writer Jigsaw</Title>
                <City>San Mateo</City> <State>CA</State>
                <Email>terry.martin@salesforce.com</Email>
                <FirstName>Terry</FirstName>
                <ContactId>33011763</ContactId>
                <IsInactive>false</IsInactive>
                <Zip>94404-5059</Zip>
            </entity>
        <matchDiffs>Zip</matchDiffs>
        <matchDiffs>Phone</matchDiffs>
        </matchRecords>
    </MatchResult>
</Match>
```

Company POST Requests

For the best chance of matching with Data.com company records with your own, it's important that your Salesforce records have accurate and complete values for certain fields. These fields are:

- Name — the official name of the company.
- Street — the physical address where the company is located.
- Phone — a telephone number for a corporate office.
- Website — the URL for the corporate website, for example, www.salesforce.com.

Use the URL and the POST command to send a match request.

```
https://your
instance/services/data/v29/match/DatacloudMatchEngine/DatacloudCompany/
```

Minimum required fields

There are no minimum field requirements; however, it is recommended that you use a company name or website when possible.

 Note: You can search on any of the supported fields. The more fields included in the request the more the match is narrowed and focused on specific information.

JSON

The following is an example of a company match request.

```
{
    "entities": [
        {
            "attributes": {
            "type": "DatacloudCompany"
            },
            "Name": "Dell Inc",
            "Website": "www.dell.com",
            "Phone": "+1.512.338.4400",
            "city": "Red Rock"
        }
    ],
    "fields": [
        "AnnualRevenue",
        "City",
        "CompanyId",
        "Country",
        "Description",
        "DunsNumber",
        "Fax",
        "Industry",
        "IsInactive",
        "NaicsCode",
        "NaicsDesc",
        "Name",
        "NumberOfEmployees",
        "Ownership",
        "Phone",
        "Sic",
        "SicDesc",
        "State",
        "Street",
        "TickerSymbol",
        "TradeStyle",
```

```
        "Website",
        "YearStarted",
        "Zip",
        "Site"
    ]
}
```

XML

```xml
<DatacloudMatchInput
xmlns:xsi="http://www.w3.org/2001/XMLSchema-instance">
<entities xsi:type="DatacloudCompany">
    <type>DatacloudCompany</type>
    <Name>Dell Inc</Name>
    <Website>www.dell.com</Website>
    <Phone>+1.512.338.4400</Phone>
    <city>Red Rock</city>
</entities>
    <fields>AnnualRevenue</fields>
    <fields>City</fields>
    <fields>CompanyId</fields>
    <fields>Country</fields>
    <fields>Description</fields>
    <fields>DunsNumber</fields>
    <fields>Fax</fields>
    <fields>Industry</fields>
    <fields>IsInactive</fields>
    <fields>NaicsCode</fields>
    <fields>NaicsDesc</fields>
    <fields>Name</fields>
    <fields>NumberOfEmployees</fields>
    <fields>Ownership</fields>
    <fields>Phone</fields>
    <fields>Sic</fields>
    <fields>SicDesc</fields>
    <fields>State</fields>
    <fields>Street</fields>
    <fields>TickerSymbol</fields>
    <fields>TradeStyle</fields>
    <fields>Website</fields>
    <fields>YearStarted</fields>
    <fields>Zip</fields>
    <fields>Site</fields>
 </DatacloudMatchInput>
```

In XML "entities" contain elements that are attributes. The attributes for Data.com are the names of fields in records.

The attributes or field names included in the match request are compared against records in the Data.com database.

The fields elements are a list of fields returned in a successful request.

Fields

Include fields in the request entities to indicate which fields to match against the Data.com database. The more fields you include in the request element, the more restricted your match will be.

List the fields you want returned from the match request in a JSON `"fields"`: list or in an XML `<fields>` element.

Field	Type	Description	Since Version
AnnualRevenue	String	The amount of money the company makes in one year.	29.0
City	String	The name of the where the company is located.	29.0
CompanyId	String	Unique numerical identifier for the company.	29.0
Country	String	A string representing the standard abbreviation for the country where the company is located.	29.0
Description	Sting	A brief summary about the company.	29.0
DunsNumber	String	A randomly generated nine-digit number assigned by Dun & Bradstreet (D&B) to identify unique business establishments	29.0
Fax	String	The telephone number used sending and receiving faxes.	29.0
Industry	String	A seven digit number that has two logical parts. The first three digits followed by four zeros identify an industry, for example 1010000 is the number for Agriculture & Mining. The last four digits indicate a sub-industry. Four zeros, 101**0000**, indicate all sub-industries.	29.0

Field	Type	Description	Since Version
IsInactive	String	A true or false response. True means the record is no longer active. False indicates the contact us still valid and active.	29.0
NaicsCode	String	North American Industry Classification System (NAICS) codes were created to provide more details about a business's service orientation. The code descriptions are focused more on what a business does.	29.0
NaicsDesc	String	A description of the NAICS classification.	29.0
Name	String	The company's name.	29.0
NumberOfEmployees	String	The total number of employees working for the company.	29.0
Ownership	String	The type of ownership of the company: • Public • Private • Government • Other	29.0
Phone	String	A numerical string containing the direct dial phone number for the contact	29.0
Sic	Integer	Standard Industrial Codes (SIC) is a numbering convention that indicates what type of service a business provides. It is a 4 digit value.	29.0
SicDesc	String	A description of the SIC classification.	29.0
Site	String	They type of location of the company such as "Headquarters."	29.0

Field	Type	Description	Since Version
State	String	The two letter standard abbreviation for a state.	29.0
Street	String	A postal address for the company.	29.0
TickerSymbol	String	The symbol the uniquely identifies companies traded on public stock exchanges.	29.0
TradeStyle	String	A legal name under which a company conducts business.	29.0
Website	String	The standard URL for the companies home page.	29.0
YearStarted	Sting	The year that the company was founded.	29.0
Zip	String	A numeric postal code designation for the address	29.0

Company Responses

Here is an example of a successful response body.

JSON

```
[ { "errorCode" : 0,
    "errorMessage" : null,
    "matchRecords" : [ { "entity" : {
            "AnnualRevenue" : 61494000000.0,
            "City" : "Round Rock",
            "CompanyId" : 34179,
            "Country" : "United States",
            "Description" : "Dell wants its name to ring from
the desktop to the data center. The world's #3 supplier of PCs
(behind #1 HP and #2 Lenovo), the company offers a broad range
of technology products for the consumer, education, enterprise,
and government sectors. In addition to a full line of desktop
and notebook PCs, Dell offers network servers, data storage
systems, printers, Ethernet switches, and peripherals, such as
displays and projectors. It also markets third-party software
and hardware. The company's growing services unit provides asset
 recovery, financing, infrastructure consulting, support, systems
 integration, and training. Dell generates nearly half of its
revenues outside the US.",
```

```
            "DunsNumber" : "114315195",
            "Fax" : "",
            "Industry" : "Electronics",
            "IsInactive" : false,
            "NaicsCode" : "334111",
          "NaicsDesc" : "Electronic Computer Manufacturing",

            "Name" : "Dell Inc.",
            "NumberOfEmployees" : 100300,
            "Ownership" : "Public",
            "Phone" : "+1.512.338.4400",
            "Sic" : "3571",
            "SicDesc" : "Electronic Computers",
            "Site" : "Headquarters",
            "State" : "TX",
            "Street" : "1 Dell Way",
            "TickerSymbol" : "DELL",
            "TradeStyle" : "",
            "Website" : "www.dell.com",
            "YearStarted" : "1984",
            "Zip" : "78682-7000",
            "attributes" : { "type" : "DatacloudCompany" }
          },
        "matchDiffs" : [ "Name",
            "City"
          ]
      } ]
  } ]
```

XML

```
<?xml version="1.0" encoding="UTF-8"?>
<Match xmlns:xsi="http://www.w3.org/2001/XMLSchema-instance">
  <MatchResult>
    <errorCode>0</errorCode>
      <errorMessage xsi:nil="true"/>
    <matchRecords>
    <entity type="DatacloudCompany">
      <Id xsi:nil="true"/>
      <SicDesc>Electronic Computers</SicDesc>
      <NaicsCode>334111</NaicsCode>
      <Description>Dell wants its name to ring from the desktop
to the data center. The world's #3 supplier of PCs (behind #1 HP
 and #2 Lenovo), the company offers a broad range of technology
 products for the consumer, education, enterprise, and government
sectors. In addition to a full line of desktop and notebook PCs,
 Dell offers network servers, data storage systems, printers,
Ethernet switches, and peripherals, such as displays and
projectors. It also markets third-party software and hardware.
The company's growing services unit provides asset recovery,
financing, infrastructure consulting, support, systems
integration, and training. Dell generates nearly half of its
revenues outside the US.</Description>
      <Phone>+1.512.338.4400</Phone>
```

```
      <Street>1 Dell Way</Street>
      <TickerSymbol>DELL</TickerSymbol>
      <Site>Headquarters</Site>
      <CompanyId>34179</CompanyId>
      <Website>www.dell.com</Website>
      <Fax/>
      <YearStarted>1984</YearStarted>
      <Country>United States</Country>
      <AnnualRevenue>6.1494E10</AnnualRevenue>
      <City>Round Rock</City>
      <Name>Dell Inc.</Name>
      <NumberOfEmployees>100300</NumberOfEmployees>
      <TradeStyle/>
      <State>TX</State>
      <NaicsDesc>Electronic Computer Manufacturing</NaicsDesc>
      <IsInactive>false</IsInactive>
      <Sic>3571</Sic>
      <Ownership>Public</Ownership>
      <Zip>78682-7000</Zip>
      <Industry>Electronics</Industry>
    </entity>
    <matchDiffs>Name</matchDiffs>
    <matchDiffs>City</matchDiffs>
  </matchRecords>
  </MatchResult>
</Match>
```

Contact GET request and response

The GET contact request doesn't require a request body.

URI

Send a GET request to the URL without a request body to list the fields available in this API.

```
/services/data/v29/match/DatacloudMatchEngine/DatacloudContact/
```

Response

The response lists all available fields and the "maxBatchSize" or number of requests that can be sent.

```
{ "fieldSets" : "[FirstName, Zip, IsInactive, Country,
Phone, LastName, IsOwned, ContactId, Street, CompanyId,
Email, Title, State, CompanyName, City]",
"maxBatchSize" : "30" }
```

Company GET request and response

The GET company request doesn't require a request body.

URI

Send a GET request to the URL without a request body to list the fields available in this API.

```
/services/data/v29/match/DatacloudMatchEngine/DatacloudCompany/
```

Response

The response lists all available fields and the "maxBatchSize" or the number of requests that can be sent.

```
{"fieldSets": "[Industry, IsOwned, Fax, AnnualRevenue,
TradeStyle, City, State, NaicsDesc, Name, Website, Zip,
SicDesc, IsInactive, Ownership, Phone, NumberOfEmployees,
 TickerSymbol, Street, DunsNumber, NaicsCode,
YearStarted, CompanyId, Country, Sic, Description, Site]",
"maxBatchSize": "30" }
```

Considerations

Searching

- When you use LIKE in a query, the Data.com Search API implicitly appends wildcards to the end of filter strings.
- The Data.com Search API does not support queryMore(). Use OFFSET and LIMIT to page through results or to retrieve more results.

Filtering by Website

The Data.com Search API does not support filtering by company website URL. Filter by name and use LIKE to achieve the same results:

```
SELECT City,State,STreet,CompanyId
FROM DatacloudCompany
WHERE Name like 'Cisco.com'
```

Matching

- The more fields you include in your Data.com Match API request, the more specific your match is likely to be.

- While there are no minimum fields for matching, include a contact's email address for best results when matching contacts. For company matches, include accurate information for name, street, phone, and website.

## Chapter 12

SOQL and SOSL

Salesforce Object Query Language (SOQL) and Salesforce Object Search Language (SOSL) are a data query language and a data search language, respectively, used within many other Salesforce APIs.

When to Use SOQL

Use SOQL whenever you need to construct powerful data query strings. SOQL isn't used directly, but rather through another Salesforce API environment. Some examples of where SOQL is used include:

- The `queryString` parameter in the `query()` and `queryAll()` SOAP API calls.
- The query request parameter used in the REST API query and queryAll resources.
- The query portion of a bulk query request in Bulk API.
- The query field in a PushTopic record that defines the basis of a Streaming API channel.
- The query strings for regular and dynamic SOQL statements in Apex.

SOQL is used to specify objects and fields, using a syntax similar to the SELECT statement in Structured Query Language (SQL). For example, the following SOQL statement returns the Id field for all Merchandise custom object records that have a Name value of "My Merchandise":

```
SELECT Id FROM Merchandise__c WHERE Name = 'My Merchandise'
```

When to Use SOSL

Use SOSL whenever you need to construct data search strings. SOSL isn't used directly, but rather through another Salesforce API environment. Some examples of where SOSL is used include:

- The `searchString` parameter in the `search()` SOAP API call.
- The search request parameter used in the REST API search resource.

- The search strings for regular and dynamic SOSL statements in Apex.
- Visualforce controllers and getter methods.

SOSL is used to specify text to search for across all records in your organization, using a specialized search syntax. For example, the following SOSL statement returns the IDs of all records in your organization that contain the text "Joe Smith" or "Dan Fielding" in the Name field of any object:

```
FIND {"Joe Smith" OR "Dan Fielding"}
IN NAME FIELDS
```

Supported Editions and Platforms

Since SOQL and SOSL aren't directly accessed APIs, refer to the supported editions and platforms information for the API you are using that uses SOQL or SOSL.

Note that not every API supports SOQL and SOSL, and some APIs that do use them only support a subset of the available SOQL clauses. For example, a bulk query in Bulk API does not support nested queries or the COUNT, ROLLUP, SUM, GROUP BY CUBE, or OFFSET clauses. See the individual developer guides for the API you are using to determine how SOQL and SOSL are supported in that API.

Resources

Search on the Salesforce Developer's Network at http://developer.salesforce.com/docs for the following resources on SOQL and SOSL.

- SOQL and SOSL Reference Guide
- APIs and Integration forums

Chapter 13

Apex

Apex is an object-oriented, on-demand programming language that lets you add business logic and triggers for your organization's data on Salesforce.

When to Use Apex

Apex is a strongly typed, object-oriented programming language that allows developers to execute flow and transaction control statements on the Force.com platform server in conjunction with calls to the Force.com API. Using syntax that looks like Java and acts like database stored procedures, Apex enables developers to add business logic to most system events, including button clicks, related record updates, and Visualforce pages. Apex code can be initiated by Web service requests and from triggers on objects.

Use Apex if you want to:

- Create Web services.
- Create email services.
- Perform complex validation over multiple objects.
- Create complex business processes that are not supported by workflow.
- Create custom transactional logic (logic that occurs over the entire transaction, not just with a single record or object).
- Attach custom logic to another operation, such as saving a record, so that it occurs whenever the operation is executed, regardless of whether it originates in the user interface, a Visualforce page, or from SOAP API.

Supported Editions and Platforms

Apex is included in Enterprise Edition, Performance Edition, Unlimited Edition, Developer Edition, and Database.com. If you are an existing Salesforce customer and want to upgrade to Enterprise, Unlimited, or Performance Edition, contact your account representative.

Apex Quick Start

Once you have a Developer Edition or sandbox organization, you may want to learn some of the core concepts of Apex. Because Apex is very similar to Java, you may recognize much of the functionality.

After reviewing the basics, you are ready to write your first Apex program—a very simple class, trigger, and unit test.

In addition, there is a more complex shipping invoice example that you can also walk through. This example illustrates many more features of the language.

 Note: The Hello World and the shipping invoice samples require custom fields and objects. You can either create these on your own, or download the objects, fields and Apex code as a managed packaged from Force.com AppExchange. For more information, see `wiki.developerforce.com/index.php/Documentation`.

Writing Your First Apex Class and Trigger

This step-by-step tutorial shows how to create a simple Apex class and trigger. It also shows how to deploy these components to a production organization.

This tutorial is based on a custom object called Book that is created in the first step. This custom object is updated through a trigger.

Creating a Custom Object

Prerequisites:

A Salesforce account in a sandbox **Performance**, **Unlimited**, or **Enterprise** Edition organization, or an account in a Developer organization.

For more information about creating a sandbox organization, see "Sandbox Overview" in the Salesforce online help. To sign up for a free Developer organization, see the Developer Edition Environment Sign Up Page.

In this step, you create a custom object called Book with one custom field called Price.

1. Log into your sandbox or Developer organization.
2. From Setup, click **Create** > **Objects** and click **New Custom Object**.
3. Enter Book for the label.

4. Enter `Books` for the plural label.

5. Click **Save**.

   Ta dah! You've now created your first custom object. Now let's create a custom field.

6. In the **Custom Fields & Relationships** section of the Book detail page, click **New**.

7. Select Number for the data type and click **Next**.

8. Enter `Price` for the field label.

9. Enter 16 in the length text box.

10. Enter 2 in the decimal places text box, and click **Next**.

11. Click **Next** to accept the default values for field-level security.

12. Click **Save**.

You've just created a custom object called Book, and added a custom field to that custom object. Custom objects already have some standard fields, like Name and CreatedBy, and allow you to add other fields that are more specific to your implementation. For this tutorial, the Price field is part of our Book object and it is accessed by the Apex class you will write in the next step.

Adding an Apex Class

Prerequisites:

- A Salesforce account in a sandbox **Performance**, **Unlimited**, or **Enterprise** Edition organization, or an account in a Developer organization.
- The Book custom object.

In this step, you add an Apex class that contains a method for updating the book price. This method is called by the trigger that you will be adding in the next step.

1. From Setup, click **Develop** > **Apex Classes** and click **New**.

2. In the class editor, enter this class definition:

   ```
   public class MyHelloWorld {

   }
   ```

   The previous code is the class definition to which you will be adding one method in the next step. Apex code is generally contained in *classes*. This class is defined as `public`, which means the class is available to other Apex classes and triggers. For more information, see Classes, Objects, and Interfaces.

3. Add this method definition between the class opening and closing brackets.

   ```
   public static void applyDiscount(Book__c[] books) {
       for (Book__c b :books){
           b.Price__c *= 0.9;
       }
   }
   ```

This method is called `applyDiscount`, and it is both public and static. Because it is a static method, you don't need to create an instance of the class to access the method—you can just use the name of the class followed by a dot (.) and the name of the method. For more information, see Static and Instance.

This method takes one parameter, a list of Book records, which is assigned to the variable `books`. Notice the __c in the object name `Book__c`. This indicates that it is a *custom object* that you created. Standard objects that are provided in the Salesforce application, such as Account, don't end with this postfix.

The next section of code contains the rest of the method definition:

```
for (Book__c b :books){
    b.Price__c *= 0.9;
}
```

Notice the __c after the field name `Price__c`. This indicates it is a *custom field* that you created. Standard fields that are provided by default in Salesforce are accessed using the same type of dot notation but without the __c, for example, `Name` doesn't end with __c in `Book__c.Name`. The statement `b.Price__c *= 0.9;` takes the old value of `b.Price__c`, multiplies it by 0.9, which means its value will be discounted by 10%, and then stores the new value into the `b.Price__c` field. The `*=` operator is a shortcut. Another way to write this statement is `b.Price__c = b.Price__c * 0.9;`. See Understanding Expression Operators.

4. Click **Save** to save the new class. You should now have this full class definition.

```
public class MyHelloWorld {
    public static void applyDiscount(Book__c[] books) {
        for (Book__c b :books){
            b.Price__c *= 0.9;
        }
    }
}
```

You now have a class that contains some code that iterates over a list of books and updates the Price field for each book. This code is part of the `applyDiscount` static method called by the trigger that you will create in the next step.

Adding an Apex Trigger

Prerequisites:

- A Salesforce account in a sandbox **Performance, Unlimited,** or **Enterprise** Edition organization, or an account in a Developer organization.
- The MyHelloWorld Apex class.

In this step, you create a trigger for the `Book__c` custom object that calls the `applyDiscount` method of the `MyHelloWorld` class that you created in the previous step.

A *trigger* is a piece of code that executes before or after records of a particular type are inserted, updated, or deleted from the Force.com platform database. Every trigger runs with a set of context variables that provide access to the records that caused the trigger to fire. All triggers run in bulk; that is, they process several records at once.

1. From Setup, click **Create** > **Objects** and click the name of the object you just created, Book.
2. In the triggers section, click **New**.
3. In the trigger editor, delete the default template code and enter this trigger definition:

```
trigger HelloWorldTrigger on Book__c (before insert) {

    Book__c[] books = Trigger.new;

    MyHelloWorld.applyDiscount(books);
}
```

The first line of code defines the trigger:

```
trigger HelloWorldTrigger on Book__c (before insert) {
```

It gives the trigger a name, specifies the object on which it operates, and defines the events that cause it to fire. For example, this trigger is called HelloWorldTrigger, it operates on the `Book__c` object, and runs before new books are inserted into the database.

The next line in the trigger creates a list of book records named `books` and assigns it the contents of a trigger context variable called `Trigger.new`. Trigger context variables such as `Trigger.new` are implicitly defined in all triggers and provide access to the records that caused the trigger to fire. In this case, `Trigger.new` contains all the new books that are about to be inserted.

```
Book__c[] books = Trigger.new;
```

The next line in the code calls the method `applyDiscount` in the `MyHelloWorld` class. It passes in the array of new books.

```
MyHelloWorld.applyDiscount(books);
```

You now have all the code that is needed to update the price of all books that get inserted. However, there is still one piece of the puzzle missing. Unit tests are an important part of writing code and are required. In the next step, you will see why this is so and you will be able to add a test class.

Adding a Test Class

Prerequisites:

- A Salesforce account in a sandbox **Performance**, **Unlimited**, or **Enterprise** Edition organization, or an account in a Developer organization.
- The HelloWorldTrigger Apex trigger.

In this step, you add a test class with one test method. You also run the test and verify code coverage. The test method exercises and validates the code in the trigger and class. Also, it enables you to reach 100% code coverage for the trigger and class.

 Note: Testing is an important part of the development process. Before you can deploy Apex or package it for the Force.com AppExchange, the following must be true.

- At least 75% of your Apex code must be covered by unit tests, and all of those tests must complete successfully.

  Note the following.

  ◊ When deploying to a production organization, every unit test in your organization namespace is executed.
  ◊ Calls to System.debug are not counted as part of Apex code coverage.
  ◊ Test methods and test classes are not counted as part of Apex code coverage.
  ◊ While only 75% of your Apex code must be covered by tests, your focus shouldn't be on the percentage of code that is covered. Instead, you should make sure that every use case of your application is covered, including positive and negative cases, as well as bulk and single records. This should lead to 75% or more of your code being covered by unit tests.

- Every trigger must have some test coverage.
- All classes and triggers must compile successfully.

1. From Setup, click **Develop** > **Apex Classes** and click **New**.
2. In the class editor, add this test class definition, and then click **Save**.

```
@isTest
private class HelloWorldTestClass {
    static testMethod void validateHelloWorld() {
        Book__c b = new Book__c(Name='Behind the Cloud',
Price__c=100);
        System.debug('Price before inserting new book: ' +
b.Price__c);

        // Insert book
        insert b;

        // Retrieve the new book
```

```
        b = [SELECT Price__c FROM Book__c WHERE Id =:b.Id];
        System.debug('Price after trigger fired: ' +
b.Price__c);

        // Test that the trigger correctly updated the price
        System.assertEquals(90, b.Price__c);
    }
}
```

This class is defined using the `@isTest` annotation. Classes defined as such can only contain test methods. One advantage to creating a separate class for testing is that classes defined with `isTest` don't count against your organization limit of 3 MB for all Apex code. You can also add the `@isTest` annotation to individual methods. For more information, see `IsTest` Annotation and Understanding Execution Governors and Limits.

The method `validateHelloWorld` is defined as a `testMethod`. This means that if any changes are made to the database, they are automatically rolled back when execution completes and you don't have to delete any test data created in the test method.

First the test method creates a new book and inserts it into the database temporarily. The `System.debug` statement writes the value of the price in the debug log.

```
Book__c b = new Book__c(Name='Behind the Cloud',
Price__c=100);
System.debug('Price before inserting new book: ' +
b.Price__c);

// Insert book
insert b;
```

Once the book is inserted, the code retrieves the newly inserted book, using the ID that was initially assigned to the book when it was inserted, and then logs the new price that the trigger modified:

```
// Retrieve the new book
b = [SELECT Price__c FROM Book__c WHERE Id =:b.Id];
System.debug('Price after trigger fired: ' + b.Price__c);
```

When the `MyHelloWorld` class runs, it updates the `Price__c` field and reduces its value by 10%. The following line is the actual test, verifying that the method `applyDiscount` actually ran and produced the expected result:

```
// Test that the trigger correctly updated the price
System.assertEquals(90, b.Price__c);
```

3. Now let's switch to the Developer Console to run this test and view code coverage information. Click **Your Name** > **Developer Console**.
    The Developer Console window opens.
4. In the Developer Console, click **Test** > **New Run**.
5. To add your test class, click **HelloWorldTestClass**, and then click **>**.
6. To run the test, click **Run**.
    The test result displays in the *Tests* tab. Optionally, you can expand the test class in the *Tests* tab to view which methods were run. In this case, the class contains only one test method.
7. The *Overall Code Coverage* pane shows the code coverage of this test class. To view the lines of code in the trigger covered by this test, which is 100%, double-click the code coverage line for **HelloWorldTrigger**. Also, because the trigger calls a method from the `MyHelloWorld` class, this class has some coverage too (100%). To view the class coverage, double-click **MyHelloWorld**.
8. To open the log file, in the *Logs* tab, double-click the most recent log line in the list of logs. The execution log displays, including logging information about the trigger event, the call to the `applyDiscount` class method, and the debug output of the price before and after the trigger.

By now, you have completed all the steps necessary for writing some Apex code with a test that runs in your development environment. In the real world, after you've sufficiently tested your code and you're satisfied with it, you want to deploy the code along with any other prerequisite components to a production organization. The next step will show you how to do this for the code and custom object you've just created.

Deploying Components to Production

Prerequisites:

*   A Salesforce account in a sandbox **Performance, Unlimited,** or **Enterprise** Edition organization.
*   The HelloWorldTestClass Apex test class.
*   A deployment connection between the sandbox and production organizations that allows inbound change sets to be received by the production organization. See "Change Sets Overview" in the Salesforce online help.
*   Create and Upload Change Sets user permissions to create, edit, or upload outbound change sets.

In this step, you deploy the Apex code and the custom object you created previously to your production organization using change sets.

This procedure doesn't apply to Developer organizations since change sets are available only in **Performance, Unlimited, Enterprise,** or Database.com Edition organizations. If you have a Developer Edition account, you can use other deployment methods. For more information, see Deploying Apex.

1. From Setup, click **Deploy** > **Outbound Changesets**.
2. If a splash page appears, click **Continue**.
3. In the Change Sets list, click **New**.
4. Enter a name for your change set, for example, `HelloWorldChangeSet`, and optionally a description. Click **Save**.
5. In the Change Set Components section, click **Add**.
6. Select Apex Class from the component type drop-down list, then select the MyHelloWorld and the HelloWorldTestClass classes from the list and click **Add to Change Set**.
7. Click **View/Add Dependencies** to add the dependent components.
8. Select the top checkbox to select all components. Click **Add To Change Set**.
9. In the Change Set Detail section of the change set page, click **Upload**.
10. Select the target organization, in this case production, and click **Upload**.
11. After the change set upload completes, deploy it in your production organization.

    a. Log into your production organization.
    b. From Setup, click **Deploy** > **Inbound Change Sets**.
    c. If a splash page appears, click **Continue**.
    d. In the change sets awaiting deployment list, click your change set's name.
    e. Click **Deploy**.

In this tutorial, you learned how to create a custom object, how to add an Apex trigger, class, and test class. Finally, you also learned how to test your code, and how to upload the code and the custom object using Change Sets.

Best Practices

Consider the best practices in this section.

Developing Code in the Cloud

The Apex programming language is saved and runs in the cloud—the Force.com multitenant platform. Apex is tailored for data access and data manipulation on the platform, and it enables you to add custom business logic to system events. While it provides many benefits for automating business processes on the platform, it is not a general purpose programming language. As such, Apex cannot be used to:

- Render elements in the user interface other than error messages
- Change standard functionality—Apex can only prevent the functionality from happening, or add additional functionality

- Create temporary files
- Spawn threads

 Tip:

All Apex code runs on the Force.com platform, which is a shared resource used by all other organizations. To guarantee consistent performance and scalability, the execution of Apex is bound by governor limits that ensure no single Apex execution impacts the overall service of Salesforce. This means all Apex code is limited by the number of operations (such as DML or SOQL) that it can perform within one process.

All Apex requests return a collection that contains from 1 to 50,000 records. You cannot assume that your code only works on a single record at a time. Therefore, you must implement programming patterns that take bulk processing into account. If you don't, you may run into the governor limits.

Writing Tests

Testing is the key to successful long-term development and is a critical component of the development process. We strongly recommend that you use a *test-driven development* process, that is, test development that occurs at the same time as code development.

To facilitate the development of robust, error-free code, Apex supports the creation and execution of *unit tests*. Unit tests are class methods that verify whether a particular piece of code is working properly. Unit test methods take no arguments, commit no data to the database, send no emails, and are flagged with the testMethod keyword or the isTest annotation in the method definition. Also, test methods must be defined in test classes, that is, classes annotated with isTest.

In addition, before you deploy Apex or package it for the Force.com AppExchange, the following must be true.

- At least 75% of your Apex code must be covered by unit tests, and all of those tests must complete successfully.

  Note the following.

  ◊ When deploying to a production organization, every unit test in your organization namespace is executed.
  ◊ Calls to System.debug are not counted as part of Apex code coverage.
  ◊ Test methods and test classes are not counted as part of Apex code coverage.

◊   While only 75% of your Apex code must be covered by tests, your focus shouldn't be on the percentage of code that is covered. Instead, you should make sure that every use case of your application is covered, including positive and negative cases, as well as bulk and single records. This should lead to 75% or more of your code being covered by unit tests.

- Every trigger must have some test coverage.
- All classes and triggers must compile successfully.

For more information on writing tests, see Testing Apex.

Understanding Execution Governors and Limits

Because Apex runs in a multitenant environment, the Apex runtime engine strictly enforces a number of limits to ensure that runaway Apex doesn't monopolize shared resources. If some Apex code ever exceeds a limit, the associated governor issues a runtime exception that cannot be handled.

The Apex limits, or *governors*, track and enforce the statistics outlined in the following tables and sections.

- Per-Transaction Apex Limits
- Per-Transaction Certified Managed Package Limits
- Force.com Platform Apex Limits
- Static Apex Limits
- Size-Specific Apex Limits
- Miscellaneous Apex Limits

In addition to the core Apex governor limits, email limits are also included later in this topic for your convenience.

Per-Transaction Apex Limits

These limits count for each Apex transaction. For Batch Apex, these limits are reset for each execution of a batch of records in the `execute` method.

This table lists limits for synchronous Apex and asynchronous Apex (Batch Apex and future methods) when they're different. Otherwise, this table lists only one limit that applies to both synchronous and asynchronous Apex.

Description	Synchronous Limit	Asynchronous Limit
Total number of SOQL queries issued[1]	100	200
Total number of records retrieved by SOQL queries	50,000	
Total number of records retrieved by `Database.getQueryLocator`	10,000	
Total number of SOSL queries issued	20	
Total number of records retrieved by a single SOSL query	2,000	
Total number of DML statements issued[2]	150	
Total number of records processed as a result of DML statements, `Approval.process`, or `database.emptyRecycleBin`	10,000	
Total stack depth for any Apex invocation that recursively fires triggers due to `insert`, `update`, or `delete` statements[3]	16	
Total number of callouts (HTTP requests or Web services calls) in a transaction	10	
Maximum timeout for all callouts (HTTP requests or Web services calls) in a transaction	120 seconds	
Total number of methods with the `future` annotation allowed per Apex invocation	10	
Total number of `sendEmail` methods allowed	10	
Total number of describes allowed[4]	100	
Total heap size[5]	6 MB	12 MB
Maximum CPU time on the Salesforce servers[6]	10,000 milliseconds	60,000 milliseconds
Maximum execution time for each Apex transaction	10 minutes	
Maximum number of unique namespaces referenced[7]	10	

[1] In a SOQL query with parent-child relationship sub-queries, each parent-child relationship counts as an additional query. These types of queries have a limit of three times the number for top-level queries. The row counts from these relationship queries contribute to the row counts of the overall code execution. In addition to static SOQL statements, calls to the following methods count against the number of SOQL statements issued in a request.

- `Database.countQuery`

- `Database.getQueryLocator`
- `Database.query`

[2] Calls to the following methods count against the number of DML queries issued in a request.

- `Approval.process`
- `Database.convertLead`
- `Database.emptyRecycleBin`
- `Database.rollback`
- `Database.setSavePoint`
- `delete` and `Database.delete`
- `insert` and `Database.insert`
- `merge` and `Database.merge`
- `undelete` and `Database.undelete`
- `update` and `Database.update`
- `upsert` and `Database.upsert`
- `System.runAs`

[3] Recursive Apex that does not fire any triggers with `insert`, `update`, or `delete` statements exists in a single invocation, with a single stack. Conversely, recursive Apex that fires a trigger spawns the trigger in a new Apex invocation, separate from the invocation of the code that caused it to fire. Because spawning a new invocation of Apex is a more expensive operation than a recursive call in a single invocation, there are tighter restrictions on the stack depth of these types of recursive calls.

[4] Describes include the following methods and objects.

- ChildRelationship objects
- RecordTypeInfo objects
- PicklistEntry objects
- `fields` calls
- `fieldsets` calls

[5] Email services heap size is 36 MB.

[6] CPU time is calculated for all executions on the Salesforce application servers occurring in one Apex transaction—for the executing Apex code, and any processes that are called from this code, such as package code and workflows. CPU time is private for a transaction and is isolated from other transactions. Operations that don't consume application server CPU time aren't counted toward CPU time. For example, the portion of execution time spent in the database for DML, SOQL, and SOSL isn't counted, nor is waiting time for Apex callouts.

[7] In a single transaction, you can only reference 10 unique namespaces. For example, suppose you have an object that executes a class in a managed package when the object is updated. Then that class updates a second object, which in turn executes a different class in a different

package. Even though the second package wasn't accessed directly by the first, because it occurs in the same transaction, it's included in the number of namespaces being accessed in a single transaction.

 Note:

- Limits apply individually to each `testMethod`.
- Use the Limits methods to determine the code execution limits for your code while it is running. For example, you can use the `getDMLStatements` method to determine the number of DML statements that have already been called by your program, or the `getLimitDMLStatements` method to determine the total number of DML statements available to your code.

Per-Transaction Certified Managed Package Limits

Certified managed packages, that is, managed packages that have passed the security review for AppExchange, get their own set of limits for per-transaction limits with the exception of some limits. Certified managed packages are developed by salesforce.com ISV Partners, are installed in your organization from Force.com AppExchange, and have unique namespaces.

Here is an example that illustrates the separate certified managed package limits for DML statements. If you install a certified managed package, all the Apex code in that package gets its own 150 DML statements, in addition to the 150 DML statements your organization's native code can execute. This means more than 150 DML statements might execute during a single transaction if code from the managed package and your native organization both execute. Similarly, the certified managed package gets its own 100 SOQL queries limit for synchronous Apex, in addition to the organization's native code limit of 100 SOQL queries, and so on.

All per-transaction limits count separately for certified managed packages with the exception of:

- The total heap size
- The maximum CPU time
- The maximum transaction execution time
- The maximum number of unique namespaces

These limits count for the entire transaction, regardless of how many certified managed packages are running in the same transaction.

Also, if you install a package from AppExchange that isn't created by a salesforce.com ISV Partner and isn't certified, the code from that package doesn't have its own separate governor limit count. Any resources it uses counts against the total for your organization. Cumulative resource messages and warning emails are also generated based on managed package namespaces as well.

For more information on salesforce.com ISV Partner packages, see salesforce.com Partner Programs.

Force.com Platform Apex Limits

The limits in this table aren't specific to an Apex transaction and are enforced by the Force.com platform.

Description	Limit
The maximum number of asynchronous Apex method executions (Batch Apex, future methods, and scheduled Apex) per a 24-hour period[1]	250,000 or the number of user licenses in your organization multiplied by 200, whichever is greater
Number of synchronous concurrent requests for long-running requests that last longer than 5 seconds for each organization. [2]	10
Maximum simultaneous requests to URLs with the same host for a callout request[3]	20
Maximum number of Apex classes scheduled concurrently	100
Maximum number of Batch Apex jobs running concurrently	5
Maximum number of Batch Apex job `start` method concurrent executions[4]	1
Total number of test classes that can be queued per a 24-hour period[5]	The greater of 500 or 10 multiplied by the number of test classes in the organization
Maximum number of query cursors open concurrently per user[6]	50
Maximum number of query cursors open concurrently per user for the Batch Apex `start` method	15
Maximum number of query cursors open concurrently per user for the Batch Apex `execute` and `finish` methods	5

[1] For Batch Apex, method executions include executions of the `start`, `execute`, and `finish` methods. This is an organization-wide limit and is shared with all asynchronous Apex: Batch Apex, scheduled Apex, and future methods. The licenses that count toward this limit are full Salesforce user licenses or Force.com App Subscription user licenses. Chatter Free, Chatter customer users, Customer Portal User, and partner portal User licenses aren't included.

[2] If additional requests are made while the 10 long-running requests are still running, they're denied.

[3] The host is defined by the unique subdomain for the URL, for example, `www.mysite.com` and `extra.mysite.com` are two different hosts. This limit is calculated across all organizations that access the same host. If this limit is exceeded, a `CalloutException` will be thrown.

[4] Batch jobs that haven't started yet remain in the queue until they're started. Note that this limit doesn't cause any batch job to fail and `execute` methods of batch Apex jobs still run in parallel if more than one job is running.

[5] This limit applies to tests running asynchronously. This includes tests started through the Salesforce user interface including the Developer Console or by inserting `ApexTestQueueItem` objects using SOAP API.

[6] For example, if 50 cursors are open and a client application still logged in as the same user attempts to open a new one, the oldest of the 50 cursors is released. Cursor limits for different Force.com features are tracked separately. For example, you can have 50 Apex query cursors, 15 cursors for the Batch Apex `start` method, 5 cursors for the Batch Apex `execute` and `finish` methods each, and 5 Visualforce cursors open at the same time.

Static Apex Limits

Description	Limit
Default timeout of callouts (HTTP requests or Web services calls) in a transaction	10 seconds
Maximum size of callout request or response (HTTP request or Web services call)[1]	3 MB
Maximum SOQL query run time before the transaction can be canceled by Salesforce	120 seconds
Maximum number of class and trigger code units in a deployment of Apex	5,000
For loop list batch size	200
Maximum number of records returned for a Batch Apex query in `Database.QueryLocator`	50 million

[1] The HTTP request and response sizes count towards the total heap size.

Size-Specific Apex Limits

Description	Limit
Maximum number of characters for a class	1 million
Maximum number of characters for a trigger	1 million
Maximum amount of code used by all Apex code in an organization[1]	3 MB
Method size limit [2]	65,535 bytecode instructions in compiled form

[1] This limit does not apply to certified managed packages installed from AppExchange (that is, an app that has been marked AppExchange Certified). The code in those types of packages belong to a namespace unique from the code in your organization. For more information on AppExchange Certified packages, see the Force.com AppExchange online help. This limit also does not apply to any code included in a class defined with the @isTest annotation.

[2] Large methods that exceed the allowed limit cause an exception to be thrown during the execution of your code.

Miscellaneous Apex Limits

SOQL Query Performance

For best performance, SOQL queries must be selective, particularly for queries inside of triggers. To avoid long execution times, non-selective SOQL queries may be terminated by the system. Developers will receive an error message when a non-selective query in a trigger executes against an object that contains more than 100,000 records. To avoid this error, ensure that the query is selective. See More Efficient SOQL Queries.

Event Reports

The maximum number of records that an event report returns for a user who is not a system administrator is 20,000; for system administrators, 100,000.

Data.com Clean

If you use the Data.com Clean product and its automated jobs, and you have set up Apex triggers with SOQL queries to run when account, contact, or lead records, the queries may interfere with Clean jobs for those objects. Your Apex triggers (combined) should not exceed 200 SOQL queries per batch. If they do, your Clean job for that object will fail. In addition, if your triggers call `future` methods, they will be subject to a limit of 10 `future` calls per batch.

Email Limits

Inbound Email Limits

Email Services: Maximum Number of Email Messages Processed (Includes limit for On-Demand Email-to-Case)	Number of user licenses multiplied by 1,000, up to a daily maximum of 1,000,000
Email Services: Maximum Size of Email Message (Body and Attachments)	10 MB[1]
On-Demand Email-to-Case: Maximum Email Attachment Size	10 MB
On-Demand Email-to-Case: Maximum Number of Email Messages Processed (Counts toward limit for Email Services)	Number of user licenses multiplied by 1,000, up to a daily maximum of 1,000,000

[1] The maximum size of email messages for Email Services varies depending on language and character set.

When defining email services, note the following:

- An email service only processes messages it receives at one of its addresses.
- Salesforce limits the total number of messages that all email services combined, including On-Demand Email-to-Case, can process daily. Messages that exceed this limit are bounced, discarded, or queued for processing the next day, depending on how you configure the failure response settings for each email service. Salesforce calculates the limit by multiplying the number of user licenses by 1,000, up to a daily maximum of 1,000,000. For example, if you have 10 licenses, your organization can process up to 10,000 email messages a day.
- Email service addresses that you create in your sandbox cannot be copied to your production organization.
- For each email service, you can tell Salesforce to send error email messages to a specified address instead of the sender's email address.
- Email services reject email messages and notify the sender if the email (combined body text, body HTML, and attachments) exceeds approximately 10 MB (varies depending on language and character set).

Outbound Email: Limits for Single and Mass Email Sent Using Apex

Using the API or Apex, you can send single emails to a maximum of 1,000 external email addresses per day based on Greenwich Mean Time (GMT). Single emails sent using the Salesforce application don't count toward this limit. There's no limit on sending individual emails to contacts, leads, person accounts, and users in your organization directly from account, contact, lead, opportunity, case, campaign, or custom object pages.

When sending single emails, keep in mind:

- You can send 100 emails per `SingleEmailMessage`.
- If you use `SingleEmailMessage` to email your organization's internal users, specifying the user's ID in `setTargetObjectId` means the email doesn't count toward the daily limit. However, specifying internal users' email addresseses in `setToAddresses` means the email does count toward the limit.

You can send mass email to a maximum of 1,000 external email addresses per day per organization based on Greenwich Mean Time (GMT). The maximum number of external addresses you can include in each mass email depends on your edition:

Edition	External Address Limit per Mass Email
Personal, Contact Manager, and Group Editions	Mass email not available
Professional Edition	250
Enterprise Edition	500
Unlimited and Performance Edition	1,000

Note: Note the following about email limits:

- The single and mass email limits don't take unique addresses into account. For example, if you have `johndoe@example.com` in your email 10 times, that counts as 10 against the limit.
- You can send an unlimited amount of email to your organization's internal users, which includes portal users.
- In Developer Edition organizations and organizations evaluating Salesforce during a trial period, your organization can send mass email to no more than 10 external email addresses per day. This lower limit does not apply if your organization was created before the Winter '12 release and already had mass email enabled with a higher limit. Additionally, your organization can send single emails to a maximum of 15 email addresses per day.

Resources

Search on the Salesforce Developer's Network at `http://developer.salesforce.com/docs` for the following resources on Apex.

- Apex Code Developer's Guide
- Apex Cheat Sheet
- Apex Workbook
- Apex development forums

## Chapter 14

Visualforce

Visualforce is a framework that allows developers to build sophisticated, custom user interfaces that can be hosted on Salesforce, using a tag-based markup language, similar to HTML.

When to Use Visualforce

Visualforce consists of a tag-based markup language that gives developers a more powerful way of building applications and customizing the Salesforce user interface. With Visualforce you can:

- Build wizards and other multistep processes.
- Create your own custom flow control through an application.
- Define navigation patterns and data-specific rules for optimal, efficient application interaction.

In the Visualforce markup language, each Visualforce tag corresponds to a coarse or fine-grained user interface component, such as a section of a page, related list, or field. The behavior of Visualforce components can either be controlled by the same logic that is used in standard Salesforce pages, or developers can associate their own logic with a controller class written in Apex.

Supported Editions and Platforms

Visualforce is available in Contact Manager, Group, Professional, Enterprise, Unlimited, Performance, and Developer Editions.

Visualforce development requires various permissions, depending on the specific activity.

User Permissions Needed	
To enable Visualforce development mode:	"Customize Application"
To create, edit, or delete Visualforce pages:	"Customize Application"

User Permissions Needed	
To create and edit custom Visualforce components:	"Customize Application"
To edit custom Visualforce controllers or Apex	"Author Apex"
To set Visualforce page security:	"Manage Users" AND "Customize Application"
To set version settings for Visualforce pages:	"Customize Application"
To create, edit, or delete static resources:	"Customize Application"
To create Visualforce Tabs:	"Customize Application"

Quick Start

To showcase the essential elements of Visualforce, this chapter includes a set of examples that demonstrate features of the language. While the examples do not go into every detail, rule, or exception for every tag or controller, new Visualforce developers can use this tutorial to understand how Visualforce works.

Creating Your First Page

With development mode enabled, you can create your first Visualforce page by entering a URL for the page in your browser's address bar as follows:

```
https://Salesforce_instance/apex/myNewPageName
```

For example, if you want to create a page called "HelloWorld" and your salesforce.com organization uses na3.salesforce.com, enter http://na3.salesforce.com/apex/HelloWorld.

Because the page does not yet exist, you are directed to an intermediary page from which you can create your new page. Click **Create Page <myNewPageName>** to create it automatically.

Note: If you do not have Visualforce development mode enabled, you can also create a new page from Setup by clicking **Develop** > **Pages**, and then clicking **New**.

Visualforce pages can always be edited from this part of setup, but to see the results of your edits you have to navigate to the URL of your page. For that reason, most developers prefer to work with development mode enabled so they can view and edit pages in a single window.

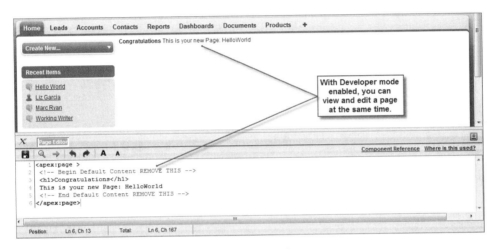

Figure 1: A New Visualforce Page

You now have a Visualforce page that includes default text. To edit your new page, click the **Page Editor** bar that appears at the bottom of the browser. It expands to show you the following Visualforce markup:

```
<apex:page>
    <!-- Begin Default Content REMOVE THIS -->
    <h1>Congratulations</h1>
    This is your new Apex Page: HelloWorld
    <!-- End Default Content REMOVE THIS -->
</apex:page>
```

This default markup includes the only required tag for any page— the `<apex:page>` tag that begins and ends any page markup. Embedded within the start and close `<apex:page>` tags is plain text, some of which is formatted with a standard HTML tag, `<h1>`.

As long as you keep the required `<apex:page>` tag you can add as much plain text or valid HTML to this page as you want. For example, after entering the following code and clicking **Save** in the Page Editor, the page displays the text "Hello World!" in bold:

```
<apex:page>
    <b>Hello World!</b>
</apex:page>
```

 Tip: Pay attention to warnings—the Visualforce editor displays a warning if you save a page with HTML that does not include a matching end tag for every opened tag. Although the page saves, this malformed HTML might cause problems in your rendered page.

Displaying Field Values with Visualforce

Visualforce pages use the same expression language as formulas—that is, anything inside `{ ! }` is evaluated as an expression that can access values from records that are currently in context. For example, you can display the current user's first name by adding the `{!$User.FirstName}` expression to a page:

```
<apex:page>
    Hello {!$User.FirstName}!
</apex:page>
```

`$User` is a global variable that always represents the current user record. All global variables are referenced with a $ symbol. For a list of global variables that you can use in Visualforce, see Global Variables.

To access fields from a record that is not globally available, like a specific account, contact, or custom object record, you need to associate your page with a *controller*. Controllers provide pages with the data and business logic that make your application run, including the logic that specifies how to access a particular object's records. While you can define a custom controller for any page with Apex, Salesforce includes standard controllers for every standard and custom object.

For example, to use the standard controller for accounts, add the `standardController` attribute to the `<apex:page>` tag, and assign it the name of the account object:

```
<apex:page standardController="Account">
    Hello {!$User.FirstName}!
</apex:page>
```

After you save your page, the Accounts tab is highlighted for the page, and the look-and-feel for the components on the page match the Accounts tab. Additionally, you can now access fields on the account record currently in context by using {!account.**<fieldName>**} expression syntax.

For example, to display an account's name on a page, use {!account.name} in the page markup:

```
<apex:page standardController="Account">
    Hello {!$User.FirstName}!
    <p>You are viewing the {!account.name} account.</p>
</apex:page>
```

The {!account.name} expression makes a call to the getAccount() method in the standard Account controller to return the record ID of the account currently in context. It then uses dot notation to access the name field for that record.

 Note: You cannot access parent objects using this expression language. In other words, {!account.parent.name} will return an error.

 Note: When you save a page, the value attribute of all input components—<apex:inputField>, <apex:inputText>, and so on—is validated to ensure it's a single expression, with no literal text or white space, and is a valid reference to a single controller method or object property. An error will prevent saving the page.

To bring an account record into the current context, you must add a query parameter to the page URL that specifies the ID of the record. To do this:

1. Find the ID of an account by any means you wish. One easy way is to view the detail page of an account record and copy the character code at the end of the URL. For example, if you navigate to an account detail page with the following URL:

    https://na3.salesforce.com/001D000000IRt53

    Then 001D000000IRt53 is the ID for the account.

2. Back on your page, add the account ID as a query string parameter to the URL in your browser's address bar. For example, if your page is located at:

    https://na3.salesforce.com/apex/HelloWorld2

    Add ?id=001D000000IRt53 to the end of the URL:

    https://**Salesforce_instance**/apex/HelloWorld2?id=001D000000IRt53

Note: If you use the id parameter in a URL, it must refer to the same entity referred to in the standard controller.

Once an account ID is specified in the URL, the page displays the appropriate account name, as shown in the following figure.

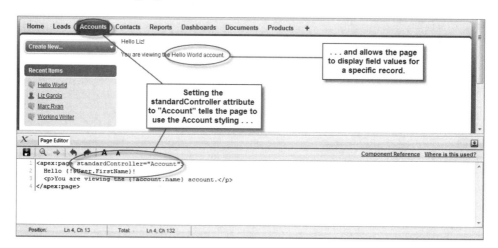

Figure 2: Displaying Account Data in a Visualforce Page

Using the Visualforce Component Library

Up to this point, the only Visualforce tag that has been used in the examples is the mandatory `<apex:page>` tag that must be placed at the start and end of all Visualforce markup. However, just as you can insert images or tables into an HTML document with the `<img>` or `<table>` tags, respectively, you can add user interface components to your Visualforce pages using tags that are defined in the Visualforce component library.

For example, to add a component that looks like a section on a detail page, use the `<apex:pageBlock>` component tag:

```
<apex:page standardController="Account">
    <apex:pageBlock title="Hello {!$User.FirstName}!">
            You are viewing the {!account.name} account.
    </apex:pageBlock>
</apex:page>
```

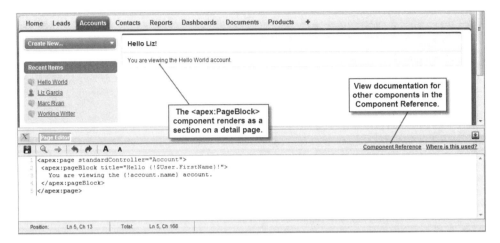

Figure 3: The `<apex:pageBlock>` Component

Tags also exist for other common Salesforce interface components, such as related lists, detail pages, and input fields. For example, to add the content of a detail page, use the `<apex:detail>` component tag:

```
<apex:page standardController="Account">
    <apex:pageBlock title="Hello {!$User.FirstName}!">
        You are viewing the {!account.name} account.
    </apex:pageBlock>
    <apex:detail/>
</apex:page>
```

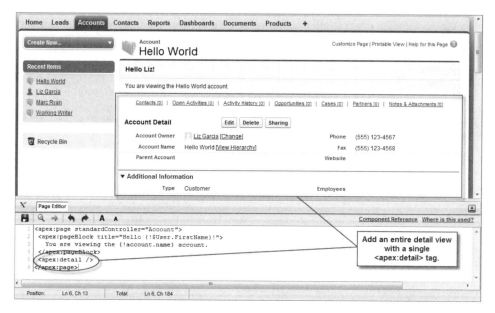

Figure 4: The `<apex:detail>` Component Without Attributes

Without any specified attributes on the tag, `<apex:detail>` displays the complete detail view for the context record. If you want to modify properties such as which record details are displayed, or whether related lists or the title appear, you can use attributes on the tag. For example, the following markup displays the details of the context account's owner, without related lists or a colored title bar:

```
<apex:page standardController="Account">
    <apex:pageBlock title="Hello {!$User.FirstName}!">
        You are viewing the {!account.name} account.
    </apex:pageBlock>
    <apex:detail subject="{!account.ownerId}" relatedList="false"
title="false"/>
</apex:page>
```

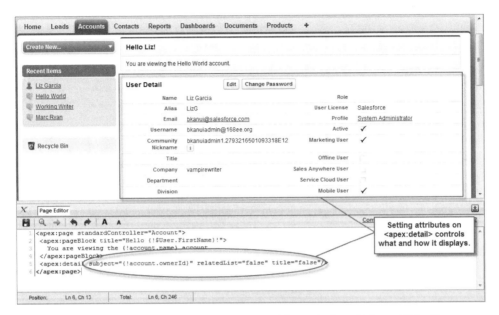

Figure 5: The `<apex:detail>` Component Without Related List or Title Elements

To browse the component library, click **Component Reference** in the Page Editor. From this page you can drill down into any component to see the attributes that are available for each, including any custom components that you define.

Using Input Components in a Page

So far the examples in this quick start tutorial show ways that you can display data in a Visualforce page. To capture input from a user, use the `<apex:form>` tag with one or more input components and a `<apex:commandLink>` or `<apex:commandButton>` tag to submit the form.

The input component tag that is most often used in a form is `<apex:inputField>`. This tag renders the appropriate input widget based on a standard or custom object field's type. For example, if you use an `<apex:inputField>` tag to display a date field, a calendar widget displays on the form. If you use an `<apex:inputField>` tag to display a picklist field, a drop-down list displays instead. The `<apex:inputField>` tag can be used to capture user input for any standard or custom object field, and respects any metadata that is set on the field definition, such as whether the field is required or unique, or whether the current user has permission to view or edit it.

For example, the following page allows users to edit and save the name of an account:

Note: Remember, for this page to display account data, the ID of a valid account record must be specified as a query parameter in the URL for the page. For example:

```
https://Salesforce_instance/apex/myPage?id=001x000xxx3Jsxb
```

Displaying Field Values with Visualforce on page 188 has more information about retrieving the ID of a record.

```
<apex:page standardController="Account">
    <apex:form>
        <apex:pageBlock title="Hello {!$User.FirstName}!">
            You are viewing the {!account.name} account. <p/>
            Change Account Name: <p/>
            <apex:inputField value="{!account.name}"/> <p/>
            <apex:commandButton action="{!save}" value="Save New
Account Name"/>
        </apex:pageBlock>
    </apex:form>
</apex:page>
```

Notice in the example that:

- The `<apex:inputField>` tag is bound to the account name field by setting the tag's value attribute. The expression contains the familiar `{!account.name}` dot-notation used to display the field's value elsewhere in the page.
- The `<apex:commandButton>` tag has an `action` attribute. The value for this attribute invokes the save action of the standard Account controller, which performs identically to the **Save** button on the standard Account edit page.

 Note: When you save a page, the `value` attribute of all input components—`<apex:inputField>`, `<apex:inputText>`, and so on—is validated to ensure it's a single expression, with no literal text or white space, and is a valid reference to a single controller method or object property. An error will prevent saving the page.

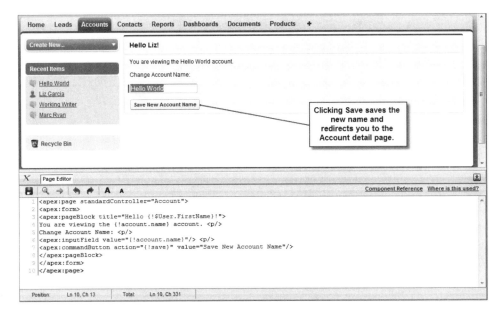

Figure 6: The <apex:form> Component with a Single Input Field

The only fields that the `<apex:inputField>` tag cannot display are those defined as member variables of a custom controller class written in Apex. To gather data for these variables, use the `<apex:inputCheckbox>`, `<apex:inputHidden>`, `<apex:inputSecret>`, `<apex:inputText>`, or `<apex:inputTextarea>` tags instead.

Adding and Customizing Input Field Labels

When used inside of a `<apex:pageBlockSection>` component, Visualforce input components and some output components automatically display a form label for the field. For components that map to standard or custom object fields, the displayed label is the object field label by default. To override the default value, and for components that aren't mapped directly to object fields, you can set the label using the `label` attribute of the component. For example:

```
<apex:page standardController="Contact">
    <apex:form>
        <apex:pageBlock title="Quick Edit: {!Contact.Name}">
            <apex:pageBlockSection title="Contact Details"
columns="1">
                <apex:inputField value="{!Contact.Phone}"/>
                <apex:outputField value="{!Contact.MobilePhone}"
                    label="Mobile #"/>
                <apex:inputText value="{!Contact.Email}"
                    label="{!Contact.FirstName + ''s Email'}"/>
            </apex:pageBlockSection>
            <apex:pageBlockButtons >
```

```
                    <apex:commandButton action="{!save}" value="Save"/>
                </apex:pageBlockButtons>
            </apex:pageBlock>
        </apex:form>
</apex:page>
```

Note: For this page to display contact data, the ID of a valid contact record must be specified as a query parameter in the URL for the page. For example,

https://***Salesforce_instance***/apex/myPage?id=003D000000Q513R

Displaying Field Values with Visualforce on page 188 has more information about retrieving the ID of a record.

The label attribute may be a string, or an expression that evaluates to a string. If you set label to an empty string, the form label for that field will be suppressed.

The label attribute can be set on the following Visualforce components:

- <apex:inputCheckbox>
- <apex:inputField>
- <apex:inputSecret>
- <apex:inputText>
- <apex:inputTextarea>
- <apex:outputField>
- <apex:outputText>
- <apex:selectCheckboxes>
- <apex:selectList>

• `<apex:selectRadio>`

Custom Labels and Error Messages

When set, the `label` attribute will be used for component-level error messages, for example, when a field is required or must be unique. Custom labels won't be used in custom error messages, and the default object field label will be used instead. If you set a `label` attribute to an empty string, the default object field label will be used in all error messages.

Adding Dependent Fields to a Page

Dependent fields provide a way to filter the field values displayed on a Visualforce page. Dependent fields consist of two parts: a controlling field that determines the filtering, and a dependent field that has its values filtered. Dependent fields can dynamically filter values in fields such as picklists, multi-select picklists, radio buttons, and checkboxes. Dependent picklists can only be displayed on Visualforce pages with Salesforce API version 19.0 or higher. For more information, see About Dependent Picklists in the Salesforce online help.

For this example, we'll be adding a dependent picklist, Subcategories, to a Visualforce page. First, create this custom picklist:

1. From Setup, click **Customize** > **Accounts** > **Fields**.
2. Click **New** in the Custom Fields & Relationships section of the page.
3. Choose **Picklist** and click **Next**.
4. Enter `Subcategories` for the **Field Label**.
5. Enter the following terms for the list of values:

   • Apple Farms
   • Cable
   • Corn Fields
   • Internet
   • Radio
   • Television
   • Winery

6. Click **Next** twice, then click **Save**.

To define the field dependencies for Subcategories:

1. From Setup, click **Customize** > **Accounts** > **Fields**.
2. Click **Field Dependencies**.
3. Click **New**.

4. Choose Industry as a controlling field, and Subcategories as a dependent field.

5. Click **Continue**.

6. Each value in the controlling field (from Industry) is listed in the top row and each value in the dependent field (from Subcategory) is displayed in the column below it. Set your field dependencies to match this image:

Industry:	Agriculture	Communications
Subcategories:	Apple Farms	Apple Farms
	Cable	Cable
	Corn Fields	Corn Fields
	Internet	Internet
	Radio	Radio
	Television	Television
	Winery	Winery

Figure 7: The Field Dependency Matrix for Subcategories

You can disregard any other Industry types that aren't shown above.

7. Click **Save**.

Now, create a Visualforce page called `dependentPicklists` that looks like this:

```
<apex:page standardController="Account">
    <apex:form >
        <apex:pageBlock mode="edit">
            <apex:pageBlockButtons >
                <apex:commandButton action="{!save}" value="Save"/>
            </apex:pageBlockButtons>
            <apex:pageBlockSection title="Dependent Picklists"
columns="2">
                <apex:inputField value="{!account.industry}"/>
                <apex:inputField value="{!account.subcategories__c}"/>
            </apex:pageBlockSection>
        </apex:pageBlock>
    </apex:form>
</apex:page>
```

When you select Agriculture from the Industry picklist, the Subcategories picklist contains Apple Farms, Corn Fields, and Winery. If you select Communication, your Subcategories picklist contains all the Communication types defined earlier.

Dependent Picklist Considerations

Consider the following when using dependent picklists in Visualforce pages:

• You can mix controlling and dependent fields across various field types, such as picklists, multi-picklists, radio buttons, and checkboxes.

• There's a limit of 10 dependent picklist pairs per page. This is totalled across all objects. Thus, you could have five dependent picklists on Account, and five on Contact, but no more. However, you can repeat the same pair of dependent picklists, such as in an iterative tag like `<apex:repeat>`, without counting more than once against your limit.

- If the user viewing the page has **read-only** access to the controlling field, a dependent picklist might not behave as expected. In this case, the dependent picklist shows all possible values for the picklist, instead of being filtered on the read-only value. This is a known limitation in Visualforce.
- Pages must include the controlling field for a dependent picklist. Failing to include the controlling field on the page causes a runtime error when the page displays.

- Don't mix inline edit-enabled fields with regular input fields from the same dependency group. For example, don't mix a standard input field for a controlling field with an inline edit-enabled dependent field:

```
<apex:page standardController="Account">
    <apex:form>
        <!-- Don't mix a standard input field... -->
        <apex:inputField value="{!account.Controlling__c}"/>
        <apex:outputField value="{!account.Dependent__c}">
            <!-- ...with an inline-edit enabled dependent field
-->
            <apex:inlineEditSupport event="ondblClick" />
        </apex:outputField>
    </apex:form>
</apex:page>
```

- If you combine inline edit-enabled dependent picklists with Ajax-style partial page refreshes, refresh all fields with dependent or controlling relationships to each other as one group. Refreshing fields individually isn't recommended and might result in inconsistent undo/redo behavior. Here's an example of the recommended way to partially refresh a form with inline edit-enabled dependent picklists:

```
<apex:form>
    <!-- other form elements ... -->

    <apex:outputPanel id="locationPicker">
        <apex:outputField value="{!Location.country}">
            <apex:inlineEditSupport event="ondblClick" />
        </apex:outputField>
        <apex:outputField value="{!Location.state}">
            <apex:inlineEditSupport event="ondblClick" />
        </apex:outputField>
        <apex:outputField value="{!Location.city}">
            <apex:inlineEditSupport event="ondblClick" />
        </apex:outputField>
    </apex:outputPanel>
    <!-- ... -->
    <apex:commandButton value="Refresh Picklists"
 reRender="locationPicker" />
</apex:form>
```

All of the inline edit-enabled picklists are wrapped in the <apex:outputPanel> component. The <apex:outputPanel> rerenders when the <apex:commandButton> action method fires.

Creating Visualforce Dashboard Components

Visualforce pages can be used as dashboard components. A *dashboard* shows data from source reports as visual components, which can be charts, gauges, tables, metrics, or Visualforce pages. The components provide a snapshot of key metrics and performance indicators for your organization. Each dashboard can have up to 20 components.

Visualforce pages that use the Standard Controller can't be used in dashboards. To be included in a dashboard, a Visualforce page must have either no controller, use a custom controller, or reference a page bound to the StandardSetController Class. If a Visualforce page does not meet these requirements, it does not appear as an option in the dashboard component `Visualforce Page` drop-down list.

Create a Visualforce page called `VFDashboard`. The following markup shows an example of a Visualforce page that uses a standard list controller and can be used within a dashboard. It displays a list of the cases associated with your organization:

```
<apex:page standardController="Case" recordSetvar="cases">
    <apex:pageBlock>
        <apex:form id="theForm">
            <apex:panelGrid columns="2">
                <apex:outputLabel value="View:"/>
                <apex:selectList value="{!filterId}" size="1">
                    <apex:actionSupport event="onchange"
rerender="list"/>
                    <apex:selectOptions value="{!listviewoptions}"/>

                </apex:selectList>
            </apex:panelGrid>
            <apex:pageBlockSection>
                <apex:dataList var="c" value="{!cases}" id="list">
                {!c.subject}
                </apex:dataList>
            </apex:pageBlockSection>
        </apex:form>
    </apex:pageBlock>
</apex:page>
```

To create a dashboard that uses this Visualforce page:

1. View the dashboard and click **Edit**.
2. Click **Add Component** from the top of any column.
3. Choose a **Visualforce Page** as the component type.
4. Optionally, enter a header to display at the top of the dashboard component.
5. Optionally, enter a footer to display at the bottom of the dashboard component.
6. From the `Visualforce Page` drop-down list, select `VFDash`.
7. Click **Save**.

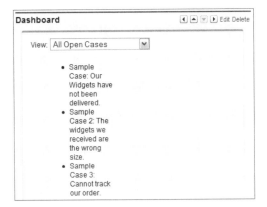

Figure 8: Sample Visualforce Page Running in a Dashboard

For a more complex example that uses a custom list controller, see Advanced Visualforce Dashboard Components.

Best Practices

Consider the best practices explained in this section.

Best Practices for Improving Visualforce Performance

Visualforce was designed to provide developers with the ability to match the functionality, behavior, and performance of standard Salesforce pages. If your users experience delays, unexpected behavior, or other issues specifically around Visualforce, there are several actions you can take to not only improve their experience, but to also make for improved coding.

First, determine whether Visualforce is the problem by ensuring that:

- The problems aren't confined to a single user's computer by testing expected Visualforce functionality on other machines as well as using different browsers.
- Slow load times aren't the result of a network issue by checking the load time of other Salesforce pages. If they're also slow, it could be the result of bandwidth or latency issues to Salesforce. To check on the status of the Salesforce servers, visit trust.salesforce.com. You should also check the status of your network connections and ensure they're functioning properly.
- You're following general Web design best practices, such as the minification of JavaScript and CSS, optimizing images for the Web, and avoiding iframes whenever possible.

- You've used the Developer Console to step through the request and determine which items in the request used the most system resources. See "Using the Developer Console" in the Salesforce online help.

The following is a list of commonly encountered Visualforce performance issues and their possible solutions:

View State Size

The view state size of your Visualforce pages must be under 135KB. By reducing your view state size, your pages can load quicker and stall less often.

You can monitor view state performance through the View State tab in the development mode footer and take the following actions:

- Use the `transient` keyword in your Apex controllers for variables that aren't essential for maintaining state and aren't necessary during page refreshes.
- If you notice that a large percentage of your view state comes from objects used in controllers or controller extensions, consider refining your SOQL calls to return only data that's relevant to the Visualforce page.
- If your view state is affected by a large component tree, try reducing the number of components your page depends on.

Load Times

Large page sizes directly affects load times. To improve Visualforce page load times:

- Cache any data that is frequently accessed, such as icon graphics.
- Avoid SOQL queries in your Apex controller getter methods.
- Reduce the number of records displayed on a page by:

    ◊ Limiting the data coming back from SOQL calls in your Apex controllers. For example, using AND statements in your WHERE clause, or removing null results
    ◊ Taking advantage of pagination with a list controller to present fewer records per page

- "Lazy load" Apex objects to reduce request times.
- Consider moving any JavaScript outside of the `<apex:includeScript>` tag and placing it into a `<script>` tag right before your closing `<apex:page>` tag. The `<apex:includeScript>` tag places JavaScript right before the closing `<head>` element; thus, Visualforce attempts to load the JavaScript before any other content on the page. However, you should only move JavaScript to the bottom of the page if you're certain it doesn't have any adverse effects to your page. For example, JavaScript code snippets requiring `document.write` or event handlers should remain in the `<head>` element.

In all cases, Visualforce pages must be under 15 MB.

Multiple Concurrent Requests

Concurrent requests are long-running tasks that could block other pending tasks. To reduce these delays:

- Action methods used by `<apex:actionPoller>` should be lightweight. It's a best practice to avoid performing DML, external service calls, and other resource-intensive operations in action methods called by an `<apex:actionPoller>`. Carefully consider the effect of your action method being called repeatedly by an `<apex:actionPoller>` at the interval you specify, especially if it's used on a page that will be widely distributed, or open continuously.
- Increase the time interval for calling Apex from your Visualforce page. For example, when using the `<apex:actionPoller>` component, you could adjust the `interval` attribute to 30 seconds instead of 15.
- Move non-essential logic to an asynchronous code block using Ajax.

Queries and Security

By using the `with sharing` keyword when creating your Apex controllers, you have the possibility of improving your SOQL queries by only viewing a data set for a single user.

Preventing Field Values from Dropping Off the Page

If your page contains many fields, including large text area fields, and has master-detail relationships with other entities, it may not display all data due to limits on the size of data returned to Visualforce pages and batch limits. The page displays this warning: "You requested too many fields to display. Consider removing some to prevent field values from being dropped from the display."

To prevent field values from being dropped from the page, remove some fields to reduce the amount of data returned. Alternatively, you can write your own controller extensions to query child records to be displayed in the related lists.

Best Practices for Accessing Component IDs

To refer to a Visualforce component in JavaScript or another Web-enabled language, you must specify a value for the `id` attribute for that component. A DOM ID is constructed from a combination of the `id` attribute of the component and the `id` attributes of all components that contain the element.

Use the `$Component` global variable to simplify referencing the DOM ID that is generated for a Visualforce component, and reduce some of the dependency on the overall page structure. To reference a specific Visualforce component's DOM ID, add a component path specifier to `$Component`, using dot notation to separate each level in the component hierarchy of the page. For example, use $Component.*itemId* to reference a component at the same level in the Visualforce component hierarchy, or use $Component.*grandparentId.parentId.itemId* to specify a more complete component path.

A $Component path specifier is matched against the component hierarchy:

- At the current level of the component hierarchy where $Component is used; and then
- At each successive higher level in the component hierarchy, until a match is found, or the top-level of the component hierarchy is reached.

There is no backtracking, so if the ID you're trying to match requires a traversal up and then back down, it won't match.

The following example illustrates several uses of $Component:

```
<apex:page >

    <style>
    .clicker { border: 1px solid #999; cursor: pointer;
        margin: .5em; padding: 1em; width: 10em; text-align: center;
}
    </style>

    <apex:form id="theForm">
        <apex:pageBlock id="thePageBlock" title="Targeting IDs with
$Component">
            <apex:pageBlockSection id="theSection">
                <apex:pageBlockSectionItem id="theSectionItem">
                    All the alerts refer to this component.

                    <p>The full DOM ID resembles something like
this:<br/>

j_id0:theForm:thePageBlock:theSection:theSectionItem</p>
                </apex:pageBlockSectionItem>

                <!-- Works because this outputPanel has a parent in
common
                    with "theSectionItem" component -->
                <apex:outputPanel layout="block" styleClass="clicker"

                    onclick="alert('{!$Component.theSectionItem}');">

                    First click here
                </apex:outputPanel>
            </apex:pageBlockSection>

        <apex:pageBlockButtons id="theButtons" location="bottom">

                <!-- Works because this outputPanel has a grandparent
("theSection")
                    in common with "theSectionItem" -->
```

```
                <apex:outputPanel layout="block" styleClass="clicker"

onclick="alert('{!$Component.theSection.theSectionItem}');">
                    Second click here
                </apex:outputPanel>

                <!-- Works because this outputPanel has a distant
ancestor ("theForm")
                    in common with "theSectionItem" -->
                <apex:outputPanel layout="block" styleClass="clicker"

                    onclick="alert('

{!$Component.theForm.thePageBlock.theSection.theSectionItem}');">
                    Third click here
                </apex:outputPanel>
            </apex:pageBlockButtons>

        </apex:pageBlock>

        <!-- Works because this outputPanel is a sibling to
"thePageBlock",
            and specifies the complete ID path from that sibling
-->
        <apex:outputPanel layout="block" styleClass="clicker"

onclick="alert('{!$Component.thePageBlock.theSection.theSectionItem}');">

            Fourth click here
        </apex:outputPanel>

        <hr/>

        <!-- Won't work because this outputPanel doesn't provide a
path
            that includes a sibling or common ancestor -->
        <apex:outputPanel layout="block" styleClass="clicker"

onclick="alert('{!$Component.theSection.theSectionItem}');">
            This won't work
        </apex:outputPanel>

        <!-- Won't work because this outputPanel doesn't provide a
path
            that includes a sibling or common ancestor -->
        <apex:outputPanel layout="block" styleClass="clicker"
            onclick="alert('{!$Component.theSectionItem}');">
            Won't work either
        </apex:outputPanel>

    </apex:form>
</apex:page>
```

Using Unique IDs

Within each hierarchy segment in a page, the component id must be unique. However, Salesforce recommends you use an id that is unique on the page for every component you need to reference, and any components above it in the component hierarchy that are needed to reference it.

For example, suppose you had two data tables in a single page. If both data tables are contained in the same page block, they must have unique id attributes. If each is contained in a separate page block, it's possible to give them the same component id. If you do so, however, the only way to reference a specific data table is to assign an id to every component and then reference the data table component using the complete hierarchy, rather than letting Visualforce do it automatically. If the page hierarchy ever changes, your program will no longer work.

Iterating with Component IDs

Some components, such as tables and lists, support iteration over a collection of records. After you assign an ID for these types of components, the system assigns a unique "compound ID" to each iteration of the component based on the initial ID.

For example, the following page contains a data table with an ID set to theTable.

```
<apex:page standardController="Account" recordSetVar="accounts"
id="thePage">
    <apex:dataTable value="{!accounts}" var="account" id="theTable">

        <apex:column id="firstColumn">
            <apex:outputText value="{!account.name}"/>
        </apex:column>
        <apex:column id="secondColumn">
            <apex:outputText value="{!account.owner.name}"/>
        </apex:column>
    </apex:dataTable>
</apex:page>
```

When the page is rendered, the `<apex:dataTable>` component results in the following HTML:

```
<table id="thePage:theTable" border="0" cellpadding="0"
cellspacing="0">
<colgroup span="2"/>
<tbody>
    <tr class="">
        <td id="thePage:theTable:0:firstColumn">
            <span id="thePage:theTable:0:accountName">Burlington
Textiles</span>
        </td>
        <td id="thePage:theTable:0:secondColumn">
            <span id="thePage:theTable:0:accountOwner">Vforce
Developer</span>
        </td>
    </tr>
```

```
    <tr class="">
        <td id="thePage:theTable:1:firstColumn">
            <span id="thePage:theTable:1:accountName">Dickenson</span>

        </td>
        <td id="thePage:theTable:1:secondColumn">
            <span id="thePage:theTable:1:accountOwner">Vforce
Developer</span>
        </td>
    </tr>
</table>
```

Each table cell has a unique ID based on the ID value of the containing components. The first table cell in the first row has the ID `thePage:theTable:0:firstColumn`, the second cell in the first row has the ID `thePage:theTable:0:secondColumn`, the first cell in the second row has the ID `thePage:theTable:1:firstColumn`, and so on.

To refer to all entries in a column, you have to iterate across the table rows, referring to each `<td>` element that has an ID following the format of the column.

The same type of ID generation is done for elements within the table cells. For example, the account name in the first row is generated as a `span` with the ID `thePage:theTable:0:accountName`. Notice that ID does not include the value of the ID for the column it's in.

Best Practices for Static Resources

Displaying the Content of a Static Resource with the `action` Attribute on `<apex:page>`

You can use the `action` attribute on a `<apex:page>` component to redirect from a Visualforce page to a static resource. This functionality allows you to add rich, custom help to your Visualforce pages. For example, to redirect a user to a PDF:

1. Upload the PDF as a static resource named `customhelp`.
2. Create the following page:

```
<apex:page sidebar="false" showHeader="false"
standardStylesheets="false"
        action="{!URLFOR($Resource.customhelp)}">
</apex:page>
```

Notice that the static resource reference is wrapped in a URLFOR function. Without that, the page does not redirect properly.

This redirect is not limited to PDF files. You can also redirect a page to the content of any static resource. For example, you can create a static resource that includes an entire help system composed of many HTML files mixed with JavaScript, images, and other multimedia files. As long as there is a single entry point, the redirect works. For example:

1. Create a zip file that includes your help content.
2. Upload the zip file as a static resource named `customhelpsystem`.
3. Create the following page:

```
<apex:page sidebar="false" showHeader="false"
standardStylesheets="false"
        action="{!URLFOR($Resource.customhelpsystem,
'index.htm')}">
</apex:page>
```

When a user visits the page, the `index.htm` file in the static resource displays.

Best Practices for Controllers and Controller Extensions

Enforcing Sharing Rules in Controllers

Like other Apex classes, all controllers and controller extensions run in system mode.

Typically, you want a controller or controller extension to respect a user's organization-wide defaults, role hierarchy, and sharing rules. You can do that by using the `with sharing` keywords in the class definition. For information, see "Using the `with sharing` or `without sharing` Keywords" in the *Force.com Apex Code Developer's Guide*.

Note that if a controller extension extends a standard controller, the logic from the standard controller does not execute in system mode. Instead, it executes in user mode, in which the permissions, field-level security, and sharing rules of the current user apply.

Controller Constructors Evaluate Before Setter Methods

Do not depend on a setter method being evaluated before a constructor. For example, in the following component, the component's controller depends on the setter for `selectedValue` being called before the constructor method:

```
<apex:component controller="CustCmpCtrl">
    <apex:attribute name="value" description=""
                type="String" required="true"
                assignTo="{!selectedValue}">
    </apex:attribute>
    //...
```

```
        //...
    </apex:component>

    public class CustCmpCtrl {

        // Constructor method
        public CustCmpCtrl() {
            if (selectedValue != null) {
                EditMode = true;
            }
        }

        private Boolean EditMode = false;

        // Setter method
        public String selectedValue { get;set; }
    }
```

Since the constructor is called before the setter, `selectedValue` will always be null when the constructor is called. Thus, `EditMode` will never be set to true.

Methods may evaluate more than once — do not use side-effects

Methods, including methods in a controller, action attributes, and expressions, may be called more than once. Do not depend on evaluation order or side-effects when creating custom methods in a controller or controller extension.

Resources

Search on the Salesforce Developer's Network at `http://developer.salesforce.com/docs` for the following resources on Visualforce.

- Visualforce Developer's Guide
- Visualforce Cheat Sheet
- Visualforce Workbook
- Visualforce development forums

## Chapter 15

Force.com Canvas

Force.com Canvas is a set of tools and JavaScript APIs that you can use to expose an application as a canvas app.

When to Use Force.com Canvas

Force.com Canvas enables you to easily integrate a third-party application in Salesforce. This means you can take your new or existing applications and make them available to your users as part of their Salesforce experience. Instead of redesigning and reintegrating your external applications, you can now use these tools to integrate your technology within Force.com Canvas. The third-party app that you want to expose as a canvas app can be written in any language. The only requirement is that the app has a secure URL (HTTPS).

From a high-level view, there are two common scenarios where Force.com Canvas is implemented.

- Application integration—You're a partner, systems integrator, or customer that builds cloud apps, and you'd like to integrate these applications with Salesforce.
- Application rationalization/enterprise desktop—You're a large organization that has many existing apps that your users access in addition to Salesforce. You'd like to integrate these apps into Salesforce so that users can accomplish all of their tasks in one place.

Supported Editions and Platforms

Force.com Canvas supports these Salesforce editions:

Edition	Create a canvas app	Publish a canvas app	Install a canvas app
Performance Edition	Yes	No	Yes
Unlimited Edition	Yes	No	Yes

Edition	Create a canvas app	Publish a canvas app	Install a canvas app
Enterprise Edition	Yes	No	Yes
Professional Edition	No	No	Yes*
Professional Edition with Force.com Canvas enabled	Yes	No	Yes
Developer Edition	Yes	Yes	Yes

*Professional Edition organizations must have Force.com Canvas enabled in order for a canvas app to appear in the specified location.

Force.com Canvas supports the following browsers:

- Mozilla® Firefox® (preferred)
- Google Chrome™
- Microsoft® Internet Explorer® version 8, 9, and 10 (be sure Compatibility Mode is disabled)
- Apple® Safari® (be sure to set the Block Cookies setting to Never)

If your app uses session cookies, you might need to set your P3P header to allow for third-party cookies or change the browser settings to allow all session cookies.

The following Salesforce user permissions are required to create canvas apps and view them in the Canvas App Previewer:

- Customize Application
- Modify All Data

Quick Start

This simple quick start shows you how to get started with Force.com Canvas by using the Heroku Quick Start. The Heroku Quick Start creates a "hello world" app on Heroku in either Java or Ruby, depending on the template you select. At the same time, it creates a corresponding canvas app in Salesforce.

The Heroku app is a "hello world" Web page that calls the Force.com Canvas SDK to display information about the current user and lets you post to the current user's Chatter feed.

Prerequisites

You need the appropriate access and tools to complete the quick start steps.

- Access to a Developer Edition organization.

  If you are not already a member of the Force.com developer community, go to `http://developer.force.com/join` and follow the instructions for signing up for a Developer Edition organization. Even if you already have Enterprise Edition, Unlimited Edition, or Performance Edition, use Developer Edition for developing, staging, and testing your solutions against sample data to protect your organization's live data. This is especially true for applications that insert, update, or delete data (as opposed to simply reading data).

  If you have an existing Developer Edition organization, and, from Setup, you don't see the menu item **Canvas App Previewer**, contact salesforce.com.

- "Customize Application" and "Modify All Data" user permissions. If you're an administrator, you most likely already have these permissions. Otherwise, you need to add them so that you can see the Canvas App Previewer and create canvas apps.
- A Heroku account. Go here to create a Heroku account: `https://api.heroku.com/signup`.

Create the App

In this step, you'll create both the Heroku "hello world" app and the associated canvas app in your Salesforce organization.

1. In Salesforce, from Setup, click **Canvas App Previewer**.
2. Click **Heroku Quick Start**.
3. In the `Template` field, select Java – Quick Start Template.
4. In the `Canvas App Name` field, enter a unique name of up to 30 characters.
5. In the `Heroku App Name` field, enter a unique name of up to 30 characters that begins with a letter and contains only lowercase letters, numbers, and dashes. The *newappName* must be unique across all Heroku apps. This name becomes part of the URL for your app, for example, *newappName*`.herokuapp.com`.
6. In the `Heroku Username` field, enter the username for the account used to log in to Heroku. This is typically an email address. The Heroku app is created under this user's credentials.

    Note: This field has a maximum length of 30 characters. If your Heroku username is longer than 30 characters, you'll need to use the API key associated with your account. You can find this value on the Heroku `My Account` page.

7. In the `Heroku Password` field, enter the password for the account used to log in to Heroku.

 Tip: Instead of using the username and password for the Heroku account, you can use the account's associated API key. You can find this value on the Heroku `Account` page.

8. Click **Create**. The app displays in the left navigation pane.

If you see an error like "Error [Read timed out] executing POST to Heroku clone REST service," this means the operation has timed out trying to contact Heroku. You can check the status of Heroku at `http://status.heroku.com`.

9. Click the link to your new app on the left.

The app appears and you'll see the message `Hello` *User.FullName*, as well as other information about the current user.

You just created a canvas app—congratulations! You'll only be able to see your canvas app in the Canvas App Previewer until you set the locations where it can appear by following the steps in Set the App Location. This defines where a user sees your app after it's installed in their organization.

Behind the scenes, the Heroku Quick Start sets the canvas app's `Permitted Users`, which includes admin-approved users and your profile. For example, if your user profile is System Administrator, that profile is added to the canvas app you just created, and any users with that profile can access the canvas app.

Set the App Location

In this step, you'll specify where your canvas app can display to a user in Salesforce.

 Note: Support for Force.com Canvas apps in the publisher, the Chatter feed, and Chatter Mobile is currently available through a pilot program and is available in all new Development Edition organizations. For information on enabling it for your organization, contact salesforce.com.

1. In Salesforce, from Setup, click **Create** > **Apps**.
2. In the Connected Apps related list, click the app you just created and then click **Edit**.

3. In the Canvas Apps Settings section, in the `Locations` field, select where the canvas app can appear to the user. For this walkthrough, select **Chatter Tab**.

- **Chatter Feed**—The canvas app appears in the Chatter feed. If this option is selected, you must create a CanvasPost feed item and ensure that the current user has access to the canvas app.
- **Chatter Tab**—The canvas app appears in the app navigation list on the Chatter tab. If this option is selected, the canvas app appears there automatically.
- **Open CTI**—The canvas app appears in the call control tool. If this option is selected, you must specify the canvas app in your call center's definition file for it to appear.
- **Publisher**—The canvas app appears in the publisher. If this option is selected, you must also create a canvas custom action and add it to the global layout or to an object layout.
- **Salesforce Console**—The canvas app appears in the footer or sidebars of a Salesforce console. If this option is selected, you must choose where the canvas app appears in a console by adding it as a custom console component.
- **Visualforce Page**—The canvas app can appear on a Visualforce page. If you add an `<apex:canvasApp>` component to expose a canvas app on a Visualforce page, be sure to select this location for the canvas app; otherwise, you'll receive an error.

4. Click **Save**.

Because you selected **Chatter Tab**, your canvas app now appears in the left navigation pane on the Chatter tab.

Best Practices

Consider the best practices explained in this section.

Referencing the Force.com Canvas SDK

The Force.com Canvas SDK is available on GitHub, and you have two options for referencing it from your canvas app.

- Host the SDK on your own Web server and access it there
- Access the SDK hosted on the Salesforce server

For example, here's what the include statement looks like if you host the SDK on your own Web server:

```
<script type="text/javascript" src="/sdk/js/canvas-all.js"></script>
```

Here's what the include statement looks like if you reference the hosted SDK:

```
<script type="text/javascript"
src="https://<instance>.salesforce.com/canvas/sdk/js/29.0/canvas-all.js"></script>
```

The ability to reference the SDK on the Salesforce server is useful when you want to include one of the SDK files in a Web app or from a Visualforce page.

User Interface Considerations

Here are some things to be aware of when designing and implementing the user interface for your canvas app.

Canvas size

The frame size for canvas apps varies depending on the location where the app appears. When using the SDK, these values are returned in the Dimensions Canvas object.

Logo image

The logo image associated with a canvas app is displayed when someone installs your canvas app or during OAuth authentication when the user is prompted to allow the app to run. We recommend that you use an image of size 256 pixels (high) by 256 pixels (wide).

Icon image

The icon image associated with a canvas app is displayed in these locations:
- To the left of the link to your canvas app on the Chatter tab, in the Chatter apps list.
- To the left of the link to your canvas app in the Canvas App Previewer.

Thumbnail image

The thumbnail image associated with a canvas app feed item is displayed when someone accesses your canvas app in the feed. If specified, this image appears next to the feed item title and description.

We recommend that you use an image of size 120 pixels (high) by 120 pixels (wide) or smaller.

Visualforce Considerations with Force.com Canvas

Keep the following considerations in mind when using the <apex:canvasApp> component:

- The <apex:canvasApp> component is available only in organizations that have Force.com Canvas enabled and in Visualforce pages at version 27.0 or higher.
- If you include a canvas app on an object detail layout, you must provide the height of the canvas app in the page layout as well as in the <apex:canvasApp> component.

- Location—If the canvas app is in a Visualforce page, then the `Environment.displayLocation` field contains the value `Visualforce`.

Force.com Canvas Limits

Because Force.com Canvas runs in a multitenant environment, limits are enforced to ensure protection of shared resources.

Description	Limit
Number of canvas apps per user that can be displayed on the Chatter tab. Only the first 50 canvas apps are displayed (sorted alphabetically).	50
Number of Force.com Canvas calls per day per user (24–hour period)	5,000 This includes SDK calls to get context and signed request calls. Note that when you call a SignedRequest method, there are actually two calls that are made—one call for the method and one call for internal logging.
Heroku Quick Start calls per day per user	100 Heroku accounts have their own limits on the number of calls you can make.

Cross-Domain XHR

Canvas apps are loaded on a Salesforce page in an iFrame. Therefore, the canvas app (in its own domain) can't make XHR (XML HTTP request) calls back to the *.salesforce.com domain. You can develop and deploy your own proxies as part of the SDK, however, Force.com Canvas provides a client-side proxy written in JavaScript. This proxy enables client-side XHR calls back to Salesforce.

If you use this proxy from the client to make an XHR request, the API forwards the request to the outer iFrame and the request is submitted on your behalf. When the request is complete, the SDK calls the client's callback function with the results.

 Note: The SDK supports cross-domain XHR calls, however, it shouldn't be used to make same-domain calls.

Resources

Search on the Salesforce Developer's Network at `http://developer.salesforce.com/docs` for the following resources on Force.com Canvas.

- Force.com Canvas Developer's Guide
- APIs and Integration forum (see posts tagged with "Canvas")

Chapter 16

Tooling API

Use Tooling API to build custom development tools for Salesforce applications.

When to Use Tooling API

Tooling API provides SOAP and REST interfaces that allow you to build custom development tools for Force.com applications. Tooling API exposes objects used in developer tooling that you can access through REST or SOAP, and works just like the Salesforce REST API and SOAP API.

For example, using Tooling API you can:

- Add features and functionality to your existing Force.com tools.
- Build dynamic modules for Force.com development into your enterprise integration tools.
- Build specialized development tools for a specific application or service.

To accomplish these goals, Tooling API gives you calls to do the following:

- Manage working copies of Apex classes and triggers and Visualforce pages and components.
- Manage working copies of static resource files.
- Check for updates and errors in working copies of Apex classes and triggers and Visualforce pages and components, and commit changes to your organization.
- Set heap dump markers.
- Overlay Apex code or SOQL statements on an Apex execution.
- Execute anonymous Apex.
- Set checkpoints to generate log files for yourself or for other users.
- Access debug log and heap dump files.
- Manage custom fields on custom objects.
- Access code coverage results.

The following Java code snippet uses the SOAP-based interface of Tooling API to programmatically create an Apex class with a single method called SayHello.

```
String classBody = "public class Messages {\n"
    + "public string SayHello() {\n"
    + " return 'Hello';\n" + "}\n"
    + "}";

// create a new ApexClass object and set the body
ApexClass apexClass = new ApexClass();
apexClass.Body = classBody;
ApexClass[] classes = { apexClass };

// call create() to add the class
SaveResult[] saveResults = sforce.create(classes);
for (int i = 0; i < saveResults.Length; i++)
    {
    if (saveResults[i].success)
        {
        Console.WriteLine("Successfully created Class: " +
           saveResults[i].id);
        }
    else
        {
        Console.WriteLine("Error: could not create Class ");
        Console.WriteLine("    The error reported was: " +
        saveResults[i].errors[0].message + "\n");
        }
    }
```

Supported Editions and Platforms

To use Tooling API, your organization must use Enterprise Edition, Performance Edition, Unlimited Edition, or Developer Edition. If you are an existing Salesforce customer and want to upgrade to Enterprise, Unlimited, or Performance Edition, contact your account representative.

Resources

Search on the Salesforce Developer's Network at http://developer.salesforce.com/docs for the following resources on Tooling API.

- Tooling API Developer's Guide
- APIs and Integration forums

Chapter 17

Analytics API

The REST-based Analytics API provides programmatic access to your report data in Salesforce.

When to Use Analytics API

Analytics API lets you integrate report data as defined in the report builder into any web or mobile application, inside or outside the Salesforce platform. For example, you might use the API to trigger a Chatter post with a snapshot of top-performing reps each quarter.

Using the Analytics API, you can:

- Integrate report data into custom objects.
- Define rich visualizations on top of the API to animate the data.
- Build custom dashboards.
- Automate reporting tasks.

At a high level, the API resources let you query and filter report data. You can:

- Run tabular, summary, or matrix reports synchronously or asynchronously.
- Filter for specific data on the fly.
- Query report metadata.

As an example, you could use the Analytics API execute async REST resource to asynchronously run a report. You'd use a REST resource URL of the form:

```
/services/data/<latest API version>/analytics/reports/<report
ID>/instances
```

In your POST request, you'd provide JSON data indicating the desired groupings and filters. After a successful request, Salesforce will queue the report to be run and return JSON response data containing information on where to get the report status and results, that might look something like this:

```
{
    "id": "0LGD000000000IjOAI",
    "requestDate": "2013-08-12T18:39:06Z",
    "status": "New",
    "ownerId": "005D0000001KvxRIAS",
    "url":
"/services/data/v29.0/analytics/reports/000D0000001ZbP7MAK/instances/0LGD000000000IjOAI",

    "hasDetailRows": false,
    "completionDate": null
}
```

Supported Editions and Platforms

To use Analytics API, your organization must use Enterprise Edition, Performance Edition, Unlimited Edition, or Developer Edition. If you are an existing Salesforce customer and want to upgrade to Enterprise, Unlimited, or Performance Edition, contact your account representative.

Best Practices

Consider the best practices explained in this section.

Use JSON for Request and Response Data

Analytics API supports request and response data in JSON, and not in XML. While using the Analytics API with a request body, use `Content-Type: application/json` in your request headers.

Analytics API Limits

Analytics API has the following limitations:

- Cross filters, standard report filters, and filtering by row limit are unavailable when filtering data.
- Historical trend reports in tabular format are unavailable.
- The API can process only reports that contain up to 100 fields selected as columns.
- The List resource returns up to 200 reports that the API user recently viewed.
- Your organization can request as many as 500 synchronous report runs per hour through the Execute Sync resource.
- The API supports as many as 20 synchronous report run requests at a time.
- The Instances List resource returns up to 2000 instances of a report that was run asynchronously.

- The API supports as many as 200 requests at a time to get results of asynchronous report runs.
- Your organization can request as many as 1200 asynchronous requests per hour through the Execute Async resource.
- Asynchronous report run results are available within a 24-hour rolling period.

Resources

Search on the Salesforce Developer's Network at `http://developer.salesforce.com/docs` for the following resources on Analytics API.

- Analytics API Developer's Guide
- APIs and Integration forums

COLLABORATION

Chapter 18

Chatter REST API

Use Chatter REST API for programmatic access to Chatter feeds, groups, and social data in your Salesforce organization.

When to Use Chatter REST API

Chatter REST API provides programmatic access to Chatter feeds and social data such as users, groups, followers, and files. Use Chatter REST API to integrate Chatter into a variety of applications such as mobile applications, intranet sites, and third-party Web applications. Chatter REST API is similar to APIs offered by other companies with feeds, such as Facebook and Twitter.

Use Chatter REST API to:

- Build a mobile client that displays a Chatter feed.
- Integrate a third-party Web application with Chatter so it can notify groups of users about events.
- Display the Chatter feed on an external system, such as an intranet site, after users are authenticated.
- Make feeds actionable and integrated with third-party sites. For example, an app that posts a Chatter item to Twitter whenever the post includes #tweet hashtag.
- Create simple games that interact with the feed for notifications. Games might include things like sales incentive competitions.
- Creating a custom, branded skin for Chatter for your organization.

Chatter REST API complements the SOAP API and the REST API by making it easy to interact with Chatter data. Many Chatter REST API resource actions are also exposed as static methods on Apex classes in the `ConnectApi` namespace. This namespace is also referred to

225

as *Chatter in Apex*. Use Chatter in Apex to develop Chatter applications on the Force.com platform without using HTTP callouts from Apex.

Supported Editions and Platforms

Chatter REST API is available in all editions except Personal Edition. Also, most features require Chatter to be enabled for the organization.

Quick Start

Create a sample application in your development environment to see the power and flexibility of the Chatter REST API.

Prerequisites

Complete these prerequisites before you begin the quick start.

- Install your development platform according to its product documentation.
- Become familiar with cURL, the tool used to execute REST requests in this quick start. If you use another tool, you should be familiar enough with it to translate the example code.
- Become familiar with JavaScript Object Notation (JSON), which is the data format returned in this quick start.
- Enable an SSL endpoint in your application server.
- Become familiar with OAuth 2.0, which requires some setup. We provide the steps, but it will help if you familiarize yourself with its terms and concepts.

Step One: Set Up Authorization

Create a connected app in a Salesforce organization and enable OAuth. The client connects to the connected app.

1. Decide where to create your connected app.

   Your connected app does not have to reside in the same organization as your users. The connected app you create can be used to sign into any organization.

2. In the appropriate organization, from Setup, click **Create** > **Apps**, and in the Connected Apps section, click **New** to create a new connected app.

3. Enter a connected app name.

4. Enter the contact email, as well as any other information appropriate to your application.

5. Select `Enable OAuth Settings`.
6. Enter a `Callback URL`. It must be secure: `http://` does not work, only `https://`. For development environments, the callback URL is generally the instance plus whatever URL you want the user to be redirected to, for example:

   `https://`***`instance_name`***`/ConnectTest/oauth/_callback`.
7. Enter an OAuth scope. Select `Access and manage your Chatter feed` in addition to any other scope you want your connected app to allow access to.
8. Click Save.

   The `Consumer Key` is created and displayed, and a `Consumer Secret` is created (click the link to reveal it).

Step Two: Connect to Chatter REST API Using OAuth

Use OAuth to connect to the connected app and get an access token. Pass the access token in a request to Chatter REST API.

Complete Step One: Set Up Authorization and create a connected app before starting this task.

This quick start uses the username-password OAuth authentication flow. Please note that Salesforce Communities doesn't support the username-password authentication flow. To complete this quick start, don't use a Communities URL.

 Note: The username-password authentication flow involves passing the user's credentials back and forth. Use this authentication flow only when necessary. No refresh token will be issued.

This table maps the terms used in the connected app you just created to the OAuth properties used in the examples. The OAuth 2.0 specification uses the word "client" instead of "consumer."

Connected App Application Label	Value in Example
`Consumer Key`	`client_id`
`Consumer Secret`	`client_secret`

This example uses the following values:

Property	Value
Server instance	na1.salesforce.com For communities, instead of an instance name, it's the following: ***communitydomain***`.force.com/`***communitypath***

Property	Value
username	admin@seattleapps.com
client_id	3MVG9PhR6g6B7ps4xDycwGrI4PvjVZvK9
client_secret	8870355475032095511
grant_type	password
	The value of grant_type depends on the OAuth authentication flow you are using
password	1Lsfdc!

1. Generate the access token.

   The following is an example of the cURL command to generate an access token:

   ```
   curl --form client_id=3MVG9PhR6g6B7ps4xDycwGrI4PvjVZvK9
         --form client_secret=8870355475032095511
         --form grant_type=password
         --form username=admin@seattleapps.com
         --form password=1Lsfdc!
         https://na1.salesforce.com/services/oauth2/token
   ```

   The following is the response that includes the access token:

   ```
   {
   "id":"https://login.na1.salesforce.com/id/00DD0000000FJ6TMAW/

        005D0000001B5T4IAK",
   "issued_at":"1302907727777",
   "instance_url":"https://na1.salesforce.com",
   "signature":"5jcevY5fUai0lWntuSxkwBzWcvRjd01RCOkIBZpyGv0=",
   "access_token":"00DD0000000FJ6T!AQkAQPde_DMF2vGzddfZmBRS95GojDbtA

   rKkgukAgZP0OVFYY5KkAqhLw9ejeKIlpJ3FgwGAWeRlBiWRt8mfXEuAZGbZNosk"
   }
   ```

2. Access Chatter REST API using the access token.

   ```
   curl -X GET
   https://na1.salesforce.com/services/data/v29.0/chatter/users/me

        -H 'Authorization: Bearer
   00DD0000000FJ6T!AQkAQPde_DMF2vGzddfZmBRS95Goj

   DbtArKkgukAgZP0OVFYY5KkAqhLw9ejeKIlpJ3FgwGAWeRlBiWRt8mfXEuAZGbZNosk'
   ```

Connecting to Salesforce Communities

To use OAuth to connect to a Salesforce community, replace the server instance name with the full path to the community URL.

To connect to Communities, you can use the OAuth Web server and user-agent workflows. To authenticate a user using the authorize URL:

```
https://login.salesforce.com/services/oauth2/authorize?
response_type=token&client_id=your_app_id&redirect_uri=your_redirect_uris
```

Replace the `login.salesforce.com` host name with the full path to the community URL. For example:

```
https://acme.force.com/customers/services/oauth2/authorize?
response_type=token&client_id=your_app_id&redirect_uri=your_redirect_uri
```

When implemented successfully, this URL directs users to your app's branded login page. Once they authorize the app, you then set a user access token and refresh token for future authentication. In requests for the token endpoint, you should similarly replace the host with the community, like this:

```
https://acme.force.com/customers/services/oauth2/token
```

To request a Chatter REST API resource, you can use the Salesforce host name and specify the community ID:

```
https://na1.salesforce.com/services/data/v29.0/connect
/communities/communityId/chatter/feeds/news/me/feed-items
```

Or you can replace the host name with the full path to the community URL:

```
https://communitydomain.force.com/communitypath/services/data/v29.0/connect
/communities/communityId/chatter/feeds/news/me/feed-items
```

Best Practices

Consider the best practices in this section.

Chatter REST API Limits

Chatter REST API requests are subject to rate limiting. Chatter REST API has a per user, per application, per hour rate limit. When you exceed the rate limit, all Chatter REST API resources return a 503 Service Unavailable error code for both the user and application. When polling for feed updates or private messages, use the `/feeds/news/me` `|`**`userId`**`/is-modified` endpoint and do not exceed one poll per minute.

Using Wildcards to Match Text Patterns

Use wildcard characters to match text patterns in Chatter REST API and Chatter in Apex searches. A common use for wildcards is searching a feed. Pass a search string and wildcards in the q parameter. This example is a Chatter REST API request:

```
/chatter/feed-items?q=chat*
```

This example is a Chatter in Apex method call:

```
ConnectApi.ChatterFeeds.searchFeedItems(null, 'chat*');
```

Understanding Response Body Encoding

Chatter REST API serves user-submitted content that is often not filtered at input and may come from many different sources including third-party mobile and web applications. Therefore, developers creating applications that consume Chatter REST API output must take care to properly process the output for the context in which they use the data.

Chatter REST API strings are minimally HTML entity encoded by default, which is suitable in most cases for display between HTML tags, but not necessarily in other HTML contexts.Chatter REST API output may be used in many contexts. Developers should not assume that the default entity encoding is appropriate for all contexts. In particular, using Chatter REST API output inside HTML attribute values, inside URLs, with javascript, inside script tags and inside CSS all require different encoding and whitelisting.

For non-HTML contexts, such as native mobile applications, Chatter REST API clients may request raw (unencoded) output by setting the `X-Chatter-Entity-Encoding` HTTP header in your request to `false`.

Chatter REST API does special encoding of any URL values included in response payloads. The main part of the URL is URL-encoded as per RFC2396, and the query string is HTML-form encoded. This encoding cannot be turned off.

Resources

Search on the Salesforce Developer's Network at `http://developer.salesforce.com/docs` for the following resources on Chatter REST API.

- Chatter REST API Developer's Guide
- Chatter Code Recipes

- Chatter REST API Cheat Sheet
- Chatter development forum

Chapter 19

GoInstant API

GoInstant is a JavaScript API for building real-time, collaborative applications. It provides the tools for integrating multi-user capabilities into your application's interface, using real-time, publish and submission messaging for data synchronization, and a real-time data store. GoInstant includes automatic scaling and security features, and works across desktop and mobile platforms. The API also includes pre-defined widgets, such as a User List and Form widget, for faster application development.

When to Use GoInstant API

Use GoInstant API when you want to incorporate collaborative experiences into your website, web application, or mobile application. For example, you can add real-time collaboration to an internal workflow, allowing multiple users to interact through the workflow simultaneously. You can also collaborate on a sales lead, allowing users to share notes, update information, and discuss the opportunity all at once. Whether you want to guide customers through a hands-on support experience, or enable customer-to-customer interactions, GoInstant API gives you the ability to develop collaborative, real-time experiences for two or more users across web or mobile applications.

Supported Editions and Platforms

GoInstant is available at http://goinstant.com

GoInstant Quickstart

Before you begin, sign up for a free GoInstant account at http://goinstant.com.

Once you've signed up, create an App by providing a name for it. After you have an Account Name and an App Name, you can execute the code samples that follow.

Step One: Create a Synchronized Form

This code sample shows you how to build a synchronized form that propagates input across users, and shows you who's typing. A synchronized, multi-user form is ideal for guiding people through your web application—for sales or support—in real time.

 Tip: To step through creating the form, visit the GoInstant website.

```html
<html>
  <head>
    <title>Text Synchronization App</title>
    <script
src="https://cdn.goinstant.net/v1/platform.min.js"></script>
    <script
src="https://cdnjs.cloudflare.com/ajax/libs/jquery/1.9.1/jquery.min.js"></script>

  </head>
  <body>
    <div>

      <!-- The Form that you'll be synchronizing -->
      <form id="example-form" action="">
        <input type="text" name="name" id="sync" />
      </form>

      <!-- Now you connect to the GoInstant API -->
      <script>
        $(document).ready(function () {
          // The connection url is provided to you by viewing the
application from the
          // GoInstant dashboard. This url tells platform where your
 application and
          // account are located in order to connect.
          var url = 'https://goinstant.net/YOURACCOUNT/YOURAPP';

          goinstant.connect(url, function (err, connection, lobby)
{
            if (err) {
              // Could not connect to platform
              throw err;
            }

// Retrieve a reference to the key where we will store the value of
the input field
          var name = lobby.key('name');

          // Retrieve a jQuery reference to the input element
          var el = $('input[name="name"]');

// Every time another user changes the value of the input field,
```

```
            // update the value displayed to the user
            name.on('set', function(value, context) {
                el.val(value);
            });

            // When the user changes the value of the field, propagate
    that value to other users
            el.on('keyup', function() {
                name.set($(this).val());
            });
        });
    });
    </script>
    </div>
    </body>
</html>
```

In the next sections, you'll learn how to build something a bit more complex—an actual form page that includes text fields, a text area, a slider, check boxes, and radio buttons. Imagine this form is on your website or in your web application, and now you want to make it collaborative.

You'll use GoInstant widgets to enhance the functionality of the API. These pre-defined widgets provide collaborative functionality.

Step Two: Create a Simple HTML Document

```
<!doctype html>
<html>
<head>
  <!-- The Platform script from our CDN -->
  <script src="https://cdn.goinstant.net/v1/platform.min.js"></script>


  <!-- All of our widgets -->
  <script src="https://cdn.goinstant.net/widgets/form/latest/form.js">

  </script>
  <link rel="stylesheet"
href="https://cdn.goinstant.net/widgets/form/latest/form.css" />

  <script
src="https://cdn.goinstant.net/widgets/user-colors/latest/user-colors.min.js">

  </script>

  <script
src="https://cdn.goinstant.net/widgets/user-list/latest/user-list.min.js">

  </script>
  <link rel="stylesheet"
href="https://cdn.goinstant.net/widgets/user-list/latest/user-list.css"
  />
```

```
  <script
src="https://cdn.goinstant.net/widgets/click-indicator/latest/click-indicator.min.js">

  </script>
  <link rel="stylesheet"
href="https://cdn.goinstant.net/widgets/click-indicator/latest/click-indicator.css"
 />

  <script>
    // !!!!!!!!!!!!!!!!!!!!!!!!!!!!!!!!!!!!!
    //
    // Place your setup functions below here
    //
    // !!!!!!!!!!!!!!!!!!!!!!!!!!!!!!!!!!!!!
  </script>

  <script>
  window.onload = function() {
    var url = 'https://goinstant.net/YOUR_ACCOUNT/YOUR_APP';
    goinstant.connect(url, function (err, connection, lobby) {
      if (err) {
        // Could not connect to platform
        throw err;
      }

      setupForm(lobby);
      setupColors(lobby);
      setupUserList(lobby);
      setupClickIndicators(lobby);
    });
  };
  </script>
</head>
<body>
  <!-- Place your markup here -->
</body>
</html>
```

Step Three: Create a Form Inside the Body Tag

```
<form id="personal-information" action="" method="GET">

  <div>
    <label for="first_name">First Name</label>
    <input type="text" name="first_name" id="first_name" />
  </div>

  <div>
    <label for="last_name">Last Name</label>
    <input type="text" name="last_name" id="last_name" />
  </div>

  <div>
```

```
   <label for="male">Male</label>
   <input type="radio" name="gender" id="male" value="m" />
</div>

<div>
   <label for="female">Female</label>
   <input type="radio" name="gender" id="female" value="female" />
</div>

<div>
   <label for="unspec">Unspecified</label>
   <input type="radio" name="gender" id="unspec" value="unspec" />
</div>

<div>
   <label for="employed">Employed</label>
   <input type="checkbox" name="employed" id="employed"
value="Employed" />
</div>

<div>
   <label for="job_title">Job Title</label>
   <input type="text" name="job_title" id="job_title" />
</div>

<div>
   <label for="income">Income Range</label>
   <input step="1000" min="0" max="10000000" type="range"
name="income" />
</div>

</form>
```

Step Four: Create Your GoInstant Connection

```
goinstant.connect(url, function (err, connection, lobby) {
  if (err) {
    // Could not connect to platform
    throw err;
  }

  // You'll add setup functions here
});
```

Step Five: Create a Form Widget

The Form Widget lets you see who's interacting with a form, and propagates form input between users.

```
function setupForm(lobby) {
  // Using a room and a key from an existing connection
  var formEl = document.getElementById('personal-information');

  var form = new goinstant.widgets.Form({
    el: formEl,
    key: lobby.key('form-key-name'),
    room: lobby
  });

  form.initialize(function(err) {
    if (err) {
      throw err;
    }

    console.log('Now your form is ready to go!');
  });
}
```

Step Six: Open a Browser

Open your page in two separate browsers (for example, in Safari and Chrome). You will see that the forms are synchronized with gray indicators.

Step Seven: Add Color

Don't settle for boring gray indicators for every user. Add color for users by adding the User Colors widget to the page.

```
function setupColors(lobby) {
  var userColors = new goinstant.widgets.UserColors({
    room: lobby
  });

  // This will choose a color for your current user.
  userColors.choose(function(err) {
    if (err) {
      throw err;
    }
```

```
      console.log('A color has been assigned for the user in this
browser!');
  });
}
```

Step Eight: Add the User List Widget

How can you tell who is interacting with the page? Add the User List widget and you will
always have the answer.

```
function setupUserList(lobby) {
  // Using a room and a key from an existing connection
  var userList = new goinstant.widgets.UserList({
    room: lobby
  });

  userList.initialize(function(err) {
    if (err) {
      throw err;
    }

    console.log('Now your user list is ready to go!');
  });
}
```

Step Nine: Add the Click Indicator Widget

Your users are doing more than interacting with the form. See what else they're up to by adding
the Click Indicator widget.

```
function setupClickIndicators(lobby) {
  // Using a room and a key from an existing connection
  var clickIndicator = new goinstant.widgets.ClickIndicator({
    room: lobby,
    element: document.body
  });

  clickIndicator.initialize(function(err) {
    if (err) {
      throw err;
    }

    console.log('Now your click indicators are ready to go!');
  });
}
```

In a few simple steps you've taken a form and turned it into a real-time, collaborative experience.
Users on the form can see who else is typing, as well as what they are typing.

GoInstant and AngularJS Quickstart

The GoInstant API makes it easy for you to build real-time, multi-user applications. It also lets you integrate your applications with popular client-side development frameworks. One such integration—GoAngular—integrates GoInstant with AngularJS.

GoAngular is a simple-to-use integration that transforms any AngularJS application into a real-time, multi-user experience. With GoAngular you can:

- Quickly make your application a multi-user application, with real-time controller synchronization.
- Control which models are synchronized.
- Auto-magically synchronize models that meet specified criteria.

In this example, we'll show you how to build a multi-user form with GoAngular.

Step One: Create a Basic Form Using AngularJS

```
<!DOCTYPE html>
<html ng-app="FormSync">
  <head>
    <title>GoAngular Form Synchronization</title>
    <script
src="https://ajax.googleapis.com/ajax/libs/angularjs/1.0.7/angular.min.js"></script>

  </head>
  <body>
    <div ng-controller="SyncCtrl">
      <input ng-model="name" type="text"/>
      <br>
      <p>Name is: {{ name }}</p>
    </div>
    <script>
      angular.module('FormSync', []);

      function SyncCtrl($scope) {
        $scope.name = '';
      }
    </script>
  </body>
</html>
```

Step Two: Connect to GoInstant

Connect to GoInstant by including the GoInstant and GoAngular libraries in the form's
<head> tag:

```
<script src="https://cdn.goinstant.net/v1/platform.min.js"></script>
<script
src="https://cdn.goinstant.net/integrations/goangular/latest/goangular.min.js"></script>
```

Next, specify the `goinstant` module as a dependency for your app and configure your
connection with the platform service (`platformProvider`):

```
angular.module('FormSync', ['goinstant']).
  config(function(platformProvider) {

platformProvider.set('https://goinstant.net/YOURACCOUNT/YOURAPP');
  });
```

Step Three: Add GoAngular to Your Controller

Add GoAngular to your controller, and make the form a multi-user form.

Create a new instance and initialize it. Then pass in your controller's $scope and choose a
namespace.

```
function SyncCtrl($scope, GoAngular) {
  $scope.name = 'Bob';

  var goAngular = new GoAngular($scope, 'SyncCtrl');

  // Begin synchronization
  goAngular.initialize();
}
```

The entire code block for your real-time, multi-user form looks like this:

```
<!DOCTYPE html>
<html ng-app="FormSync">
  <head>
    <title>GoAngular Form Synchronization</title>
    <script
src="https://ajax.googleapis.com/ajax/libs/angularjs/1.0.7/angular.min.js"></script>

    <script
src="https://cdn.goinstant.net/v1/platform.min.js"></script>
    <script
```

```
src="https://cdn.goinstant.net/integrations/goangular/latest/goangular.min.js"></script>

    </head>
    <body>
      <div ng-controller="SyncCtrl">
        <input ng-model="name" type="text"/>
        <br>
        <p>Name is: {{ name }}</p>
      </div>
      <script>
        angular.module('FormSync', ['goinstant']).
          config(function(platformProvider) {

platformProvider.set('https://goinstant.net/YOURACCOUNT/YOURAPP');
          });

        function SyncCtrl($scope, GoAngular) {
          $scope.name = 'Bob';

          var goAngular = new GoAngular($scope, 'SyncCtrl');

          goAngular.initialize();
        }
      </script>
    </body>
</html>
```

How GoInstant Works

GoInstant enables multi-user experiences by synchronizing real-time data across users. The GoInstant model has several inherent benefits over others:

- Late-joining users only need to fetch the latest state, and don't need to replay events from the beginning. Supporting late-joining user scenarios is important when one person has partially completed a process (for example, filling out a form) and another person joins them to help out.
- With state propagation you can regulate frequent data changes without becoming de-synchronized. This helps optimize performance.
- Reconnecting users can quickly re-synchronize, even if they have connection issues and miss one or more data changes.

Data Structure

GoInstant stores data in a tree structure where each node in the tree is a key. This tree is essentially one big multi-dimensional map (or associative array) where the value of any non-leaf key is another key. The data is stored in the leaf keys (a key that has no children) of the tree.

Here's a simple visualization of how the data structure works:

```
{
    a = {
        b = 2,
        c = {
            d = 3,
            e = 4
        },
    }
}
```

Each letter is a key. The tree starts with "A" which then has two children, "B" and "C". "B" is a leaf key (with no additional children) and therefore it's storing a value. "C" has additional children, "D" and "E" which are each leaf keys storing values.

This data structure makes it simple for you to organize the state of your application because it allows you to easily group your data.

For example, in a chat room implementation, you'd group all of the chat messages together. Each chat message would then be a child key under the main 'messages' key.

Sometimes, applications require broadly- or deeply-nested data structures. This is no problem for GoInstant. Here are a few important points that have to do with how we store data:

- You can access all data in a branch from a higher-level (parent) node.
- You can add listeners to let you know when data changes.
- You can add a bubbling-listener on a parent key to let you know of any changes to the values of its children keys.

Bubbling is valuable because it allows you to have a single listener for an entire collection of data, which makes managing hierarchical data much easier. For example, you could use bubbling to detect additions to a group of messages in a chat room.

Here's how it works:

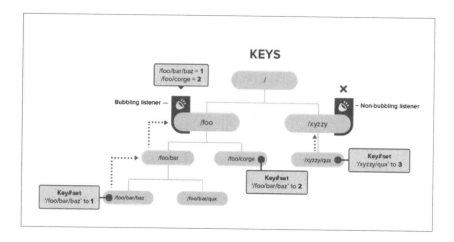

The key /foo/bar/baz is several levels down the tree and has a value set to "1". There's a bubbling listener on /foo, and so /foo becomes aware that /foo/bar/baz has changed. Another child key, /foo/corge also has its value set (to "2"), which then bubbles up to notify its parent key, /foo.

On the other hand, when key /xyzzy/qux changes to "3," that change doesn't bubble up to its parent key, because /xyzzy doesn't have a bubbling listener on it.

Bubbling with a tree-like structure gives you a great deal of flexibility on how you manage data within your application.

Security

GoInstant has engineered strict transport, authentication, data, and access control security to provide in-depth defense against potential security breaches.

Transport Security

GoInstant enforces an HTTPS connection to its web servers, with only strong cryptographic cipher-suites enabled. HSTS is deployed to prevent browsers from accidentally connecting to HTTP, which is an active deterrent to MITM downgrade attacks. All HTTP access is denied (other than the initial redirect to establish HSTS) to GoInstant web servers. The net result is that no data or commands ever leave your application in unencrypted form.

Authentication Security

GoInstant uses JSON Web Token (JWT) IETF-draft-standard technology for authentication. JWT allows you to implement Single Sign-On (SSO) simply and securely.

To implement, your web server authenticates a user by whatever means you've already developed and then encodes a specifically-formatted JSON object, attaching a cryptographic signature (for example, HMAC-SHA256). This token is passed to the GoInstant client. A GoInstant server in turn verifies the signature as coming from your server, authenticating that user to use GoInstant.

JWT also gives you the flexibility to import identity-based attributes for each user, called "claims", into GoInstant. These claims can be used to control each user's permissions within your application (see Access Control Security below). Client-side application code doesn't need to know how to encode/decode JWTs; the GoInstant system handles it for you.

The REST API uses the industry-standard OAuth 2.0 instead of cookies for authentication. Passwords used to log in to the dashboard are stored with a salted, iterative, cryptographic hash function.

Data Security

All data is kept in a firewall-controlled, restricted access network in GoInstant's virtual private cloud. Every server in the GoInstant cloud is subject to strict OS- and network-layer firewalls, including between servers at the same logical layer of the stack. Systems are actively monitored for access, intrusion, and malware. In the unlikely event of a problem our Operations team will be notified within seconds.

GoInstant's Internet-facing servers are routinely subject to external monitoring and professional third-party penetration testing. The GoInstant stack's architecture and code is reviewed periodically by a third-party security firm, in addition to being scrutinized continuously during the GoInstant code-review process.

Your application data is kept separate from other applications. Additionally, within your application, data is compartmentalized by GoInstant Rooms. Users can only connect to the Rooms to which you give them access.

Access Control Security

Access Control Lists (ACLs) can be specified on a per-app and per-Room basis to control who has permission to log in and who can access what data. Inside each ACL, you define fine-grained, per-field permissions, which can effectively protect private and/or sensitive data. The permission to join a Room can be predicated on any of the claims contained in the user's JWT (including the fact that they're a guest). Storing one or more "groups" in your JWT allows for fully-customizable role-based access control.

The ACLs control, with as much or as little granularity as you want, which users can read and/or write various Keys. ACLs can differentiate between the different kinds of writes (supporting our full range of operations). ACLs also control who can join a Room, based on attributes stored in their JWT (see Authentication Security above). By default, all users and operations are disallowed, so it's easier to build a secure ACL. Data restricted by ACL will ensure that it is never transmitted to an unauthorized user.

API Reference

GoInstant's API has 5 key sections: Connection, Room, Key, Channel, and Users.

Connection

The Connection object is the root object you'll use for accessing and manipulating GoInstant. You'll need an application URL and account (both of which you receive when you sign up). Once connected, you'll be able to join a Room which can be used to manipulate Keys and listen to connection-lifecycle events.

Here's an example for connecting to GoInstant as an unauthenticated user:

```
var url = 'https://goinstant.net/YOURACCOUNT/YOURAPP';

var connection = new goinstant.Connection(url);
connection.connect(function (err) {
  if (err) {
    // there was an error connecting OR the token was invalid.
    return;
  }

  var room = connection.room('public-stocks');
  room.join(function(err) {
    if (err) {
      // there as an error joining the room
      return;
    }

    var key = room.key('/stock-prices/CRM');
    key.get(function(err, value, context) {
      if (err) {
        // could not retrieve the value
      }

      // display the data.
    });
  });
});
```

There's also a helper function called `goinstant.connect` that takes care of instantiating and creating a Connection object and joining one or more Rooms. By default, `goinstant.connect` joins the "lobby" Room, which makes it easy to get started without having to dig into the Room concept further.

In the subsequent example, you'll see how `goinstant.connect` works. We're also providing a custom name for guest users.

```
var url = 'https://goinstant.net/YOURACCOUNT/YOURAPP';
var userDefaults = {displayName: 'Roger User'};
goinstant.connect(url, {user: userDefaults}, function(err, connection,
  room) {
  if (err) {
    console.log('Error connecting to GoInstant:', err);
    return;
  }

  // you're connected and in the `lobby` room. with the displayName
  'Roger User'
});
```

Room

Rooms are instances of your application within GoInstant. Each room holds a number of users and keys. A user must be in a room to interact with other users or manipulate keys. A user can be in more than one room at a time, using a single connection.

```
var url = 'https://goinstant.net/MYACCOUNT/MYAPP';
var token = 'eyJ...(base64url)...p9Q';

// Initialize a connection to GoInstant
var connection = new goinstant.Connection(url);
connection.connect(token, function (err) {
  if (err) {
    console.log('could not connect:', err);
    return;
  }

  // Connected!
  // Now join a room
  var room = connection.room('my-room');
  room.join(function(err) {
    if (err) {
      console.log('Error joining the room:',err);
      return;
    }

    // In the room, get a key and print its value
    var key = room.key('/legumes/peanut');
    key.get(function(err, value) {
      console.log('peanut details:', value);

      // Done with the room. Now leave.
      room.leave(function(err) {
        if (err) {
          console.log('error while leaving the room:', err);
        }
      });
    });
  });
```

```
    });
});
```

Key

The key is the primary interface for accessing and manipulating data in GoInstant. A Key refers to a key-value store. The Key object provides the interface for managing and monitoring a value in our server-side data store. Key values are limited to 32 KB in size.

Keys are initially instantiated from a Room:

```
var foo = room.key('/foo');
```

There are a number of commands you can use on Keys, including: Key#get (read the current value of the key), Key#set (writing to keys), Key#remove (destroying keys), Key#watch (to retrieve a key's current value and listen for future changes) and Key#unwatch (to stop listening).

Channel

A Channel is a full-duplex messaging interface for broadcasting to all users who are listening to that channel in a room. Unlike a Key, a Channel does not store state, so you cannot retrieve the previous messages from the channel. You can create a Channel using the Room object through the .channel(name) method.

```
var channel = room.channel('/a/channel');
```

Here's an example of using a Channel:

```
channel.message({ time: Date.now(), msg: 'hi'}, function(err) {
    if (err) {
      // Messaging the channel was not successful!
    }

    // The message was sent!
});

channel.on('message', function(msg) {
    // received a msg from another user
});
```

Users

GoInstant supports unauthenticated users (guests) and authenticated users. It's best to start with unauthenticated users to familiarize yourself with the User Object and how GoInstant works.

Guests always belong to the GoInstant-provided group { id: 'guests', displayName: 'Guests' }. A Group is a collection of users with specific permissions based on the Access Control Lists. Guests can also be identified at runtime by:

```
// user.provider === 'goinstant' && user.id.match(/^guest:/)
```

Here's an example guest object:

```
var userObject = {
  provider: 'yourdomain.com',
  id: 'bsmith',
  displayName: 'Bob Smith',
  groups: [
    { id: 'developers', displayName: 'Developers' },
    { id: 'technical-staff', displayName: 'Technical Staff' }
  ]
};
```

Best Practices

The fastest way to get started with GoInstant API is to use a GoInstant widget. These widgets are self-contained pieces of functionality that are incredibly easy to implement and use. Add multiple widgets to your application and realize the benefits of real-time, multi-user applications within minutes.

After that, explore the API further. You'll discover extensibility around authentication, security, data management, and more.

Resources

Use the following resources to get more information about GoInstant API

* Sign up for GoInstant: http://goinstant.com
* GoInstant Documentation: https://developers.goinstant.com/v1/
* Multi-user map demos: https://maps.goinstant.com
* GoAngular Documentation: https://developers.goinstant.com/v1/GoAngular

MOBILE

## Chapter 20

Salesforce Mobile SDK

The Salesforce Mobile SDK provides a set of frameworks and tools that let you easily create sophisticated mobile apps that integrate with Salesforce.

When to Use Mobile SDK

Salesforce Mobile SDK lets you develop native Objective-C apps for iOS and Java apps for Android. You can also use it to provide a native container for hybrid apps written in HTML5 and JavaScript. Npm scripts for iOS and Android help you get started building native and hybrid apps. Salesforce Mobile SDK provides:

- Native device services. You can access device features such as the camera, GPS, and contacts across a broad range of iOS and Android devices.
- Secure offline storage and data synchronization. You can build applications which continue to function with limited or no network connectivity. The data stored on the device is securely encrypted and safe, even if the device is lost or stolen.
- Client OAuth authentication support. You're free from having to rebuild login pages and general authentication in mobile apps. Mobile SDK apps quickly and easily integrate with enterprise security management.

The Mobile SDK also seamlessly integrates with the Force.com cloud architecture by providing:

- SmartSync Data Framework for accessing Salesforce data through JavaScript
- Secure offline storage
- Data syncing for hybrid apps
- Implementation of Force.com Connected App policy that works out of the box
- OAuth credentials management, including persistence and refresh capabilities
- Wrappers for Salesforce REST APIs

- Libraries for building native iOS and Android applications
- Containers for building hybrid applications

Supported Editions and Platforms

You'll need the following to use the Mobile SDK:

- To build iOS applications (hybrid or native), you'll need Mac OS X "Lion" or higher, iOS 6.0 or higher, and Xcode 4.5 or higher.
- To build Android applications (hybrid or native), you'll need the Java JDK 6, Eclipse, Android ADT plugin, and the Android SDK.
- To build remote hybrid applications, you'll need an organization that has Visualforce.
- Most of our resources are on GitHub, a social coding community. You can access all of our files in our public repository, but we think it's a good idea to join. https://github.com/forcedotcom

Depending on how you use the Mobile SDK to integrate with Salesforce, you might also end up using Visualforce, Apex, or the REST API. See the sections in this guide on these APIs to understand what Salesforce editions are supported, and what additional requirements might be needed.

When to Use Salesforce1 Platform vs. Creating a Custom App

When it comes to developing functionality for your Salesforce mobile users, you have options. Here are some differences between extending Salesforce1 and creating custom apps using the Mobile SDK.

- Has a defined user interface.
- Has full access to Salesforce data.
- You can create an integrated experience with functionality developed in the Salesforce1 Platform.
- Publisher actions give you a way to include your own apps/functionality.
- You can customize Salesforce1 with point-and-click or programmatic customizations.
- Functionality can be added programmatically through Visualforce pages or Force.com Canvas apps.
- Salesforce1 customizations or apps adhere to the Salesforce1 navigation. So, for example, a Visualforce page can be called from the navigation menu or from the publisher.
- You can leverage existing Salesforce development experience, both point-and-click and programmatic.
- Included in all Salesforce editions and supported by salesforce.com.

Custom apps can be either free-standing apps you create with Salesforce Mobile SDK or browser apps using plain HTML5 and JQuery Mobile/Ajax. With custom apps, you can:

- Define a custom user experience.
- Access Salesforce data using REST APIs in native and hybrid local apps, or with Visualforce in hybrid apps using JavaScript Remoting. In HTML5 apps, do the same using JQueryMobile and Ajax.
- Brand your user interface for customer-facing exposure.
- Create standalone mobile apps, either with native APIs using Java for Android or Objective-C for iOS, or through a hybrid container using JavaScript and HTML5 (Mobile SDK only).
- Distribute apps through mobile industry channels, such as the Apple App Store or Google Play (Mobile SDK only).
- Configure and control complex offline behavior (Mobile SDK only).
- Use push notifications (Developer Preview in Winter '14; available for Mobile SDK native apps only).
- Design a custom security container using your own OAuth module (Mobile SDK only).
- Other important Mobile SDK considerations:

  ◊ Open-source SDK, downloadable for free through npm installers as well as from GitHub. No licensing required.

  ◊ Requires you to develop and compile your apps in an external development environment (Xcode for iOS, Eclipse or similar for Android).

  ◊ Development costs range from $0 to $1M or more, plus maintenance costs.

About Native, HTML5, and Hybrid Development

Many factors play a part in your mobile strategy, such as your team's development skills, required device functionality, the importance of security, offline capability, interoperability, and so on. In the end, it's not just a question of what your app will do, but how you'll get it there. The Mobile SDK offers three ways to create mobile apps:

- **Native** apps are specific to a given mobile platform (iOS or Android) and use the development tools and language that the respective platform supports (for example, Xcode and Objective-C with iOS, Eclipse and Java with Android). Native apps look and perform best but require the most development effort.
- **HTML5** apps use standard web technologies—typically HTML5, JavaScript and CSS—to deliver apps through a mobile Web browser. This "write once, run anywhere" approach to mobile development creates cross-platform mobile applications that work on multiple devices. While developers can create sophisticated apps with HTML5 and JavaScript alone,

some challenges remain, such as session management, secure offline storage, and access to native device functionality (such as camera, calendar, notifications, and so on).

- **Hybrid** apps combine the ease of HTML5 Web app development with the power of the native platform by wrapping a Web app inside the Salesforce container. This combined approach produces an application that can leverage the device's native capabilities and be delivered through the app store. You can also create hybrid apps using Visualforce pages delivered through the Salesforce hybrid container.

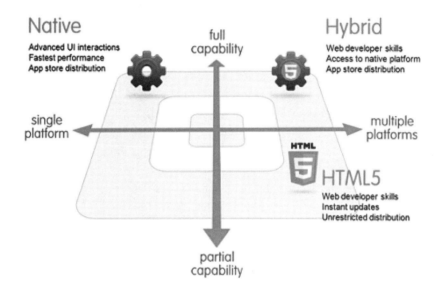

Native Apps

Native apps provide the best usability, the best features, and the best overall mobile experience. There are some things you get only with native apps:

- **Fast graphics API**—the native platform gives you the fastest graphics, which might not be a big deal if you're showing a static screen with only a few elements, or a very big deal if you're using a lot of data and require a fast refresh.
- **Fluid animation**—related to the fast graphics API is the ability to have fluid animation. This is especially important in gaming, highly interactive reporting, or intensely computational algorithms for transforming photos and sounds.
- **Built-in components**—The camera, address book, geolocation, and other features native to the device can be seamlessly integrated into mobile apps. Another important built-in component is encrypted storage, but more about that later.

- **Ease of use**—The native platform is what people are accustomed to. When you add that familiarity to the native features they expect, your app becomes that much easier to use.

Native apps are usually developed using an integrated development environment (IDE). IDEs provide tools for building, debugging, project management, version control, and other tools professional developers need. You need these tools because native apps are more difficult to develop. Likewise, the level of experience required is higher than in other development scenarios. If you're a professional developer, you don't have to be sold on proven APIs and frameworks, painless special effects through established components, or the benefits of having all your code in one place.

HTML5 Apps

An HTML5 mobile app is basically a web page, or series of web pages, that are designed to work on a small mobile device screen. As such, HTML5 apps are device agnostic and can be opened with any modern mobile browser. Because your content is on the web, it's searchable, which can be a huge benefit for certain types of apps (shopping, for example).

If you're new to mobile development, the technological bar is lower for Web apps; it's easier to get started here than in native or hybrid development. Unfortunately, every mobile device seems to have its own idea of what constitutes usable screen size and resolution. This diversity imposes an additional burden of testing on different devices. Browser incompatibility is especially common on Android devices, for example.

An important part of the "write once, run anywhere" HTML5 methodology is that distribution and support is much easier than for native apps. Need to make a bug fix or add features? Done and deployed for all users. For a native app, there are longer development and testing cycles, after which the consumer typically must log into a store and download a new version to get the latest fix.

If HTML5 apps are easier to develop, easier to support, and can reach the widest range of devices, where do these apps lose out?

- **Secure offline storage** — HTML5 browsers support offline databases and caching, but with no out-of-the-box encryption support. You get all three features in Mobile SDK native applications.
- **Security** — In general, implementing even trivial security measures on a native platform can be complex tasks for a mobile Web developer. It can also be painful for users. For example, a web app with authentication requires users to enter their credentials every time the app restarts or returns from a background state.
- **Native features** — the camera, address book, and other native features are accessible on limited, if any, browser platforms.
- **Native look and feel** — HTML5 can only emulate the native look, while customers won't be able to use familiar compound gestures.

Hybrid Apps

Hybrid apps are built using HTML5 and JavaScript wrapped inside a thin container that provides access to native platform features. For the most part, hybrid apps provide the best of both worlds, being almost as easy to develop as HTML5 apps with all the functionality of native. In addition, hybrid apps can use the SmartSync Data Framework in JavaScript to model Salesforce data, query and search it, edit it, securely cache it for offline use, and synchronize it with the Salesforce server.

You know that native apps are installed on the device, while HTML5 apps reside on a Web server, so you might be wondering whether hybrid apps store their files on the device or on a server? You can implement a hybrid app locally or remotely.

Local

> You can package HTML and JavaScript code inside the mobile application binary, in a structure similar to a native application. In this scenario you use REST APIs and Ajax to move data back and forth between the device and the cloud.

Server

> Alternatively, you can implement the full web application from the server (with optional caching for better performance). Your container app retrieves the full application from the server and displays it in a browser window.

Both types of hybrid development are covered in this guide.

Native, HTML5, and Hybrid Summary

The following table sums up how the three mobile development scenarios stack up.

	Native	HTML5	Hybrid
Graphics	Native APIs	HTML, Canvas, SVG	HTML, Canvas, SVG
Performance	Fastest	Fast	Fast
Look and feel	Native	Emulated	Emulated
Distribution	App store	Web	App store
Camera	Yes	Browser dependent	Yes
Notifications	Yes	No	Yes
Contacts, calendar	Yes	No	Yes
Offline storage	Secure file system	Shared SQL	Secure file system, shared SQL
Geolocation	Yes	Yes	Yes

	Native	HTML5	Hybrid
Swipe	Yes	Yes	Yes
Pinch, spread	Yes	Yes	Yes
Connectivity	Online, offline	Mostly online	Online, offline
Development skills	Objective C, Java	HTML5, CSS, JavaScript	HTML5, CSS, JavaScript

Installing Mobile SDK

Salesforce Mobile SDK provides two installation paths:

- You can install the SDK in a ready-made development setup using a Node Packaged Module (npm) script.
- You can download the Mobile SDK open source code from GitHub.

Mobile SDK npm Packages

Many mobile developers want to use the SDK as a "black box" and begin creating Mobile SDK apps as quickly as possible. These developers prefer the npm installers. Salesforce provides two npm packages: **forceios** for the iOS Mobile SDK, and **forcedroid** for the Android version of the Mobile SDK. These packages provide a static snapshot of an SDK release. In the case of iOS, the npm installer package provides binary modules rather than uncompiled source code. In the case of Android, the npm installer package provides a snapshot of the SDK source code rather than binaries. You use the npm script both to install Mobile SDK and to create new template projects.

Npm packages for the Salesforce Mobile SDK reside at https://www.npmjs.org.

 Note: Npm packages do not support source control, so you can't update your installation dynamically for new releases. Instead, you install each release separately. To upgrade to new versions of the SDK, go to the npmjs.org website and download the new package.

iOS Installation

For the fastest, easiest route to iOS development, use npm to install Salesforce Mobile SDK for iOS.

1. If you've already successfully installed Node.js and npm, skip to step 4.
2. Install Node.js on your system. The Node.js installer automatically installs npm.

   a. Download Node.js from www.nodejs.org/download.

   b. Run the downloaded installer to install Node.js and npm. Accept all prompts asking for permission to install.

3. At a command prompt, type npm and press Return to make sure your installation was successful. If you don't see a page of usage information, revisit Step 2 to find out what's missing.
4. Use the forceios package to install the Mobile SDK either globally (recommended) or locally.

   a. To install Salesforce Mobile SDK in a global location, use the sudo command and append the "global" option, -g:

   ```
   sudo npm install forceios -g
   ```

   With the -g option, you can run npm install from any directory. The npm utility installs the package under /usr/local/lib/node_modules, and links binary modules in /usr/local/bin. Most users need the sudo option because they lack read-write permissions in /usr/local.

   b. To install Salesforce Mobile SDK in a local folder, cd to that folder and use the npm command without sudo or -g:

   ```
   npm install forceios
   ```

   This command installs Salesforce Mobile SDK in a node_modules folder under your current folder. It links binary modules in ./node_modules/.bin/. In this scenario, you rarely use sudo because you typically install in a local folder where you already have read-write permissions.

Android Installation

For the fastest, easiest route to Android development, use npm to install Salesforce Mobile SDK for Android.

1. If you've already successfully installed Node.js and npm, skip to Step 4.

2. Install Node.js and npm on your system.

a. a. Download Node.js from www.nodejs.org/download.

b. b. Run the downloaded installer to install Node.js and npm. Accept all prompts asking for permission to install.

3. At a command prompt, type `npm` and press `Return` to make sure your installation was successful. If you don't see a page of usage information, revisit Step 2 to find out what's missing.

4. Use the forcedroid package to install the Mobile SDK either globally (recommended) or locally.

   a. To install Salesforce Mobile SDK in a global location, append the "global" option, `-g`, to the end of the command. For non-Windows environments, use the `sudo` command:

   ```
   sudo npm install forcedroid -g
   ```

   On Windows:

   ```
   npm install forcedroid -g
   ```

   With the `-g` option, you run `npm install` from any directory. In non-Windows environments, the npm utility installs the package under `/usr/local/lib/node_modules`, and links binary modules in `/usr/local/bin`. Most users need the `sudo` option because they lack read-write permissions in `/usr/local`. In Windows environments, global packages are installed in `%APPDATA%\npm\node_modules`, and binaries are linked in `%APPDATA%\npm`.

   b. To install Salesforce Mobile SDK in a local directory, `cd` to that directory and use the npm command without `sudo` or the `-g` option:

   ```
   npm install forcedroid
   ```

   This command installs Salesforce Mobile SDK in a `node_modules` directory under your current directory. It links binary modules in `./node_modules/.bin/`. In this scenario, you rarely use `sudo` because you typically install in a local folder where you already have read-write permissions.

Uninstalling Mobile SDK npm Packages

If you need to uninstall an npm package, use the npm script.

Uninstalling the Forcedroid Package

The instructions for uninstalling the forcedroid package vary with whether you installed the package globally or locally.

If you installed the package globally, you can run the uninstall command from any folder. Be sure to use the -g option. On a Unix-based platform such as Mac OS X, use sudo as well.

```
$ pwd
/Users/joeuser
$ sudo npm uninstall forcedroid -g
$
```

If you installed the package locally, run the uninstall command from the folder where you installed the package. For example:

```
cd <my_projects/my_sdk_folder>
npm uninstall forcedroid
```

If you try to uninstall a local installation from the wrong directory, you'll get an error message similar to this:

```
npm WARN uninstall not installed in /Users/joeuser/node_modules:
"my_projects/my_sdk_folder/node_modules/forcedroid"
```

Uninstalling the Forceios Package

Instructions for uninstalling the forceios package vary with whether you installed the package globally or locally. If you installed the package globally, you can run the uninstall command from any folder. Be sure to use sudo and the -g option.

```
$ pwd
/Users/joeuser
$ sudo npm uninstall forceios -g
$
```

To uninstall a package that you installed locally, run the uninstall command from the folder where you installed the package. For example:

```
$ pwd
/Users/joeuser
cd <my_projects/my_sdk_folder>
npm uninstall forceios
```

If you try to uninstall a local installation from the wrong directory, you'll get an error message similar to this:

```
npm WARN uninstall not installed in /Users/joeuser/node_modules:
"my_projects/my_sdk_folder/node_modules/forceios"
```

Mobile SDK GitHub Repository

More adventurous developers who want to delve into the SDK, keep up with the latest changes, and possibly contribute to SDK development can clone the open source repository from GitHub. Using GitHub allows you to monitor source code in public pre-release development branches. In this scenario, both iOS and Android apps include the SDK source code, which is built along with your app.

You don't need to sign up for GitHub to access the Mobile SDK, but we think it's a good idea to be part of this social coding community. https://github.com/forcedotcom

You can always find the latest Mobile SDK releases in our public repositories:

- `https://github.com/forcedotcom/SalesforceMobileSDK-iOS`
- `https://github.com/forcedotcom/SalesforceMobileSDK-Android`

iOS: Cloning the Mobile SDK GitHub Repository (Optional)

1. Clone the Mobile SDK iOS repository to your local file system by issuing the following command at the OS X Terminal app: `git clone git://github.com/forcedotcom/SalesforceMobileSDK-iOS.git`

 Note: If you have the GitHub app for Mac OS X, click **Clone in Mac**. In your browser, navigate to the Mobile SDK iOS GitHub repository: `https://github.com/forcedotcom/SalesforceMobileSDK-iOS.`

2. In the OS X Terminal app, change to the directory where you installed the cloned repository. By default, this is the SalesforceMobileSDK-iOS directory.
3. Run the install script from the command line: `./install.sh`

Android: Cloning the Mobile SDK GitHub Repository (Optional)

1. In your browser, navigate to the Mobile SDK Android GitHub repository: https://github.com/forcedotcom/SalesforceMobileSDK-Android.
2. Clone the repository to your local file system by issuing the following command: `git clone git://github.com/forcedotcom/SalesforceMobileSDK-Android.git`

3. Open a command prompt in the directory where you installed the cloned repository, and run the install script from the command line: `./install.sh`

 Note: Windows users: Run `cscript install.vbs`.

Chapter 21

HTML5 Development

HTML5 lets you create lightweight mobile interfaces without installing software on the target device. Any mobile, touch or desktop device can access these mobile interfaces. HTML5 now supports advanced mobile functionality such as camera and GPS, making it simple to use these popular device features in your Salesforce mobile app.

You can create an HTML5 application that leverages the Force.com platform by:

*   Using Visualforce to deliver the HTML content
*   Using JavaScript remoting to invoke Apex controllers for fetching records from Force.com

In addition, you can repurpose HTML5 code in a standalone Mobile SDK hybrid app, and then distribute it through an app store. Converting to hybrid involves creating a Mobile SDK project to get the native container, then importing your HTML5 files into the project.

Getting Started

If you're already a web developer, you're set up to write HTML5 apps that access Salesforce. HTML5 apps can run in a browser and don't require Salesforce Mobile SDK. You simply call Salesforce APIs, capture the return values, and plug them into your logic and UI. The same advantages and challenges of running any app in a mobile browser apply. However, Salesforce and its partners provide tools that help streamline mobile web design and coding.

If you want to build your HTML5 app as standalone in a native mobile container and distribute it in the Apple AppStore or an Android marketplace, you'll need to create a hybrid app using the Mobile SDK.

Using HTML5 and JavaScript

You don't need a professional development environment such as Xcode or Microsoft Visual Studio to write HTML5 and JavaScript code. Most modern browsers include sophisticated developer features including HTML and JavaScript debuggers. You can literally write your application in a text editor and test it in a browser. However, you do need a good knowledge of currently available industry libraries that you can leverage to minimize your coding effort.

The recent growth in mobile development has led to an explosion of new web technology toolkits. Often, these JavaScript libraries are open-source and don't require licensing. Most of the tools provided by Salesforce for HTML5 development are built on these third-party technologies.

HTML5 Development Requirements

If you're planning to write a browser-based HTML5 Salesforce application, you don't need Salesforce Mobile SDK.

- You'll need a Force.com organization.
- Some knowledge of Apex and Visualforce is necessary.

 Note: This type of development uses Visualforce. You can't use Database.com.

HTML5 Development Tools

Salesforce provides a suite of tools that makes HTML5 development surprisingly simple. Some of these tools are built on popular open source JavaScript frameworks, while others are home-grown solutions. Also, a group of third-party, open source Mobile Packs brings the power of industry-standard architectures to Salesforce app development.

Introduction to Hybrid Development

Hybrid apps combine the ease of HTML5 Web app development with the power and features of the native platform. They run within the Salesforce Mobile Container, a native layer that translates the app into device-specific code.

Hybrid apps depend on HTML and JavaScript files. These files can be stored on the device or on the server.

- **Device**—Hybrid apps developed with `forcetk.mobilesdk` wrap a Web app inside the Salesforce Mobile Container. In this scenario, the JavaScript and HTML files are stored on the device.
- **Server** — Hybrid apps developed using Visualforce technology store their HTML and JavaScript files on the Salesforce server and are delivered through the Salesforce Mobile Container.

If you're creating libraries or sample apps for use by other developers, we recommend posting your public modules in a version-controlled online repository such as GitHub (https://github.com). For smaller examples such as snippets, GitHub provides *gist*, a low-overhead code sharing forum (https://gist.github.com).

iOS Hybrid Development

In order to develop hybrid applications, you'll need to meet some of the prerequisites for both the iOS native and the vanilla HTML5 scenarios.

1. Make sure you meet the requirements for HTML5 Development on page 263.
2. Follow the installation instructions for iOS on page 257.
3. After installing Mobile SDK for iOS, create a new hybrid app as described in Creating an iOS Project on page 268. For the `apptype` parameter:

   - Use `--apptype="hybrid_local"` for a hybrid app with all code in the local project. Put your HTML and JavaScript files in `${target.dir}/assets/www/`.
   - Use `--apptype="hybrid_remote"` for a hybrid app with code in a Visualforce app on the server

Android Hybrid Development

To develop hybrid applications, you'll need to meet some of the prerequisites for both the Android native and the plain HTML5 scenarios.

1. Make sure you meet the requirements for HTML5 Development on page 263.
2. Follow the installation instructions for Android Native on page 258.
3. After installing Mobile SDK for Android, create a new hybrid app as described in Creating an Android Project on page 280. For the `apptype` parameter:

- Use --apptype="hybrid_local" for a hybrid app with all code in the local project. Put your HTML and JavaScript files in ${target.dir}/assets/www/.
- Use --apptype="hybrid_remote" for a hybrid app with code in a Visualforce app on the server

Chapter 22

Native iOS Development

Salesforce Mobile SDK delivers libraries and sample Xcode projects for developing mobile apps on iOS.

Two main things that the iOS native SDK provides are:

- Automation of the OAuth2 login process, making it easy to integrate OAuth with your app.
- Access to the REST API with infrastructure classes (including third-party libraries such as RestKit) to make that access as easy as possible.

When you create a native app using the forceios application, your project starts as a fully functioning native sample app. This simple app allows you to connect to a Salesforce organization and run a simple query. It doesn't do much, but it lets you know things are working as designed.

iOS Native Quick Start

Use the following procedure to get started quickly.

1. Make sure you meet all of the native iOS requirements.
2. Install the Mobile SDK for iOS. If you prefer, you can install the Mobile SDK for iOS from GitHub instead.
3. Run the template app.

Native iOS Requirements

- Xcode—4.5 is the minimum, but we recommend the latest version.
- iOS 6.0 or higher.
- Mac OS X "Lion" or higher.
- Install the Mobile SDK.
- A Developer Edition organization with a connected app.

For important information on using various versions of XCode, see the Readme at https://github.com/forcedotcom/SalesforceMobileSDK-iOS/blob/master/readme.md.

Creating an iOS Project

To create a new app, use forceios again on the command line. You have two options for configuring your app.

- Configure your application options interactively as prompted by the forceios app.
- Specify your application options directly at the command line.

Specifying Application Options Interactively

To enter application options interactively, do one of the following:

- If you installed Mobile SDK globally, type `forceios create`.
- If you installed Mobile SDK locally, type *<forceios_path>*`/node_modules/.bin/forceios create`.

The forceios utility prompts you for each configuration value.

```
rwhitley-ltm1:Downloads rwhitley$ forceios create
Enter your application type (native, hybrid_remote, or hybrid_local): native
Enter your application name: MyNativeiOSApp
Enter your company identifier (com.mycompany): com.acme.goodapps
Enter your organization name (Acme, Inc.): GoodApps, Inc.
Enter the output directory for your app (defaults to the current directory):
Enter your Connected App ID (defaults to the sample app's ID):
Enter your Connected App Callback URI (defaults to the sample app's URI):
Creating app in /Users/rwhitley/Downloads/MyNativeiOSApp
Successfully created native app 'MyNativeiOSApp'.
```

Specifying Application Options Directly

You can also specify your configuration directly by typing the full forceios command string. To see usage information, type `forceios` without arguments. The list of available options displays:

```
$ forceios
Usage:
forceios create
    --apptype=<Application Type> (native, hybrid_remote, hybrid_local)

    --appname=<Application Name>
    --companyid=<Company Identifier> (com.myCompany.myApp)
    --organization=<Organization Name> (Your company's/organization's
name)
    --startpage=<App Start Page> (The start page of your remote app.
Only required for hybrid_remote)
    [--outputdir=<Output directory> (Defaults to the current working
directory)]
    [--appid=<Salesforce App Identifier> (The Consumer Key for your
app. Defaults to the sample app.)]
    [--callbackuri=<Salesforce App Callback URL (The Callback URL
for your app. Defaults to the sample app.)]
```

Using this information, type `forceios create`, followed by your options and values. For example:

```
$ forceios create --apptype="native" --appname="package-test"
--companyid="com.acme.mobile_apps" --organization="Acme Widgets,
Inc." --outputdir="PackageTest" --packagename="com.test.my_new_app"
```

Running the New Project in XCode

Apps created with the forceios template are ready to run "right out of the box". After the app creation script finishes, you can open and run the project in Xcode.

1. In Xcode, select **File** > **Open**.
2. Navigate to the output folder you specified.
3. Open your app's `xcodeproj` file.
4. Click the **Run** button in the upper left corner to see your new app in action.

forceios Command Parameters

These are the descriptions of the forceios command parameters:

Parameter Name	Description
`--apptype`	One of the following: • "native" • "hybrid_remote" (server-side hybrid app using VisualForce) • "hybrid_local" (client-side hybrid app that doesn't use VisualForce)
`--appname`	Name of your application
`--companyid`	A unique identifier for your company. This value is concatenated with the app name to create a unique app identifier for publishing your app to the App Store. For example, "com.myCompany.apps".
`--organization`	The formal name of your company. For example, "Acme Widgets, Inc.".
`--packagename`	Package identifier for your application. For example, "com.acme.app".
`--startpage`	(hybrid remote apps only) Server path to the remote start page. For example: `/apex/MyAppStartPage`.
`--outputdir`	(Optional) Folder in which you want your project to be created. If the folder doesn't exist, the script creates it. Defaults to the current working directory.

Parameter Name	Description
`--appid`	(Optional) Your connected app's Consumer Key. Defaults to the consumer key of the sample app. **Note:** If you don't specify the value here, you're required to change it in the app before you publish to the App Store.
`--callbackuri`	(Optional) Your connected app's Callback URL. Defaults to the callback URL of the sample app. **Note:** If you don't specify the value here, you're required to change it in the app before you publish to the App Store.
`--usesmartstore=true`	(Optional) Include only if you want to use SmartStore for offline data. Defaults to false if not specified.

Running the Xcode Project Template App

The Xcode project template includes a sample application you can run right away.

1. Press **Command-R** and the default template app runs in the iOS simulator.
2. On startup, the application starts the OAuth authentication flow, which results in an authentication page. Enter your credentials, and click **Login**.
3. Tap **Allow** when asked for permission

You should now be able to compile and run the sample project. It's a simple app that logs you into an org via OAuth2, issues a `select Name from Account` SOQL query, and displays the result in a `UITableView` instance.

Developing a Native iOS App

The Salesforce Mobile SDK for native iOS provides the tools you need to build apps for Apple mobile devices. Features of the SDK include:

- Classes and interfaces that make it easy to call the Salesforce REST API
- Fully implemented OAuth login and passcode protocols
- SmartStore library for securely managing user data offline

The native iOS SDK requires you to be proficient in Objective-C coding. You also need to be familiar with iOS application development principles and frameworks. If you're a newbie, Start Developing iOS Apps Today is a good place to begin learning. See Native iOS Requirements on page 268 for additional prerequisites.

In a few Mobile SDK interfaces, you're required to override some methods and properties. SDK header (.h) files include comments that indicate mandatory and optional overrides.

About Login and Passcodes

To access Salesforce objects from a Mobile SDK app, the user logs into an organization on a Salesforce server. When the login flow begins, your app sends its connected app configuration to Salesforce. Salesforce responds by posting a login screen to the mobile device.

Optionally, a Salesforce administrator can set the connected app to require a passcode after login. The Mobile SDK handles presentation of the login and passcode screens, as well as authentication handshakes. Your app doesn't have to do anything to display these screens. However, you do need to understand the login flow and how OAuth tokens are handled. See About PIN Security and OAuth2 Authentication Flow.

About Memory Management

Beginning in Mobile SDK 2.0, native iOS apps use Automatic Reference Counting (ARC) to manage object memory. You don't have to allocate and then remember to deallocate your objects. See the Mac Developer Library at https://developer.apple.com for ARC syntax, guidelines, and best practices.

Overview of Application Flow

When you create a project with the forceios application, your new app defines three classes: AppDelegate, InitialViewController, and RootViewController. The AppDelegate object loads InitialViewController as the first view to show. After the authentication process completes, the AppDelegate object displays the view associated with RootViewController as the entry point to your app.

The workflow demonstrated by the template app is merely an example. You can tailor your AppDelegate and supporting classes to achieve your desired workflow. You can retrieve data through REST API calls and display it, launch other views, perform services, and so on. Your app remains alive in memory until the user quits it, or until the device is rebooted.

Native iOS apps built with the Mobile SDK follow the same design as other iOS apps. The main.m source file creates a UIApplicationMain object that is the root object for the rest of the application. The UIApplicationMain constructor creates an AppDelegate object that manages the application lifecycle.

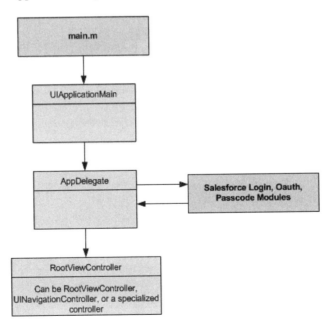

AppDelegate Class

The AppDelegate class is the true entry point for an iOS app. In Mobile SDK apps, AppDelegate implements the standard iOS UIApplicationDelegate interface. The

Mobile SDK template application for creating native iOS apps implements most of the Salesforce-specific startup functionality for you.

To customize the `AppDelegate` template, populate the following static variables with information from your Force.com Connected Application:

- `RemoteAccessConsumerKey`

```
static NSString * const RemoteAccessConsumerKey =
@"3MVG9Iu66FKeHhINkB1l7xt7kR8czFcCTUhqoA8Ol2LtfleYHOU4SqQRSEitYFDUpqRWooQ2.dBv_a1Dyu5xa";
```

- `OAuthRedirectURI`

```
static NSString * const OAuthRedirectURI =
@"testsfdc:///mobilesdk/detect/oauth/done";
```

OAuth functionality resides in an independent module. This separation makes it possible for you to use Salesforce authentication on demand. You can start the login process from within your `AppDelegate` implementation, or you can postpone login until it's actually required—for example, you can call OAuth from a sub-view.

Initialization

The following high-level overview shows how the `AppDelegate` initializes the template app. Keep in mind that you can change any of these details to suit your needs.

1. When the `[AppDelegate init]` message runs, it:

   - Initializes configuration items, such as Connected App identifiers, OAuth scopes, and so on.
   - Adds notification observers that listen to `SFAuthenticationManager`, `logoutInitiated`, and `loginHostChanged` notifications.

     The `logoutInitiated` notification lets the app respond when a user logs out voluntarily or is logged out involuntarily due to invalid credentials. The `loginHostChanged` notification lets the app respond when the user changes the login host (for example, from Production to Sandbox). See the `logoutInitiated:` and `loginHostChanged:` handler methods in the sample app.

   - Initializes authentication "success" and "failure" blocks for the `[SFAuthenticationManager loginWithCompletion:failure:]` message. These blocks determine what happens when the authentication process completes.

2. `application:didFinishLaunchingWithOptions:`, a
`UIApplicationDelegate` method, is called at app startup. The template app uses
this method to initialize the `UIWindow` property, display the initial view (see
`initializeAppViewState`), and initiate authentication. If authentication succeeds,
the `SFAuthenticationManager` executes `initialLoginSuccessBlock` (the
"success" block).

3. `initialLoginSuccessBlock` calls `setupRootViewController`, which creates
and displays the app's `RootViewController`.

You can customize any part of this process. At a minimum, change
`setupRootViewController` to display your own controller after authentication. You can
also customize `initializeAppViewState` to display your own launch page, or the
`InitialViewController` to suit your needs. You can also move the authentication details
to where they make the most sense for your app. The Mobile SDK does not stipulate when—or
if—actions must occur, but standard iOS conventions apply. For example, `self.window`
must have a `rootViewController` by the time
`application:didFinishLaunchingWithOptions:` completes.

UIApplication Event Handlers

You can also use the application delegate class to implement `UIApplication` event handlers.
Important event handlers that you might consider implementing or customizing include:

`application:didFinishLaunchingWithOptions:`

First entry point when your app launches. Called only when the process first starts (not
after a backgrounding/foregrounding cycle).

`applicationDidBecomeActive`

Called every time the application is foregrounded. The iOS SDK provides no default
parent behavior; if you use it, you must implement it from the ground up.

For a list of all `UIApplication` event handlers, see "UIApplicationDelegate Protocol
Reference" in the iOS Developer Library.

About View Controllers

In addition to the views and view controllers discussed with the `AppDelegate` class, Mobile
SDK exposes the `SFAuthorizingViewController` class. This controller displays the login
screen when necessary.

To customize the login screen display:

1. Override the `SFAuthorizingViewController` class to implement your custom display logic.
2. Set the `[SFAuthenticationManager sharedManager].authViewController` property to an instance of your customized class.

The most important view controller in your app is the one that manages the first view that displays, after login or—if login is postponed—after launch. This controller is called your root view controller because it controls everything else that happens in your app. The Mobile SDK for iOS project template provides a skeletal class named `RootViewController` that demonstrates the minimal required implementation.

If your app needs additional view controllers, you're free to create them as you wish. The view controllers used in Mobile SDK projects reveal some possible options. For example, the Mobile SDK iOS template project bases its root view class on the `UITableViewController` interface, while the `RestAPIExplorer` sample project uses the `UIViewController` interface. Your only technical limits are those imposed by iOS itself and the Objective-C language.

RootViewController Class

The `RootViewController` class exists only as part of the template project and projects generated from it. It implements the `SFRestDelegate` protocol to set up a framework for your app's interactions with the Salesforce REST API. Regardless of how you define your root view controller, it must implement `SFRestDelegate` if you intend to use it to access Salesforce data through the REST APIs.

RootViewController Design

As an element of a very basic app built with the Mobile SDK, the `RootViewController` class covers only the bare essentials. Its two primary tasks are:

- Use Salesforce REST APIs to query Salesforce data
- Display the Salesforce data in a table

To do these things, the class inherits `UITableViewController` and implements the `SFRestDelegate` protocol. The action begins with an override of the `UIViewController:viewDidLoad` method:

```
- (void)viewDidLoad
{
    [super viewDidLoad];
    self.title = @"Mobile SDK Sample App";

    //Here we use a query that should work on either Force.com or
Database.com
```

```
    SFRestRequest *request = [[SFRestAPI sharedInstance]
requestForQuery:@"SELECT Name FROM User LIMIT 10"];
    [[SFRestAPI sharedInstance] send:request delegate:self];
}
```

The iOS runtime calls `viewDidLoad` only once in the view's life cycle, when the view is first loaded into memory. The intention in this skeletal app is to load only one set of data into the app's only defined view. If you plan to create other views, you might need to perform the query somewhere else. For example, if you add a detail view that lets the user edit data shown in the root view, you'll want to refresh the values shown in the root view when it reappears. In this case, you can perform the query in a more appropriate method, such as `viewWillAppear`.

After calling the superclass method, this code sets the title of the view, then issues a REST request in the form of an asynchronous SOQL query. The query in this case is a simple SELECT statement that gets the Name property from each User object and limits the number of rows returned to ten. Notice that the `requestForQuery` and `send:delegate:` messages are sent to a singleton shared instance of the `SFRestAPI` class. Use this singleton object for all REST requests. This object uses authenticated credentials from the singleton `SFAccountManager` object to form and send authenticated requests.

The Salesforce REST API responds by passing status messages and, hopefully, data to the delegate listed in the send message. In this case, the delegate is the `RootViewController` object itself:

```
[[SFRestAPI sharedInstance] send:request delegate:self];
```

The `RootViewController` object can act as an `SFRestAPI` delegate because it implements the `SFRestDelegate` protocol. This protocol declares four possible response callbacks:

- `request:didLoadResponse:` — Your request was processed. The delegate receives the response in JSON format. This is the only callback that indicates success.
- `request:didFailLoadWithError:` — Your request couldn't be processed. The delegate receives an error message.
- `requestDidCancelLoad` — Your request was canceled by some external factor, such as administrator intervention, a network glitch, or another unexpected event. The delegate receives no return value.
- `requestDidTimeout` — The Salesforce server failed to respond in time. The delegate receives no return value.

The response arrives in one of the callbacks you've implemented in `RootViewController`. Place your code for handling Salesforce data in the `request:didLoadResponse:` callback. For example:

```
- (void)request:(SFRestRequest *)request
      didLoadResponse:(id)jsonResponse {
    NSArray *records = [jsonResponse objectForKey:@"records"];
    NSLog(@"request:didLoadResponse: #records: %d", records.count);
    self.dataRows = records;
```

```
        [self.tableView reloadData];
}
```

As the use of the `id` data type suggests, this code handles JSON responses in generic Objective-C terms. It addresses the `jsonResponse` object as an instance of `NSDictionary` and treats its records as an `NSArray` object. Because `RootViewController` implements `UITableViewController`, it's simple to populate the table in the view with extracted records.

A call to `request:didFailLoadWithError:` results from one of the following conditions:

- If you use invalid request parameters, you get a `kSFRestErrorDomain` error code. For example, if you pass nil to `requestForQuery:`, or you try to update a non-existent object.
- If an OAuth access token expires, the framework tries to obtain a new access token and, if successful, retries the query. If a request for a new access token or session ID fails, you get a `kSFOAuthErrorDomain` error code. For example, if the access token expires, and the OAuth refresh token is invalid. This scenario rarely occurs.
- If the low-level HTTP request fails, you get an `RKRestKitErrorDomain` error code. For example, if a Salesforce server becomes temporarily inaccessible.

The other callbacks are self-describing, and don't return an error code. You can choose to handle the result however you want: display an error message, write to the log, retry the request, and so on.

Chapter 23

Native Android Development

Salesforce Mobile SDK delivers libraries and sample projects for developing native mobile apps on Android.

The Android native SDK provides two main features:

- Automation of the OAuth2 login process, making it easy to integrate the process with your app.
- Access to the Salesforce REST API, with utility classes that simplify that access.

The Android Salesforce Mobile SDK includes several sample native applications. It also provides an `ant` target for quickly creating a new application.

Android Native Quick Start

Use the following procedure to get started quickly.

1. Make sure you meet all of the native Android requirements.
2. Install the Mobile SDK for Android.
3. At the command line, run the forcedroid application to create a new Android project, and then run that app in Eclipse or from the command line.
4. Set up sample projects in Eclipse.

Native Android Requirements

- Java JDK 6.
- Apache Ant 1.8 or later.

- Android SDK, version 21 or
  later—http://developer.android.com/sdk/installing.html.

   Note: For best results, install all previous versions of the Android SDK as well as your target version.

- Eclipse 3.6 or later. See http://developer.android.com/sdk/requirements.html for other versions.
- Android ADT (Android Development Tools) plugin for Eclipse, version 21 or later—http://developer.android.com/sdk/eclipse-adt.html#installing.
- In order to run the application in the Emulator, you need to set up at least one Android Virtual Device (AVD) that targets Platform 2.2 or above (we recommend 4.0 or above). To learn how to set up an AVD in Eclipse, follow the instructions at http://developer.android.com/guide/developing/devices/managing-avds.html.
- A Developer Edition organization with a connected app.

The SalesforceSDK project is built with the Android 3.0 (Honeycomb) library. The primary reason for this is that we want to be able to make a conditional check at runtime for file system encryption capabilities. This check is bypassed on earlier Android platforms; thus, you can still use the salesforcesdk.jar in earlier Android application versions, down to the mininum-supported Android 2.2.

Creating an Android Project

To create a new app, use forcedroid again on the command line. You have two options for configuring your app.

- Configure your application options interactively as prompted by the forcedroid app.
- Specify your application options directly at the command line.

Specifying Application Options Interactively

To enter application options interactively, do one of the following:

- If you installed Mobile SDK globally, type forcedroid create.
- If you installed Mobile SDK locally, type
  <forcedroid_path>/node_modules/.bin/forcedroid create.

The forcedroid utility prompts you for each configuration option.

```
rwhitley-ltm1:Downloads rwhitley$ forcedroid create
Enter your application type (native, hybrid_remote, or hybrid_local): native
Enter your application name: MyNativeAndroidApp
Enter the target directory of your app: /Users/rwhitley/Development/AndroidApps
Enter the package name for your app (com.mycompany.my_app): com.acme.goodapps
Do you want to use SmartStore in your app? [yes/NO] ('No' by default)
Adjusting SalesforceSDK library project reference in project.properties.
Renaming application class to MyNativeAndroidAppApp in source.
Renaming application to MyNativeAndroidApp in source.
Renaming package name to com.acme.goodapps in source.
Moving source files to proper package path.
Renaming the app class filename to MyNativeAndroidAppApp.java.

Your application project is ready in /Users/rwhitley/Development/AndroidApps.
```

Specifying Application Options Directly

You can also specify your configuration directly by typing the full forcedroid command string. To see usage information, type `forcedroid` without arguments. The list of available options displays:

```
$ node_modules/.bin/forcedroid
Usage:
forcedroid create
    --apptype=<Application Type> (native, hybrid_remote, hybrid_local)

    --appname=<Application Name>
    --targetdir=<Target App Folder>
    --packagename=<App Package Identifier> (com.my_company.my_app)
    --apexpage=<Path to Apex start page> (/apex/MyPage - Only
required/used for 'hybrid_remote')
    [--usesmartstore=<Whether or not to use SmartStore>
(--usesmartstore=true - false by default)]
```

Using this information, type `forcedroid create`, followed by your options and values. For example:

```
$ node_modules/.bin/forcedroid create --apptype="native"
--appname="package-test" --targetdir="PackageTest"
--packagename="com.test.my_new_app"
```

Building and Running Your App From the Command Line

After the command line returns to the command prompt, the forcedroid script prints instructions for running Android utilities to configure and clean your project. Follow these instructions only if you want to build and run your app from the command line.

1. Before building the new application, build the SalesforceSDK project by running the following commands at the command prompt:

    ```
    cd $SALESFORCE_SDK_DIR/native/SalesforceSDK
    $ANDROID_SDK_DIR/tools/android update project -p . -t <id>
    ant clean debug
    ```

where `SALESFORCE_SDK_DIR` points to your Salesforce SDK installation directory, and `ANDROID_SDK_DIR` points to your Android SDK directory.

 Note: The `-t <id>` parameter specifies API level of the target Android version. Use `android.bat list targets` to see the IDs for API versions installed on your system. See Native Android Requirements on page 279 for supported API levels.

2. Build the SmartStore project by running the following commands at the command prompt:

```
cd $SALESFORCE_SDK_DIR/hybrid/SmartStore
$ANDROID_SDK_DIR/tools/android update project -p . -t <id>
ant clean debug
```

where `SALESFORCE_SDK_DIR` points to your Salesforce SDK installation directory, and `ANDROID_SDK_DIR` points to your Android SDK directory.

3. To build the new application, run the following commands at the command prompt:

```
cd <your_project_directory>
$ANDROID_SDK_DIR/tools/android update project -p . -t <id>
ant clean debug
```

where `ANDROID_SDK_DIR` points to your Android SDK directory.

4. If your emulator is not running, use the Android AVD Manager to start it. If you're using a device, connect it.

5. Type the following command at the command prompt:

```
ant installd
```

 Note: You can safely ignore the following warning:

```
It seems that there are sub-projects. If you want to update
them please use the --subprojects parameter.
```

The Android project you created contains a simple application you can build and run.

Importing and Building Your App in Eclipse

The forcedroid script also prints instructions for running the new app in the Eclipse editor.

1. Launch Eclipse and select the `-targetdir` directory as your workspace directory.

2. Select **Window** > **Preferences**, choose the **Android** section, and enter the Android SDK location.

3. Click OK.

4. Select **File** > **Import** and select **General** > **Existing Projects into Workspace**.

5. Click Next.

6. Specify the `forcedroid/native` directory as your root directory. Next to the list that displays, click **Deselect All**, then browse the list and check the SalesforceSDK project.

7. If you set `-use_smartstore=true`, check the SmartStore project as well.

8. Click **Import**.

9. Repeat Steps 4–8. In Step 6, choose your target directory as the root, then select only your new project.

When you've finished importing the projects, Eclipse automatically builds your workspace. This process can take several minutes. When the status bar reports zero errors, you're ready to run the project.

1. In your Eclipse workspace, Control-click or right-click your project.
2. From the popup menu, choose **Run As** > **Android Application**.

Eclipse launches your app in the emulator or on your connected Android device.

forcedroid Command Parameters

These are descriptions of the forcedroid command parameters:

Parameter Name	Description
`--apptype`	One of the following: • "native" • "hybrid_remote" (server-side hybrid app using VisualForce) • "hybrid_local" (client-side hybrid app that doesn't use VisualForce)
`--appname`	Name of your application

Parameter Name	Description
`--targetdir`	Folder in which you want your project to be created. If the folder doesn't exist, the script creates it.
`--packagename`	Package identifier for your application (for example, "com.acme.app").
`--apexpage`	(hybrid remote apps only) Server path to the Apex start page. For example: `/apex/MyAppStartPage`.
`--usesmartstore=true`	(Optional) Include only if you want to use SmartStore for offline data. Defaults to false if not specified.

Setting Up Sample Projects in Eclipse

The repository you cloned has other sample apps you can run. To import those into Eclipse:

1. Launch Eclipse and select `–target_dir` as your workspace directory.
2. If you haven't done so already, select **Window** > **Preferences**, choose the **Android** section, and enter the Android SDK location. Click OK.
3. Select **File** > **Import** and select **General** > **Existing Projects into Workspace**.
4. Click Next.
5. Select `forcedroid/native` as your root directory and import the projects listed in Android Project Files.

Android Project Files

Inside the $NATIVE_DIR, you will find several projects:

1. `SalesforceSDK`—The SalesforceSDK, which provides support for OAuth2 and REST API calls
2. `test/SalesforceSDKTest`—Tests for the SalesforceSDK project

3. `TemplateApp`—Template used when creating new native applications using SalesforceSDK

4. `test/TemplateAppTest`—Tests for the TemplateApp project

5. `SampleApps/RestExplorer`—App using SalesforceSDK to explore the REST API calls

6. `SampleApps/NativeSqlAggregator` —A native app that uses SmartStore

Developing a Native Android App

The native Android version of the Salesforce Mobile SDK empowers you to create rich mobile apps that directly use the Android operating system on the host device. To create these apps, you need to understand Java and Android development well enough to write code that uses Mobile SDK native classes.

Android Application Structure

Typically, native Android apps that use the Mobile SDK require:

- An application entry point class that extends `android.app.Application`.
- At least one activity that extends `android.app.Activity`.

With the Mobile SDK, you:

- Create a stub class that extends `android.app.Application`.
- Implement `onCreate()` in your `Application` stub class to call `SalesforceSDKManager.initNative()`.
- Extend `SalesforceActivity`, `SalesforceListActivity`, or `SalesforceExpandableListActivity`. This extension is optional but recommended.

The top-level `SalesforceSDKManager` class implements passcode functionality for apps that use passcodes, and fills in the blanks for those that don't. It also sets the stage for login, cleans up after logout, and provides a special event watcher that informs your app when a system-level account is deleted. OAuth protocols are handled automatically with internal classes.

The `SalesforceActivity`, `SalesforceListActivity`, and `SalesforceExpandableListActivity` classes offer free handling of application pause and resume events and related passcode management. We recommend that you extend one of these classes for all activities in your app—not just the main activity. If you use a different base class for an activity, you're responsible for replicating the pause and resume protocols found in `SalesforceActivity`.

Within your activities, you interact with Salesforce objects by calling Salesforce REST APIs. The Mobile SDK provides the `com.salesforce.androidsdk.rest` package to simplify the REST request and response flow.

You define and customize user interface layouts, image sizes, strings, and other resources in XML files. Internally, the SDK uses an R class instance to retrieve and manipulate your resources. However, the Mobile SDK makes its resources directly accessible to client apps, so you don't need to write code to manage these features.

Native API Packages

Salesforce Mobile SDK groups native APIs into seven packages. Here's a quick overview of these packages and points of interest within them.

Package name	Description
app	Contains `SalesforceSDKManager`, the entry point class for all Mobile SDK applications. This package also contains app utility classes for internal use.
auth	Internal use only. Handles login, OAuth authentication, and HTTP access.
phonegap	Internal classes used by hybrid applications to create a bridge between native code and Javascript code. Includes plugins that implement Mobile SDK Javascript libraries. If you want to implement your own Javascript plugin within an SDK app, extend `ForcePlugin` and implement the abstract `execute()` function. See ForcePlugin Class.
rest	Provides classes for handling REST API activities. These classes manage the communication with the Salesforce instance and handle the HTTP protocol for your REST requests. See `ClientManager` and `RestClient` for information on available synchronous and asynchronous methods for sending requests.
security	Internal classes that handle passcodes and encryption. If you provide your own key, you can use the `Encryptor` class to generate hashes. See `Encryptor`.
ui, ui.sfhybrid, ui.sfnative	Mostly internal classes that define the UI activities common to all Mobile SDK apps. These packages include `SalesforceActivity`, `SalesforceListActivity`, and

Package name	Description
	`SalesforceExpandableListActivity`, which are intended to serve individually as potential base classes for all app activities.
`util`	Contains utility and test classes. These classes are mostly for internal use, with some notable exceptions.
	• You can register an instance of the `TokenRevocationReceiver` class to detect when an OAuth access token has been revoked.
	• You can implement the `EventObserver` interface to eavesdrop on any event type.
	• The `EventsListenerQueue` class is useful for implementing your own tests.
	• Browse the `EventsObservable` source code to see a list of all supported event types.

Using REST APIs

To query, describe, create, or update data from a Salesforce org, native apps call Salesforce REST APIs. Salesforce REST APIs honor SOQL strings and can accept and return data in either JSON or XML format. REST APIs are fully documented at REST API Developer's Guide. You can find links to related Salesforce development documentation at the Force.com developer documentation website..

With Android native apps, you do only minimal coding to access Salesforce data through REST calls. The classes in the `com.salesforce.androidsdk.rest` package initialize the communication channels and encapsulate low-level HTTP plumbing. These classes include:

• `ClientManager`—Serves as a factory for RestClient instances. It also handles account logins and handshakes with the Salesforce server. Implemented by the Mobile SDK.
• `RestClient`—Handles protocol for sending REST API requests to the Salesforce server. Don't directly create instances of `RestClient`. Instead, call the `ClientManager.getRestClient()` method. Implemented by the Mobile SDK.

- `RestRequest`—Formats REST API requests from the data your app provides. Also serves as a factory for instances of itself. Don't directly create instances of `RestRequest`. Instead, call an appropriate `RestRequest` static getter function such as `RestRequest.getRequestForCreate()`. Implemented by the SDK.
- `RestResponse`—Formats the response content in the requested format, returns the formatted response to your app, and closes the content stream. The `RestRequest` class creates instances of `RestResponse` and returns them to your app through your implementation of the `RestClient.AsyncRequestCallback` interface. Implemented by the SDK.

The `RestRequest` class natively handles the standard Salesforce data operations offered by the Salesforce REST and SOAP APIs. Supported operations are:

Operation	Parameters	Description
Versions	None	Returns Salesforce version metadata
Resources	API version	Returns available resources for the specified API version, including resource name and URI
Metadata	API version, object type	
DescribeGlobal	API version	Returns a list of all available objects in your org and their metadata
Describe	API version, object type	Returns a description of a single object type
Create	API version, object type, map of field names to value objects	Creates a new record in the specified object
Retrieve	API version, object type, object ID, list of fields	Retrieves a record by object ID
Update	API version, object type, object ID, map of field names to value objects	Updates an object with the given map
Upsert	API version, object type, external ID field, external ID, map of field names to value objects	Updates or inserts an object from external data, based on whether the external ID

Operation	Parameters	Description
		currently exists in the external ID field
Delete	API version, object type, object ID	Deletes the object of the given type with the given ID

To obtain an appropriate `RestRequest` instance, call the `RestRequest` static method that matches the operation you want to perform. Here are the RestRequest static methods.

- `getRequestForCreate()`
- `getRequestForDelete()`
- `getRequestForDescribe()`
- `getRequestForDescribeGlobal()`
- `getRequestForMetadata()`
- `getRequestForQuery()`
- `getRequestForResources()`
- `getRequestForRetrieve()`
- `getRequestForSearch()`
- `getRequestForUpdate()`
- `getRequestForUpsert()`
- `getRequestForVersions()`

These methods return a `RestRequest` object which you pass to an instance of `RestClient`. The `RestClient` class provides synchronous and asynchronous methods for sending requests: `sendSync()` and `sendAsync()`. Use `sendAsync()` when you're sending a request from a UI thread. Use `sendSync()` only on non-UI threads, such as a service or a worker thread spawned by an activity.

Here's the basic procedure for using the REST classes on a UI thread:

1. Create an instance of `ClientManager`.

    a. Use the `SalesforceSDKManager.getInstance().getAccountType()` method to obtain the value to pass as the second argument of the `ClientManager` constructor.

    b. For the `LoginOptions` parameter of the `ClientManager` constructor, call `SalesforceSDKManager.GetInstance().getLoginOptions()`.

2. Implement the `ClientManager.RestClientCallback` interface.

3. Call `ClientManager.getRestClient()` to obtain a `RestClient` instance, passing it an instance of your `RestClientCallback` implementation. This code from the `native/SampleApps/RestExplorer` sample app implements and instantiates `RestClientCallback` inline:

```
String accountType =
SalesforceSDKManager.getInstance().getAccountType();

LoginOptions loginOptions =
SalesforceSDKManager.getInstance().getLoginOptions();
// Get a rest client
new ClientManager(this, accountType, loginOptions,
SalesforceSDKManager.getInstance().shouldLogoutWhenTokenRevoked()).getRestClient(this,

  new RestClientCallback() {
    @Override
    public void authenticatedRestClient(RestClient client) {
      if (client == null) {

SalesforceSDKManager.getInstance().logout(ExplorerActivity.this);

        return;
      }
      // Cache the returned client
      ExplorerActivity.this.client = client;
    }
  });
```

4. Call a static `RestRequest()` getter method to obtain the appropriate `RestRequest` object for your needs. For example, to get a description of a Salesforce object:

```
request = RestRequest.getRequestForDescribe(apiVersion,
objectType);
```

5. Pass the `RestRequest` object you obtained in the previous step to `RestClient.sendAsync()` or `RestClient.sendSync()`. If you're on a UI thread and therefore calling `sendAsync()`:

   a. Implement the `ClientManager.AsyncRequestCallback` interface.
   b. Pass an instance of your implementation to the `sendAsync()` method.
   c. Receive the formatted response through your `ASyncRequestCallback.onSuccess()` method.

The following code implements and instantiates `ASyncRequestCallback` inline:

```
private void sendFromUIThread(RestRequest restRequest) {
  client.sendAsync(restRequest, new AsyncRequestCallback() {
```

```
private long start = System.nanoTime();
@Override
public void onSuccess(RestRequest request, RestResponse result) {
  try
  {
    // Do something with the result
  }
  catch (Exception e) {
    printException(e);
  }
  EventsObservable.get().notifyEvent(EventType.RenditionComplete);
}
@Override
public void onError(Exception exception)
{
  printException(exception);
  EventsObservable.get().notifyEvent(EventType.RenditionComplete);

}
});
```

If you're calling the `sendSync()` method from a service, use the same procedure with the following changes:

1. To obtain a `RestClient` instance call `ClientManager.peekRestClient()` instead of `ClientManager.getRestClient()`.

2. Retrieve your formatted REST response from the `sendSync()` method's return value.

Resources

Search on the Salesforce Developer's Network at `http://developer.salesforce.com/docs` for the following resources on Salesforce Mobile SDK.

- Salesforce Mobile SDK Development Guide
- Platform Mobile Services site
- Mobile SDK release notes
- Mobile development forums

MARKETING CLOUD

Chapter 24

ExactTarget API

ExactTarget's core offerings include an award-winning product, called Fuel, that powers multi-channel marketing programs for many of the world's top brands. The foundation of the ExactTarget Marketing Cloud, Fuel is open to third-party development, enabling you to build upon, extend, and integrate with ExactTarget's industry-leading digital marketing products.

If you're reading this, you're probably a developer who works for an ExactTarget customer or partner, and you're probably wondering how to get started. The next few sections will introduce you to Fuel and how to leverage the ExactTarget Marketing Cloud to build innovative customer touchpoints.

- **Using Fuel to Send Email** — provides a guided tutorial for using Fuel to create a highly personalized email communication that utilizes a number of ExactTarget messaging, data, and content technologies.
- **Email Communication as the Universal Medium** — goes deeper into the capabilities and use cases available for developers sending email through Fuel.
- **SMS Communication to Mobile Phones** — details the SMS capabilities that Fuel provides to communicate to mobile phones.
- **Push Communication to Mobile Apps** — details the Push messaging capabilities that Fuel provides to communicate to mobile applications.
- **Resources** — points you to detailed product documentation and other information on the above topics.

Using Fuel to Send Email

One of the most common uses of Fuel is to send email. This section walks you through the process of sending an email to a list of subscribers. This example is designed to illustrate many of the basic concepts that you will need to use Fuel programatically to send email, both promotionally and transactionally.

Specifically, we will show you how to add attributes associated with purchase activity to the subscriber data model. We will show you how to create a list, add a subscriber to that list, create an email, send the email to the list, and get back tracking events from the send, all programatically. Finally, we will look at how you can use content scripting to build a highly personalized message using additional data sets.

Subscribers, Attributes, Lists, and Emails

Before we get started, we need to introduce a few key Marketing Cloud concepts: subscribers, profile attributes, lists, and emails. These four concepts are the basis of any email communications initiative tying contacts, subscription, and content together.

Subscribers are contacts that have an email address and status. A subscriber can be active, unsubscribed, or held. If a subscriber is active, the Marketing Cloud can send email to that email address. If a subscriber is unsubscribed, the Marketing Cloud will prevent email from being sent to that email address. If a subscriber is held, previous attempts to send email to that email address were unsuccessful.

Subscribers are contained in lists. Lists represent the simplest way to send email to multiple subscribers. Every account in the Marketing Cloud has an "All Subscribers" list that, as the name implies, contains all subscribers on all lists. All lists in an account are considered children of the "All Subscribers" list, so if a subscriber is unsubscribed on the "All Subscribers" list, they are considered unsubscribed on all lists, and the Marketing Cloud will not allow email to be sent to that subscriber.

Profile attributes are arbitrary name/value pairs that can be associated with each subscriber. For example, you might store the subscriber's first name in a profile attribute called FirstName that enables you to address your email to that subscriber ("Hi %%FirstName%%!"). Profile attributes exist at the "All Subscribers" list level and apply to all child lists that are created. You can create up to 200 profile attributes in an account. A more flexible attribute model exists with data extensions. Data extensions are described at the end of the chapter when we personalize our message even further.

Emails are delivered to subscribers on lists. Every email is a template that can be personalized with substitution strings represented by your profile attributes. The concept of a template in the Marketing Cloud is tied to the workflow of how an email goes from being a skeleton of structure to being a fully formed email capable of production sending against a production data source. You will create an email in the tutorial using our Fuel SDKs.

The tutorial will use the Fuel SDKs to configure an organization with a new profile attribute, list and subscriber. Next, you will create a new email message and send that email message to the list. Finally, you will get a tracking result back for the send that you initiated.

A summary of the objects we are going to interact with via Fuel to send email.

Before starting to code, you need to set up your development environment.

Setting Up Your Development Environment

The first step is to create an account on Code@ExactTarget, ExactTarget's developer community (http://code.exacttarget.com).

Code@ExactTarget (Code@ for short) is the central source of information about Fuel and the home of our API and other developer documentation. You can read much more about the technologies introduced in this book at Code@.

Code@ also features a powerful question and answer forum that you can use to get your questions answered by ExactTarget Developer Advocates and other members of the developer community.

Finally, Code@ is the home of App Center, the tool we'll be using to create and manage our app and get access tokens for authenticating with the API. You'll need an account to use App Center, so go ahead and create one and log in to it.

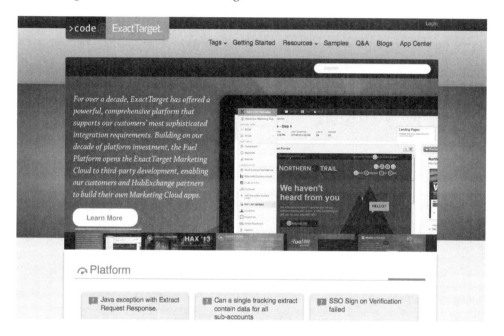

Fuel SDKs

Next, you should download the Fuel SDK for your preferred environment. You can find the SDKs under the Code@ Resources dropdown or directly at https://code.exacttarget.com/sdks.

The Fuel SDKs are wrappers around Fuel's APIs that enable developers to integrate with those APIs using native language constructs. There are currently Fuel SDKs available for Java, .NET, PHP, Python, and Ruby. We'll be using the PHP SDK to build our app, but all Fuel SDKs employ common patterns, so you'll be able to adapt the example code to any of the other SDKs fairly easily.

The SDKs provide protocol agnostic interfaces across Fuel's SOAP and REST APIs as well as automated token management and other features designed to reduce development time. Our SOAP API is our oldest and most comprehensive API, but its functionality is limited to the ExactTarget email application and, like all SOAP APIs, it is fairly heavyweight. Our REST API is newer and less comprehensive, but it exposes a broader set of Marketing Cloud capabilities and is much more lightweight and easy to use (and is getting more comprehensive with every release).

By using the SDKs, you get the best of both worlds. And, in most cases, it is possible to accomplish the same task with far less code using the SDKs. Finally, we have encapsulated common patterns and best practices directly in to the SDKs. So they are the preferred way to integrate with the Fuel Platform.

If there's no SDK for your preferred environment, or if you'd rather not use an SDK, don't worry—you can always access the APIs directly. We'll show you a few examples of how to do that, but we won't be able to be comprehensive. You can find much more information about how to use the API directly at Code@ExactTarget.

App Center

Once you've created an account on Code@ExactTarget, logged in to that account, and downloaded the appropriate Fuel SDK (if applicable), the next step is to connect an application to ExactTarget using App Center. App Center is the central development console for building applications and integrating with the Fuel Platform. An extension to the Code@ExactTarget developer community, App Center enables ExactTarget developers to obtain API keys for authenticating with Fuel APIs as well as create and manage their Marketing Cloud apps.

App Center is accessed via the Code@ExactTarget top menu bar.

1. Create a new account on Code@. Just click the **Login** link in the upper-right corner to get to the next screen.
2. Log in if you already have a user account, or create a new account. Once you log in or create an account, notice that your account does not currently have access to the App Center.
3. The App Center button appears in your main navigation bar once logged in. You can now proceed with the registration process. Simply fill out the form and click **Continue**.
4. Accept the End User License Agreement to proceed.

After you accept the EULA, you can create your first app.

Each app in App Center represents an application that has been connected to the Fuel Platform. There are currently three types of connected apps.

Server-to-Server	Marketing Cloud	MobilePush
A Server-to-Server App should be created when you want to use Fuel's APIs to automate tasks or integrate business systems.	Marketing Cloud Apps are apps that live within the ExactTarget Marketing Cloud and are launched via the Marketing Cloud's app menu.	MobilePush Apps are apps built for the iOS, Android, or Blackberry mobile platforms that use MobilePush to communicate with their users via push messages.

- **Server-to-Server Apps** are secure, API-based server-to-server integrations. A Server-to-Server App should be created when you want to use Fuel's APIs to automate tasks or integrate business systems. Server-to-Server Apps utilize an OAuth2 client credentials flow to acquire access tokens directly from Fuel's authentication service.

- **Marketing Cloud Apps** are apps that live within the ExactTarget Marketing Cloud and are launched via the Marketing Cloud's app menu. Marketing Cloud Apps can be custom apps built by your organization or apps installed from the ExactTarget AppExchange. Marketing Cloud Apps utilize a JSON Web Token (JWT) to acquire access tokens on behalf of logged in users.

- **MobilePush Apps** are apps built for the iOS, Android, or Blackberry mobile platforms that use MobilePush to communicate with their users via push messages (for more information about MobilePush, see the ExactTarget corporate web site at http://www.exacttarget.com/products/mobile-marketing). MobilePush Apps are classified as consumer-grade applications and utilize long-lived limited access tokens.

Connect an App

Since we are building an API-based integration with ExactTarget, we will be creating a Server-to-Server App, so click "Server-to-Server App". Give the app a name and description, and specify "myapp" as your package name (packages are identifiers that uniquely identify the app in the Fuel Platform).

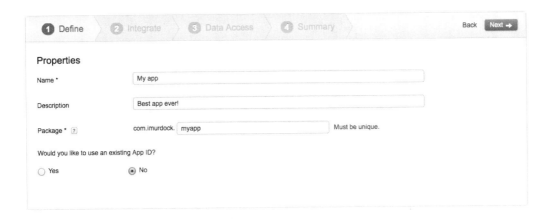

Link Your App to an Account

Next, you need to link your app to an ExactTarget Marketing Cloud account. This is the account your app will access when it makes API calls and can be thought of as your app's development environment.

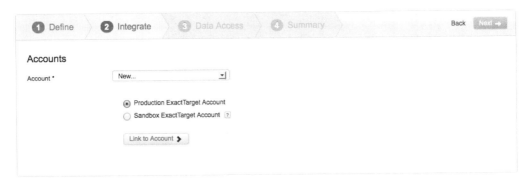

The first time you link an app to an account, you need to select "New…" from the dropdown menu. App Center saves account references, so if you want to use the same account for future apps, you can select that account from the dropdown menu rather than linking a new one.

When you link an account, you need to tell App Center what type of account it is. A **Production ExactTarget Account** is what most developers have access to and use for development purposes. A **Sandbox ExactTarget Account** is a special type of account that some organizations have purchased that is used in conjunction with a production account for testing. If you're not sure which type of account to choose, you should choose Production ExactTarget Account.

After you have selected what type of ExactTarget account you want to link to your app, click the "Link to Account" button. A new browser window will open showing the Marketing Cloud login screen asking for a username and password. You may need to ask your administrator to create a user account for you if you do not have existing credentials.

Note: Don't confuse the username and password you used to log into Code@ExactTarget with Marketing Cloud credentials—they're different!

Specify Account Features

Upon completion of the login process, you will automatically be moved to the next step of the wizard. In this step, you need to tell App Center what account features your app will need to use. Your app will only be able to access the account features you specify here, and for other app types, like Marketing Cloud Apps, the users of your app must also have access to those features to use your app in their Marketing Cloud account.

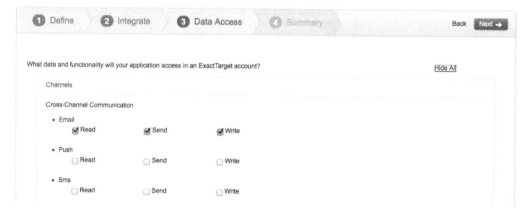

Our app will need to modify the subscriber data model, create lists, create email content and send email content. So, in this step, you should give the app access to the following assets and operations.

- **Channels - Email**: Read, Write, Send
- **Contacts - List and Subscribers** : Read, Write
- **Data - Data Extensions**: Read, Write
- **Data - Tracking Events**: Read

Finishing Up

After completing this step of the wizard, you'll be shown a summary screen. If everything looks good, click **Finish**.

Among other things, the summary screen shows you the connected app's OAuth client credentials, which will be used with the Fuel Platform's authentication service to get OAuth tokens that will authenticate our app with other Fuel APIs.

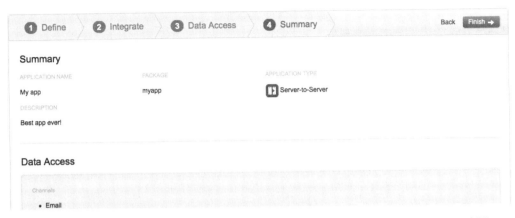

The Courtesy Limit is a soft capped limit. If your app needs to make more than 50,000 API calls per day, it will not be prevented from making them. However, the Fuel Platform monitors the usage of each app and can rate limit or throttle apps that are either intentionally or accidentally abusing Marketing Cloud resources.

 Note: The connected app's OAuth client credentials represent pre-authorized access to the account granted through the authorization step of the App Center wizard. You should NEVER expose the client secret on the client side via JavaScript, and you should ALWAYS take steps to ensure that the client secret is stored securely in your application, as knowledge of the client secret will give anyone full access to the linked account!

You can get back to the app's summary screen at any time from the App Center main window.

Now your application is connected to a Marketing Cloud account and you have OAuth credentials to that account. Let's write some code!

Building the App

As mentioned previously, we'll be building our app using the PHP SDK. The other SDKs use similar patterns, so you can apply the example code to the other SDKs.

If you haven't already done so, download the PHP SDK from https://code.exacttarget.com/sdks. To configure the SDK, you'll need to add your OAuth credentials to config.php (the SDK contains a template file you can use to create config.php). Note that it's safe to include the client ID and client secret in `config.php`, because `config.php` is hosted server-side and not exposed to the client.

```php
<?php
return array(
    'appsignature' => 'none',
        'clientid' => 'YOUR_CLIENT_ID_FROM_APP_CENTER',
        'clientsecret' => 'YOUR_CLIENT_SECRET_FROM_APP_CENTER',
        'defaultwsdl' =>
'https://webservice.exacttarget.com/etframework.wsdl'
);
?>
```

Initialize the Fuel SDK

Now that the PHP SDK is configured, the first step is to initialize the SDK by instantiating an ET_Client object.

```php
require('ET_Client.php');

$myclient = new ET_Client();
```

The ET_Client object is the central object in all Fuel SDKs and performs a number of tasks for you automatically, including acquiring and refreshing OAuth access tokens using the client ID and client secret you specify in config.php.

Create a Profile Attribute (a.k.a. Define your Subscriber Data Model)

Next, let's create a profile attribute to hold the subscriber's first name so we can personalize the email to that subscriber. Here's how to create a profile attribute using the SDK:

```php
$profileAttribute = new ET_ProfileAttribute();
$profileAttribute->authStub = $myclient;

$profileAttribute->props = array("Name" => "FirstName", "PropertyType"
```

```
=> "string", "Description" => "The subscriber's first name");

$response = $profileAttribute->post();
```

This is a typical interaction with a Fuel SDK object and highlights the patterns common to all Fuel SDKs.

1. Instantiate the object you want to interact with (in this case, `ET_ProfileAttribute`).
2. Supply the ExactTarget account context via the `authStub` property on the object (`$profileAttribute->authStub = $myclient`).
3. Set the appropriate properties that govern the operation (in this case, we want to create a profile attribute called `FirstName`, which is a string and contains the subscriber's first name).
4. Perform a REST-like operation (`get`, `post`, `patch`, or `delete`) on the object depending on whether you want to retrieve, create, update, or delete it. In our example, we're creating a profile attribute, so we perform a `post`.

Create a List

Next, we'll create a list to hold our subscribers using the same pattern we used to create a profile attribute.

```
$list = new ET_List();
$list->authStub = $myclient;

$list->props = array("ListName" => "Important Customers");

$response = $list->post();
```

When an object is created, a unique identifier is assigned to that object. The unique identifier can be found in the response object's NewID property. We save that value in a variable so we can refer to the list in later calls:

```
$listID = $response->results[0]->NewID;
```

Add a Subscriber to the List

Next, we'll create a subscriber and add that subscriber to the list we just created. For the `FirstName` property, use your email address. Note how we pass `$listID` to reference the list we just created.

```
$subscriber = new ET_Subscriber();
$subscriber->authStub = $myclient;

$subscriber->props = array("EmailAddress" => "myemail@mycompany.com",
  "Lists" => array("ID" => $listID));
```

```
// specify profile attributes
$subscriber->props['Attributes'] = array(array('Name' => 'FirstName',
 'Value' => 'MyFirstName'));

$response = $subscriber->post();
```

Note that if your account is enabled with `SubscriberKey`, the previous code sample will not work unless you specify a `SubscriberKey` attribute in `props`. For more information about `SubscriberKey`, please see http://help.exacttarget.com/en/documentation/exacttarget/subscribers/subscriber_key.

Create an Email

Next, we'll create an email to send to the list. As when we created a list, we save the ID of the email in a variable so we can refer to it in later calls:

```
$email = new ET_Email();
$email->authStub = $myclient;

// store the email in a variable
$email = <<<EMAIL
<html>
<body>
<p>%%FirstName%%,</p>

<p>We're pretty sure you would love our products!</p>

<small>
  <p>This email was sent by:</p>

  <p>
    %%Member_Busname%%
    <br />
    %%Member_Addr%%
    <br />
    %%Member_City%%, %%Member_State%%, %%Member_PostalCode%%
    <br />
    %%Member_Country%%
  </p>

  <a href="%%profile_center_url%%">Profile Center</a>
  <br />
  <a href ="%%unsub_center_url%%">Unsubscribe</a></small>

<custom name="opencounter" type="tracking">
</body>
</html>
EMAIL;

$email->props = array("CustomerKey" => "123", "Name" => "Important
Purchases Dreamforce Edition", "Subject" => "Hi %%FirstName%%, we
think you will like this", "HTMLBody" => $emailbody, "IsHTMLPaste"
=> true);
```

```
$response = $email->post();

$emailID = $response->results[0]->NewID;
```

This operation is much more complex than previous operations. Let's use this call to highlight a few important concepts and features.

1. We've added a property called `CustomerKey` to the `ET_Email` object. This property is on every object in ExactTarget, and you can use it to attach your own identifier to an object. This makes it easier to integrate ExactTarget with your existing infrastructure.

2. A customer opening an email is an important touchpoint. To have ExactTarget track when customers open HTML email, we've added the following tag to the email body: `<custom name="opencounter" type="tracking">`.

3. Both the email subject (the `Subject` property) and the email body (the `HTMLBody` property) contain substitution strings, denoted by `%%` on either side of the substitution string name. Some of these substitution strings are user-defined in profile attributes (like `FirstName`), and others are automatically resolved by ExactTarget.

User-defined substitution strings enable you to personalize your email to the recipient. A good email subject line is critical in creating a successful customer touchpoint, as a good subject line increases the chance that the recipient will open an email. Subject lines in ExactTarget can be personalized in a number of ways, including using substitution strings (for example, "Thanks for your purchase, `%%FirstName%%`!").

Once the recipient has opened your email, the content of the email will determine whether or not the recipient will engage (e.g., buy a product) or disengage (e.g., unsubscribe). In addition to substitution strings, ExactTarget provides many features to help you innovate and make your content more relevant, including the AMPscript content scripting language, HTTPGet content scraping, and sophisticated dynamic content functionality.

Substitution strings are automatically resolved by ExactTarget make it easy for you to ensure your content complies with CAN-SPAM laws for commercial sending. To help marketers comply with CAN-SPAM, ExactTarget requires every email to contain the following personalization strings:

```
%%Member_Busname%%
%%Member_Addr%%
%%Member_City%%
%%Member_State%%
%%Member_PostalCode%%
%%Member_Country%%
```

These substitution strings contain the elements of the sending organization's physical address, as required by CAN-SPAM, and will be automatically filled in by ExactTarget based on the account information.

In addition, ExactTarget requires every email to contain a link to a profile center to manage subscription preferences, as well as a link to a URL where the recipient of the email can opt out of future communications. ExactTarget builds and hosts these profile centers. To comply with CAN-SPAM, all you have to do is include the following substitution strings..

```
%%profile_center_url%%
%%unsub_center_url%%
```

Finally, you'll note the `"IsHTMLPaste"` => `true` property. We set this property to `true` so users of the Marketing Cloud UI can only edit the content using the HTML editor. By default, and when `IsHTMLPaste` is set to `false`, the WYSIWYG editor will be the editing experience, but the content must provide templating hooks to be editable. If you're doing an API-only integration, you don't need to specify this value.

Send the Email

Now that we've created a list, added a subscriber to that list, and created an email to send to that list, we're ready to send our first email! Sending an email using the Fuel SDK only takes one line.

```
$response = new ET_Post($myclient, 'Send', array("List"=> array("ID"
=> $listID), "Email" => array("ID" => $emailID)));

$sendID = $response->results[0]->NewID;
```

Note that this example uses a slightly different SDK pattern—rather than calling a method on the email object, the code is calling an SDK method directly.

As before, we save the send ID in a variable. The send ID can be used to retrieve summary and raw individual statistics about the send, get the status of the send, pause the send, cancel it, or restart it. Let's take a look at one example of receiving information about a send.

Retrieve Statistics

Retrieving event data from ExactTarget is how you can measure the success of any customer touchpoint. ExactTarget captures a variety of events for each send.

Delivery events related to the send enable you to know if your data is of good quality. These events are `SentEvent`, which indicates that the email was rendered and sent; and `BounceEvent`, which indicates that the email bounced (was not delivered) either synchronously or asynchronously.

Engagement events related to the send enable you to know how a customer engaged with your email content. These events are `UnsubEvent`, which indicates that the recipient unsubscribed from the list either by spam complaint, reply mail management, or profile center; `OpenEvent`, which indicates that the recipient opened the email (this only works for HTML emails that include the tracking pixel above, and after the recipient allows images to load); and

`ClickEvent`, which indicates that the recipient clicked on a link in the email (this only works if ExactTarget wraps the links).

In this example, we get all of the SentEvents for the send we just performed and print them to the browser window or console.

```
$sentEvent = new ET_SentEvent();
$sentEvent->authStub = $myclient;

$sentEvent->props = array("SubscriberKey", "EventDate");

$sentEvent->filter = array("Property" => "SendID", "SimpleOperator"
 => "equals", "Value" => array($sendID));

$response = $sentEvent->get();

// Loop through the first page of results
for ($x=0; $x<count($response->results); $x++) {
 print_r('SubscriberKey:
'.$response->results[$x]->SubscriberKey."\n");
 print_r('EventDate: '.$response->results[$x]->EventDate."\n");
}

// If there are more pages of results, utilize a while loop to get
them all
while ($response->moreResults) {
 $response = $sentEvent->GetMoreResults();
 print_r('SubscriberKey:
'.$response->results[$x]->SubscriberKey."\n");
 print_r('EventDate: '.$response->results[$x]->EventDate."\n");
}
```

Using the API Directly

If you're using a language or platform where the SDKs are not available or are otherwise not a viable solution, you can use the API directly rather than going through the SDK.

Getting an Access Token

The first step in any API-based integration is getting an access token, which will be used to authenticate other API calls. To get an access token, you will use Fuel's authentication service. The code sample below demonstrates how to use an HTTP POST request to acquire an access token:

```
POST https://auth.exacttargetapis.com/v1/requestToken
Content-Type: application/json
{
    "clientId": "YOUR_CLIENT_ID_FROM_APP_CENTER",
    "clientSecret": "YOUR_CLIENT_SECRET_FROM_APP_CENTER"
}
```

```
200 OK
{
    "accessToken": "dfy3dsnqw3gre6e3pbatcr4s"
    "expiresIn": 3600
}
```

The access token is returned in the accessToken property. You can use this token to authenticate other API calls by either specifying it via the query string parameter access_token or via the Authorization header field with the Bearer HTTP authorization scheme, e.g.,

```
GET
https://www.exacttargetapis.com/platform/v1/endpoints?access_token=dfy3dsnqw3gre6e3pbatcr4s
Accept: application/json
```

or

```
GET https://www.exacttargetapis.com/platform/v1/endpoints
Accept: application/json
Authorization: Bearer dfy3dsnqw3gre6e3pbatcr4s
```

Fuel access tokens can be used to authenticate with ExactTarget's SOAP API as well. Here is an example of using the same access token to authenticate with the SOAP API:

```
<s:Envelope xmlns:s="http://schemas.xmlsoap.org/soap/envelope/">
  <s:Header>
    <h:fueloauth xmlns="http://exacttarget.com"
                 xmlns:h="http://exacttarget.com">
      dfy3dsnqw3gre6e3pbatcr4s
    </h:fueloauth>
  </s:Header>
  [...]
</s:Envelope>
```

Refreshing an Access Token

Note the `expiresIn` property in the HTTP response to the `requestToken` API call. Fuel access tokens expire one hour after they're issued. If you attempt to use an expired token, you'll receive a 401 Unauthorized HTTP response. If this happens, you'll need to refresh your access token.

Important Considerations When Using the API Directly

There are a few important considerations to keep in mind if you use the API directly and do your own OAuth token management rather than using the SDKs.

First of all, you should NOT request a new token for every API call you make—each token is good for an hour and should be reused. Making two API calls for every one operation is inefficient and may result in throttling.

Secondly, and we cannot say this enough, be careful where you store your client secret. In particular, you should NOT store your client secret in a mobile application because a mobile device is not a secure environment; it is recommended that you utilize an Authorization Code or Implicit Grant OAuth flow instead.

Using Data Extensions and AMPscript for Advanced Personalization

In this section, we'll make our message even more personalized and relevant through the use of two advanced Marketing Cloud technologies: data extensions and AMPscript.

A data extension is a flexible table of almost any type of data and can be used for personalization, segmentation, or as a sending data source. Data extensions are very powerful constructs and can be thought of as cloud-based, relational marketing databases.

AMPscript is the Marketing Cloud's content scripting language and can be used to programmatically personalize the content of an email, SMS message, or landing page. AMPscript can interact with data extensions, so you can read data from data extensions in your messages and write data to your data extensions in your landing pages.

In our example, we'll use a data extension to store information about products that we can use to further personalize the email we sent in the last section. Specifically, we'll use the subscriber's previous purchase behavior to include a relevant offer in our email designed to drive the next purchase.

Create a Data Extension

First, we'll create a data extension called Products to store information about our products. In our example, each product will have a unique identifier, a name, a price, and an image URL.

id	name	price	image
...	...	...	...

Let's go ahead and create the data extension using the SDK.

```
$de = new ET_DataExtension();
$de->authStub = $myclient;

$de->props = array("Name" => "Products", "CustomerKey" => "products");

// specify the data extension columns
$de->columns = array();
$de->columns[] = array("Name" => "id", "FieldType" => "Number",
```

```
"IsPrimaryKey" => "true", "IsRequired" => "true");
$de->columns[] = array("Name" => "name", "FieldType" =>
"Text","MaxLength" => "100");
$de->columns[] = array("Name" => "price", "FieldType" => "Decimal",
 "Precision" => "18", "Scale" => "2");
$de->columns[] = array("Name" => "image", "FieldType" =>
"Text","MaxLength" => "100");

$response = $de->post();
```

Populate the Data Extension

Next, we'll add some product data to the Products data extension. In essence, we'll be adding two new rows to the Products database.

id	name	price	image
1234	iPhone 5c	$99.00	http://bit.ly/H76rMz
5678	iPhone 5c case	$29.00	http://bit.ly/Hesctp

Let's go ahead and create the two new rows.

```
$deRow = new ET_DataExtension_Row();
$deRow->authStub = $myclient;

// specify the name of the data extension
$deRow->Name = "Products";

// specify the values of data extension row #1
$deRow->props = array("id" => "1234", "name" => "iPhone 5c", "price"
 => "$99", "image" => "http://bit.ly/H76rMz");

$response = $deRow->post();

// specify the values of data extension row #2
$deRow->props = array("id" => "5678", "name" => "iPhone 5c case",
"price" => "$29", "image" => "http://bit.ly/Hesctp");

$response = $deRow->post();
```

The approach above is ideal for small- to medium-sized data sets like real-time or near real-time updates to single rows or small batches of data in periodic updates. For example, if you want to send ExactTarget purchase data as it happens or on a frequent basis (say hourly), utilizing the API approach is ideal.

Other scenarios require bulk loading of data into a data extension. For example, if you want to load millions of products into ExactTarget regularly, a file-based approach may be more efficient from a bandwidth and processing standpoint. Importing compressed files dropped onto an FTP site is the most efficient way to bulk load millions of rows of data into a data extension.

Extend the Subscriber Data Model

Next, we'll create another profile attribute, this time to store the ID of the product to recommend next.

```
$profileAttribute = new ET_ProfileAttribute();
$profileAttribute->authStub = $myclient;

$profileAttribute->props = array("Name" => "productID", "PropertyType"
  => "string", "Description" => "ID of next product recommendation");

$response = $profileAttribute->post();
```

In a real world use case, a background process might be running that analyzes past purchases and populates the productID profile attribute with the product it determines is most relevant to include next for each subscriber. In our case, we'll need to populate the productID profile attribute manually. Go ahead and set it to 5678. We won't include a code sample this time because by now you should know the pattern well.

Use AMPscript to Bring it All Together

Finally, we'll update the email to include AMPscript that uses the profile attribute productID to read details about that product from the Products data extension and include those details in the email message. Note that this time we use patch because we are updating an existing email.

```
$email = new ET_Email();
$email->authStub = $myclient;

// store the email in a variable
$updatedEmail = <<<EMAIL
<html>
<body>
<p>%%FirstName%%,</p>

<p>We're pretty sure you would love the following product:</p>

<p>
  <b>%%=Lookup("Products", "name", "id", productID)=%%</b>
  <br />
  <i>%%=Lookup("Products", "price", "id", productID)=%%</i>
</p>

<img src="%%=Lookup("Products", "image", "id", productID)=%%"
width="25%" />

<p>We appreciate your continued business!</p>

<small>
  <p>This email was sent by:</p>

  <p>
    %%Member_Busname%%
```

```
    <br />
    %%Member_Addr%%
    <br />
    %%Member_City%%, %%Member_State%%, %%Member_PostalCode%%
    <br />
    %%Member_Country%%
</p>

<a href="%%profile_center_url%%">Profile Center</a>
<br />
<a href="%%unsub_center_url%%">Unsubscribe</a>
</small>


<custom name="opencounter" type="tracking">
</body>
</html>
EMAIL;

// set the subject line and HTML email body
$email->props = array("ID" => "4303065", "Subject" => "Hi
%%FirstName%%, may we suggest for your next purchase...", "HTMLBody"
 => $updatedEmail);

// update the ET_Email object
$response = $email->patch();
```

The AMPscript used in the email above is the Lookup function. The Lookup function returns a single field value for a single row in a data extension. For example, in our case, the AMPscript:

```
%%=Lookup("Products", "price", "id", productID)=%%
```

produces this output:

```
$29
```

In this example, we are looking up the value of the price field from the Products data extension. The Products data extension has one primary key, and the final two parameters of the Lookup function provide the name and value of that primary key. In our case, the value of this key is the product ID data specified in the subscriber's profile attribute `productID`.

Now that the email content has been updated, let's do another send. You can preview the send via the UI to see the results as well.

```
$response = new ET_Post($myclient, 'Send', array("List" => array("ID"
 => $listID), "Email" => array("ID" => $emailID)));
```

You should receive an email that looks like this.

Hi Ian, may we suggest for your next purchase...

 ExactTarget
to me ▾

Ian,

We're pretty sure you would love the following product:

iPhone 5c case
$29

We appreciate your continued business!

This email was sent by:

ExactTarget
20 N. Meridian St.
Indianapolis, IN, 46204
USA

Profile Center

Now It's Your Turn

You've finished building a relatively sophisticated email communication using a number of ExactTarget technologies and concepts. This exercise, hopefully, has you thinking of creative ways to use your organization's data to create more personalized and beneficial customer touchpoints.

Many of the concepts you've learned in this section translate to how you personalize content on other channels (like SMS). We'll dive deeper into the email, SMS, and Push channels in the following sections.

Email Communication as The Universal Medium

Email is a technology available to almost everyone on every type of computing device you can imagine. For that reason, utilizing email as a customer touchpoint will allow you to reach customers at almost any stage of digital adoption. Did you setup your email account first or your social media account? For millions, it's the same answer -- email.

This section describes the types of email communication and how the Fuel Platform allows you to utilize a wide range of email techniques. The goal is to help you understand and provide email solutions to your organization through ExactTarget.

Types of Email Communication

List-Based Communications

When you send to a list of individuals with a common goal, you are sending list-based communications. Everything from a newsletter communication to a recurring birthday notification can be considered list-based because the send goes out at a particular time to a group of people with one key aggregation point -- the individual send event to the group. These types of communication are generally classified as purposely commercial under the CAN-SPAM Act.

ExactTarget provides multiple ways to send a list-based communication -- both at the definition level and the data source level.

	Classic Send	Email Send Definition
Audience		
— Marketing List	✓	✓
— Data Extension		✓
Automation		
— Single and Scheduled	✓	✓
— Recurring		✓
Management		
— Send Status	✓	✓
— Pause and Restart	✓	✓
Usage		
— Reusable with Perform Start		✓
— One-off Immediate	✓	

	Classic Send	Email Send Definition
Requirements		
— Email and List	☑	
— Name, Email, List, and Send Classification		☑

If you wanted to send to a list filled with movie attenders, you could create a Send object via the SOAP API by specifying the Email ID and List ID. Immediately, a Send ID will be created and returned and the send will process asynchronously. While this method is simple, it lacks the sophisticated options available to the Email Send Definition.

```
<s:Envelope xmlns:s="http://schemas.xmlsoap.org/soap/envelope/">
    <s:Header xmlns:wsa="http://www.w3.org/2005/08/addressing">
        <h:fueloauth xmlns:h="http://exacttarget.com"
xmlns="http://exacttarget.com">fuelauthtoken</h:fueloauth>
    </s:Header>
    <s:Body>
        <CreateRequest xmlns="http://exacttarget.com/wsdl/partnerAPI">

            <Options/>
            <Objects xsi:type="Send">
                <ObjectID xsi:nil="true"/>
                <Email>
                    <ID>12345</ID>
                </Email>
                <List>
                    <ID>3456242</ID>
                </List>
            </Objects>
        </CreateRequest>
    </s:Body>
</s:Envelope>
```

If you wanted to send to a data extension filled with movie attendees, you first would create a EmailSendDefinition object via the Email SOAP API and specify the required values. To use this definition to send, you'll need one more API call -- the Perform method -- that accepts an EmailSendDefinition object and an action of "start".

```
<s:Envelope xmlns:s="http://schemas.xmlsoap.org/soap/envelope/">
    <s:Header xmlns:wsa="http://www.w3.org/2005/08/addressing">
        <h:fueloauth xmlns:h="http://exacttarget.com"
xmlns="http://exacttarget.com">fuelauthtoken</h:fueloauth>
    </s:Header>
    <s:Body xmlns:xsi="http://www.w3.org/2001/XMLSchema-instance"
xmlns:xsd="http://www.w3.org/2001/XMLSchema">
        <CreateRequest xmlns="http://exacttarget.com/wsdl/partnerAPI">

            <Options></Options>
            <Objects xsi:type="EmailSendDefinition">
```

```
                    <ObjectID xsi:nil="true"></ObjectID>
                    <CustomerKey>movie_notification</CustomerKey>
                    <Name>Movie Notification</Name>
                    <SendClassification>

   <ObjectID>51422ad6-6f65-de11-bf42-001e0bbb7678</ObjectID>
                    </SendClassification>
                    <SendDefinitionList>

   <SendDefinitionListType>SourceList</SendDefinitionListType>

   <CustomObjectID>729860f8-7d66-de11-bf42-001e0bbb7678</CustomObjectID>

                        <DataSourceTypeID>CustomObject</DataSourceTypeID>

                    </SendDefinitionList>
                    <Email>
                        <ID>542894</ID>
                    </Email>
                </Objects>
            </CreateRequest>
        </s:Body>
   </s:Envelope>
```

Transactional Communications

For systems communicating to customers based on activities in near real-time like purchases or rental confirmations, you should utilize transactional one-to-one email. In the Marketing Cloud transactional email is an important customer touchpoint for marketers as well as a developer technology. The basic model that allows this marketer and developer interaction is the triggered send definition. The triggered send definition exposes itself as the `TriggeredSend` object in the Fuel SDKs, the `MessageDefinitionSend` resource in the REST API, and a `TriggeredSendDefinition` object in the SOAP API.

The basic model of an ExactTarget transactional send is a definition containing:

- The email template
- Default from name
- Email reply logic
- The recipient data storage (either a Marketing List or a Data Extension)
- Any exclusion lists needed to scrub the individual subscriber
- Logging of Send Data

All that's left for a send is to perform a very lightweight API call, containing just a reference to the `TriggeredSend`, information about the recipient's address, and any additional data needed to populate the template.

Here are three examples of transactional reminder messages being sent by ExactTarget via Fuel technologies:

1. Transactional Sending and the Fuel PHP SDK

```php
require('ET_Client.php');
$myclient = new ET_Client();
$triggeredsend = new ET_TriggeredSend();
$triggeredsend->authStub = $myclient;
$triggeredsend->props = array("CustomerKey" => "password");
$triggeredsend->subscribers =
array(array("EmailAddress"=>"jsmith@example.com",
"SubscriberKey" => "jsmith@example.com");
$triggeredsend->send();
```

2. Transactional Sending and the REST API

```
POST messaging/v1/messageDefinitionSends/key:reminder/send
Authorization: Bearer exampletoken1
{
  "From": {
      "Address": "code@exacttarget.com",
      "Name": "Code@"
  },
  "To": {
      "Address": "jsmith@example.com",
      "SubscriberKey": "jsmith@example.com",
      "ContactAttributes": {
          "SubscriberAttributes": {
              "ResetLink": "https://..."
          }
      }
  }
}
```

3. Transactional Sending and the SOAP API

```xml
<s:Envelope
xmlns:s="http://schemas.xmlsoap.org/soap/envelope/">
  <s:Header>
 <h:fueloauth xmlns:h="http://exacttarget.com"
xmlns="http://exacttarget.com">fuelauthtoken</h:fueloauth>
  </s:Header>
  <s:Body
xmlns:xsi="http://www.w3.org/2001/XMLSchema-instance"
xmlns:xsd="http://www.w3.org/2001/XMLSchema">
 <CreateRequest
xmlns="http://exacttarget.com/wsdl/partnerAPI">
      <Options/>
      <Objects xsi:type="TriggeredSend">
          <TriggeredSendDefinition>
              <CustomerKey>reminder</CustomerKey>
          </TriggeredSendDefinition>
          <Subscribers>
              <EmailAddress>jsmith@example.com</EmailAddress>
              <SubscriberKey>jsmith@example.com</SubscriberKey>

          </Subscribers>
      </Objects>
```

```
     </CreateRequest>
</s:Body>
```

Managing Email Delivery

One of the most difficult aspects of utilizing email as a customer touchpoint from a developer perspective is deliverability. By sometimes mysterious means, an email will fail to get into a user's inbox and it can fall to the development team to figure out why. The Marketing Cloud helps you manage deliverability by utilizing a number of fully managed techniques to ensure the success your organization's email operations.

The aspects of email delivery that should be top of mind for any developer is:

- My email always goes out on an IP address and sending domain.
- The ISPs know, validate, and record my IP address and my domain.
- The ISPs reject any email it doesn't know about and records it.
- The recipient of my emails either are going to like it, ignore it or hate it.
- The ISPs record whether the recipients like, ignore or hate my email.
- An ISPs recorded history of my IP address and sending domain becomes my email-sending reputation.

The center of the story for deliverability is DNS configuration, data quality, content quality and delivery timing. If you fail miserably on any of these areas, ISPs will generally give your IP address and/or sending domain a bad reputation.

Using Fuel's SDKs and APIs, you can enforce data quality relevant to deliverability in ExactTarget by updating the status of subscribers or pulling deliverability data from the Marketing Cloud. You may want to update the status of a subscriber if you are synchronizing email statuses from an external system or are building a custom profile center by selecting Unsubscribe from All.

This sample shows how to update the status of a subscriber using the C# SDK.

```
Using FuelSDK;
ET_Client myclient = new ET_Client();
ET_Subscriber subscriber = new ET_Subscriber();
subscriber.AuthStub = myclient;
subscriber.SubscriberKey = "SDKSubscriber";
subscriber.Status = SubscriberStatus.Unsubscribed;
PatchReturn results = subscriber.Patch();
Console.WriteLine("Patch Status: " + results.Status.ToString());
```

In this example, the subscriber status is changing to Unsubscribed for a subscriber with an externally supplied identifier, SubscriberKey. The Patch() on the subscriber is then called causing the update to occur.

Here are a few practical recommendations for making sense of deliverability.

- Ensure your DNS is configured properly for DKIM (Domain Keys Identified Mail), and SPF (Sender Policy Framework), and SenderID. The Marketing Cloud Team can help manage this on your behalf to remove the guess work.
- Cleanse data that you're sending against lists of email addresses known to cause reputation problems. The Marketing Cloud provides a list detective service on every email that is sent.
- Check your content before you send it against a content filter. If you or your marketing team is sending content that contains certain key phrases, you will have problems.
- Ask your marketing team for new content on a regular basis. Recipients will eventually think you are spamming them as you get less and less relevant and timely from a content perspective.
- Send only the email you need. Every customer touchpoint is something to be valued—don't waste your opportunities by yelling at customers when communicating too frequently. Customers will hit the "Spam" button and ISPs won't like your IP address or domain as much.

SMS Communication to Mobile Phones

Every phone number in the world associated with mobile phone adds a customer touchpoint that gives developers and marketers the ability to communicate valuable information and build a deeper relationship. To innovate on the SMS customer touchpoint, developers must recognize the reach of SMS as a communication medium and provide high value SMS messages and offers.

ExactTarget's MobileConnect application provides the features and capabilities needed for marketers to effectively build SMS-based communication programs. These capabilities are exposed to developers via Fuel REST APIs and provide a solid foundation for building mobile communications solutions -- simple and complex.

MobileConnect allows you to create, send, receive, and track mobile (SMS) messages. You can use MobileConnect to manage your available keywords, conduct sends to subscriber, automatically respond to incoming messages, and many other tasks. You can send and receive SMS messages using a short code within the United States and using short or long codes in other countries around the world. Each country requires its own short code, but you can use long codes to reach several different countries (depending on the general region).

Inbound and Outbound SMS

When you talk about SMS messages, it's always in the context of a mobile device.

The term MO message (mobile-originated message) is a message that a subscriber sent from a mobile device into the Marketing Cloud. Setting up your system to respond to MO messages is similar to setting up a triggered email: you create content and the system sends it out automatically whenever anyone triggers the message. In the case of SMS, people trigger the message by sending you a keyword in a MO message.

The term MT message (mobile-terminated message) refers to a message that goes out from the Marketing Cloud and is received by the subscriber's mobile device. Setting up an MT message is similar to setting up a user-initiated email: you choose the content and select the subscribers, and send the message at the time you choose.

Even more so than email communication, SMS communication to customers must be carefully crafted from a timing and content perspective. Marketing Cloud users with a private or shared short code can set up their organization to respond to MO message as well as send MT messages. Every MobileConnect installation must provision HELP and STOP keywords so that mobile phone users receiving messages or initiating conversations from your Marketing Cloud account can request assistance or stop any further messages.

Private and Shared Short Codes

A short code is a 5-6 digit phone number used for SMS messages. When you decide to begin using SMS, you need to decide whether to use a Shared Short Code or Private Short Code. The Marketing Cloud team will help guide you through the process of acquiring a short code.

Shared Short Code

If you choose to use a Shared Short Code, you will lease a Short Code that may be used by other ExactTarget clients.

Since the code is shared by multiple organizations, keywords (the words texted to a short code to prompt a response message or action) can only be used by one organization on that particular short code. Therefore, some of the more popular keywords, like SALE, ALERTS, or DEALS, may not be available for your campaigns.

Shared Short Codes are ideal for organizations that don't need many keywords and organizations that need to send campaigns immediately.

Example: A movie theatre may use "Text ALERTS to 12345 to receive new movie notifications via SMS."

Private Short Code

If you choose to get a Private Short Code, ExactTarget will lease it from the Common Short Code Administration (CSCA). Your organization will be the only ExactTarget client using the Short Code. Keywords availability is unlimited.

Private Short Codes are ideal for organizations needing unlimited keywords and organizations that do not want to share a Short Code with other ExactTarget clients.

You can also choose a Vanity Short Code (specific numbers that spell out a word -- i.e., OAKLEY - 625539) or a randomly assigned Private Short Code.

The following table shows the difference between private and shared short codes.

Property	Private Short Code	Shared Short Code
Definition	Five- or six-digit number assigned to a single entity for use in sending and receiving SMS messages	Five- or six-digit number shared across multiple entities for use in sending and receiving SMS messages
How Keywords Work	Can use any keyword and account for intentional or unintentional misspellings	• Limited to 5 keywords per account (additional keywords can be purchased) • Must be registered by a Marketing Cloud representative
Double Opt-In	Can add users through a mobile device to a publication list for future MT sends	Can add users through a mobile device to a publication list for future MT sends
Triggered MT Sends	Can send MT messages using data extensions and publication lists	Can send MT messages using data extensions and publication lists
Tracking	Messages Sent, MO/MT Traffic	Messages Sent, MO/MT Traffic
AMPscript	Full Support	Full Support

The SMS Fuel REST API

The SMS Fuel REST API comprises of the following endpoints:

- Contacts — Resource for importing into or refreshing existing lists
- Keyword — Resource for creating and deleting keywords
- Message — Used to change the status of a message
- MessageContact — Used for sending mobile-terminated (MT) messages through MobileConnect
- MessageList — Used for sending mobile-terminated (MT) messages through MobileConnect to a predefined list of subscribers
- QueueMO — Used for programmatically initiating a Mobile Originated (MO) message that is defined within the MobileConnect interface

Sending a Mobile-Terminated SMS to a Customer

The MessageContact service represents a MT (mobile-terminated) SMS message sent via the SMS API. Using this service, you can send SMS messages and check the status to ensure they were delivered.

If you wanted to send a MT message to a contact telling them how to subscribe to movie notifications, you could use an API call similar to the one below.

```
POST
https://www.exacttargetapis.com/sms/v1/messageContact/MzA6Nzg6MA/send
Authorization: Bearer exampletoken1
Content-Type: application/json
{
    "mobileNumbers": [
    "13175551212"
    ],
    "Subscribe": true,
    "Resubscribe": true,
    "keyword": "ALERTS",
    "Override": true,
    "messageText": "Text ALERTS to 12345 to receive new movie
notifications via SMS.",
    "BlackoutWindow": {
    "UtcOffset": "-0500",
    "WindowStart": "1500",
    "WindowEnd": "2200"
    },
    "SendTime": "2012-10-05 20:01"
}
```

In this use case, you may want to initiate a mobile conversation with a contact via an MT because they walked into the theater and are registered in your system to get movie offers, but have yet to register for new movie alerts.

You'll notice that this API call specifies an array of phone numbers to send the SMS message, the message, and specific data related modifiers -- `SendTime` and `BlackoutWindow` -- to ensure a quality delivery. Use the `Subscribe` and `Resubscribe` options when a keyword is specified.

Sending a Mobile-Terminated SMS to a List

The MessageList Send service allows you to initiate an SMS message using this API in order to send to a list of contacts. That request optionally allows you to pass the text of the message to override the message specified in the definition.

```
POST
https://www.exacttargetapis.com/sms/v1/messageList/MzA6Nzg6MA/send
Authorization: Bearer exampletoken1
Content-Type: application/json
```

```
{
    "TargetListIds": [
        "bzZ0cENGam1FZUtNX0poTDRYZzhlQTo2Mzow"
    ],
    "OverrideTemplateTargetLists": "true",
    "OverrideTemplateExclusionLists": "false",
    "IgnoreExclusionLists": "true",
    "OverrideMessageText": "false",
    "BlackoutWindow": {
        "UtcOffset": "-0500",
        "WindowStart": "1500",
        "WindowEnd": "2200"
    },
    "AllowDuplication": "false"
}
```

In this use case, you may want to send out a new movie alert to all contacts who have opted-in to the movie alert campaign when a new movie is released in the movie theater.

This API call allows an array of one or more List ID strings. The contacts in these Lists will be included in the send and will overwrite the Message's default marketing lists.

Queuing an MO for System Initiated SMS Conversations

You can use the QueueMO service to initiate a MO keyword and opt-in contacts to your mobile campaign that requires a double opt-in process. The contacts indicates interest by signing up on your website or other external system. This contact then receives an SMS message to which they can respond in order to continue with the double opt-in process. This process ensures the contacs provides a valid number belonging to the contact.

The above example does not represent the only use for this call. You can use this service any time you must start an MO keyword from a system other than the subscriber's mobile phone. This same call can be used to initiate 2-way SMS conversations with a contact to collect CRM data such as zip code, state or general feedback through a survey.

The QueueMO service validates the short code and keyword combination and ensures the account has permission to use the short code. Any country code associated with the calls derives from the location of the mobile number and produces an error if the short code does not have permission to send in the country code.

```
PPOST https://www.exacttargetapis.com/sms/v1/queueMO/
Authorization: Bearer exampletoken1
Content-Type: application/json
{
  "mobileNumbers" : [
  "15555551212"
  ],
  "shortCode" : "12345",
  "messageText" : "ALERTS"
}
```

In this API call, suppose the contact registered for movie alerts from the movie theater's web site. The web site could make this call to the Marketing Cloud to initiate the opt-in conversation to replicate the scenario of the user registering from their mobile phone.

Push Communication to Mobile Apps

Each application installed on a mobile device with an application ecosystem (like iOS, Android, Windows Phone, and Blackberry) adds a customer touchpoint that gives your marketers the ability to add value to the customer lifecycle with your organization. To innovate on this customer touchpoint, developers play a critical role because a push notification works only after an application is built to support it. Marketers want access to this new customer touchpoint as well. Therefore, developers need access to a marketer-friendly push notification platform. The push notification technology that meets this need is provided by ExactTarget MobilePush.

ExactTarget MobilePush allows you to create and send targeted push messages based on cross-channel consumer data to encourage app usage and deliver increased ROI. With MobilePush, you view how users navigate through your app. From the products they view to the amount of time spent on each page, you gain a window into how users interact with your app across their smartphones and tablets. Because MobilePush is built on the Interactive Marketing Hub, you can easily integrate push message campaigns with any email, SMS, or social campaigns. The message wizard and preview features make it simple to create, deliver, and track push notifications to smartphones and tablets on iOS, Android, and Blackberry operating systems.

MobilePush allows you to:

- Drive engagement and mCommerce
- Gain valuable user insight
- Easily build cross-channel campaigns
- Segment and schedule messages

Integrating MobilePush push messaging into a mobile application requires registering your application with the Marketing Cloud (as the push provider), registering your application with the platform providers (Apple, Google, etc), utilizing the MobilePush SDK in your mobile application to capture events and data, and leveraging the data to deliver push notifications from the Marketing Cloud to the device. Let's walk through each of the steps needed to get to the point you can receive messages in your app from the ExactTarget Marketing Cloud.

Step 1: Organization, Configuration, and Registration

In order to use MobilePush capabilities, you need to have an ExactTarget account with the MobilePush application licensed and installed. For more information on getting the MobilePush application licensed and installed, contact your Marketing Cloud customer relationship manager. Additionally, your ExactTarget user must be provisioned with MobilePush. If not, contact your Marketing Cloud administrator.

Next, register your mobile app with the Marketing Cloud using the Code@ App Center as a Device connected application so it will appear in MobilePush Marketing Cloud application. Make sure the organization business unit used to link your connected mobile app matches the organization business unit that your marketing department will be using to manage push notification customer touchpoints. If you don't, your marketing team won't know which Marketing Cloud organization the mobile application is associated with.

Most mobile application development cycles involve development and production version of applications. Therefore, you'll want to create two applications in App Center, one representing development and the other production.

Step 2 (iOS): Register with Apple's App Store

Follow the steps below to register your mobile app with Apple. You must repeat this process for both development and production environments

- Register your Bundle ID with Apple
- Register the Push SSL certificates for both your development and production environments

For details of these steps, see: https://developer.apple.com/library/ios/navigation.

Read the instructions to generate a Certificate Signing Request (CSR) and click **Continue**.

1. Open Keychain Access.
2. Select Certificate Assistant.
3. Select Request a Certificate From a Certificate Authority... .
4. Enter the following information in the Certificate Information screen:

   - The developer email address
   - The common name of the application

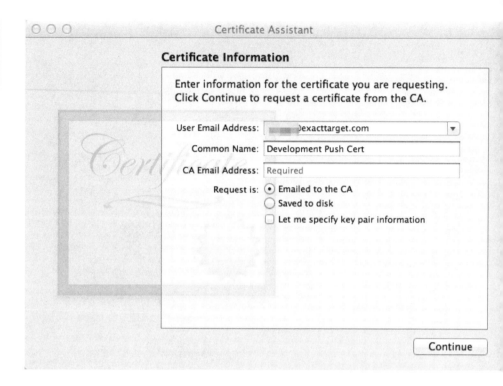

5. Select **Saved to disk** in the **Request is:** field.
6. Click **Continue**.

7. Review the notification regarding your SSL certificate and click **Continue**.

8. Select the private key you wish to download.
9. Click **Download** to save the certificate to your developer environment.

 Your certificate is ready.

Download, Install and Backup
Download your certificate to your Mac, then double click the .cer file to install in Keychain Access. Make sure to save a backup copy of your private and public keys somewhere secure.

Name:	Apple Development iOS Push Services: com.exacttarget.
Type:	APNs Development iOS
Identifier ID:	
Expires:	Oct 22, 2014

Download

Documentation
For more information on using and managing your certificates read:

App Distribution Guide

Add Another   Done

10. In Keychain Access, select the certificates and keys to export.

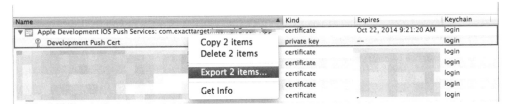

Name		Kind	Expires	Keychain
▼ Apple Development IOS Push Services: com.exacttarget.		certificate	Oct 22, 2014 9:21:20 AM	login
Development Push Cert	Copy 2 items	private key	--	login
	Delete 2 items	certificate		login
		certificate		login
	Export 2 items...	certificate		login
		certificate		login
	Get Info	certificate		login

11. Right-click on your selected items and select Export (n) items... .
12. Enter a name for your certificate files in the Save As field.
13. Select the folder for your mobile app.
14. Click Save.
15. Enter a password for your certificates and click OK.

16. Provide these certificates to MobilePush@ExactTarget.com in order to integrate your apps with MobilePush.

Step 2 (Android): Register with Google Play

1. Review the Google documentation regarding setting up your Android project for GCM (Google Cloud Messaging).http://developer.android.com/google/gcm/gs.html
2. Log into the Google API console.https://code.google.com/apis/console
3. Click Create and create your Android project.
4. Copy the project number in the dashboard of your new project.
5. Click Services in the project screen.

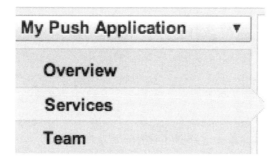

6. Scroll to Google Cloud Messaging for Android and select ON.

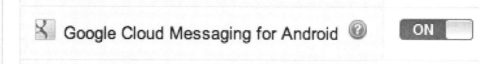

7. Click API Access:
8. Copy any existing API key.
9. If the field does not contain an existing value, click Create new Server key.

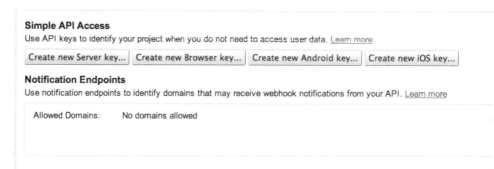

10. Record your Project Number and API Key values.

11. Provide these certificates to MobilePush@ExactTarget.com in order to integrate your apps with MobilePush.

Step 3: SDK Integration

Download the MobilePush SDKs to integrate push functionality into your mobile app. This download also includes methods for implementing OpenDirect, custom sounds, and custom keys inside your app.

This iOS snippet from the iOS SDK demonstrates the initial configuration of the SDK in your iOS application.

```
...
#import "ETAppDelegate.h"
#import "ETViewController.h"
#import "OpenDirectDemoViewController.h"

@implementation ETAppDelegate

- (BOOL)application:(UIApplication *)application
didFinishLaunchingWithOptions:(NSDictionary *)launchOptions
{

    NSLog(@"Launch Options: %@", launchOptions);

    [[ETPush pushManager] configureSDKWithAppID:@""
andAccessToken:@""];
    [[ETPush pushManager] setOpenDirectDelegate:self];
    [[ETPush pushManager] setDisplayLocalNotificationsTo:YES];

    [[ETPush pushManager] registerForRemoteNotificationTypes:
        UIRemoteNotificationTypeAlert|UIRemoteNotificationTypeBadge|

        UIRemoteNotificationTypeSound];
    [[ETPush pushManager] resetBadgeCount];
    [[ETPush pushManager]
applicationLaunchedWithOptions:launchOptions];
...
```

You will see how you can easily include the ETPush classes into your application and specify the intial configuration operations and methods. Set the value on the configureSDKWithAppID and andAccessToken methods on the pushManager object with the string values you received from registering your application in App Center in Step 1.

Here's another snippet that demonstrates another MobilePush SDK feature -- the ability to send tags to the Marketing Cloud about the user of an application or what the user is doing.

```
-(void)textFieldDidEndEditing:(UITextField *)textField
{
    if (textField == _firstName) {
```

```
            [[ETPush pushManager] addAttributeNamed:@"FirstName"
value:textField.text];
            [[NSUserDefaults standardUserDefaults] setValue:textField.text
    forKey:@"FirstName"];
        } else if (textField == _lastName) {
            [[ETPush pushManager] addAttributeNamed:@"LastName"
value:textField.text];
            [[NSUserDefaults standardUserDefaults] setValue:textField.text
    forKey:@"LastName"];
        } else if (textField == _subscriberKey) {
            [[ETPush pushManager] setSubscriberKey:textField.text];
            [[NSUserDefaults standardUserDefaults] setValue:textField.text
    forKey:@"SubKey"];


    }
}
```

In this case, the iOS application has three defined UITextField objects that trigger a message to the text field delegate upon textFieldDidEndEditing. The text fields are capturing FirstName, LastName, and a contact identifier (SubKey), storing it in the application user defaults and sending the data to the ExactTarget Marketing Cloud.

What could you use this data for? If you capture a contact identifier in your application that correlates to other contact identifiers your organization captures in other ways, you will be on your way to providing a cross-channel view of your contact inside the Marketing Cloud and allowing mobile data to influence how a contact is messages across other channels. If you don't capture any personally identifiable information, you can still communicate with all the relevance you would otherwise, just not without the cross-channel connection.

An Android snippet from the Android SDK demonstrates the initial configuration of the SDK and setting some initial tags in your Android application.

```
...
import com.exacttarget.etpushsdk.AnalyticActivity;
import com.exacttarget.etpushsdk.ETPush;

public class HomeActivity extends AnalyticActivity {
  private static final String TAG = "Home Activity";

  private static String FirstNameKey = "FirstName";
  private static String LastNameKey = "LastName";
  private static String EmailAddressKey = "EmailAddress";
  private static String PreferencesKey = "ETDemoPreferences";

  @Override
  public void onCreate(Bundle savedInstanceState) {
    super.onCreate(savedInstanceState);
    setContentView(R.layout.activity_home);

    final EditText txtFirstName = (EditText)
findViewById(R.id.txtFirstName);
    final EditText txtLastName = (EditText)
findViewById(R.id.txtLastName);
```

```
  final EditText txtEmailAddress = (EditText)
findViewById(R.id.txtEmailAddress);

  final ToggleButton tglPushEnabled = (ToggleButton)
findViewById(R.id.togglePushEnabled);

  ETPush pushManager = ETPush.pushManager();

  pushManager.configureSDKWithAppIdAndAccessToken("", "");
  pushManager.setNotificationRecipientClass(HomeActivity.class);
  pushManager.setOpenDirectRecipient(OpenDirectDemo.class);
  pushManager.setGcmSenderID("");


  pushManager.addTag("Android");
  pushManager.addTag("6.0");
...
```

In this code sample, you specify your Device connected application ApplicationID and Access Token from App Center as parameters in the `configureSDKWithAppIdAndAccessToken` method. The Google Cloud Messaging Sender ID is also specified here as well.

The last few lines show a simple, but important, use of tags. A tag is being added specifying "Android" and "6.0". To push a notification to all Android users of your application, just send a push notification to the "Android" tag. If your application is on version 6.0, you'll be able to communicate directly to all customers who have this version installed.

Step 4: Using The Push Fuel REST API

This member of the Fuel API Family exposes MobilePush technology to send push messages programmatically without the need to access the MobilePush interface. The Push Fuel REST API takes the data acquired from devices and allows developers to utilize the data in unique ways to deliver push messages back to devices. As a developer, you can target specific groups of device users (even individuals) with a unique message, specify custom data for your notification, schedule the notification and more.

The top-level services exposed by the Push Fuel REST API are:

- MessageContact — Used for sending push messages to specific mobile devices
- MessageTag — Used for sending push messages to mobile devices based on a tag
- MessageApp — Used for sending push messages to all users of a mobile app

To use the Push API, you will need to register a Server-to-Server or ExactTarget AppExchange connected application in App Center. The Push API cannot use the same access token that a device application uses and should be considered a distinct integration than that of the native device SDK integrations in Step 3.

The MessageContact Send service allows you to initiate a push message to one or many specific devices.

```
POST
https://www.exacttargetapis.com/push/v1/messageContact/OE18ODow/send

Authorization: Bearer exampletoken1
Content-Type: application/json
{
    "DeviceTokens": [
        "DeviceToken1",
        "DeviceToken2",
        "DeviceToken3"
    ],
    "Override": true,
    "MessageText": "Free Tickets to ET: the Marketing Cloud Movie!",

    "SendTime": "2013-11-17 09:00",
    "Sound": "tada.caf",
    "Badge": "+1",
    "OpenDirect": "OD01",
    "CustomKeys": {
        "keyA": "keyA_value",
        "keyB": "keyB_value"
    },
    "CustomPayload": "{ \"availableSeats\": \"34\" }"
}
```

In this code sample, you're sending a special message in the MessageText property to the customers associated with three devices who have installed your movie notification application about receiving free tickets to movie. You've scheduled the message using the SendTime property and are passing some custom information to the application about the number of available seats using the CustomPayload property. As you can see, the possiblities of interacting with mobile device users is almost unlimited using the Push Fuel REST API.

The MessageTag Send service allows you to initiate a push message to a group of devices that have provided the same tag value to the Marketing Cloud. Instead of targeting an set of individual devices, you can now target a much larger set of customers.

```
POST https://www.exacttargetapis.com/push/v1/messageTag/OE18ODow/send
Authorization: Bearer exampletoken1
Content-Type: application/json
{
    "InclusionTags": [
        "Salesforce", "ExactTarget"
    ],
    "ExclusionTags": [
        "Competitors"
    ],
    "Override": true,
    "MessageText": "Cloudy with a Chance of Customers - Now playing!",

    "Sound": "lightning.caf",
```

```
    "Badge": "+1",
    "OpenDirect": "OD01",
    "CustomKeys": {
        "keyA": "keyA_value",
        "keyB": "keyB_value"
    },
    "CustomPayload": "{ \"availableSeats\": \"2 billion\" }"
}
```

In the above example, any device owner who has expressed an affinity for Salesforce or ExactTarget and has installed your movie notification application will receive an email that a new movie named "Cloudy with a Chance of Customers" is now playing in theaters. Any competitors are excluded from getting the notification. This represents the essence of customer touchpoint development-giving customers what they want by communicating a specific message with good content to those who want to hear it and giving them useful information that will make them value your organization more!

Resources

General Developer Resources

- Code@ExactTarget Developer Community: https://code.exacttarget.com
- Code@ExactTarget App Center: https://code.exacttarget.com/appcenter
- Fuel APIs: https://code.exacttarget.com/api
- Fuel SDKs: https://code.exacttarget.com/sdks
- Fuel Cloud Editor: https://code.exacttarget.com/cloudeditor
- Fuel UX: https://code.exacttarget.com/fuelux
- ExactTarget AppExchange Developer Documentation: https://code.exacttarget.com/appexchange

Email Communication

- ExactTarget Email Developer Documentation: https://code.exacttarget.com/sdks
- ExactTarget Email Product Documentation: http://help.exacttarget.com/en/documentation/exacttarget
- ExactTarget Email Product Information: http://www.exacttarget.com/products/email-marketing
- Email Content Syndication: http://help.exacttarget.com/en/documentation/exacttarget/content/content_syndication
- Email Personalization Strings: http://help.exacttarget.com/en/documentation/exacttarget/content/personalization_strings
- AMPScript Documentation: http://help.exacttarget.com/en/documentation/exacttarget/content/ampscript

SMS Communication

- SMS Fuel REST API Developer Documentation:
  https://code.exacttarget.com/api/fuel-api-family-sms
- MobileConnect Product Documentation:
  http://help.exacttarget.com/en/documentation/mobileconnect/
- ExactTarget Marketing Cloud Mobile Products Information:
  http://www.exacttarget.com/products/mobile-marketing

Push Communication

- MobilePush Developer Documentation:
  https://code.exacttarget.com/getting-started/mobilepush
- MobilePush Product Documentation:
  http://help.exacttarget.com/en/documentation/mobilepush
- ExactTarget Marketing Cloud Mobile Products Information:
  http://www.exacttarget.com/products/mobile-marketing

Chapter 25

Radian6 API

Radian6 enables you to listen, analyze, and engage in your customers' conversations about your company, products, and competitors.

Use the Radian6 API to extend the functionality of the Salesforce Marketing Cloud. With the Radian6 API, you can:

- Create custom reporting and make your own visualizations.
- Extract post data directly from your Topic Profiles.
- Extract the data from visualizations or widgets from the Radian6 Dashboard.
- Access appended post data like post tags and source tags.
- Access Radian6 Insights data like demographics, sentiment, and entities, and so on.

Then, you can use this data to drive integration, from creating custom internal reporting to enhancing the value of your applications and services.

Supported Browsers

Radian6 supports the following browsers:

- Mozilla® Firefox®
- Google Chrome™
- Microsoft® Internet Explorer®
- Apple® Safari®

Older versions of Internet Explorer might not support the Summary Dashboard. We recommend Internet Explorer 9 and above, or another browser listed above.

Supported Salesforce Editions

Radian6 supports these Salesforce Editions:

- Developer Edition
- Enterprise Edition
- Unlimited Edition

If you're an existing Salesforce customer and want to upgrade to any of these editions, contact your account representative.

Quick Start

The Radian6 REST API retrieves, analyzes, and modifies social media posts and data from any Topic profile in your Radian6 account.

Before your begin, make sure that you have:

- A valid username and password
- A unique application key for your application

If you don't already have an application key, contact your account representative.

The following endpoints are available for access to the Radian6 API.

Development endpoint

```
https://demo-api.radian6.com/socialcloud/v1/
```

All development work should be performed and tested on the development endpoint before running your application against production.

Production endpoint

```
https://api.radian6.com/socialcloud/v1/
```

Run your application against the production endpoint after you have tested it on the development endpoint.

If you currently have an account on only one of the two environments, please contact apisupport@radian6.com in order to have your account replicated and available at both endpoints.

To get started with the Radian6 API, follow these steps.

1. Authenticate with the API.
2. Issue a basic call to one of the API methods.
3. Fetch some data from the Radian6 system.

Step One: Authenticate with the API

You must authenticate with the API before issuing calls.

The API currently only supports a basic authentication mechanism. An initial call needs to be made to the authentication service in order to fetch an authentication token used in subsequent API calls.

```
https://api-endpoint/auth/authenticate
```

This call expects the following request headers for an authentication check.

Parameter	Description
auth_user	The username on your account
auth_pass	The password in plain text
auth_appkey	The API key to include in your header parameter

All parameters are required. If authentication was successful, XML containing basic user account information and a token tag will be returned in the following format:

```
<token>70d756801c703f3e78f81726c11b00249fb81770a446958b2577cd223811e</token>
```

This is the token used to perform subsequent API requests.

```
<auth>
<token>e008252b4dce9b29c4c8155f0010cc8e128290b9e3ae99c8e9d15c
</token>
<UserDetails>
 <user>
  <userId>132972</userId>
  <clientId>1226</clientId>
  <displayName>Joe User</displayName>
  <emailAddress>joe.user@radian6.com</emailAddress>
  <packages />
 </user>
 <Packages>
  <feature>
   <featureId>1</featureId>
   <description>Workflow</description>
```

```
    </feature>
    <feature>
     <featureId>4</featureId>
     <description>Admin Portal Full</description>
    </feature>
    <feature>
     <featureId>6</featureId>
     <description>Require PO Number</description>
    </feature>
    <feature>
      <featureId>8</featureId>
        <description>SENTIMENT</description>
    </feature>
   </Packages>
  </UserDetails>
 </auth>
```

Step Two: Issue a Call to a Method

After authenticating with the Radian6 API, issue a call to an API method.

Now that you have the authentication token and API application key, you can make a call to one of the API methods. Fetching data requires the use of Topic Profiles, so let's start by getting a list of Topics. The call used to fetch the list of topics is `TopicService.fetchTopicList`.

```
https://api-endpoint/topics
```

As with all other calls, you must provide two request headers, `auth_token` and `auth_appkey`, obtained in Step One: Authenticate with the API.

You should receive an XML response containing a list of Topic Profiles and related information.

Sample XML Response Format

```
<topicFilters>
    <topicFilter>
        <name><![CDATA[2013 Candidates]]></name>
        <public>1</public>
        <status>1</status>
        <estimateVolume>317900</estimateVolume>
        <competeEnabled>0</competeEnabled>
        <bCode></bCode>
        <creatorId>2</creatorId>
        <creatorName>Chris Doe</creatorName>
        <creatorEmail>someguy@radian6.com</creatorEmail>
        <createDate>20080124</createDate>
        <topicFilterId>232</topicFilterId>
        <sentiment>0</sentiment>
```

```
<postTopicIgnoreStatus>-1</postTopicIgnoreStatus>
<inboundOnTopicLinksCount>0</inboundOnTopicLinksCount>
<number_queries>13</number_queries>
<filterGroups>
    <filterGroup>
        <filterGroupId>541</filterGroupId>
        <name><![CDATA[Group 1]]></name>
        <filterGroupTypeId>1</filterGroupTypeId>
        <filterQueries>
            <filterQuery>
                <query>"John" AND "president"</query>
                <filterQueryId>2031</filterQueryId>
                <isExcludeQuery>false</isExcludeQuery>
            </filterQuery>
            <filterQuery>
                <query>"Jane" AND "ceo"</query>
                <filterQueryId>2039</filterQueryId>
                <isExcludeQuery>false</isExcludeQuery>
            </filterQuery>
        </filterQueries>
    </filterGroup>
</filterGroups>
<sentimentQueries></sentimentQueries>
<includeSourceFilterList>
    <filterIds></filterIds>
</includeSourceFilterList>
<excludeSourceFilterList>
    <filterIds></filterIds>
</excludeSourceFilterList>
<includeAllSourceFilterList>
    <filterIds></filterIds>
</includeAllSourceFilterList>
<languages></languages>
<mediaType></mediaType>
<projects></projects>
<regions></regions>
    </topicFilter>
</topicFilters>
```

Step Three: Fetch Data

After authenticating with the Radian6 API and getting a list of topics, you can now fetch some data for a topic.

This example shows you how to fetch the most recent 100 items from the Radian6 system for a topic over the last 24 hours. The call used to fetch this data is `DataService.fetchRecentTopicPosts`.

```
https://api-endpoint/data/topicdata/recent/{recentXhours}/{topics}
/{mediatypes}/{PageIndex}/{pageSize}
```

recentXHours

> 24 (the last 24 hours of data)

topics

> 232 (a topicId fetched from the call in Step Two: Issue a Call to a Method)

mediatypes

> 1,2,3,4 (fetched from `LookupService.fetchMediaTypes`)

PageIndex

> 1 (the first page)

pageSize

> 100 (all items on current page)

For example, the call to development endpoint would look like this:

```
https://sandbox-insights.radian6.com/socialcloud/v1/data/topicdata
/realtime/24/232/1,2,3,4/1/100
```

This call returns a list of matching posts, sorted by default sort by `publish_date`. Each item in the result set is defined by an `<Article>` tag.

```
<radian6_RiverOfNews_export>
    <report_date>Fri Oct 30 10:22:06 ADT 2009</report_date>
    <user_name>Jane Smith</user_name>
    <RoN_sort_order>publishedDate</RoN_sort_order>
    <article_count>1</article_count>
    <article ID="1934621185">
        <description charset="UTF-8">
            <headline><![CDATA[ TWEET FROM: ACME]]>
            </headline>
            <author><![CDATA[ ACME]]>
            </author>
            <content><![CDATA[ The content of the Tweet]]>
            </content>
        </description>
        <source><![CDATA[ TWEET FROM: ACME]]></source>
        <host><![CDATA[ twitter.com]]></host>
        <article_url> <![CDATA[
http://twitter.com/username/statuses/4735539663]]>
        </article_url>
        <media_provider>TWITTER</media_provider>
        <media_type_id>8</media_type_id>
        <spam_rating>TODO</spam_rating>
        <publish_date>Oct 09, 2009 11:31 AM</publish_date>
        <harvest_date>Oct 09, 2009 11:31 AM</harvest_date>
        <PostDynamicsIteration>
            <PostDynamicsDefinition>
                <fieldId>9</fieldId>
```

```
                    <label>Following</label>
                    <value>0</value>
                    <sortOrder>1</sortOrder>
            </PostDynamicsDefinition>
            <PostDynamicsDefinition>
                    <fieldId>8</fieldId>
                    <label>Followers</label>
                    <value>0</value>
                    <sortOrder>2</sortOrder>
            </PostDynamicsDefinition>
            <PostDynamicsDefinition>
                    <fieldId>10</fieldId>
                    <label>Updates</label>
                    <value>0</value>
                    <sortOrder>3</sortOrder>
            </PostDynamicsDefinition>
            <PostDynamicsDefinition>
                    <fieldId>21</fieldId>
                    <label>Sentiment</label>
                    <shortLabel>S</shortLabel>
                    <sortOrder>4</sortOrder>
                    <value>15418,0</value>
                    <exceptionValue>15418,false</exceptionValue>
                    <reportValue>Neutral</reportValue>
                    <tooltip />
            </PostDynamicsDefinition>
            <reportFormatedData><![CDATA[ <span
style="font-weight:bold; color: #FF9900; font-size: 11pt"> Following:
    </span>0  <span style="font-weight:bold; color: #FF9900; font-size:
11pt"> Followers:
    </span>0  <span style="font-weight:bold; color: #FF9900; font-size:
11pt"> Updates:  </span>0  <span style="font-weight:bold; color:
#FF9900; font-size: 11pt"> Sentiment:  </span>Neutral  ]]>
            </reportFormatedData>
        </PostDynamicsIteration>
    </article>
</radian6_RiverOfNews_export>
```

Using the Services

Access and manage your posts, users, insights, topics, and other data.

This section walks you through common operations for each of the services. See theRadian6 API Reference at `http://socialcloud.radian6.com/docs/` for a full list of examples and response details.

Post Service

The Post Service enables you to perform operations such as assigning users to posts, setting the engagement type on posts, and adding tags to posts.

Calls can be made no more than once every 30 seconds.

Get Post Details

Fetch post details, such as the content, title, author, and published date.

```
GET /post
```

Parameters	Type	Description
auth_token	HeaderParam	Required. Request header containing the token returned from authentication with the API.
auth_appkey	HeaderParam	Required. Application key unique to your account.
url	PathParam	URL of the post.

Example

```
http://api.radian6.com/socialcloud/v1/post?url=http://twitter.com
/username/statuses/13...4
```

Request Headers

```
GET /socialcloud/v1/post?url HTTP/1.1
Host: api.radian6.com
auth_token: NotARealToken
auth_appkey: NotARealAppKey
```

Response Headers

```
HTTP/1.1 200 OK
Date: Thu, 29 Sep 2011 17:17:16 GMT
Content-Type: application/xml
Content-Length: 705
Keep-Alive: timeout=15, max=100
Connection: Keep-Alive
```

Response

```
<?xml version="1.0" encoding="iso-8859-1"?>
<PostDetails>
```

```
    <blogPost>
        <Post>
            <postId>12....</postId>
            <title>
                <![CDATA[Tweet from username (r6ts) ]]>
            </title>
            <author>
                <![CDATA[username]]>
            </author>
            <content>
                <![CDATA[]]>
            </content>
            <publishedDate>1321898901000</publishedDate>
            <link>

<![CDATA[http://twitter.com/username/statuses/13.....3]]>
            </link>
            <providerId>10</providerId>
            <mediaTypeId>1</mediaTypeId>
            <languageId>1</languageId>
            <regionId>235</regionId>
            <postStatusId>0</postStatusId>
        </Post>
    </blogPost>
    <blog>
        <blogId>44....7</blogId>
        <title>
            <![CDATA[Twitter / username]]>
        </title>
        <feed>

<![CDATA[http://twitter.com/statuses/user_timeline/username.atom]]>

        </feed>
        <link>
            <![CDATA[http://twitter.com/username]]>
        </link>
        <languageId>1</languageId>
        <languageAccuracy>0.99</languageAccuracy>
    </blog>
</PostDetails>
```

Resources for Post Service

The following list shows other operations you can use with the Post Service.

Operations	Example
Assign user to post	POST /post/workflow/assign/{postId}/{userId} /{topicList}

Operations	Example
Assign post classification	`POST /post/workflow/classification/{postId}/{classificationTypeId}`
Set post engagement	`POST /post/workflow/engagement/{postId}/{engagementTypeId}`
Assign post sentiment	`POST /post/workflow/sentiment/{postId}/{TopicId}/{sentimentValue}`
Add post note	`POST /post/workflow/note/{postId}`
Add post note reply	`POST /post/workflow/notereply/{postId}`
Add tags to posts	`POST /post/workflow/tags/{postId}`
Toggle spam	`POST /post/workflow/toggleSpam/{postList}/{topicList}/{spamValue}`
Get post dynamics	`GET /post/metrics/{postId}`
Get post workflow updates	`GET /post/workflow/updates/{epoch}/{postIdList}`
Remove tags and notes	`POST /post/workflow/removeTagsAndNotes/{tagAndNoteIds}`
Get child posts count	`GET /v1/post/{parentPostId}/childcount`
Get child posts count for multiple posts	`GET /v1/post/list/{parentPostIdList}/childcount`

The `auth_token` and `auth_appkey` header parameters are required for all calls. See the Post Service reference in the Radian6 API Documentation for details on each of these operations.

User Service

The User Service enables you to perform operations such as retrieving user details and their dashboards.

Calls can be made no more than once every 30 seconds.

Get User

Return basic information for the user making the request.

```
GET /user
```

Parameters	Type	Description
auth_token	HeaderParam	Required. Request header containing the token returned from authentication with the API.
auth_appkey	HeaderParam	Required. Application key unique to your account.

Example

```
http://api.radian6.com/socialcloud/v1/user
```

Request Headers

```
GET /socialcloud/v1/smm/user HTTP/1.1
Host: api.radian6.com
auth_token: NotARealToken
auth_appkey: NotARealAppKey
```

Response Headers

```
HTTP/1.1 200 OK
Date: Thu, 29 Sep 2011 17:17:16 GMT
Content-Type: application/xml
Content-Length: 705
Keep-Alive: timeout=15, max=100
Connection: Keep-Alive
```

Response

```
<user>
    <userId>538</userId>
    <clientId>1</clientId>
    <displayName>
        <![CDATA[John Doe]]>
```

```
    </displayName>
    <emailAddress>John.Doe@example.com</emailAddress>
    <timezone>GMT</timezone>
</user>
```

Resources for User Service

The following list shows other operations you can use with the User Service.

Operations	Example
Get user details	GET /socialcloud/v1/user/details
Get client	GET /client
Get dashboard widgets	GET /user/dashboard
Set avatar	GET /user/avatar

The `auth_token` and `auth_appkey` header parameters are required for all calls. See the User Service reference in the Radian6 API Documentation for details on each of these operations.

Insight Service

The Insight Service enables you to perform operations such as aggregating insights and returning the insight types.

Get Insight Types

Fetch a list of the associated Insight Types for an Insights Package. The client must have access to the provided Topic Profile, and the Topic Profile must be subscribed to the provided Insights Package.

```
GET /socialcloud/v1/insights/insightTypes
```

Parameters	Type	Description
auth_token	HeaderParam	Required. Request header containing the token returned from authentication with the API.
auth_appkey	HeaderParam	Required. Application key unique to your account.
packageId	QueryParam	The ID of the Insights Package for which to fetch a list of Insight Types.

Parameters	Type	Description
topicProfileId	QueryParam	The ID of the Topic Profile that is subscribed to the provided Insights Package.

Example

```
http://api.radian6.com/socialcloud/v1/insights/insightTypes
```

Request Headers

```
GET
/socialcloud/v1/insights/insightTypes?packageId=1...2&topicProfileId=1...2
 HTTP/1.1
Host: api.radian6.com
auth_token: NotARealToken
auth_appkey: NotARealAppKey
```

Response Headers

```
HTTP/1.1 200 OK
Date: Mon, 05 Dec 2011 14:24:31 GMT
Server: Apache-Coyote/1.1
Content-Type: application/xml
Content-Length: 135
```

Response

```
<insightTypes>
    <insightType>
        <dataDescriptor>multi-value</dataDescriptor>
        <description>Retweeted usernames</description>
        <displayName>Retweeted Usernames</displayName>
        <isPrivacyRelated>false</isPrivacyRelated>
        <name>retweet_username</name>
        <objectId>4d6...bbb</objectId>
        <providerName>radian6</providerName>
    </insightType>
    ...
</insightTypes>
```

Resources for Insight Service

The following list shows other operations you can use with the Insight Service.

Operations	Example
Aggregate insights	POST /socialcloud/v1/insights /aggregateInsightsByTopic

Operations	Example
Get package subscriptions	`GET /socialcloud/v1/insights/packageSubscriptions`
Filter values	`GET /socialcloud/v1/insights/fetchFilterValues /{topicFilterId}`
Source insights	`GET /socialcloud/v1/insights/fetchInsightsBySource /{topicProfileId}/{blogIds}/{providers}`

The `auth_token` and `auth_appkey` header parameters are required for all calls. See the Insight Service reference in the Radian6 API Documentation for details on each of these operations.

Topic Service

The Insight Service enables you to perform operations such as creating topic profiles, filter groups, and filter queries.

Create or Update Topic Profile

Create or update a topic.

```
POST /topics/createTP/{topicId}/{name}/{isPublic}/{mediatypes}
/{languages}/{regions}
```

Parameters	Type	Description
`auth_token`	HeaderParam	Required. Request header containing the token returned from authentication with the API.
`auth_appkey`	HeaderParam	Required. Application key unique to your account.
`topicId`	PathParam	Unique Id of topic (required when updating)
`name`	PathParam	Display name of the topic filter
`isPublic`	PathParam	Integer value indicating if the topic is public or private
`mediatypes`	PathParam	Comma delimited list of valid media types for the topic

Parameters	Type	Description
languages	PathParam	Comma delimited list of valid languages for the topic
regions	PathParam	Comma delimited list of valid regions for the topic
billingCode	QueryParam	The billing code for the topic. Default is an empty string.
isTrial	QueryParam	Integer value indicating if the topic is a trial. Default is 1.

Example

```
http://api.radian6.com/socialcloud/v1/topics/createTP/1/My
Topic/1/8/1/2
```

Request Headers

```
GET /socialcloud/v1/topics/createTP/{topicId}/{name}/{isPublic}
/{mediatypes}/{languages}/{regions} HTTP/1.1
Host: api.radian6.com
auth_token: NotARealToken
auth_appkey: NotARealAppKey
```

Response Headers

```
HTTP/1.1 200 OK
Date: Thu, 29 Sep 2011 17:17:16 GMT
Content-Type: application/xml
Content-Length: 705
Keep-Alive: timeout=15, max=100
Connection: Keep-Alive
```

Response

```
<topicFilter>
    <name>
        <![CDATA[My Topic]]>
    </name>
    <public>0</public>
    <status>2</status>
    <estimateVolume>-1</estimateVolume>
    <competeEnabled>0</competeEnabled>
    <topicFilterTypeId>1</topicFilterTypeId>
    <bCode>
        <![CDATA[]]>
    </bCode>
    <creatorId>538</creatorId>
    <creatorName>
        <![CDATA[Jane Smith]]>
```

```
        </creatorName>
        <creatorEmail>Jane.Smith@...</creatorEmail>
        <topicFilterId>3...3</topicFilterId>
        <inboundOnTopicLinksCount>0</inboundOnTopicLinksCount>
        <languages/>
        <mediaType>8,12,14,13,11,10,9,5,2,1,16,4</mediaType>
        <projects/>
        <regions/>
        <deactivationDate>null</deactivationDate>
        <evp>false</evp>
        <topicFilterTier>
            <topicFilterTierId>-1</topicFilterTierId>
            <name/>
            <lowerTrafficLimit>-1</lowerTrafficLimit>
            <upperTrafficLimit>-1</upperTrafficLimit>
        </topicFilterTier>
        <number_queries>0</number_queries>
        <filterGroups>
            <filterGroup>
                <filterGroupId>2...9</filterGroupId>
                <name>
                    <![CDATA[Group 1]]>
                </name>
                <filterGroupTypeId>1</filterGroupTypeId>
                <filterQueries/>
            </filterGroup>
        </filterGroups>
        <sentimentQueries/>
        <includeSourceFilterList>
            <filterIds/>
        </includeSourceFilterList>
        <excludeSourceFilterList>
            <filterIds/>
        </excludeSourceFilterList>
        <includeAllSourceFilterList>
            <filterIds/>
        </includeAllSourceFilterList>
</topicFilter>
```

Resources for Topic Service

The following list shows other operations you can use with the Topic Service.

Operations	Example
Get multiple topic profiles	GET /topics
Get topic profile	GET /topics/{topicId}
Get topic profile usage	GET /topics/usage
Delete topic profile	POST /topics/remove/{topicId}

Operations	Example
Create source filter association	`POST /topics/{topicId}/sourcefilters`
Get multiple filter groups	`GET /topics/{topicId}/filterGroups`
Get filter group	`GET /topics/{topicId}/filterGroups/{filterGroupId}`
Get source filters	`GET /topics/{topicId}/sourcefilters`
Delete filter group	`DELETE /topics/{topicId}/filterGroups /{filterGroupId}`
Create filter group	`POST /topics/{topicId}/filterGroups`
Update filter group	`PUT /topics/{topicId}/filterGroups/{filterGroupId}`
Get multiple filter queries	`GET /topics/{topicId}/filterGroups /{filterGroupId}/filterQueries`
Create filter query	`GET /topics/{topicId}/filterGroups /{filterGroupId}/filterQueries`
Get filter query	`GET /topics/{topicId}/filterGroups /{filterGroupId}/filterQueries/{filterQueryId}`
Delete filter query	`DELETE /topics/{topicId}/filterGroups /{filterGroupId)/filterQueries/{filterQueryId}`
Get insight subscription window	`GET /topics/{topicId}/subscriptionWindow`

The `auth_token` and `auth_appkey` header parameters are required for all calls. See the Topic Service reference in the Radian6 API Documentation for details on each of these operations.

Data Service

The Data Service enables you to perform operations such as fetching posts and topic comparison data.

Get Post Data

Fetch posts matching given query parameters.

```
GET /data/topicdata/realtime/{recentXhours}/{topics}/{mediatypes}
/{pageIndex}/{pageSize}
```

Parameters	Type	Description
auth_token	HeaderParam	Required. Request header containing the token returned from authentication with the API.
auth_appkey	HeaderParam	Required. Application key unique to your account.
recentXhours	PathParam	Number of hours to go back. For example, setting this to 48 will return all posts within the last two days. This references the published date as they are returned within the response.
topics	PathParam	Comma delimited list of topic profile ids to get posts for.
mediaTypes	PathParam	Comma delimited list of media types from which post will be returned.
pageIndex	PathParam	Specifies which page of data to return.
pageSize	PathParam	Number of posts to return per page.

Example

```
http://api.radian6.com/socialcloud/v1/data/topicdata/realtime
/2/3..9/1,2,4,5,8,10,9,11,12,13,14,16/1/20?includeWorkflow=1&includeSpam=0
&merged=1&token=1321987774350&extendedMediaTypes=2,3,4
```

Request Headers

```
GET /socialcloud/v1/data/topicdata/realtime/{recentXhours}/{topics}
/{mediatypes}/{pageIndex}/{pageSize} HTTP/1.1
Host: api.radian6.com
auth_token: NotARealToken
auth_appkey: NotARealAppKey
```

Response Headers

```
HTTP/1.1 200 OK
Date: Thu, 29 Sep 2011 17:17:16 GMT
Content-Type: application/xml
Content-Length: 705
Keep-Alive: timeout=15, max=100
Connection: Keep-Alive
```

Response

```
<?xml version="1.0" encoding="UTF-8"?>
<radian6_RiverOfNews_export>
    <report_date>2012-07-11 02:24:04 +1200</report_date>
    <user_name>Jane.Smith@...</user_name>
    <RoN_sort_order>publishedDate</RoN_sort_order>
    <article_count>2</article_count>
    <total_article_count>101</total_article_count>
    <article ID="2...9">
        <description charset="UTF-8">
            <headline/>
            <author fbid="-1" externalId="3...2"/>
            <author_full_name />
            <recipient/>
            <content/>
            <external_id>2...73</external_id>
            <parentExternalId>2...70</parentExternalId>
        </description>
        <avatar/>
        <source/>
        <host>
            <![CDATA[twitter.com]]>
        </host>
        <article_url>
            <![CDATA[2...73]]>
        </article_url>
        <media_provider>TWITTER</media_provider>
        <media_type_id>8</media_type_id>
        <language_id>16</language_id>
        <spam_rating>0</spam_rating>
        <publish_date epoch="1341901361000">2012-07-10 18:22:41
+1200</publish_date>
        <harvest_date epoch="1341901379000">2012-07-10 18:22:59
+1200</harvest_date>
        <PostInsights>
            <PostInsight>
                <Provider>
                    <![CDATA[provider_name]]>
                </Provider>
                <Type>
                    <![CDATA[type_name]]>
                </Type>
                <Value>
                    <![CDATA[some_value]]>
                </Value>
            </PostInsight>
        </PostInsights>
        <SourceInsights>
            <SourceInsight>
                <Provider>
                    <![CDATA[provider_name]]>
                </Provider>
                <Type>
                    <![CDATA[type_name]]>
                </Type>
                <Value>
```

```
                        <![CDATA[some_value]]>
                    </Value>
                <SourceInsight>
            </SourceInsights>
            <PostDynamicsIteration>
                <PostDynamicsDefinition>
                    <fieldId>9</fieldId>
                    <label>Following</label>
                    <value/>
                    <sortOrder>1</sortOrder>
                </PostDynamicsDefinition>
                <PostDynamicsDefinition>
                    <fieldId>8</fieldId>
                    <label>Followers</label>
                    <value/>
                    <sortOrder>2</sortOrder>
                </PostDynamicsDefinition>
                <PostDynamicsDefinition>
                    <fieldId>10</fieldId>
                    <label>Updates</label>
                    <value/>
                    <sortOrder>3</sortOrder>
                </PostDynamicsDefinition>
                <PostDynamicsDefinition>
                    <fieldId>21</fieldId>
                    <label>Sentiment</label>
                    <shortLabel>S</shortLabel>
                    <sortOrder>4</sortOrder>
                    <value/>
                    <exceptionValue>2860,false</exceptionValue>
                    <reportValue>Neutral</reportValue>
                    <tooltip/>
                </PostDynamicsDefinition>
                <reportFormatedData/>
            </PostDynamicsIteration>
    </article>
    <article ID="252359343">
        <description charset="UTF-8">
            <headline>
                <![CDATA[Post from Facebook user]]>
            </headline>
            <author fbid="1769972299" externalId="1769972299">
                <![CDATA[Facebook user]]>
            </author>
            <recipient>
                <![CDATA[None]]>
            </recipient>
            <content>
                <![CDATA[Facebook post content...]]>
            </content>
            <external_id>17...9_22...4</external_id>
        </description>
        <source ID="1...2">
            <![CDATA[Post from Facebook user]]>
        </source>
        <host>
            <![CDATA[www.facebook.com]]>
```

```
        </host>
        <article_url>

<![CDATA[http://www.facebook.com/permalink.php?story_fbid=22...4&id=17...9]]>

        </article_url>
        <media_provider>facebook.com Discussions</media_provider>
        <media_type_id>12</media_type_id>
        <language_id>1</language_id>
        <spam_rating>0</spam_rating>
        <publish_date epoch="1341886037000">2012-07-10 14:07:17
+1200</publish_date>
        <harvest_date epoch="1341886905000">2012-07-10 14:21:45
+1200</harvest_date>
        <PostDynamicsIteration>
            <PostDynamicsDefinition>
                <fieldId>21</fieldId>
                <label>Sentiment</label>
                <shortLabel>S</shortLabel>
                <sortOrder>1</sortOrder>
                <value>
                    <![CDATA[2860,0]]>
                </value>
                <exceptionValue>2860,false</exceptionValue>
                <reportValue>Neutral</reportValue>
                <tooltip/>
            </PostDynamicsDefinition>
            <reportFormatedData>
                <![CDATA[<span style="font-weight:bold; color:
#FF9900; font-size: 11pt"> Sentiment:  </span>Neutral  ]]>
            </reportFormatedData>
        </PostDynamicsIteration>
    </article>
</radian6_RiverOfNews_export>
```

For a complete list of parameters for this operation, see Get Post Data in the Radian6 API Documentation.

Resources for Data Service

The following list shows other operations you can use with the Data Service.

Operations	Example
Get data by range	GET /data/topicdata/realtime/{daterangeStart} /{daterangeEnd}/{topics}/{mediatypes}/{pageIndex}/{pageSize}
Get tag cloud data	GET /data/tagclouddata/{recentXhours}/{topics} /{mediatypes}/{advancedQueryFilters}

Operations	Example
Get tag cloud data by range	`GET /data/tagclouddata/{daterangeStart}` `/{daterangeEnd}/{topics}/{mediatypes}/{advancedQueryFilters}`
Get topic match data	`GET /data/comparisondata/{recentXhours}/{topics}` `/{mediatypes}/{segmentation}/{countBy}`
Get topic match data by range	`GET /data/comparisondata/{daterangeStart}` `/{daterangeEnd}/{topics}/{mediatypes}/{segmentation}/{countBy}`
Get widget data	`GET /data/widget/{widgetId}`

The `auth_token` and `auth_appkey` header parameters are required for all calls. See the Data Service reference in the Radian6 API Documentation for details on each of these operations.

Blog Service

The Blog Service enables you to perform operations such as fetching a list of posts for a given site and adding notes to a site.

Get Blog Details

Fetch a list of posts for a given site including workflow details.

`GET /blog/workflow/{blogId}/{topicId}`

Parameters	Type	Description
`auth_token`	HeaderParam	Required. Request header containing the token returned from authentication with the API.
`auth_appkey`	HeaderParam	Required. Application key unique to your account.
`blogId`	PathParam	Blog Ids for which to get posts for.
`topicId`	PathParam	Comma delimited list of topic Ids.
`maxPostCount`	QueryParam	Total number of post to return per request.

Parameters	Type	Description
pageNum	QueryParam	The page index to return posts for. For example if the total count of posts for the request exceeds the maximum number of posts (as indicated by the maxPostCount paramter), the page number can be incremented to fetch those posts not returned in the current request.

Example

```
http://api.radian6.com/socialcloud/v1/blog/workflow/5...5/2...7
```

Request Headers

```
GET /socialcloud/v1/blog/workflow/{blogId}/{topicId} HTTP/1.1
Host: api.radian6.com
auth_token: NotARealToken
auth_appkey: NotARealAppKey
```

Response Headers

```
HTTP/1.1 200 OK
Date: Thu, 29 Sep 2011 17:17:16 GMT
Content-Type: application/xml
Content-Length: 705
Keep-Alive: timeout=15, max=100
Connection: Keep-Alive
```

Response

```
<?xml version="1.0" encoding="UTF-8"?>
<radian6_RiverOfNews_export>
    <report_date>2012-07-11 02:24:04 +1200</report_date>
    <user_name>Jane.Smith@...</user_name>
    <RoN_sort_order>publishedDate</RoN_sort_order>
    <article_count>1</article_count>
    <total_article_count>1</total_article_count>
    <article ID="2...3">
        <description charset="UTF-8">
            <headline>
                <![CDATA[Post from Facebook user]]>
            </headline>
            <author fbid="17...9" externalId="17...9">
                <![CDATA[Facebook user]]>
            </author>
            <recipient>
                <![CDATA[None]]>
            </recipient>
            <content>
                <![CDATA[Facebook post content...]]>
```

```
            </content>
            <external_id>17...9_22...4</external_id>
        </description>
        <source ID="1...2">
            <![CDATA[Post from Facebook user]]>
        </source>
        <host>
            <![CDATA[www.facebook.com]]>
        </host>
        <article_url>

<![CDATA[http://www.facebook.com/permalink.php?story_fbid=22...4&id=17...9]]>

        </article_url>
        <media_provider>facebook.com Discussions</media_provider>
        <media_type_id>12</media_type_id>
        <language_id>1</language_id>
        <spam_rating>0</spam_rating>
        <publish_date epoch="1341886037000">2012-07-10 14:07:17
+1200</publish_date>
        <harvest_date epoch="1341886905000">2012-07-10 14:21:45
+1200</harvest_date>
        <PostDynamicsIteration>
            <PostDynamicsDefinition>
                <fieldId>21</fieldId>
                <label>Sentiment</label>
                <shortLabel>S</shortLabel>
                <sortOrder>1</sortOrder>
                <value>
                    <![CDATA[2860,0]]>
                </value>
                <exceptionValue>2860,false</exceptionValue>
                <reportValue>Neutral</reportValue>
                <tooltip/>
            </PostDynamicsDefinition>
            <reportFormatedData>
                <![CDATA[<span style="font-weight:bold; color:
#FF9900; font-size: 11pt"> Sentiment:  </span>Neutral  ]]>
            </reportFormatedData>
        </PostDynamicsIteration>
    </article>
</radian6_RiverOfNews_export>
```

Resources for Blog Service

The following list shows other operations you can use with the Blog Service.

Operations	Example
Add note to a site	POST /blog/workflow/note/{blogIdList}
Add note by post Id	POST /blog/workflow/noteByPostId/{blogPostId}
Add tag by post Id	POST /blog/workflow/tagsByPostId/{blogPostId}

Operations	Example
Get site metrics	`GET /blog/metrics/{siteId}/{topicId}`
Get tagged blogs	`GET /blog/sourcetagged/{tags}`
Remove tags and notes	`POST /blog/workflow/removeTagsAndNotes /{tagAndNoteIds}`

The `auth_token` and `auth_appkey` header parameters are required for all calls. See the Blog Service reference in the Radian6 API Documentation for details on each of these operations.

Authentication Service

The Authentication Service enables you to authenticate a user in the Radian6 system.

Responds with authentication token to be used for subsequent requests as request header called `auth_token`. `auth_appkey` must also be provided for every request.

```
GET /socialcloud/v1/auth/authenticate
```

Parameters	Type	Description
`auth_user`	`HeaderParam`	Required. Request header containing username.
`auth_pass`	`HeaderParam`	Required. Request header containing the plain text password.
`auth_token`	`HeaderParam`	Required. Request header containing the token returned from authentication with the API.
`auth_appkey`	`HeaderParam`	Required. Application key unique to your account.
`fields`	`QueryParam`	Comma delimited list of elements to return such as `userdetails` and `clientattributes`.

Example

```
https://api.radian6.com/socialcloud/v1/auth/authenticate
?fields=userdetails,clientattributes
```

Request Headers

```
GET /socialcloud/v1/auth/authenticate HTTP/1.1
Host: api.radian6.com
```

```
auth_user: mikemullen
auth_pass: NotARealPassword
auth_appkey: NotARealAppKey
```

Response Headers

```
HTTP/1.1 200 OK
Date: Thu, 29 Sep 2011 17:17:16 GMT
Content-Type: application/xml
Content-Length: 705
Keep-Alive: timeout=15, max=100
Connection: Keep-Alive
```

Response

```
<auth>
  <token>b65e06d1b5383...</token>
  <UserDetails>
    <user>
      <userId>12345</userId>
      <clientId>99</clientId>
      <displayName><![CDATA[Mike Mullen]]></displayName>
      <emailAddress>Mike.Mullen@...</emailAddress>
      <timezone>GMT</timezone>
      <packages></packages>
      <userRoleId>1</userRoleId>
      <createdDate>Jun 22, 2010 05:18 PM</createdDate>
      <enabled>true</enabled>
      <aihUsers><aihUser>
      <userKey>84ba97...</userKey>
      <registerDate>2010</registerDate>
      <type>1</type>
      </aihUser></aihUsers>
    </user>
    <avatar
userId="12345"><![CDATA[http://path-to-avatar-image.jpg]]></avatar>
    <Packages></Packages>
    <ClientAttributes>
      <attribute>
        <id>12</id>
        <description>IDLE_TIMEOUT</description>
        <value>10800000</value>
      </attribute>
      ...
    </ClientAttributes>
  </UserDetails>
</auth>
```

Lookup Service

The Lookup Service enables you to perform operations such as fetching a list of media types, languages, users, and workflow items.

Get Media Types

Fetch a list of valid media types. Media types are used to indicate the type and source of social media posts within the Radian6 API. They can be used to create source filters within the Analysis Dashboard (Topic Profile Configuration) and can also be used to filter results in the calls of the Data Service. This call shows you the name and id of all the media types in the system.

```
GET /lookup/mediaproviders
```

Parameters	Type	Description
auth_token	HeaderParam	Required. Request header containing the token returned from authentication with the API.
auth_appkey	HeaderParam	Required. Application key unique to your account.

Example

```
http://api.radian6.com/socialcloud/v1/lookup/mediaproviders
```

Request Headers

```
GET /socialcloud/v1/lookup/mediaproviders HTTP/1.1
Host: api.radian6.com
auth_token: NotARealToken
auth_appkey: NotARealAppKey
```

Response Headers

```
HTTP/1.1 200 OK
Date: Thu, 29 Sep 2011 17:17:16 GMT
Content-Type: application/xml
Content-Length: 705
Keep-Alive: timeout=15, max=100
Connection: Keep-Alive
```

Response

```
<?xml version="1.0" encoding="utf-8"?>
<MediaTypeList>
    <MediaTypeItem>
        <mediaTypeId>1</mediaTypeId>
        <mediaTypeName>Blogs</mediaTypeName>
        <displayOrder>1</displayOrder>
    </MediaTypeItem>
    <MediaTypeItem>
        <mediaTypeId>2</mediaTypeId>
        <mediaTypeName>Videos</mediaTypeName>
        <displayOrder>2</displayOrder>
```

```
        </MediaTypeItem>
        <MediaTypeItem>
            <mediaTypeId>4</mediaTypeId>
            <mediaTypeName>Images</mediaTypeName>
            <displayOrder>3</displayOrder>
        </MediaTypeItem>
        <MediaTypeItem>
            <mediaTypeId>5</mediaTypeId>
            <mediaTypeName>Mainstream News</mediaTypeName>
            <displayOrder>4</displayOrder>
        </MediaTypeItem>
        <MediaTypeItem>
            <mediaTypeId>8</mediaTypeId>
            <mediaTypeName>MicroMedia</mediaTypeName>
            <displayOrder>5</displayOrder>
        </MediaTypeItem>
        <MediaTypeItem>
            <mediaTypeId>10</mediaTypeId>
            <mediaTypeName>Forums</mediaTypeName>
            <displayOrder>6</displayOrder>
        </MediaTypeItem>
        <MediaTypeItem>
            <mediaTypeId>9</mediaTypeId>
            <mediaTypeName>Forum Replies</mediaTypeName>
            <displayOrder>7</displayOrder>
        </MediaTypeItem>
        <MediaTypeItem>
            <mediaTypeId>11</mediaTypeId>
            <mediaTypeName>Comments</mediaTypeName>
            <displayOrder>8</displayOrder>
        </MediaTypeItem>
        <MediaTypeItem>
            <mediaTypeId>12</mediaTypeId>
            <mediaTypeName>Facebook</mediaTypeName>
            <displayOrder>9</displayOrder>
        </MediaTypeItem>
        <MediaTypeItem>
            <mediaTypeId>13</mediaTypeId>
            <mediaTypeName>Aggregator</mediaTypeName>
            <displayOrder>10</displayOrder>
        </MediaTypeItem>
        <MediaTypeItem>
            <mediaTypeId>14</mediaTypeId>
            <mediaTypeName>Buy/Sell</mediaTypeName>
            <displayOrder>11</displayOrder>
        </MediaTypeItem>
        <MediaTypeItem>
            <mediaTypeId>16</mediaTypeId>
            <mediaTypeName>MySpace</mediaTypeName>
            <displayOrder>13</displayOrder>
        </MediaTypeItem>
</MediaTypeList>
```

Resources for Lookup Service

The following list shows other operations you can use with the Lookup Service.

Operations	Example
Get sort types	`GET /lookup/sorttypes`
Get languages	`GET /lookup/languages`
Get timezones	`GET /lookup/timezones`
Get filter types	`GET /lookup/filtertypes`
Get count types	`GET /lookup/counttypes`
Get users	`GET /lookup/users`
Get tags	`GET /lookup/tags`
Get advanced filter types	`GET /lookup/advancedfiltertypes`
Get regions	`GET /lookup/regions`
Get projects	`GET /lookup/projects`
Get influencer metrics	`GET /lookup/influencermetrics`
Get external account types	`GET /lookup/externalaccounttypes`
Get extended media types	`GET /lookup/extendedmediatypes`
Get media group types	`GET /lookup/mediagroupproviders`
Get workflow	`GET /lookup/workflow`

The `auth_token` and `auth_appkey` header parameters are required for all calls. See the Lookup Service reference in the Radian6 API Documentation for details on each of these operations.

Resources

Use the following resources to get more information about the Radian6 API.

- Radian6 API Documentation: `http://socialcloud.radian6.com/docs`
- Get started with Radian6:
  `http://www.salesforcemarketingcloud.com/products/social-media-listening/`
- Radian6 case studies:
  `http://www.salesforcemarketingcloud.com/resources/videos/`

## Chapter 26

Pardot API

Pardot enables you to create, deploy, and manage online marketing campaigns efficiently. The Pardot REST API allows your application to access prospects, visitors, activities, opportunities, and other data in Pardot.

All Pardot accounts and user roles have full access to the API. Pardot integrates and syncs automatically with Salesforce using a connector. You can use the Pardot API if you're performing custom integrations involving third-party tools and services not supported by our connectors.

You must authenticate with the API before issuing requests. All requests must use HTTP GET or POST. Although GET requests are secure due to the use of SSL, we recommend using POST, with sensitive or lengthy parameter values being part of the POST message body.

When performing update requests, only the fields specified in the request are updated, and all others are left unchanged. If a required field is cleared during an update, the request will be declined.

Objects available through the API correspond to objects within the Pardot user interface. These objects may include opportunities, prospects, users, visitors, and so on.

Supported Browsers

Pardot supports the following browsers:

- Mozilla® Firefox®
- Google Chrome™
- Microsoft® Internet Explorer®
- Apple® Safari®

If you receive an "outdated browser" warning, upgrade to the latest version of a browser listed above.

Supported Salesforce Editions

Pardot supports these Salesforce Editions:

- Professional Edition
- Enterprise Edition
- Unlimited Edition

If you're an existing Salesforce customer and want to upgrade to any of these editions, contact your account representative.

Quick Start

The Pardot API allows your application to access data within Pardot.

To get started with the Pardot API, follow these steps.

1. Authenticate with the API.
2. Issue requests using the API. You can test out API requests via the API Console.

Visit the Pardot Developer site to learn more and watch a demo on how to get your API key and learn how to query and create prospects.

Step One: Authenticate with the API

You must authenticate with the API before issuing requests.

A few prerequisites must be met to successfully authenticate a connection to the API.

1. All requests to the Pardot API must be made via SSL encrypted connection.
2. Authentication requests must use HTTP POST.
3. Obtain the `email`, `password`, and `user_key` (available in the application under **My Settings**) for the Pardot user account that will be submitting API requests.

With these requirements met, an API key must be acquired. Both User and API keys are unique to individual users. API keys are valid for 60 minutes. In contrast, user keys are valid indefinitely. To authenticate, issue the following request (having replaced the values denoted in `italics` with values for your account):

```
POST: https://pi.pardot.com/api/login/version/3
message body: email=email&password=password&user_key=user_key
```

Parameter	Description
email	The email address of your user account
password	The password of your user account
user_key	The 32-bit hexadecimal user key for your user account

All parameters are required. If authentication was successful, a 32-character hexadecimal API key will be returned in the following format:

```
<rsp stat="ok" version="1.0">
    <api_key>5a1698a233e73d7c8ccd60d775fbc68a</api_key>
</rsp>
```

Otherwise, the response will contain the following:

```
<rsp stat="fail" version="1.0">
    <err code="15">Login failed</err>
</rsp>
```

Subsequent authentication requests will return either the current valid API key or a newly generated API key if the previous one had expired.

Step Two: Issue Requests Using the Pardot API

The Pardot API handles a variety of requests for many of the objects available through the Pardot user interface.

Most requests to the API use the following standardized format. All requests must use HTTP `GET` or `POST`. Although `GET` requests are secure due to the use of SSL, we recommend using `POST`, with sensitive or lengthy parameter values being part of the `POST` message body. You're responsible for issuing requests with the following components:

```
POST:
https://pi.pardot.com/api/object/version/3/do/operator/identifier_field/identifier
message body:
api_key=your_api_key&user_key=your_user_key&parameters_for_request
```

```
GET:
https://pi.pardot.com/api/object/version/3/do/operator/identifier_field/identifier
?api_key=your_api_key&user_key=your_user_key&parameters_for_request
```

Parameter	Description
object	The object type to be returned by the API request
operator	The operation to be performed on the specified object type
identifier_field	The field to be used as the identifier for the specified object type
identifier	The identifier for the specified object(s)
your_api_key	The API key that was obtained during authentication
your_user_key	The user key that was used during authentication
format	The API data format. Either xml or json (xml is default)
parameters_for_request	Parameters specific to your request

With the exception of format and parameters_for_request, all parameters are required.

The ordering of parameters is arbitrary. Parameters are passed using conventional HTML parameter syntax, with '?' indicating the start of the parameter string (for GET requests only) and '&' as the separator between parameters. Data returned from the API is formatted using JSON or XML 1.0 with UTF-8 character encoding. Keep in mind that some characters in the response may be encoded as HTML entities, requiring client-side decoding. Also, keep in mind that all parameters specified in an API request MUST be URL-encoded before they are submitted.

In general, the API will return XML or JSON containing a current version of the target object's data. However, unsuccessful requests will return a short response containing an error code and message.

Querying Objects

Search criteria may be used together in any combination and/or order unless otherwise specified. Unless output=mobile is specified, each query request returns 200 results. This limit is not enforced for responses formatted for mobile devices. For parameter values that can be quite large such as those with comma-separated IDs, we recommend using a POST request due to the URL character limits on GET requests. When querying objects, you can include parameters to navigate through the result set, retrieve the remaining results, and sort.

Changing the API Response Format

The Pardot API supports several output formats, each of which returns different levels of detail in the XML or JSON response. Output formats are defined by specifying the `output` request parameter. Supported output formats include:

- `full`—Returns all supported data for the Pardot object and all objects associated with it.
- `simple`—Returns all supported data for the data for the Pardot object.
- `mobile`—Returns an abbreviated version of the object data. This output format is ideal for mobile applications.

If the output request parameter is not defined, the output format defaults to `full`.

Sample XML Response Format

The following examples show the XML response formats for an opportunity.

For `output=full`:

```
<rsp stat="ok" version="1.0">
    <opportunity>
        . . .
        <campaign>
            . . .
        </campaign>
        <prospects>
            <prospect>
                . . .
            </prospect>
        </prospects>
        <opportunity_activities>
            <visitor_activity>
                . . .
            </visitor_activity>
        </opportunity_activities>
    </opportunity>
</rsp>
```

For `output=simple`:

```
<rsp stat="ok" version="1.0">
    <opportunity>
        . . .
        <campaign>
            . . .
        </campaign>
        <prospects>
            <prospect>
```

```
                ...
            </prospect>
          </prospects>
      </opportunity>
  </rsp>
```

For `output=mobile`:

```
<rsp stat="ok" version="1.0">
    <opportunity>
        ...
    </opportunity>
</rsp>
```

Using the API

Each field returned by the API maps to a field within the Pardot user interface. Field mappings for individual records (prospects and leads/contacts) and accounts are set up automatically when you verify your connector.

By default, Salesforce is the master for all of these fields except for the proprietary Pardot fields (score, grade, Pardot campaign, and so on), referrer fields, and Google Analytics fields created when you install the AppExchange package.

At this time, we only sync with lead, contact, account, and opportunity fields. However, you can choose to make Pardot the master for most other fields and change most of the default mappings if you'd like.

For more information on field mapping, see the following resources.

- Getting Started with the Salesforce Integration
- Opportunities in Pardot
- Default Prospect and Account Field Mapping

For more information on fields that can be returned or updated via the API, see the Object Field References in the Pardot API Documentation.

Using Prospects

Access and manage your prospects.

Supported Operations

Supported operations for prospects are `assign`, `unassign`, `create`, `read`, `update`, `upsert`, `delete`, and `query`.

Operation	Description
assign	**Format** /api/prospect/version/3/do/assign/email/*email*?... **Required Parameters** user_key, api_key, email (user_email OR user_id OR group_id) **Description** Assigns or reassigns the prospect specified by *email* to a specified Pardot user or group. One of the following parameters must be provided to identify the target user or group: *user_email*, *user_id*, or *group_id*. Returns an updated version of the prospect.
assign	**Format** /api/prospect/version/3/do/assign/id/*id*?... **Required Parameters** user_key, api_key, id (user_email OR user_id OR group_id) **Description** Assigns or reassigns the prospect specified by *id* to a specified Pardot user or group. One of the following parameters must be provided to identify the target user or group: *user_email*, *user_id*, or *group_id* Returns an updated version of the prospect.
create	**Format** /api/prospect/version/3/do/create/email/*email*?... **Required Parameters** user_key, api_key, email **Description** Creates a new prospect using the specified data. *email* must be a unique email address. Email list subscriptions and custom field data may also be added with this request.

Operation	Description
query	**Format** /api/prospect/version/3/do/query?... **Required Parameters** user_key, api_key **Description** Returns the prospects matching the specified criteria parameters.
query	**Format** /api/opportunity/version/3/do/query?... **Required Parameters** user_key, api_key **Description** Returns the opportunities matching the specified criteria parameters.

Assigning and Reassigning Prospects

To assign or reassign a prospect, both the prospect to be assigned and the target user or group of the assignment must be defined. Prospects can be specified by their Pardot ID or email address. Users or groups can be specified by their Pardot user ID, email address, or Pardot group ID.

The following examples show possible combinations of parameters. You must substitute specific values for parameters denoted in *italics*.

```
/api/prospect/version/3/do/assign/email/?user_email=user_email
&api_key=api_key&user_key=user_key
```

```
/api/prospect/version/3/do/assign/email/?user_id=user_id
&api_key=api_key&user_key=user_key
```

```
/api/prospect/version/3/do/assign/email/?group_id=group_id
&api_key=api_key&user_key=user_key
```

```
/api/prospect/version/3/do/assign/id/?user_email=user_email
&api_key=api_key&user_key=user_key
```

```
/api/prospect/version/3/do/assign/id/?user_id=user_id
&api_key=api_key&user_key=user_key
```

```
/api/prospect/version/3/do/assign/id/?group_id=group_id
&api_key=api_key&user_key=user_key
```

Only values that are specifically named in the request are updated. All others are left unchanged. To clear a value, submit an `update` request containing a parameter with no specified value, such as `status=`.

Creating Prospects

To create a prospect via the API, only a valid and unique email address is required. Values for any other prospect fields may also be provided in the `create` request. Developers are responsible for substituting specific values for parameters denoted in *italics*.

The following example shows how to create a new prospect.

```
/api/prospect/version/3/do/create/email/new_prospect@pardot.com?first_name=first_name
&last_name=last_name&api_key=api_key&user_key=user_key
```

See Using Prospects and the Prospect field reference in the Pardot API Documentation for complete descriptions of prospects.

Updating Field Values

Modifying values of prospect data fields is done by submitting an `update` request with parameters for each field to be updated. Each parameter is formatted as `field_name=value`. Custom field values are updated using the same syntax.

The following example shows how to update the phone number of a prospect whose email address is bob@pardot.com.

```
/api/prospect/version/3/do/update/email/bob@pardot.com?phone=888-123-4567
&api_key=api_key&user_key=user_key
```

Only values that are specifically named in the request are updated. All others are left unchanged. To clear a value, submit an update request containing a parameter with no specified value, such as phone=.

Note: Any field that is set to record multiple responses cannot have its values cleared this way.

Using Opportunities

Access and manage your opportunities.

Supported Operations

Supported operations for opportunities are create, read, update, delete, undelete, and query.

Operation	Description
create	**Format** /api/opportunity/version/3/do/create/ prospect_email/prospect_email?... **Required Parameters** user_key, api_key, prospect_email, name, value, probability **Description** Creates a new opportunity using the specified data. The prospect_email parameter must correspond to an existing prospect. name, value, and probability must also be specified. **Note:** If both prospect_email and prospect_id are specified, both must correspond to the same prospect.

Operation	Description

create	**Format**
	
	`/api/opportunity/version/3/do/create/`
	`prospect_id/`*`prospect_id`*`?...`
	
	Required Parameters
	
	`user_key, api_key, prospect_email, name, value,`
	`probability`
	
	Description
	
	Creates a new opportunity using the specified data. The `prospect_id` parameter must correspond to an existing prospect. `name`, `value`, and `probability` must also be specified.

update	**Format**
	
	`/api/opportunity/version/3/do/update/id/`*`id`*`?...`
	
	Required Parameters
	
	`user_key, api_key, id`
	
	Description
	
	Updates the provided data for the opportunity specified by `id`, which is the Pardot ID for the target opportunity. Fields that are not updated by the request remain unchanged. Returns an updated version of the opportunity.

query	**Format**
	
	`/api/opportunity/version/3/do/query?...`
	
	Required Parameters
	
	`user_key, api_key`
	
	Description
	
	Returns the opportunities matching the specified criteria parameters.

Usage

Modifying values of opportunity data fields is done by submitting an `update` request with parameters for each field to be updated. Each parameter is formatted as *`field_name=value`*.

The following example updates the value of an opportunity whose Pardot ID is 27.

```
POST: /api/opportunity/version/3/do/update/id/27 message body:
value=50000&api_key=api_key&user_key=user_key
```

Only values that are specifically named in the request are updated. All others are left unchanged. To clear a value, submit an update request containing a parameter with no specified value, such as status=.

See Using Opportunities and the Opportunity field reference in the Pardot API Documentation for complete descriptions of opportunity.

Using Visitors

Access and query your visitors.

Supported Operations

Supported operations for visitors are assign, read, and query.

Operation	Description
assign	**Format** /api/visitor/version/3/do/assign/id/id?... **Required Parameters** user_key, api_key, id (prospect_email OR prospect_id) **Description** Assigns or reassigns the visitor specified by id to a specified prospect. One (and only one) of the following parameters must be provided to identify the target prospect: prospect_email or prospect_id. Returns an updated version of the visitor.
read	**Format** /api/visitor/version/3/do/read/id/id?... **Required Parameters** user_key, api_key, id

Operation	Description
	Description Returns the data for the visitor specified by `id`, including associated visitor activities, identified company data, and visitor referrers. The `id` parameter is the Pardot ID for the target visitor.

query	**Format**
	`/api/visitor/version/3/do/query?...`
	
	Required Parameters
	`user_key, api_key`
	
	Description
	Returns the visitors matching the specified criteria parameters.

Assigning and Reassigning Visitors

To assign or reassign a visitor, both the visitor to be assigned and the target prospect of the assignment must be defined. Visitors are specified by their Pardot ID. Prospects can be specified by their Pardot user ID or by their email address.

The following example shows possible combinations of parameters. You must substitute specific values for parameters denoted in *italics*.

```
/api/visitor/version/3/do/assign/id/visitor_id?prospect_email=prospect_email
&api_key=api_key&user_key=user_key
```

```
/api/visitor/version/3/do/assign/id/visitor_id?prospect_id=prospect_id
&api_key=api_key&user_key=user_key
```

See Using Visitors and the Visitor field reference in the Pardot API Documentation for complete descriptions of visitors.

Using Users

Read and query your users.

Supported Operations

Supported operations for users are `read`, and `query`. The following examples show how you can assign, read and query users.

Operation	Description

read	**Format**
	
	`/api/user/version/3/do/read/email/`*`email`*`?...`
	
	Required Parameters
	`user_key, api_key, id`
	
	Description
	Returns the data for the user specified by *email*, which is the email address of the target user.

read	**Format**
	
	`/api/user/version/3/do/read/id/`*`id`*`?...`
	
	Required Parameters
	`user_key, api_key, id`
	
	Description
	Returns the data for the user specified by *id*, which is the Pardot ID of the target user.

query	**Format**
	
	`/api/user/version/3/do/query?...`
	
	Required Parameters
	`user_key, api_key`
	
	Description
	Returns the users matching the specified criteria parameters.

Usage

See Using Users and the User field reference in the Pardot API Documentation for complete descriptions of users.

Using Visits

Read and query your users' visits.

Supported Operations

Supported operations for visits are `read` and `query`. The following examples show how you can read and query visits.

Operation	Description

read	**Format**
	
	　　`/api/visit/version/3/do/read/id/`*`id`*`?...`
	
	Required Parameters
	　　`user_key, api_key, id`
	
	Description
	　　Returns the data for the visit specified by *id*, including associated visitor page views. The *id* parameter is the Pardot ID for the target visit.

query	**Format**
	
	　　`/api/visit/version/3/do/query?...`
	
	Required Parameters
	　　`user_key, api_key, (ids, visitor_ids, prospect_ids)`
	
	Description
	　　Returns the visits matching the specified criteria parameters.

Usage

See Using Visits and the Visit field reference in the Pardot API Documentation for complete descriptions of visits.

Using Lists

Read and query your email list subscriptions.

Supported Operations

Supported operations for lists are `read` and `query`. The following examples show how you can read and query lists.

Operation	Description

read	**Format**
	
	    `/api/list/version/3/do/read/id/`*`id`*`?...`
	
	Required Parameters
	`user_key, api_key, id`
	
	Description
	Returns the data for the list specified by *`id`*, which is the Pardot ID for the target list.

query	**Format**
	
	    `/api/list/version/3/do/query?...`
	
	Required Parameters
	`user_key, api_key`
	
	Description
	Returns the lists matching the specified criteria parameters.

Usage

See Using Lists and the List field reference in the Pardot API Documentation for complete descriptions of lists.

Using Prospect Accounts

Access and manage your prospect accounts.

Supported Operations

Supported operations for prospects are `create`, `describe`, `read`, `update`, and `query`. The following examples show how you can create, read, and query prospect accounts.

Operation	Description
create	**Format** `/api/prospectAccount/version/3/do/create?...`

Operation	Description
	Required Parameters `user_key, api_key` **Description** Create a new prospect accounts.

`read`	**Format**
	`/api/prospectAccount/version/3/do/read/id/`*`id`*`?...`
	Required Parameters
	`user_key, api_key, id`
	Description
	Returns the data for the prospect account specified by *id*, which is the Pardot ID of the target prospect account.

`query`	**Format**
	`/api/prospectAccount/version/3/do/query?...`
	Required Parameters
	`user_key, api_key`
	Description
	Returns the prospect accounts matching the specified criteria parameters.

Usage

See Using Prospect Accounts and the Prospect Account field reference in the Pardot API Documentation for complete descriptions of prospect accounts.

Reading Emails

Read emails based on the Pardot ID.

Supported Operations

The following example shows how you can read emails.

Operation	Description

read	**Format**
	
	`/api/email/version/3/do/read/id/email_id?...`
	
	Required Parameters
	
	`user_key, api_key, email`
	
	Description
	
	Returns the data for the email specified by `id`, which is the Pardot ID for the target email.

Usage

For more information, see the Email field reference in the Pardot API Documentation.

Sending One to One Emails

Send an email to a prospect.

Supported Operations

The following example shows how you can send one-to-one email to a prospect.

Operation	Description

send	**Format**
	
	`/api/email/version/3/do/send/prospect_id`
	`/<prospect_id>?...`
	
	Required Parameters
	
	`user_key, api_key, campaign_id,`
	`(email_template_id OR (text_content, name, &`
	`subject)), (from_email OR from_user_id)`
	
	Description
	
	Sends a one-to-one email to the prospect identified by `<prospect_id>`.

send	**Format**
	
	`/api/email/version/3/do/send/prospect_email`
	`/<prospect_email>?...`

Operation	Description

	Required Parameters
	`user_key, api_key, campaign_id,`
	`(email_template_id OR (text_content, name, &`
	`subject)), (from_email OR from_user_id)`
	
	Description
	Sends a one-to-one email to the prospect identified by
	`<prospect_email>`.

Usage

For more information, see the Email field reference in the Pardot API Documentation.

Sending List Emails

Send emails to prospects at a scheduled date and time.

Supported Operations

The following example shows how you can send emails to prospects.

Operation	Description

send	**Format**
	`/api/email/version/3/do/send`
	
	Required Parameters
	`user_key, api_key, list_ids[], campaign_id,`
	`(email_template OR (text_content, name, &`
	`subject)), (from_email OR from_user_id)`
	
	Description
	Sends an email to all prospects in a list identified by
	`list_ids[]`.

Usage

For more information, see the Email field reference in the Pardot API Documentation.

Resources

Use the following resources to get more information about the Pardot API.

- Pardot API Documentation: `http://developer.pardot.com/`
- Object Field References:
  `http://developer.pardot.com/kb/api-version-3/object-field-references`
- Getting Started with the Salesforce Integration:
  `http://www.pardot.com/faqs/salesforce/getting-started-salesforce-com/`

SERVICE CLOUD

Chapter 27

Desk.com API

Desk.com enables you to deliver efficient all-in-one customer service, from customer and content management to business process automation and insights.

The Desk.com API provides a powerful and simple RESTful interface for interacting with your Desk.com data. With the Desk.com API, you can:

- Read all your cases
- Search for customers by name
- Create a new company
- Update an article translation
- Delete a topic

With over 100 endpoints, the Desk.com API can help you to build rich integrations and applications.

Supported Browsers

Desk.com supports the following browsers:

- Mozilla® Firefox®
- Google Chrome™
- Microsoft® Internet Explorer®
- Apple® Safari®

We recommend using the latest version of a browser listed above. Cookies and JavaScript must be enabled.

Supported Salesforce Editions

Desk.com provides deep two-way integration with these Salesforce Editions:

- Developer Edition
- Group Edition
- Professional Edition
- Enterprise Edition
- Unlimited Edition

If you're an existing Salesforce customer and want to upgrade to any of these editions, contact your account representative.

Quick Start

The Desk.com API handles requests over HTTPS and in JSON format.

Each resource represents the state of an object within Desk.com, such as a case, customer, or company, as well as its relationships with other resources. Each resource is identified by a named URI, and is accessed using HTTP methods like GET, POST, PATCH, and DELETE. Each request you make to the server must contain all information necessary to process the request as no state is stored on the server.

PATCH is used to modify a resource. If your HTTP client can't perform PATCH/DELETE requests, you can perform a POST request using an X-HTTP-Method-Override header to specify PATCH or DELETE.

```
$ curl https://yoursite.desk.com/api/v2/cases/1 \
    -u email:password \
    -H 'Accept: application/json' \
    -H 'Content-Type: application/json' \
    -H 'X-HTTP-Method-Override: PATCH' \
    -X POST \
    -d '{ "subject":"Updated" }'
```

The actions you can request on each resource is based on your role. These roles are: Agent, Reporting Agent, Workflow Manager, Knowledgebase Manager, Content Manager, Business Manager, Administrative Manager, Administrator, Knowledgebase Administrator, and Billing Administrator. See Authorization for more information on these roles and their permissions.

To get started with the Desk.com API, follow these steps.

1. Authenticate with the API.
2. Request for data.

Step One: Authenticate with the API

You must authenticate with the API before sending or receiving data.

The API supports both basic authentication over SSL/TLS and OAuth 1.0a authentication. If you require access to your own account's data only, use basic authentication with your Desk.com email and password.

```
$ curl https://yoursite.desk.com/api/v2/cases \
    -u email:password \
    -H 'Accept: application/json'
```

If you are writing an API application that needs to access other accounts on behalf of their users, OAuth 1.0a provides you the capability to use the API without storing emails and passwords of users.

Before an API call can be made, a registered Desk.com user must first go through theOAuth Authorization workflow and allow the client application to access Desk.com on behalf of the user. During the process, the user will be required to login to Desk.com and "Allow" access. As an added layer of security, we require that a site administrator authorize your application before users of that site can authorize it. The user will then be redirected to a callback URL configured for the client application with an authorization code which the application can use to retrieve an "Access Token" for subsequent API calls.

Table 5: OAuth Endpoints

Type	Endpoint
Authorize	/oauth/authorize
Request Token	/oauth/request_token
Access Token	/oauth/access_token

Your token can be found under your client application's details in **Admin** > **Settings** > **API**. The combination of your consumer key, secret, access token, and access token secret provides you everything you need to make an API request.

This example shows how you can use the standard Ruby OAuth library to authenticate with the API.

```
require 'rubygems'
require 'oauth'
```

```
# KEY and SECRET are available in Desk.com Admin -> Settings -> API
  ->
# My Applications -> Key and Secret fields
KEY    = "YOUR_OAUTH_KEY"
SECRET = "YOUR_OAUTH_SECRET"
SITE   = "https://yoursite.desk.com"

# Start the process by requesting a token
callback_url = "https://example.com/oauth/callback"
consumer     = OAuth::Consumer.new(KEY, SECRET, site: SITE)
request_token = consumer.get_request_token(oauth_callback:
callback_url)

# For demonstration purposes, visit this URL in your web browser and
  authorize
# the request. for a live application, redirect your user user to
this URL
puts request_token.authorize_url(oauth_callback: callback_url)

# After the application is authorized, Desk.com will send a request
  to your
# callback_url with two parameters, oauth_token and oauth_verifier
oauth_token    = "oauth_token_param"
oauth_verifier = "oauth_verifier_param"

# Retrieve the access token
access_token = request_token.get_access_token(oauth_token:
oauth_token,
   oauth_verifier: oauth_verifier)

# Send a GET request to Desk.com
access_token.get("/api/v2/cases")

# From here, you can store the credentials to make requests in the
future
```

Step Two: Request for data

After authenticating with the Desk.com API, request for your data.

This section walks through some sample Ruby code showing how to read, create, update, and delete Topics and Topic Translations. The purpose of it is to demonstrate basic API calls in a simple manner. A real world application would need to additionally implement error handling for HTTP calls and prompt the user to fix any validation problems that may arise from POST and PATCH calls.

The following code assumes your system has these items installed:

- Ruby 1.9.3
- Ruby gems

- JSON gem version 1.8.0
- httparty gem version 0.11.0

```ruby
require 'rubygems'
require 'json'
require 'httparty'

AUTH     = { basic_auth: { username: 'you@yoursite.com', password:
"password" } }
BASE_URI = "https://yoursite.desk.com"

# get a resource
def get(uri, opts = {})
  opts = opts.merge(AUTH)
  uri  = BASE_URI + uri

  puts "getting #{uri}"

  response = HTTParty.get(uri, opts)

  JSON.parse(response.body)
end

# patch a resource
def patch(uri, opts = {})
  opts = opts.merge(AUTH)
  uri  = BASE_URI + uri

  puts "patching #{uri}"

  HTTParty.patch(uri, opts)
end

# post a resource
def post(uri, opts = {})
  opts = opts.merge(AUTH)
  uri  = BASE_URI + uri

  puts "posting #{uri}"

  HTTParty.post(uri, opts)
end

# delete a resource
def delete(uri, opts = {})
  opts = opts.merge(AUTH)
  uri  = BASE_URI + uri

  puts "deleting #{uri}"

  HTTParty.delete(uri, opts)
end

def get_topics
  get("/api/v2/topics", { query: { per_page: 1 } } )
end
```

```
def get_topic_translations(topic)
  get(topic["_links"]["translations"]["href"])
end

# get the first topic
topics = get_topics
topic  = topics["_embedded"]["entries"].first

# get that topic's first translation
translations = get_topic_translations(topic)
translation  = translations["_embedded"]["entries"].first

puts "current translation name: #{translation['name']}"

# update the translation's name
patch(translation["_links"]["self"]["href"], { query: { name: "name
 updated via API at #{Time.now.to_s}" } } )

# get the updated translation
translation = get(translation["_links"]["self"]["href"])

puts "new translation name: #{translation['name']}"

# create a new topic
topic_options = { name: "new topic via API", allow_questions: false,
 in_support_center: false }
post("/api/v2/topics", { query: topic_options } )

# find the last topic
topics = get_topics
topics = get(topics["_links"]["last"]["href"])
topic  = topics["_embedded"]["entries"].last

puts "last topic's name: #{topic['name']}"

# delete the topic
response = delete(topic["_links"]["self"]["href"])
```

Best Practices

The Desk.com API uses a RESTful Architecture. This section explains this architecture and offers several best practices.

JSON interface

Requests and responses are in JSON format.

Authentication

Both HTTP Basic Authentication and OAuth 1.0a are supported.

Authorization

Authorization is handled transparently based on the given user's role.

Stateless

Each request from the client to the server must contain all of the information necessary to process the request. No state is stored on the server.

Caching Behavior

Responses are labeled as cacheable or non-cacheable with HTTP ETags.

Uniform Interface

All resources are accessed with a generic interface over HTTPS.

Named Resources

All resources are named using a base URI that follows your Desk.com URI.

Layered Components

The architecture of Desk.com API v2 allows for intermediaries such as proxy servers and gateways to exist between the client and the server.

Rate Limit

Rate limiting is implemented on a per-user basis, irrespective of the method of authentication. The current threshold is 60 calls per minute across all endpoints, and it is limited in one minute windows.

All responses include headers with status info about rate limiting.

`X-Rate-Limit-Limit`

Maximum number of requests per minute to the endpoint

`X-Rate-Limit-Remaining`

Available requests remaining in the current window

`X-Rate-Limit-Reset`

Seconds remaining until the next window begins

If your application hits the rate limit, an HTTP 429 error response will be returned with this body.

```
{
"message": "Too Many Requests"
}
```

Assuming it is 40 seconds into the current window, these headers will be returned::

```
{
  "X-Rate-Limit-Limit": 60,
  "X-Rate-Limit-Remaining": 0,
  "X-Rate-Limit-Reset": 20
}
```

When the limit is reached, your application should stop making requests until X-Rate-Limit-Reset seconds have elapsed.

Reducing Requests and Conserving Bandwidth

When requesting for data, you'll receive a response code with your data to indicate success or failure. Resources such as labels, groups, macros, and users also support ETag caching.

The example responses below show only the headers. If the data on the server has changed, a 200 will be returned along with the entire response body. If the data on the server has not changed, a 304 will be returned with an empty response body, signifying that your application has up-to-date data.

The following example shows a request without an ETag and its example response headers.

```
$ curl https://yoursite.desk.com/api/v2/groups \
    -u email:password \
    -I
```

```
HTTP/1.1 200 OK
Date: Fri, 24 May 2013 15:00:10 GMT
Content-Type: application/json; charset=utf-8
Connection: keep-alive
X-Rate-Limit-Remaining: 59
X-Rate-Limit-Limit: 60
X-Rate-Limit-Reset: 50
X-AppVersion: 120.1
ETag: "1369407549"
X-Frame-Options: SAMEORIGIN
X-UA-Compatible: IE=Edge
Cache-Control: no-cache, private
X-Runtime: 0.323047
X-Rack-Cache: miss
```

The following example shows a request with a current ETag and its example response headers.

```
$ curl https://yoursite.desk.com/api/v2/groups \
    -u email:password \
```

```
    -H "if-none-match \"1369407549\""
    -I


HTTP/1.1 304 Not Modified
Date: Fri, 24 May 2013 15:05:42 GMT
Connection: keep-alive
```

Embedding Resources

Related resources are linked and embedded using the HAL specification.

Most resources with a 1:1 or N:1 relationship with a second resource can embed the second one. If your application reads Cases and needs to retrieve the associated Customer, a naive approach might make a request to get the Case and another request to get the Customer. However, the Customer can be embedded within the Case, which will only count as one request:

Here is how you would request a case and embed the related customer, along with the response with embedded resource:

```
$ curl https://yoursite.desk.com/api/v2/cases/1?embed=customer \
    -u email:password \
    -H 'Accept: application/json'
```

```
{
  "subject": "Some case",
  "_links": {
    "self": {
      "href": "/api/v2/cases/1",
      "class": "case"
    },
    "customer": {
      "href": "/api/v2/customers/1",
      "class": "customer"
    }
  },
  "_embedded": {
    "customer": {
      "first_name": "John",
      "last_name": "Doe",
      "_links": {
        "self": {
          "href": "/api/v2/customers/1",
          "class": "customer"
        }
      }
    }
  }
}
```

Embedding is useful when you need to grab a particular resource or collection of resources along with the related resources. Not every relationship can be embedded, and you can only specify embedded relationships on the top level resource or collection of resources.

Selecting Fields

The fields included in a response can be limited by providing the comma separated `fields` param in the request. `_links` will be returned with all responses. The following example shows a request using field selection.

```
$ curl
https://yoursite.desk.com/api/v2/cases/:id\?fields\=subject,status
\
    -u email:password \
    -H 'Accept: application/json'
```

Adjusting Pagination

Requests to collections of resources will return a page of 50 resources by default. You can request up to 100 entries per page by using the `per_page` parameter. By default, the first page is returned unless specified with the page parameter. You can follow links to different pages using `_links` and access the resulting resources under the `_embedded` entries.

```
curl https://yoursite.desk.com/api/v2/cases?per_page=100 \
    -u email:password \
    -H 'Accept: application/json'
```

For more information, see the Desk.com API Documentation.

Using the API

Access and manage your articles, brands, cases, companies, customers, and other Desk.com data.

This section walks you through common actions for each resources. See the Desk.com API Documentation for a full list of examples and response details.

Articles

Perform actions on your articles, such as listing, creating, or updating them.

Retrieve a paginated list of all articles.

```
GET  https://yoursite.desk.com/api/v2/articles
```

Example Curl Request

```
$ curl https://yoursite.desk.com/api/v2/articles \
    -u email:password \
    -H 'Accept: application/json'
```

Example Response

The body content has been simplified in the following example.

```
{
  "total_entries": 2,
  "_links": {
    "self": {
      "href": "/api/v2/articles?page=1&per_page=30",
      "class": "page"
    },
    "first": {
      "href": "/api/v2/articles?page=1&per_page=30",
      "class": "page"
    },
    "last": {
      "href": "/api/v2/articles?page=1&per_page=30",
      "class": "page"
    },
    "next": null,
    "previous": null
  },
  "_embedded": {
    "entries": [
      {
        "subject": "Awesome Subject",
        "body": "<p>Awesome apples</p>",
        "internal_notes": "Notes to the agent here",
        "publish_at": "2013-10-14T20:41:32Z",
        "created_at": "2013-10-14T20:36:32Z",
        "updated_at": "2013-10-14T20:41:32Z",
        "_links": {
          "self": {
            "href": "/api/v2/articles/1",
            "class": "article"
          },
          "topic": {
            "href": "/api/v2/topics/1",
            "class": "topic"
          },
          "translations": {
            "href": "/api/v2/articles/1/translations",
            "class": "article_translation"
          }
        }
      },
      {
        "subject": "How to make your customers happy",
        "body": "<strong>Use Desk.com</strong>",
```

```
      "body_email": "Email just doesn't cut it",
      "internal_notes": "Notes to the agent here",
      "publish_at": "2013-10-14T20:41:32Z",
      "created_at": "2013-10-14T20:36:32Z",
      "updated_at": "2013-10-14T20:41:32Z",
      "_links": {
        "self": {
          "href": "/api/v2/articles/2",
          "class": "article"
        },
      "topic": {
        "href": "/api/v2/topics/1",
        "class": "topic"
      },
      "translations": {
        "href": "/api/v2/articles/2/translations",
        "class": "article_translation"
      }
    }
  }
  }
 ]
 }
}
```

Calls for Articles

The following list shows all other calls for your articles.

Actions	Example
Show a single article	GET https://yoursite.desk.com/api/v2/articles/:id
Create an article	POST https://yoursite.desk.com/api/v2/articles
Update an article	PATCH https://yoursite.desk.com/api/v2/articles/:id
Delete an article	DELETE https://yoursite.desk.com/api/v2/articles/:id
Search across all public articles	GET https://yoursite.desk.com/api/v2/articles/search
List translations for an article	GET https://yoursite.desk.com/api/v2/articles/ :article_id/translations
Show a single article translation	GET https://yoursite.desk.com/api/v2/articles/ :article_id/translations/:locale
Create an article translation	POST https://yoursite.desk.com/api/v2/articles/ :article_id/translations

Actions	Example
Update an article translation	`PATCH https://yoursite.desk.com/api/v2/articles/:article_id/translations/:locale`

See the Articles reference for details on each of these actions, including roles and fields.

Brands

List all your brands or retrieve them individually.

Retrieve a paginated list of all brands.

```
GET https://yoursite.desk.com/api/v2/brands
```

Retrieve a single brand.

```
GET https://yoursite.desk.com/api/v2/brands/:id
```

Example Curl Request

```
$ curl https://yoursite.desk.com/api/v2/brands/:id \
    -u email:password \
    -H 'Accept: application/json'
```

Example Response

The body content has been simplified in the following example.

```
{
  "name": "Desk.com",
  "created_at": "2013-10-14T20:36:32Z",
  "updated_at": "2013-10-14T20:36:32Z",
  "_links": {
    "self": {
      "href": "/api/v2/brands/1",
      "class": "brand"
    }
  }
}
```

See the Brands reference for details on retrieving brands.

Cases

Perform actions on your cases, such as listing, creating, or updating them.

Retrieve a paginated list of all cases.

```
GET  https://yoursite.desk.com/api/v2/cases
```

Retrieve a single case. An external id can be used by URL-encoding it and prefacing with e-, such as e-case%405-300.

```
GET  https://yoursite.desk.com/api/v2/cases/:id
```

Example Curl Request

```
$ curl https://yoursite.desk.com/api/v2/cases/1 \
    -u email:password \
    -H 'Accept: application/json'
```

Example Response

```
{
  "external_id": null,
  "subject": "Welcome",
  "priority": 5,
  "locked_until": null,
  "description": null,
  "status": "new",
  "type": "email",
  "language": "en_us",
  "created_at": "2013-10-14T20:36:32Z",
  "updated_at": "2013-10-14T20:36:32Z",
  "active_at": null,
  "received_at": "2012-05-02T21:38:48Z",
  "custom_fields": {
    "level": "vip"
  },
  "_links": {
    "self": {
      "href": "/api/v2/cases/1",
      "class": "case"
    },
    "message": {
      "href": "/api/v2/cases/1/message",
      "class": "message"
    },
    "customer": {
      "href": "/api/v2/customers/1",
      "class": "customer"
    },
```

```
    "assigned_user": {
      "href": "/api/v2/users/2",
      "class": "user"
    },
    "assigned_group": {
      "href": "/api/v2/groups/1",
      "class": "group"
    },
    "locked_by": null
  }
}
```

Calls for Cases

The following list shows all other calls for your cases.

Actions	Example
Search cases	GET https://yoursite.desk.com/api/v2/cases /search?name=John+Doe&status=open
Create a case	POST https://yoursite.desk.com/api/v2/customers /:customer_id/cases
Update a case	PATCH https://yoursite.desk.com/api/v2/cases/:id
Retrieve a message	GET https://yoursite.desk.com/api/v2/cases /:case_id/message
List all replies	GET https://yoursite.desk.com/api/v2/cases /:case_id/replies
Retrieve a reply	GET https://yoursite.desk.com/api/v2/cases/ :case_id/replies/:id
Update a draft reply	PATCH https://yoursite.desk.com/api/v2/cases /:case_id/replies/:id
Retrieve a note	GET https://yoursite.desk.com/api/v2/cases /:case_id/notes/:id
Create a private note	POST https://yoursite.desk.com/api/v2/cases /:id/notes

Actions	Example
Retrieve all case attachments	GET https://yoursite.desk.com/api/v2/cases/:case_id /attachments
Retrieve all message attachments	GET https://yoursite.desk.com/api/v2/cases/:case_id /message/attachments
Retrieve all reply attachments	GET https://yoursite.desk.com/api/v2/cases/:case_id /replies/:reply_id/attachments
Retrieve an attachment	GET https://yoursite.desk.com/api/v2/cases/:case_id /attachments/:id
Create a case attachment	POST https://yoursite.desk.com/api/v2/cases/:id /attachments
Create a reply attachment	POST https://yoursite.desk.com/api/v2/cases/:case_id /replies/:reply_id/attachments

See the Cases reference for details on each of these actions, including roles and fields.

Companies

Perform actions on your companies, such as listing, creating, or updating them.

Retrieve a paginated list of all companies.

```
GET   https://yoursite.desk.com/api/v2/companies
```

Retrieve a single company.

```
GET   https://yoursite.desk.com/api/v2/companies/:id
```

Example Curl Request

```
$ curl https://yoursite.desk.com/api/v2/companies/:id \
    -u email:password \
    -H 'Accept: application/json'
```

Example Response

```
{
  "name": "Acme Inc",
  "domains": [
    "acmeinc.com",
    "acmeinc.net"
  ],
  "created_at": "2013-10-16T17:25:16Z",
  "updated_at": "2013-10-16T17:25:16Z",
  "custom_fields": {
    "employer_id": "123456789"
  },
  "_links": {
    "self": {
      "href": "/api/v2/companies/1",
      "class": "company"
    },
    "customers": {
      "href": "/api/v2/companies/1/customers",
      "class": "customer"
    }
  }
}
```

Calls for Companies

The following list shows all other calls for your companies.

Actions	Example
Create a company	POST https://yoursite.desk.com/api/v2/companies
Update a company	PATCH https://yoursite.desk.com/api/v2/companies/:id
Search	GET https://yoursite.desk.com/api/v2/companies /search

See the Companies reference for details on each of these actions, including roles and fields.

Custom Fields

List all your custom fields or retrieve them individually.

Retrieve a paginated list of all custom fields.

```
GET https://yoursite.desk.com/api/v2/custom_fields
```

Retrieve a single brand.

```
GET https://yoursite.desk.com/api/v2/brands/:id
```

Example Curl Request

```
$ curl https://yoursite.desk.com/api/v2/custom_fields/:id \
    -u email:password \
    -H 'Accept: application/json'
```

Example Response

```
{
  "name": "frequent_buyer",
  "label": "Frequent Buyer",
  "type": "customer",
  "active": true,
  "data": {
    "type": "boolean"
  },
  "_links": {
    "self": {
      "href": "/api/v2/custom_fields/1",
      "class": "custom_field"
    }
  }
}
```

See the Custom fields reference for details on retrieving custom fields.

Customers

List, create, or update customer data.

Retrieve a paginated list of all customers.

```
GET  https://yoursite.desk.com/api/v2/customers
```

Retrieve a single customer.

```
GET  https://yoursite.desk.com/api/v2/customers/:id
```

Example Curl Request

```
$ curl https://yoursite.desk.com/api/v2/customers/:id \
    -u email:password \
    -H 'Accept: application/json'
```

Example Response

```
{
  "first_name": "John",
  "last_name": "Doe",
  "company": "ACME, Inc",
  "title": "Senior Ninja",
  "external_id": null,
  "background": "Great customer!",
  "language": "en_us",
  "locked_until": null,
  "created_at": "2013-10-16T17:25:16Z",
  "updated_at": "2013-10-16T17:25:16Z",
  "custom_fields": {
    "level": "vip"
  },
  "emails": [
    {
      "type": "work",
      "value": "john@acme.com"
    },
    {
      "type": "home",
      "value": "john@home.com"
    }
  ],
  "phone_numbers": [
    {
      "type": "work",
      "value": "123-456-7890"
    }
  ],
  "addresses": [
    {
      "type": "work",
      "value": "123 Main St, San Francisco, CA 94105"
    }
  ],
  "_links": {
    "self": {
    "href": "/api/v2/customers/1",
    "class": "customer"
  },
  "cases": {
    "href": "/api/v2/customers/1/cases",
    "class": "case"
    },
    "locked_by": null
  }
}
```

Calls for Customers

The following list shows all other calls for your customers.

Actions	Example
Create a customer	GET https://yoursite.desk.com/api/v2/customers
Update a customer	PATCH https://yoursite.desk.com/api/v2/customers/:id
Search customers	GET https://yoursite.desk.com/api/v2/customers/search

See the Customers reference for details on each of these actions, including roles and fields.

Filters

List all your filters, retrieve them individually, or retrieve all cases for the given filter.

Retrieve a paginated list of all filters.

```
GET https://yoursite.desk.com/api/v2/filters
```

Retrieve a single filter.

```
GET https://yoursite.desk.com/api/v2/filters/:id
```

Retrieve cases for the given filter.

```
GET https://yoursite.desk.com/api/v2/filters/:id/cases
```

Example Curl Request

```
$ curl https://yoursite.desk.com/api/v2/filters/:id \
    -u email:password \
    -H 'Accept: application/json'
```

Example Response

```
{
  "name": "My Active Cases",
  "sort": "priority",
  "sort_field": "priority",
  "sort_direction": "desc",
  "position": 1,
  "active": true,
  "_links": {
    "self": {
      "href": "/api/v2/filters/1",
      "class": "filter"
```

```
        },
        "group": null,
        "user": null
    }
}
```

See the Filters reference for details on using filters.

Groups

Perform actions on your groups, such as listing, creating, or updating them.

Retrieve a paginated list of all groups.

```
GET  https://yoursite.desk.com/api/v2/groups
```

Retrieve a single group.

```
GET  https://yoursite.desk.com/api/v2/groups/:id
```

Example Curl Request

```
$ curl https://yoursite.desk.com/api/v2/groups/:id \
    -u email:password \
    -H 'Accept: application/json'
```

Example Response

```
{
    "name": "Support Ninjas",
    "_links": {
        "self": {
            "href": "/api/v2/groups/1",
            "class": "group"
        }
    }
}
```

Calls for Groups

The following list shows all other calls for your groups.

Actions	Example
Retrieve all filters for the given group	GET https://yoursite.desk.com/api/v2/groups/:id /filters

Actions	Example
Retrieve all users for the given group	GET https://yoursite.desk.com/api/v2/groups/:id /users

See the Groups reference for details on each of these actions, including roles and fields.

Inbound Mailboxes

List all your inbound mailboxes or retrieve them individually.

List all inbound mailboxes.

```
GET https://yoursite.desk.com/api/v2/mailboxes/inbound
```

Retrieve a single inbound mailbox.

```
GET https://yoursite.desk.com/api/v2/mailboxes/inbound/:id
```

Example Curl Request

```
$ curl https://yoursite.desk.com/api/v2/mailboxes/inbound/:id \
    -u email:password \
    -H 'Accept: application/json'
```

Example Response

```
{
  "name": "Support Mailbox",
  "enabled": true,
  "type": "imaps",
  "hostname": "mail.example.com",
  "port": 993,
  "email": "support@example.com",
  "last_checked_at": "2013-10-16T17:25:16Z",
  "created_at": "2013-10-16T17:25:16Z",
  "updated_at": "2013-10-16T17:25:16Z",
  "last_error": null,
  "inbound_address_filter": null,
  "outbound_address_filter": null,
  "_links": {
    "self": {
      "href": "/api/v2/mailboxes/inbound/1",
      "class": "inbound_mailbox"
    },
    "default_group": {
      "href": "/api/v2/groups/1",
```

```
      "class": "group"
    },
    "created_by": {
      "href": "/api/v2/users/1",
      "class": "user"
    },
    "updated_by": {
      "href": "/api/v2/users/1",
      "class": "user"
    }
  }
}
```

See the Inbound mailboxes reference for details on retrieving mailboxes.

Insights

Retrieve meta data or create a report for your business insights.

Retrieve insights meta data for the authenticated site.

```
GET https://yoursite.desk.com/api/v2/insights/meta
```

To create a report, use the following request.

```
POST https://yoursite.desk.com/api/v2/insights/reports
```

Example Curl Request

```
$ curl https://yoursite.desk.com/api/v2/insights/reports \
    -u email:password \
    -X POST \
    -H 'Accept: application/json' \
    -H 'Content-Type: application/json' \
    -d '{"resolution":"days", "min_date":"2013-06-01",
"max_date":"2013-07-30",
"dimension1_name":"*", "dimension1_values":"*",
"dimension2_name":"*", "dimension2_values":"*"}'
```

Example Request Body

```
{
   "resolution": "days",
   "min_date": "2012-06-01",
   "max_date": "2013-07-30",
   "dimension1_name": "*",
   "dimension1_values": "*",
   "dimension2_name": "*",
   "dimension2_values": "*"
}
```

See the Insights reference for details on using insights.

Integration URLs

Perform actions on your integration URLs, such as listing, creating, or updating them.

Retrieve a paginated list of all integration URLs.

```
GET  https://yoursite.desk.com/api/v2/integration_urls
```

Retrieve a single integration URL.

```
GET  https://yoursite.desk.com/api/v2/integration_urls/:id
```

Example Curl Request

```
$ curl
https://yoursite.desk.com/api/v2/integration_urls/:id\?customer_id\=1
  \
    -u email:password \
    -H 'Accept: application/json'
```

Example Response

```
{
  "name": "Sample URL",
  "description": "A sample Integration URL",
  "enabled": true,
  "markup": "http://www.example.com/name={{customer.name |
url_encode}}",
  "rendered": "http://www.example.com/name=Andrew",
  "created_at": "2013-10-16T17:25:16Z",
  "updated_at": "2013-10-16T17:25:16Z",
  "_links": {
    "self": {
      "href": "/api/v2/integration_urls/1",
      "class": "integration_url"
    }
  }
}
```

Calls for Integration URLs

The following list shows all other calls for your integration URLs.

Actions	Example
Create an integration URL	POST https://yoursite.desk.com/api/v2 /integration_urls
Update an integration URL	PATCH https://yoursite.desk.com/api/v2 /integration_urls/:id
Delete an integration URL	DELETE https://yoursite.desk.com/api/v2 /integration_urls/:id

See the Integration URLs reference for details on each of these actions, including roles and fields.

Labels

Perform actions on your labels, such as listing, creating, or updating them.

Retrieve a paginated list of all labels.

```
GET  https://yoursite.desk.com/api/v2/labels
```

Retrieve a single label.

```
GET  https://yoursite.desk.com/api/v2/labels/:id
```

Example Curl Request

```
$ curl https://yoursite.desk.com/api/v2/labels/:id \
    -u email:password \
    -H 'Accept: application/json'
```

Example Response

```
{
  "name": "MyLabel",
  "description": "My Label Description",
  "types": ["case","macro"],
  "active": true,
  "position": 1,
  "_links": {
    "self": {
      "href": "/api/v2/labels/1",
      "class": "label"
```

```
        }
      }
    }
```

Calls for Labels

The following list shows all other calls for your labels.

Actions	Example
Create a label	POST https://yoursite.desk.com/api/v2/labels
Update a label	PATCH https://yoursite.desk.com/api/v2/labels/:id
Delete a label	DELETE https://yoursite.desk.com/api/v2/labels/:id

See the Labels reference for details on each of these actions, including roles and fields.

Macros

Perform actions on your macros, such as listing, creating, or updating them.

Retrieve a paginated list of all macros.

```
GET  https://yoursite.desk.com/api/v2/macros
```

Retrieve a single macro.

```
GET  https://yoursite.desk.com/api/v2/macros/:id
```

Example Curl Request

```
$ curl https://yoursite.desk.com/api/v2/macros/:id \
    -u email:password \
    -H 'Accept: application/json'
```

Example Response

```
{
  "name": "Macro Macro",
  "description": "On repeat",
  "enabled": true,
  "position": 1,
  "folders": [
    "Sample Macros",
    "Favorites"
```

```
  ],
  "_links": {
    "self": {
      "href": "/api/v2/macros/1",
      "class": "macro"
    },
    "actions": {
      "href": "/api/v2/macros/1/actions",
      "class": "macro_action"
    }
  }
}
```

Calls for Macros

The following list shows all other calls for your macros.

Actions	Example
Create a macro	POST https://yoursite.desk.com/api/v2/macros
Update a macro	PATCH https://yoursite.desk.com/api/v2/macros/:id
Delete a macro	DELETE https://yoursite.desk.com/api/v2/macros/:id
Retrieve all actions for a macro	GET https://yoursite.desk.com/api/v2/macros/:macro_id /actions
Retrieve an action for a macro	GET https://yoursite.desk.com/api/v2/macros/:macro_id /actions/:id
Update an action	PATCH https://yoursite.desk.com/api/v2/macros/:macro_id /actions/:id

See the Macros reference for details on each of these actions, including roles and fields.

Rules

List all your rules or retrieve them individually.

Retrieve a paginated list of all rules.

```
GET https://yoursite.desk.com/api/v2/rules
```

Retrieve a single rule.

```
GET https://yoursite.desk.com/api/v2/rules/:id
```

Example Curl Request

```
$ curl https://yoursite.desk.com/api/v2/rules/:id \
    -u email:password \
    -H 'Accept: application/json'
```

Example Response

The body content has been simplified in the following example.

```
{
  "name": "Assign to Support",
  "description": "Assign inbound tweets to support group",
  "enabled": true,
  "created_at": "2013-10-16T17:25:16Z",
  "updated_at": "2013-10-16T17:25:16Z",
  "_links": {
    "self": {
      "href": "/api/v2/rules/1",
      "class": "rule"
    }
  }
}
```

See the Rules reference for details on retrieving rules.

Site Settings

List all your site settings or retrieve them individually.

Retrieve a paginated list of all site settings.

```
GET https://yoursite.desk.com/api/v2/site_settings
```

Retrieve a single rule.

```
GET https://yoursite.desk.com/api/v2/site_settings/:id
```

Example Curl Request

```
$ curl https://yoursite.desk.com/api/v2/site_settings/:id \
    -u email:password \
    -H 'Accept: application/json'
```

Example Response

```
{
  "name": "company_name",
  "value": "Cool Surfboard Co.",
  "_links": {
    "self": {
      "href": "/api/v2/site_settings/1",
      "class": "site_setting"
    }
  }
}
```

See the Sites reference for details on retrieving site settings.

System Message

Desk.com uses the system message resource to announce upcoming maintenance or any other news that may affect its users. This is a read-only endpoint that exposes the current system message if one exists.

Retrieve all system messages.

```
GET https://yoursite.desk.com/api/v2/system_message
```

Example Curl Request

```
$ curl https://yoursite.desk.com/api/v2/system_message \
    -u email:password \
    -X GET \
    -H 'Accept: application/json' \
    -H 'Content-Type: application/json'
```

Example Response

The body content has been simplified in the following example.

```
{
  "message": "We're not doing maintenance today, but if we were then
we would tell you about it here.",
  "updated_at": "2013-10-16T17:25:16Z"
}
```

See the System message reference for details on retrieving system messages.

Topics

Perform actions on your topics, such as listing, creating, or updating them.

Retrieve a paginated list of all topics.

```
GET  https://yoursite.desk.com/api/v2/topics
```

Retrieve a single topic.

```
GET  https://yoursite.desk.com/api/v2/topics/:id
```

Example Curl Request

```
$ curl https://yoursite.desk.com/api/v2/topics/:id \
    -u email:password \
    -H 'Accept: application/json'
```

Example Response

```
{
  "name": "Customer Support",
  "description": "This is key to going from good to great",
  "position": 1,
  "allow_questions": true,
  "in_support_center": true,
  "created_at": "2013-10-06T17:35:16Z",
  "updated_at": "2013-10-11T17:35:16Z",
  "_links": {
    "self": {
      "href": "/api/v2/topics/1",
      "class": "topic"
    },
    "articles": {
      "href": "/api/v2/topics/1/articles",
      "class": "article"
    },
    "translations": {
      "href": "/api/v2/topics/1/translations",
      "class": "topic_translation"
    }
  }
}
```

Calls for Topics

The following list shows all other calls for your topics.

Actions	Example
Create a topic	POST https://yoursite.desk.com/api/v2/topics
Update a topic	PATCH https://yoursite.desk.com/api/v2/topics/:id
Delete a topic	DELETE https://yoursite.desk.com/api/v2/topics/:id
Retrieve translations for a topic	GET https://yoursite.desk.com/api/v2/topics/:topic_id /translations
Retrieve a single topic translation	GET https://yoursite.desk.com/api/v2/topics/:id /translations/:locale
Create a topic translation	POST https://yoursite.desk.com/api/v2/topics/:topic_id /translations
Update a topic translation	PATCH https://yoursite.desk.com/api/v2/topics/:id /translations/:locale
Delete a topic translation	DELETE https://yoursite.desk.com/api/v2/topics/:id /translations/:locale

See the Topics reference for details on each of these actions, including roles and fields.

Twitter Accounts

Perform actions on your Twitter accounts, such as listing or creating Tweets.

Retrieve a paginated list of all Twitter accounts.

```
GET  https://yoursite.desk.com/api/v2/twitter_accounts
```

Retrieve a single Twitter account.

```
GET  https://yoursite.desk.com/api/v2/twitter_accounts/:id
```

Example Curl Request

```
$ curl https://yoursite.desk.com/api/v2/twitter_accounts/:id \
    -u email:password \
    -H 'Accept: application/json'
```

Example Response

```
{
  "handle": "desk_dev",
  "name": "Desk.com Development",
  "profile_image": "http://www.example.com/image.png",
  "active": true,
  "created_at": "2013-04-16T17:35:16Z",
  "updated_at": "2013-05-16T17:35:16Z",
  "_links": {
    "self": {
      "href": "/api/v2/twitter_accounts/1",
      "class": "twitter_account"
    }
  }
}
```

Calls for Twitter Accounts

The following list shows all other calls for your Twitter accounts.

Actions	Example
Post a Tweet from a Twitter account	POST https://yoursite.desk.com/api/v2/twitter_accounts /:id/tweets
Retrieve all Tweets for a Twitter account	GET https://yoursite.desk.com/api/v2/twitter_accounts /:id/tweets
Retrieve a Tweet	GET https://yoursite.desk.com/api/v2/twitter_accounts /:twitter_account_id/tweets/:id

See the Twitter accounts reference for details on each of these actions, including roles and fields.

Users

Retrieve users or perform other actions, such as retrieving their preferences.

Retrieve a paginated list of all users.

```
GET  https://yoursite.desk.com/api/v2/users
```

Retrieve a single user.

```
GET  https://yoursite.desk.com/api/v2/users/:id
```

Example Curl Request

```
$ curl https://yoursite.desk.com/api/v2/users/:id \
    -u email:password \
    -H 'Accept: application/json'
```

Example Response

```
{
  "name": "John Doe",
  "public_name": "John Doe",
  "email": "john@acme.com",
  "level": "agent",
  "_links": {
    "self": {
      "href": "/api/v2/users/1",
      "class": "user"
    },
    "preferences": {
      "href": "/api/v2/users/1/preferences",
      "class": "user_preference"
    }
  }
}
```

Calls for Users

The following list shows all other calls for your users.

Actions	Example
Retrieve all user's preferences	GET https://yoursite.desk.com/api/v2/users/:id /preferences

Actions	Example
Retrieve a user's preference	`GET https://yoursite.desk.com/api/v2/users/:id /preferences/:id`
Update a user's preference	`PATCH https://yoursite.desk.com/api/v2/users /:user_id/preferences/:id`

See the Users reference for details on each of these actions, including roles and fields.

Resources

Use the following resources to get more information about the Desk.com API.

- Desk.com API Documentation: `http://dev.desk.com/API/using-the-api/`
- Desk.com Integration Guides: `http://dev.desk.com/guides/`

Chapter 28

Live Agent API

Live Agent lets service organizations connect with customers or website visitors in real time through a Web-based, text-only live chat. This guide provides several examples to customize chat windows and other Live Agent components using the Deployment and Pre-Chat APIs.

With the Live Agent API, you can:

*   Customize deployments with the Deployment API.
*   Create pre-chat forms to gather information from customers before they begin a chat with an agent with the Pre-Chat API.

Besides these APIs, you can customize the appearance of customer-facing chat windows and create post-chat pages that appear to customers after a chat is complete using Visualforce pages and components. Using Visualforce is not covered in this guide. See the Live Agent Developer's Guide for more information.

You can also customize these and other Live Agent components through Salesforce settings. For more information, see Setting Up Live Agent in the Salesforce online help.

Supported Browsers

Live Agent supports the following browsers:

*   Mozilla® Firefox®
*   Google Chrome™
*   Microsoft® Internet Explorer®
*   Apple® Safari® versions 5.x and 6.x on Mac OS X

We recommend using the latest version of a browser listed above. Desktop alerts is available only in the most recent stable version of Google Chrome.

Supported Salesforce Editions

Live Agent is available with these Salesforce Editions:

- Developer Edition
- Enterprise Edition
- Unlimited Edition
- Performance Edition

If you're an existing Salesforce customer and want to upgrade to any of these editions, contact your account representative.

Quick Start

Live Agent provides the JavaScript-based Deployment API and Pre-Chat API. Different methods and parameters are available in different versions of these APIs.

Before you customize Live Agent, make sure:

- Live Agent is enabled in your organization. Refer to the Live Agent Implementation Guide for detailed information.
- Your administrator has granted you a Live Agent feature license. Although you can customize the product without a feature license, having one will allow you to access and test your customizations.
- You've created a Force.com site and uploaded images as static resources for your chat buttons and windows. Your site needs to have the following information:

  ◊ A site label and a site name
  ◊ A site contact
  ◊ The active site's home page
  ◊ A site template

  If you plan to customize Live Agent without using a Force.com site, skip this step.
- Verify your API versions.

  Deployment API

  Summer '13 and earlier releases support version 28.0 of the Deployment API. The URL for API version 28.0 looks like this:

  ```
  https://hostname.salesforceliveagent.com/content/g/deployment.js
  ```

Winter '14 supports version 29.0 of the Deployment API. The URL for API version 29.0 contains the version number:

`https://`**`hostname`**`.salesforceliveagent.com/content/g/js/`**`29.0`**`/deployment.js`

Pre-Chat Information API

Winter '14 supports version 29.0 of the Pre-Chat API. The URL for API version 29.0 contains the version number:

`https://`**`hostname`**`.salesforceliveagent.com/content/g/js/`**`29.0`**`/prechat.js`

Next, you can create a deployment and start customizing it with the Deployment API. For more examples on how to use Live Agent's API, see the Live Agent Developer's Guide.

Creating Deployments

Create a deployment to host Live Agent on your website. Each deployment includes a chat window, which visitors use to chat with support agents.

Once you create a deployment, you can customize it using the Deployment API to meet your company's needs.

To create a deployment:

1. From Setup, click **Customize** > **Live Agent** > **Deployments**.
2. Click **New**.
3. Enter a name for the deployment. This name, or a version of it, automatically becomes the `Developer Name`.
4. Enter a title for the chat window.
5. Select `Allow Visitors to Save Transcripts` to let visitors download a copy of the chat session when it ends.
6. Select the site that you'll associate with the deployment.
7. In `Chat Window Branding Image`, select the graphic that will appear in the chat window.
8. In `Mobile Chat Window Branding Image`, select the graphic that visitors using mobile devices will see in the chat window.
9. Click **Save**. Salesforce generates the deployment code.
10. Copy the deployment code and paste it on each Web page where you want to deploy Live Agent. For best performance, paste the code right before the closing body tag.

For more information on creating a deployment, see Creating Deployments in the Salesforce online help.

Using the Deployment API

Customize your deployments, such as for launching a chat request or creating records automatically.

This section provides basic information on methods and sample code for the Deployment API.

Methods

Use these methods to customize your Live Agent deployment.

This list provides an overview of the methods available with the Deployment API. You can add most of these methods as additional scripts within the code that's automatically generated when you create a deployment. See the Live Agent Developer's Guide for more information.

Log Deployment Activity

Logging lets you store information about the activity that occurs within a customer's Web browser as they chat with an agent through a particular deployment.

Method	Details
enableLogging	**Description** Enables logging on a particular deployment. Available in API versions 28.0 and later. **Syntax** `liveagent.enableLogging();`

Customize your Chat Window

Use these methods to customize the dimensions of your customer-facing chat windows.

Method	Details
setChatWindowHeight	**Description** Sets the height (in pixels) of the chat window that appears to customers. Available in API versions 28.0 and later. **Syntax** **void** setChatWindowHeight(**Number** height)

Method	Details
setChatWindowWidth	**Description** Sets the width (in pixels) of the chat window that appears to customers. Available in API versions 28.0 and later. **Syntax** **void** setChatWindowWidth(**Number** width)

Launch a Chat Request

Customize how chat requests are launched or route chats when a customer clicks a chat button.

Method	Details
startChat	**Description** Requests a chat from a button in a new window. Available in API versions 28.0 and later. **Syntax** **void** startChat(**String** buttonId)
startChatWithWindow	**Description** Requests a chat from a button using the name of a window. Available in API versions 28.0 and later. **Syntax** **void** startChatWithWindow(**String** buttonId, **String** windowName)

Customize Visitor Details

Customize visitor information when customers request to chat with an agent.

Method	Details
addCustomDetail	**Description** Adds custom details for each chat visitor. Available in API versions 28.0 and later.

Method	Details
	Syntax `addCustomDetail(`**`String`**` label, `**`String`**` value, (optional) `**`Boolean`**` displayToAgent)` **Returns** An instance of `CustomDetailMapper`.
`setName`	**Description** Overrides the visitor name displayed in the Live Agent console or the Salesforce console. Available in API versions 28.0 and later. **Syntax** `setName(`**`String`**` name)`

CustomDetailMapper

Use the `CustomDetailMapper` object to add custom details for each chat visitor to the appropriate Live Agent session records.

Method	Details
`map`	**Description** Maps the value of the custom detail to the specified field on the specified entity in the CRM chatlet in the Live Agent console or the relevant record in the Salesforce console. Available in API versions 28.0 and later. **Syntax** **`void`**` map(`**`String`**` entityName, `**`String`**` fieldName, `**`Boolean`**` fastFill, `**`Boolean`**` autoQuery, `**`Boolean`**` exactMatch)`
`saveToTranscript`	**Description** Saves the value of the custom detail to the specified field on the LiveChatTranscript record that's created at the end of the chat. Available in API versions 28.0 and later. **Syntax** `saveToTranscript(`**`String`**` fieldName)`

Create Records Automatically

Search for or create customer records automatically when an agent begins a chat with a customer.

Method	Details
findOrCreate	**Description** Finds existing records or create new ones based on certain criteria. Available in API versions 29.0 and later. **Syntax** `liveagent.findOrCreate(String EntityName)`

findOrCreate.map	**Description**
	
	Searches for or creates records that contain specific customer details. Available in API versions 29.0 and later.
	
	Syntax
	
	`liveagent.findOrCreate(Object EntityName)`
	`.map(String FieldName, String DetailName,`
	`Boolean doFind, Boolean isExactMatch,`
	`Boolean doCreate)`

findOrCreate.saveToTranscript	**Description**
	
	Saves the record you find or creates to the chat transcript associated with the chat. Available in API versions 29.0 and later.
	
	Syntax
	
	`liveagent.findOrCreate(String EntityName)`
	`.saveToTranscript(String`
	`TranscriptFieldName)`

findOrCreate.showOnCreate	**Description**
	
	Automatically opens the record you find or creates in a subtab in the Salesforce console. Available in API versions 29.0 and later.
	
	Syntax
	
	`liveagent.findOrCreate(String`
	`EntityName).showOnCreate()`

Method	Details
findOrCreate.linkToEntity	**Description** Links the record you found or created to another record type. Available in API versions 29.0 and later. **Syntax** ```liveagent.findOrCreate(String EntityName).linkToEntity(String EntityName, String FieldName)```

Customize Chat Buttons

Customize the chat buttons that appear on your website.

Method	Details
showWhenOnline	**Description** Specifies what customers see when particular button is online. Available in API versions 28.0 and later. **Syntax** ```void showWhenOnline(String buttonId, Object element)```
showWhenOffline	**Description** Specifies what customers see when particular button is offline. Available in API versions 28.0 and later. **Syntax** ```void showWhenOffline(String buttonId, element)```
addButtonEventHandler	**Description** Defines a chat button's behavior when certain events occur, such as when an agent is available to chat. Available in API versions 28.0 and later. **Syntax** ```void addButtonEventHandler(String buttonId, Function callback)```

Method	Details
	Event Types
	BUTTON_AVAILABLE: liveagent.BUTTON_EVENT.BUTTON_AVAILABLE
	BUTTON_UNAVAILABLE: liveagent.BUTTON_EVENT.BUTTON_UNAVAILABLE

Customize Automated Chat Invitations

Customize automated chat invitations that appear to customers on your website.

Method	Details
rejectChat	**Description** Rejects and retracts an invitation that's been sent to a customer. Available in API versions 28.0 and later. **Syntax** void rejectChat(**String** buttonId)
addButtonEventHandler	**Description** Defines an automated invitation's behavior when certain events occur. Available in API versions 28.0 and later. **Syntax** **void** addButtonEventHandler(**String** buttonId, **Function** callback) **Event Types** BUTTON_AVAILABLE: liveagent.BUTTON_EVENT.BUTTON_AVAILABLE BUTTON_UNAVAILABLE: liveagent.BUTTON_EVENT.BUTTON_UNAVAILABLE BUTTON_ACCEPTED: liveagent.BUTTON_EVENT.BUTTON_ACCEPTED BUTTON_REJECTED: liveagent.BUTTON_EVENT.BUTTON_REJECTED

Method	Details
setCustomVariable	**Description** Creates customized criteria in your sending rules that must be met in order for your automated invitation to be sent to customers. Available in API versions 28.0 and later. **Syntax** **void** setCustomVariable(**String** variableName, **Object** value)

Automated Chat Invitation Code Sample

Test and preview how automated chat invitations can work on your website using this code sample.

The following code is for an automated chat invitation that uses the addButtonEventHandler() method to display a customized invitation on a website. This invitation allows customers to start a chat with an agent when an agent with the correct skills is available to chat.

```
<apex:page>
  <div id="liveagent_invite_button_573x00000000010" style="display:
none; position: fixed; border: 2px solid darkblue; border-radius:
5px; background-color: lightblue; height: 100px; width: 200px;">
    <div style="cursor: pointer; padding: 5px; right: 0px; position:
absolute; color: darkred; font-weight: bold;"
onclick="liveagent.rejectChat('573x00000000010')">X</div>
    <div style="cursor: pointer; top: 42px; left: 65px; position:
absolute; font-weight: bold; font-size: 16px;"
onclick="liveagent.startChat('573x00000000010')">Start Chat</div>
  </div>

<script type='text/javascript'
src='https://c.la1s1.salesforceliveagent.com/content/g/deployment.js'></script>
<script type='text/javascript'>
function buttonCallback(e) {
  if (e == liveagent.BUTTON_EVENT.BUTTON_AVAILABLE) {

document.getElementById('liveagent_invite_button_573x00000000010').style.display
= '';

document.getElementById('liveagent_invite_button_573x00000000010').style.left
= '300px';

document.getElementById('liveagent_invite_button_573x00000000010').style.top
= '200px';
  }
```

```
  if (e == liveagent.BUTTON_EVENT.BUTTON_UNAVAILABLE) {

document.getElementById('liveagent_invite_button_573x000000000010').style.display
= 'none';
  }
  if (e == liveagent.BUTTON_EVENT.BUTTON_ACCEPTED) {

document.getElementById('liveagent_invite_button_573x000000000010').style.display
= 'none';
  }
  if (e == liveagent.BUTTON_EVENT.BUTTON_REJECTED) {

document.getElementById('liveagent_invite_button_573x000000000010').style.display
= 'none';
  }
liveagent.addButtonEventHandler('573x000000000010', buttonCallback);
liveagent.init('https://d.la1s1.salesforceliveagent.com/chat',
'572x00000000001', '00Dx00000001gEH');
</script>
</apex:page>
```

The code above results in an invitation that looks like this:

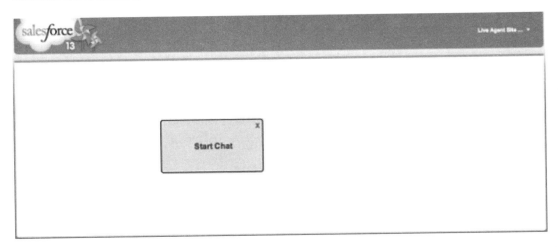

Deployment API Code Sample

Test and preview how the Deployment API can help you customize your deployments using this code sample.

The following code sample shows a chat window that uses the following Deployment API methods:

- `startChat`
- `showWhenOnline`

- showWhenOffline
- addCustomDetail
- setName
- map
- setChatWindowWidth
- setChatWindowHeight

```
<apex:page >
 <h1>Welcome</h1>
  Thank you for contacting customer support

  <!-- START Button code -->
   <img id="liveagent_button_online_573D000000000Ar" style="display:
  none; border: 0px none; cursor: pointer"
onclick="liveagent.startChat('573D000000000Ar')"
src="https://na1.salesforce.com/resource/1319587702000/Chat_Online"
 />

   <img id="liveagent_button_offline_573D000000000Ar" style="display:
  none; border: 0px none; "
src="https://na1.salesforce.com/resource/1319587748000/Chat_Offline"
 />
    <script type="text/javascript">
    if (!window._laq) { window._laq = []; }

window._laq.push(function(){liveagent.showWhenOnline('573D000000000Ar',
 document.getElementById('liveagent_button_online_573D000000000Ar'));

     liveagent.showWhenOffline('573D000000000Ar',
document.getElementById('liveagent_button_offline_573D000000000Ar'));

   });</script>
  <!-- END Button code -->

  <!-- Deployment code -->
<script type='text/javascript'

src='https://c.la1s1.saleforceliveagent.com/content/g/deployment.js'></script>

<script type='text/javascript'>
 // An auto query that searches contacts whose email field matches
"john@acme.com"
 liveagent.addCustomDetail('Contact E-mail',
'john@acme.com').map('Contact', 'Email', false, true);
 // A fast-fill to populate a contact's name with "John Doe"
 liveagent.addCustomDetail('Contact Name', 'John Doe').map('Contact',
 'Name', true, false);
 // Saves the custom detail to a custom field on LiveChatTranscript
at the end of a chat
 liveagent.addCustomDetail('Company',
'Acme').saveToTranscript('Company__c');
 // Overrides the display name of the visitor in the agent console
when engaged in a chat
 liveagent.setName('John Doe');
```

```
// Sets the width of the chat window to 500px
liveagent.setChatWindowWidth(500);
// Sets the height of the chat window to 500px
liveagent.setChatWindowHeight(500);

liveagent.init('https://d.la1s1.salesforceliveagent.com/chat',
'572D0000000002R', '00DD0000000JXbY');
</script>
</apex:page>
```

The deployment code above results in a page that looks like this:

Using the Pre-Chat API

Customize your pre-chat experience, such as for gathering and accessing a customer's information.

The pre-chat experience is what happens between the time visitors request a chat and the time they're connected to a support agent. Use pre-chat forms in Live Agent to customize this experience and collect information from visitors. This section provides a sample pre-chat form and basic information on methods for the Pre-Chat API.

Methods

Use these methods to customize your Live Agent pre-chat experience.

This list provides an overview of the methods available with the Pre-Chat API. See the Live Agent Developer's Guide for more information.

Initialize and Access Details in Chat

Access the custom details that have been passed into the chat through the `addCustomDetail` Deployment API method.

Method	Details
preChatInit	**Description** Extracts the custom details that have been passed into the chat through the addCustomDetail Deployment API method and integrates them into a pre-chat form. Available in API versions 29.0 and later. **Syntax** liveagent.details.preChatInit(**String** chatUrl, **function** detailCallback, (optional) **String** chatFormName)

The details object contains all the custom details included in the pre-chat form. It has a structure similar to the following example object:

```
{
    "geoLocation":{
        "countryCode":"US",
        "countryName":"United States",
        "longitude":-122.4294,
        "organization":"SALESFORCE.COM",
        "latitude":37.764496,
        "region":"CA",
        "city":"San Francisco"

    },
    "customDetails":[
        {
            "label":"Email",
            "value":"sonic@sega.com",
            "transcriptFields":["Email__c"],
            "entityMaps":[
                {
                    "fieldName":"Email",
                    "isAutoQueryable":true,
                    "entityName":"Contact",
                    "isExactMatchable":true,
                    "isFastFillable":false
                }]
        },
        {
            "label":"Name",
            "value":"Sonic H.",
            "transcriptFields":[],
            "entityMaps":[]
        }
    ],
    "visitorId":"251a5956-bcbc-433d-b822-a87c062e681c"
}
```

Create Records Automatically

Search for or create customer records automatically when a customer completes a pre-chat form

Method	Details
findOrCreate.map	**Description** Searches for or creates records that contain the customer data specified in the pre-chat form completed by the customer. This method maps the value of the custom details to the fields on the specified record in the Salesforce console. You can call the findOrCreate.map method as many times as necessary to find the appropriate records. You can list multiple fields and their corresponding details to map the detail values to the appropriate fields within the record. Available in API versions 29.0 and later. **Syntax** `<input type= "hidden" name= "liveagent.prechat.findorcreate.map:` **`String`** `entityName" value= "`**`String`** `fieldName,` **`String`** `detailName;"/>`
findOrCreate.map.doFind	**Description** Specifies which fields in your findOrCreate.map method to use to search for an existing record. You can search for one or more fields within records. Available in API versions 29.0 and later. **Syntax** `<input type= "hidden" name= "liveagent.prechat.findorcreate.map.doFind:` **`String`** `entityName" value= "`**`String`** `fieldName,` **`Boolean`** `find;"/>`
findOrCreate.map.isExactMatch	**Description** Specifies which fields in your findOrCreate.map method require an exact field name match when you search for existing records. You can specify this for one or more fields within records. Available in API versions 29.0 and later.

Method	Details

	Syntax
	
	```<input type= "hidden" name=```
	```"liveagent.prechat.findorcreate.map.isExactMatch:```
	```String entityName" value= "String```
	```fieldName, Boolean exactMatch;"/>```

findOrCreate.map.doCreate	**Description**
	
	Specifies which fields in your `findOrCreate.map` method to use to create a new record if an existing record isn't found. You can specify one or more fields for creating new records. Available in API versions 29.0 and later.
	
	Syntax
	
	```<input type= "hidden" name=```
	```"liveagent.prechat.findorcreate.map.doCreate:```
	```String entityName" value= "String```
	```fieldName, Boolean create;"/>```

findOrCreate.saveToTranscript	**Description**
	
	Saves the record that you found or created using `findOrCreate.map.doCreate` or `findOrCreate.map.doFind` to the chat transcript associated with the chat when the chat ends. Available in API versions 29.0 and later.
	
	Syntax
	
	```<input type= "hidden" name=```
	```"liveagent.prechat.findorcreate.saveToTranscript:```
	```String entityName" value= "String```
	```transcriptFieldName"/>```

findOrCreate.showOnCreate	**Description** Opens the record you found or created using `findOrCreate.map.doCreate` and `findOrCreate.map.doFind` automatically in a subtab in the to the Salesforce console. Available in API versions 29.0 and later.

Method	Details
	Syntax ```<input type= "hidden" name= "liveagent.prechat.findorcreate.showOnCreate: String entityName" value= "Boolean show"/>```
findOrCreate.linkToEntity	**Description** Links the record that you found or created using findOrCreate.map.doFind and findOrCreate.map.doCreate to another record of a different record type that you created using a separate findOrCreate.map API call. For example, you can link a case record you found within your organization to a contact record you create. Available in API versions 29.0 and later. **Syntax** ```<input type= "hidden" name= "liveagent.prechat.findorcreate.linkToEntity: String entityName" value= "String parentEntityName, String fieldName"/>```
findOrCreate.displayToAgent	**Description** Specifies which pre-chat details to display to an agent in the Details tab in Salesforce console when the agent receives a chat request. Available in API versions 29.0 and later. **Syntax** ```<input type= "hidden" name= "liveagent.prechat.findorcreate.displayToAgent: String detailName" value= "Boolean display"/>```

Pre-Chat Form Code Sample

Test and preview how pre-chat forms can work for your agents and customers using this code sample.

The following code is for a pre-chat form that:

- Requests a visitor's name and email address.
- Displays that information in the Details chatlet in the Live Agent console .
- Enables mapping and auto-query, which triggers a search on the visitor's email address when a support agent opens the CRM chatlet in the Live Agent console.
- Displays a drop-down list that lets visitors choose a different Live Chat button through which to route their chat request.

```
<apex:page showHeader="false">
<!-- This script takes the endpoint URL parameter passed from the
deployment page and makes it the action for the form -->
<script type="text/javascript">
    (function() {
    function handlePageLoad() {
     var endpointMatcher = new RegExp("[\\?\\&]endpoint=([^&#]*)");

      document.getElementById('prechatForm').setAttribute('action',

decodeURIComponent(endpointMatcher.exec(document.location.search)[1]));

      } if (window.addEventListener) {
            window.addEventListener('load', handlePageLoad, false);

    } else { window.attachEvent('onload', handlePageLoad, false);
            }})();
</script>
<h1>Pre-chat Form</h1>
<form method='post' id='prechatForm'>
    Name: <input type='text' name='liveagent.prechat.name'
id='prechat_field' /><br />
    Email Address: <input type='text' name='liveagent.prechat:Email'
 /><br />
        Department: <select name="liveagent.prechat.buttons">
        <!-- Values are LiveChatButton IDs. -->
        <option value="573a00000000001">Customer Service</option>

        <option value="573a00000000002">Technical Support</option>

        <option value="573a00000000001,573a00000000002">Customer
Service if online,
        otherwise Technical Support</option>
        </select><br />
        <!-- Creates an auto-query for a matching Contact record's
Email field based on the
        value of the liveagent.prechat:Email field -->
        <input type="hidden" name="liveagent.prechat.query:Email"
        value="Contact,Contact.Email" />
        <input type="hidden" name="liveagent.prechat.save:Email"
value="Email__c" />
        <input type='submit' value='Request Chat' id='prechat_submit'/>

<style type="text/css">
p {font-weight: bolder }
</style>
```

```
</form>
</apex:page>
```

The code above results in a pre-chat form that looks like this:

Resources

Search on the Salesforce Developer's Network at `http://developer.salesforce.com/docs` for the following resources on Live Agent API.

- Live Agent Developer's Guide
- Live Agent Implementation Guide

Chapter 29

Salesforce Console Integration Toolkit

The Salesforce console is designed for users in fast-paced environments who need to find, update, and create records in Salesforce quickly.

The Salesforce Console Integration Toolkit provides you with programmatic access to the Salesforce console so that you can extend it to meet your business needs. With the Salesforce Console Integration Toolkit, you can open and close tabs in the console to streamline a business process. For example, the toolkit lets you integrate third-party systems with the console, opening up an external application in the same window, in a tab.

The Salesforce Console Integration Toolkit is a browser-based JavaScript API. It uses browsers as clients to display pages as tabs in the console.

The Salesforce Console Integration Toolkit matches the API version for any given release. For example, if the current version of SOAP API is 28.0, then there's also a version 28.0 of the Salesforce Console Integration Toolkit.

This guide provides a high-level overview on the Salesforce Console Integration Toolkit and the available API methods. For more information, see the *Salesforce Console Integration Toolkit Developer's Guide*.

Supported Browsers

Salesforce Console Integration Toolkit supports the following browsers:

- Mozilla® Firefox® version 3.5 and later
- Google Chrome™, most recent stable version
- Microsoft® Internet Explorer® version 7 and later

URLs to Salesforce console pages might not work when pasted into browsers or selected from bookmarks. For known issues, see "Salesforce Console Limitations" in the Salesforce Help.

Supported Salesforce Editions

Salesforce Console Integration Toolkit is available with these Salesforce Editions, with the Service Cloud:

- Developer Edition
- Enterprise Edition
- Unlimited Edition
- Performance Edition

If you're an existing Salesforce customer and want to upgrade to any of these editions, contact your account representative.

Quick Start

Get started with the Salesforce Console Integration Toolkit by first connecting to the Toolkit using JavaScript.

Follow these steps to get started.

1. Connect to the toolkit.
2. Make asynchronous calls with the Toolkit.
3. Use Force.com Canvas to integrate the Salesforce Console with external applications that require authentication methods.

Use the Salesforce Console Integration Toolkit to do the following in the Salesforce Console:

- Open a new primary tab or subtab that displays a specified URL
- Set the title of a primary tab or a subtab
- Return the ID of a primary tab or subtab
- Close a specified primary tab or subtab

Connecting to the Toolkit

The first portion of any JavaScript code that uses the Salesforce Console Integration Toolkit must make the toolkit available to the JavaScript code. The syntax for this is different depending on whether you are embedding JavaScript in a Visualforce page, or a third-party domain.

- For Visualforce pages or any source other than a custom `onclick` JavaScript button, specify a `<script>` tag that points to the toolkit file:

```
<apex:page>
        <script src="/support/console/29.0/integration.js"
type="text/javascript"></script>
    ...
</apex:page>
```

For Visualforce, a relative path is sufficient to include `integration.js`, and is recommended.

- For a third-party domain:

```
<script
src="https://c.na1.visual.force.com/support/console/29.0/integration.js"
  type="text/javascript"></script>
```

For third-party domains, it is necessary to specify an absolute URL to `integration.js` to use the toolkit. The default instance at which you can access the toolkit library is: `c.na1.visual.force.com/support/console/29.0/integration.js`. We recommend that you use the default instance when the organization's instance cannot be determined.

The version of the Salesforce Console Integration Toolkit is in the URL.

Asynchronous Calls with the Salesforce Console Integration Toolkit

The Salesforce Console Integration Toolkit lets you issue asynchronous calls. Asynchronous calls allow the client-side process to continue instead of waiting for a callback from the server. To issue an asynchronous call, you must include an additional parameter with the API call, which is referred to as a callback function. Once the result is ready, the server invokes the callback method with the result.

Asynchronous syntax:

```
method('arg1','arg2', ..., callback_method);
```

For example:

```
//Open a new primary tab with the Salesforce home page in it
    sforce.console.openPrimaryTab(null, 'http://www.salesforce.com',

      false, 'Salesforce', callback);
```

Working with Force.com Canvas

To integrate the Salesforce Console with external applications that require authentication methods, such as signed requests or OAuth 2.0 protocols, Salesforce.com recommends you use Force.com Canvas.

Force.com Canvas and the Salesforce Console Integration Toolkit are similar—they're a set of tools and JavaScript APIs that developers can use to add third-party systems to Salesforce. However, one of the benefits of Force.com Canvas, is the ability to choose authentication methods. For more information, see the *Force.com Canvas Developer's Guide*.

 Note: For a canvas app to appear in a console, you must add it to the console as a custom console component. See "Adding Custom Console Components" in the Salesforce Help.

When developing a canvas app, and you want to include functionality from the Salesforce Console Integration Toolkit, do the following:

1. Include the console integration toolkit API in `index.jsp`.
2. If your console has a whitelist for domains, add the domain of your canvas app to the whitelist. See "Whitelisting Domains for a Salesforce Console" in the Salesforce Help.
3. Call `Sfdc.canvas.client.signedrequest()` to store the signed request needed by the console integration toolkit API. For example, if the Force.com Canvas method of authentication is a signed request, do the following:

   ```
   Sfdc.canvas.client.signedrequest('<%=signedRequest%>')
   ```

   If the Force.com Canvas method of authentication is OAuth, do the following in the callback function used to get the context as shown in "Getting Context in Your Canvas App" in the *Force.com Canvas Developer's Guide*:

   ```
   Sfdc.canvas.client.signedrequest(msg)
   ```

Consider the following when working with the Salesforce Console Integration Toolkit and canvas apps:

- The console integration toolkit API script depends on the signed request and should be added after the call to `Sfdc.canvas.client.signedrequest()` has executed. We recommend that you load the scripts dynamically.

- To retrieve the entity ID of the record that is associated with the canvas sidebar component, do the following:

```
// Get signedRequest
var signedRequest = Sfdc.canvas.client.signedrequest();
var parsedRequest = JSON.parse(signedRequest);
// get the entity Id that is associated with this canvas sidebar
component.
var entityId =
parsedRequest.context.environment.parameters.entityId;
```

- To retrieve the `entityId` for OAuth, do the following:

```
var entityId = msg.payload.environment.parameters.entityId;
```

To see an example on how to retrieve `msg.payload`, see "Getting Context in Your Canvas App" in the *Force.com Canvas Developer's Guide*.

Best Practices

- Since many of the methods in the Salesforce Console Integration Toolkit are asynchronous and return their results using a callback method, Salesforce.com recommends that you refer to the documentation for each method to understand the information for each response.
- Errors generated by the Salesforce Console Integration Toolkit are typically emitted in a way that doesn't halt JavaScript processing. Therefore, Salesforce recommends you use a tool such as Firebug for Firefox to monitor the JavaScript console and to help you debug your code.
- To display Visualforce pages properly in the Salesforce Console, Salesforce.com recommends you:

  ◊ Set `showHeader="false"` and `sidebar="false"` on the `apex:page` tag.
  ◊ Set `Behavior` on custom buttons and links that include methods from the toolkit to display in an existing window without a sidebar or header. For more information, see Defining Custom Buttons and Links" in the Salesforce online help.

- When using Firefox, Salesforce.com recommends that you don't call `closeTab()` on a tab with an active alert box because the browser may not load properly.
- Duplicate tabs might open when users initiate methods with invalid URLs. Salesforce.com recommends you check URLs for validity before you include them in methods.
- To prevent `External Page` from displaying as a tab name, Salesforce recommends you specify the `tabLabel` argument on methods such as `openPrimaryTab()` and `openSubtab()`.

- For information on how you can customize, extend, or integrate the sidebars of the Salesforce console using Visualforce, Salesforce.com recommends you see "Custom Console Components Overview" in the Salesforce online help.
- To enable the toolkit for third-party domains, you must add the domains to the whitelist of the Salesforce console. See "Whitelisting Domains for a Salesforce Console" in the Salesforce online help.

Sample Visualforce Page Using the Salesforce Console Integration Toolkit

This example shows how to change the Salesforce console user interface using the Salesforce Console Integration Toolkit.

1. Create a Visualforce page. See the *Visualforce Developer's Guide*.
2. Cut and paste the following sample code into your Visualforce page.

    This code demonstrates various functions of the Salesforce Console Integration Toolkit:

```
<apex:page standardController="Case">

    <apex:includeScript
value="/support/console/20.0/integration.js"/>
    <script type="text/javascript">
        function openPrimaryTab() {
            sforce.console.openPrimaryTab(undefined,
                'http://www.salesforce.com', true,
'salesforce');
        }

        //The callback function that openSubtab will call
    once it's got the ID for its primary tab
        var callOpenSubtab=function callOpenSubtab(result) {

            sforce.console.openSubtab(result.id,
                'http://www.yahoo.com', true, 'yahoo');
        };

        function openSubtab() {

    sforce.console.getEnclosingPrimaryTabId(callOpenSubtab);
        }

        //Sets the title of the current tab to "SFDC"
        function setTitle() {
            sforce.console.setTabTitle('SFDC');
        }

        //The callback function that closeTab will call once
```

```
it's got the ID for its tab
    var callCloseTab= function callCloseTab(result) {
        sforce.console.closeTab(result.id);
    }

    function closeTab() {
        sforce.console.getEnclosingTabId(callCloseTab);
    }
</script>

  <A HREF="#" onClick="openPrimaryTab();return false">Open
A Primary Tab</A>
  <p/><A HREF="#" onClick="openSubtab();return false">Open
A Subtab</A>
  <p/><A HREF="#" onClick="setTitle();return false">Set Title
to SFDC</A>
  <p/><A HREF="#" onClick="closeTab();return false">Close
This Tab</A>

</apex:page>
```

 Note: This example is set to run by clicking a custom link on a case. For more information, see "Defining Custom Buttons and Links" in the Salesforce online help.

After you create the above Visualforce page and add it as a custom link on cases, this page displays after you navigate to a case and click the link:

Figure 9: Output of Sample Visualforce Page

Methods

Use these methods to customize your Salesforce Console experience.

This guide provides an overview of the methods available with the Salesforce Console Integration Toolkit. See the *Salesforce Console Integration Toolkit Developer's Guide* for more information on the calls and responses.

Methods are available for the following elements:

- Primary Tabs and subtabs
- Computer-Telephony Integration (CTI)
- Application-Level Custom Console Components
- Push Notifications
- Live Agent

Methods for Primary Tabs and Subtabs

The Salesforce console displays Salesforce pages as primary tabs or subtabs:

Primary Tab

A tab in a Salesforce console that displays the main item to work on, such as an account.

Subtab

A tab that displays content related to the item on a primary tab in a Salesforce console. For example, a primary tab showing an account might have subtabs for cases and contacts.

You can use the following methods for primary tabs and subtabs:

Method	Description
closeTab()	Closes a specified primary tab or subtab. Note that closing the first tab in a primary tab closes the primary tab itself. This method is only available in API version 20.0 or later.
focusPrimaryTabById()	Focuses the browser on a primary tab that is already open with the specified ID. This method is only available in API version 22.0 or later.
focusPrimaryTabByName()	Focuses the browser on a primary tab that is already open with the specified name. This method is only available in API version 22.0 or later.
focusSubtabById()	Focuses the browser on a subtab that is already open with the specified ID. This method is only available in API version 22.0 or later.

Method	Description
focusSubtabByNameAndPrimaryTabId()	Focuses the browser on a subtab that is already open with the specified name and primary tab ID. This method is only available in API version 22.0 or later.
focusSubtabByNameAndPrimaryTabName()	Focuses the browser on a subtab that is already open with the specified name and primary tab name. This method is only available in API version 22.0 or later.
generateConsoleUrl()	Generates a URL to a tab, or group of related tabs, in the Salesforce console. If any tabs include external URLs, then add the external URLs to the console's whitelist so that they can display correctly. For more information, see "Whitelisting Domains for a Salesforce Console" in the Salesforce online help. This method is only available in API version 28.0 or later.
getEnclosingPrimaryTabId()	Returns the ID of the current primary tab. This method works within a primary tab or subtab, not within the navigation tab or custom console components. This method is only available in API version 20.0 or later.
getEnclosingPrimaryTabObjectId()	Returns the object ID of the current primary tab, which contains a subtab. For example, a case ID or account ID. This method works within a primary tab or subtab. This method is only available in API version 24.0 or later.
getEnclosingTabId()	Returns the ID of the tab that contains the current Visualforce page, which may be a primary tab or subtab. This method will work if the call is made within a component enclosed within a subtab. This method is only available in API version 20.0 or later.
getFocusedPrimaryTabId()	Returns the ID of the primary tab on which the browser is focused. This method is only available in API version 25.0 or later.

Method	Description
getFocusedPrimaryTabObjectId()	Returns the object ID of the primary tab on which the browser is focused. This method is only available in API version 25.0 or later.
getFocusedSubtabId()	Returns the ID of the subtab on which the browser is focused. For example, a case ID or account ID. This method is only available in API version 25.0 or later.
getFocusedSubtabObjectId()	Returns the object ID of the subtab on which the browser is focused. For example, a case ID or account ID. This method is only available in API version 24.0 or later.
getPageInfo()	Returns page information for the specified tab after its content has loaded. If the tab ID is null, it returns page information for the enclosing primary tab or subtab. Note that to get the page information from a custom console component, a tabId must be passed as the first parameter to this method. This method is only available in API version 26.0 or later.
getPrimaryTabIds()	Returns all of the IDs of open primary tabs. This method is only available in API version 26.0 or later.
getSubtabIds()	Returns all of the IDs of the subtabs on the primary tab specified by a primary tab ID. If the primary tab ID is null, it returns the IDs of the subtabs on the current primary tab. This method can only be called from a custom console component or a detail page overwritten by a Visualforce page. This method is only available in API version 26.0 or later.
getTabLink()	Retrieves the URL to a tab, or group of related tabs, from the Salesforce console. This method is only available in API version 28.0 or later.
isInConsole()	Determines if the page is in the Salesforce console. This method is only available in API version 22.0 or later.

Method	Description
onEnclosingTabRefresh()	Registers a function to call when the enclosing tab refreshes. This method is only available in API version 24.0 or later.
onFocusedSubtab()	Registers a function to call when the focus of the browser changes to a different subtab. This method is only available in API version 24.0 or later.
onTabSave()	Registers and calls a callback method when a user clicks **Save** in a subtab's Unsaved Changes dialog box. When using this method, you must call setTabUnsavedChanges() in the callback method. This notifies the console that the custom save operation completed. In the call to setTabUnsavedChanges(), pass the first parameter as false to indicate a successful save or true to indicate an unsuccessful save. This method is only available in API version 28.0 or later.
openConsoleUrl()	Opens a URL created by the generateConsoleUrl() method (a URL to a tab, or group of related tabs, in the Salesforce console). This method is only available in API version 28.0 or later.
openPrimaryTab()	Opens a new primary tab to display the content of the specified URL, which can be relative or absolute. You can also override an existing tab. This method is only available in API version 20.0 or later.
openSubtab()	Opens a new subtab (within a primary tab) that displays the content of a specified URL, which can be relative or absolute. You can also override an existing subtab. Use to open a new subtab on a primary tab via the primary tab's ID. This method is only available in API version 20.0 or later.
openSubtabByPrimaryTabName()	Opens a new subtab (within a primary tab) that displays the content of a specified URL, which

Method	Description
	can be relative or absolute. You can also override an existing subtab. Use to open a new subtab on a primary tab via the primary tab's name. This method is only available in API version 22.0 or later.
`refreshPrimaryTabById()`	Refreshes a primary tab specified by ID, including its subtabs. This method can't refresh subtabs with URLs to external pages or Visualforce pages. This method is only available in API version 22.0 or later.
`refreshPrimaryTabByName()`	Refreshes a primary tab specified by name, including its subtabs. This method can't refresh subtabs with URLs to external pages or Visualforce pages. This method is only available in API version 22.0 or later.
`refreshSubtabById()`	Refreshes a subtab with the last known URL with a specified ID. This method can't refresh a subtab If the last known URL is an external page or a Visualforce page. This method is only available in API version 22.0 or later.
`refreshSubtabByNameAndPrimaryTabId()`	Refreshes a subtab with the last known URL with the specified name and primary tab ID. This method can't refresh a subtab If the last known URL is an external page or a Visualforce page. This method is only available in API version 22.0 or later.
`refreshSubtabByNameAndPrimaryTabName()`	Refreshes a subtab with the last known URL with the specified name and primary tab name. This method can't refresh a subtab If the last known URL is an external page or a Visualforce page. This method is only available in API version 22.0 or later.
`resetSessionTimeOut()`	Resets a session timeout on a Visualforce page so that users can continue working without being logged out. For more information, see "Setting Session Security" in the Salesforce Help. This

Method	Description
	method is only available in API version 24.0 or later.
setTabLink()	Sets a console tab's URL attribute to the location of the tab's content. Use this method to generate secure console URLs when users navigate to tabs displaying content outside of the Salesforce domain. This method is only available in API version 28.0 or later.
setTabIcon()	Sets an icon on the specified tab. If a tab is not specified, the icon is set on the enclosing tab. Use this method to customize a tab's icon. This method is only available in API version 28.0 or later.
setTabStyle()	Sets a cascading style sheet (CSS) on the specified tab. If a tab is not specified, the CSS is set on the enclosing tab. Use this method to customize a tab's look and feel. This method is only available in API version 28.0 or later.
setTabTextStyle()	Sets a cascading style sheet (CSS) on a specified tab's text. If a tab is not specified, the CSS is set on the enclosing tab's text. Use this method to customize a tab's text style. This method is only available in API version 28.0 or later.
setTabTitle()	Sets the title of a primary tab or subtab. This method is only available in API version 20.0 or later.
setTabUnsavedChanges()	Sets the unsaved changes icon (*) on subtabs to indicate unsaved data. This method is only available in API version 23.0 or later.

Methods for Computer-Telephony Integration (CTI)

Salesforce CRM Call Center seamlessly integrates Salesforce with third-party computer-telephony integration (CTI) systems. After a lightweight CTI adapter program has been installed on a Salesforce user's machine, the user can use the features of a CTI system through the Salesforce SoftPhone, a customizable call-control tool that appears in the footer of the Salesforce console or in sidebar of every Salesforce page.

For more information on CTI, see "Call Center Overview" in the Salesforce online help.

You can use the following methods for a CTI system with the Salesforce console:

Method	Description
getCallAttachedData()	Returns the attached data of a call represented by the call object ID or null if there isn't an active call. The data is returned in JSON format. This method is for computer-telephony integration (CTI); it's only available in API version 24.0 or later.
getCallObjectIds()	Returns any active call object IDs in the order in which they arrived or null if there aren't any active calls. This method is for computer-telephony integration (CTI); it's only available in API version 24.0 or later.
onCallBegin()	Registers a function that is called when a call begins (comes in). This method is for computer-telephony integration (CTI); it's only available in API version 24.0 or later.
onCallEnd()	Registers a function that is called when a call ends. This method is for computer-telephony integration (CTI); it's only available in API version 24.0 or later.
sendCTIMessage()	Sends a message to the CTI adapter. This method is for computer-telephony integration (CTI); it's only available in API version 24.0 or later.

Methods for Application-Level Custom Console Components

Custom console components let you customize, extend, or integrate the footer, sidebars, highlights panels, and interaction logs of a Salesforce console using Visualforce, canvas apps, or lookup fields.

Administrators can add custom console components to either:

- Page layouts to display content on specific pages
- Salesforce console apps to display content across all pages and tabs

For more information, see "Custom Console Components Overview" in the Salesforce online help.

You can use the following methods for custom console components that display at the Salesforce console app-level:

Method	Description
addEventListener()	Adds a listener for a custom event type, which is called when the custom event is fired. This method is only available in API version 25.0 or later.
addToBrowserTitleQueue()	Adds a browser tab title to a list of titles, which rotates every three seconds. This method is only available in API version 28.0 or later.
blinkCustomConsoleComponentButtonText()	Blinks a button's text on an application-level custom console component that's on a page. This method is only available in API version 25.0 or later.
fireEvent()	Fires a custom event. This method is only available in API version 25.0 or later.
isCustomConsoleComponentWindowHidden()	Determines if the application-level custom console component window is hidden. This method is only available in API version 25.0 or later.
isInCustomConsoleComponent()	Determines if the page is in an application-level custom console component. This method is only available in API version 25.0 or later.
onCustomConsoleComponentButtonClicked()	Registers a function to call when a button is clicked on an application-level custom console component. This method is only available in API version 25.0 or later.
onFocusedPrimaryTab()	Registers a function to call when the focus of the browser changes to a different primary tab. This

Method	Description
	method is only available in API version 25.0 or later.
removeFromBrowserTitleQueue()	Removes a browser tab title from the list of titles, which rotates every three seconds. This method is only available in API version 28.0 or later.
scrollCustomConsoleComponentButtonText()	Scrolls a button's text on an application-level custom console component that's on a page. This method is only available in API version 25.0 or later.
setCustomConsoleComponentButtonIconUrl()	Sets the button icon URL of an application-level custom console component that's on a page. This method is only available in API version 25.0 or later.
setCustomConsoleComponentButtonStyle()	Sets the style of a button used to launch an application-level custom console component that's on a page. This method is only available in API version 25.0 or later.
setCustomConsoleComponentButtonText()	Sets the text on a button used to launch an application-level custom console component that's on a page. This method is only available in API version 25.0 or later.
setCustomConsoleComponentWindowVisible()	Sets the window visibility of an application-level custom console component that's on a page. This method is only available in API version 25.0 or later.

Methods for Push Notifications

Push notifications are visual indicators on lists and detail pages in a Salesforce console that show when a record or field has changed during a user's session. For example, if two support agents are working on the same case and one agent changes the Priority, a push notification displays to the other agent so he or she notices the change and doesn't duplicate the effort.

When administrators set up a Salesforce console, they choose when push notifications display, and which objects and fields trigger push notifications. Developers can use push notification methods to customize push notifications beyond the default visual indicators supplied by

Salesforce. For example, developers can use the methods below to create personalized notifications about objects accessible to specific console users, thereby eliminating the need for email notifications.

For more information about how to set up push notifications, see "Customizing Push Notifications for a Salesforce Console" in the Salesforce online help.

Note the following when using push notification methods:

- Push notification listener response is only available for the objects and fields selected to trigger push notifications for a console.
- When a Visualforce page includes a listener added by the addPushNotificationListener() method, the page receives notifications. The listener receives notifications when there is an update by any user to the objects selected for triggering console push notifications and the current user has access to the modified record. This functionality is slightly different from push notifications set up in the Salesforce user interface in that:

  ◊ Listeners receive update notifications for changes made by all users.
  ◊ Listeners receive notifications when an object's fields are updated or created, even if those fields aren't selected to trigger push notifications; and the notifications don't include details about what changed. For example, if Status on the Case object is set to trigger a push notification, but Priority on the Case object changes, a listener receives a notification that the case changed without specifying details.
  ◊ Listeners don't obey the Choose How Lists Refresh and Choose How Detail Pages Refresh push notifications settings in a Salesforce console.
  ◊ The only way to stop receiving notifications is to remove listeners using the removePushNotificationListener() method.

You can use the following methods for push notifications that display in the Salesforce console:

Method	Description
addPushNotificationListener()	Adds a listener for a push notification. A user can only register a listener once until he or she removes the listener, or the listener is removed by another user. This method is only available in API version 26.0 or later. For more information on push notifications, see Methods for Push Notifications on page 454.
removePushNotificationListener()	Removes a listener that gets added for a push notification. This method is only available in API

Method	Description
	version 26.0 or later. For more information on push notifications, see Methods for Push Notifications on page 454.

Methods for Live Agent

Live Agent lets you connect with customers or website visitors in real time through a Web-based, text-only live chat. See "Adding Live Agent to the Salesforce Console" in the Salesforce Help for more information. You can use the following methods to customize Live Agent in the Salesforce Console for Service:

Method	Description
acceptChat()	Accepts a chat request. Available in API version 29.0 or later.
declineChat()	Declines a chat request. Available in API version 29.0 or later.
endChat()	Ends a chat in which an agent is currently engaged. Available in API version 29.0 or later.
getAgentInput()	Returns the string of text which is currently in the agent's text input area in the chat log of a chat with a specific chat key. Available in API version 29.0 or later.
getAgentState()	Returns the agent's current Live Agent status, such as Online, Away, or Offline. Available in API version 29.0 or later.
getChatLog()	Returns the chat log of a chat associated with a specific chat key. Available in API version 29.0 or later.

Method	Description
getChatRequests()	Returns the chat keys of the chat requests that have been assigned to an agent. Available in API version 29.0 or later.
getDetailsByChatKey()	Returns the details of the chat associated with a specific chat key. Available in API version 29.0 or later.
getDetailsByPrimaryTabId()	Returns the details of the chat associated with a specific primary tab ID. Available in API version 29.0 or later.
getEngagedChats()	Returns the chat keys of the chats in which the agent is currently engaged. Available in API version 29.0 or later.
getMaxCapacity()	Returns the maximum chat capacity for the current agent, as specified in the agent's assigned agent configuration. Available in API version 29.0 or later.
onAgentSend()	Registers a function to call when an agent sends a chat message through the Salesforce console. This method intercepts the message and occurs before it is sent to the chat visitor. Available in API version 29.0 or later.
onAgentStateChanged()	Registers a function to call when agents change their Live Agent status, such as from Online to Away. Available in API version 29.0 or later.
onChatCanceled()	Registers a function to call when a chat visitor cancels a chat request. Available in API version 29.0 or later.

Method	Description
onChatCriticalWaitState()	Registers a function to call when a chat becomes critical to answer or a waiting chat is answered. Available in API version 29.0 or later.
onChatDeclined()	Registers a function to call when an agent declines a chat request. Available in API version 29.0 or later.
onChatEnded()	Registers a function to call when an engaged chat ends. Available in API version 29.0 or later.
onChatRequested()	Registers a function to call when an agent receives a chat request. Available in API version 29.0 or later.
onChatStarted()	Registers a function to call when an agent starts a new chat with a customer. Available in API version 29.0 or later.
onChatTransferredOut()	Registers a function to call when an engaged chat is transferred out to another agent. Available in API version 29.0 or later.
onCurrentCapacityChanged()	Registers a function to call when an agent's capacity for accepting chats changes—for example, if an agent accepts a new chat, ends a currently engaged chat, or otherwise changes the number of chats to which they are assigned, or if a chat request is pushed to their chat queue. Available in API version 29.0 or later.
onCustomEvent()	Registers a function to call when a custom event takes place during a chat. Available in API version 29.0 or later.

Method	Description
onNewMessage()	Registers a function to call when a new message is sent from a customer, agent, or supervisor. Available in API version 29.0 or later.
onTypingUpdate()	Registers a function to call when the customer's text in the chat window changes. If Sneak Peek is enabled, this function is called whenever the customer edits the text in the chat window. If Sneak Peek is not enabled, this function is called whenever a customer starts or stops typing in the chat window. Available in API version 29.0 or later.
sendCustomEvent()	Sends a custom event to the client-side chat window for a chat with a specific chat key. Available in API version 29.0 or later.
sendMessage()	Sends a new chat message from the agent to a chat with a specific chat key. Available in API version 29.0 or later.
setAgentInput()	Sets the string of text in the agent's text input area in the chat log of a chat with a specific chat key. Available in API version 29.0 or later.
setAgentState()	Sets an agent's Live Agent status, such as Online, Away, or Offline. Available in API version 29.0 or later.

Resources

Search on the Salesforce Developer's Network at
`http://developer.salesforce.com/docs` for the following resources on Salesforce
Console Integration Toolkit.

- Salesforce Console Integration Toolkit Developer's Guide
- "Salesforce Console Overview" in the Salesforce Help

## Chapter 30

Open CTI

Open CTI helps advanced administrators and developers build and integrate third-party computer-telephony integration (CTI) systems with Salesforce so that Salesforce users can use a SoftPhone without installing CTI adapters on their machines.

Salesforce CRM Call Center seamlessly integrates Salesforce with third-party computer-telephony integration (CTI) systems. Before the introduction of Open CTI, Salesforce users could only use the features of a CTI system after they installed a CTI adapter program on their machines. Yet such programs often included desktop software that required maintenance and didn't offer the benefits of cloud architecture. Open CTI lets developers:

- Build CTI systems that integrate with Salesforce without the use of CTI adapters.
- Create customizable SoftPhones (call-control tools) that function as fully integrated parts of Salesforce and the Salesforce console.
- Provide users with CTI systems that are browser and platform agnostic, for example, CTI for Microsoft® Internet Explorer®, Mozilla® Firefox®, Apple® Safari®, or Google Chrome™ on Mac, Linux, or Windows machines.

Open CTI is a browser-based JavaScript API. It uses browsers as clients to display SoftPhones. It matches the API version for any given release. For example, if the current version of SOAP API is 28.0, then there's also a version 28.0 of Open CTI.

This guide provides a high-level overview on how to use Open CTI and the available API methods. For more information, see the *Open CTI Developer's Guide*.

Supported Browsers

Open CTI supports the following minimum browser requirements:

- Mozilla® Firefox® 3.6
- Google Chrome™ 7
- Microsoft® Internet Explorer® 8
- Apple® Safari® 4

Supported Salesforce Editions

Open CTI is available with these Salesforce Editions:

- Developer Edition
- Professional Edition
- Enterprise Edition
- Unlimited Edition
- Performance Edition

If you're an existing Salesforce customer and want to upgrade to any of these editions, contact your account representative.

Quick Start

Get started with the Open CTI by first connecting to Open CTI using JavaScript.

Follow these steps to get started.

1. Connect to the toolkit.
2. Make asynchronous calls with Open CTI.
3. Use Force.com Canvas to integrate the Salesforce Console with external applications that require authentication methods.

Use the Open CTI to do the following in Salesforce:

- Set the height or width of a SoftPhone
- Enable or disable click-to-dial
- Return a call center definition file's settings
- Determine if a user is in the Salesforce console
- Show or hide a SoftPhone in the Salesforce console
- Return information about a page
- Execute an Apex method from an Apex class that's exposed in Salesforce
- Save or update an object in Salesforce
- Search keywords in Salesforce and screen pop any matching records as defined in a SoftPhone layout

Connecting to Open CTI

The first portion of any JavaScript code that uses the Open CTI must make the toolkit available to the JavaScript code. The syntax for this is different depending on whether you are embedding JavaScript in a Visualforce page, or a third-party domain.

- For Visualforce pages or any source other than a custom `onclick` JavaScript button, specify a `<script>` tag that points to the Open CTI file:

```
<apex:page>
            <script src="/support/api/29.0/interaction.js"
type="text/javascript"></script>
      ...
</apex:page>
```

For Visualforce, a relative path is sufficient to include `integration.js`, and is recommended.

- For a third-party domain:

```
<script
src="https://c.na1.visual.force.com/support/api/29.0/interaction.js"
  type="text/javascript"></script>
```

For third-party domains, it is necessary to specify an absolute URL to `interaction.js` to use the toolkit. The default instance at which you can access the toolkit library is: `https://c.na1.visual.force.com/support/api/29.0/interaction.js`. We recommend that you use the default instance when the organization's instance cannot be determined.

The version of Open CTI is in the URL.

Asynchronous Calls with Open CTI

Open CTI lets you issue asynchronous calls. Asynchronous calls allow the client-side process to continue instead of waiting for a callback from the server. To issue an asynchronous call, you must include an additional parameter with the API call, referred to as a callback function. Once the result is ready, the server invokes the callback method with the result.

Asynchronous syntax:

```
method('arg1','arg2', ..., callback_method);
```

For example:

```
//Set SoftPhone height
    sforce.interaction.cti.setSoftphoneHeight(300, callback);
```

 Note: The call result depends on the execution context. For example, calling `setSoftphoneWidth()` in the standard Salesforce application has no effect, but calling `setSoftphoneWidth()` in the Salesforce console resizes the width of the SoftPhone.

Working with Force.com Canvas

To integrate Open CTI with external applications that require authentication methods, such as signed requests or OAuth 2.0 protocols, Salesforce.com recommends you use Force.com Canvas.

Force.com Canvas and Open CTI are similar—they're a set of tools and JavaScript APIs that developers can use to add third-party systems to Salesforce. However, one of the benefits of Force.com Canvas, is the ability to choose authentication methods. For more information, see the *Force.com Canvas Developer's Guide*.

 Note: For a canvas app to appear in a Salesforce console, you must add it to the console as a custom console component. See "Adding Custom Console Components" in the Salesforce Help.

When developing a canvas app, and you want to include functionality from Open CTI, do the following:

1. Include the Open CTI API in `index.jsp`.
2. Call `Sfdc.canvas.client.signedrequest()` to store the signed request needed by the console integration toolkit API. For example, if the Force.com Canvas method of authentication is a signed request, do the following:

   ```
   Sfdc.canvas.client.signedrequest('<%=signedRequest%>')
   ```

   If the Force.com Canvas method of authentication is OAuth, do the following in the callback function used to get the context as shown in "Getting Context in Your Canvas App" in the *Force.com Canvas Developer's Guide*:

   ```
   Sfdc.canvas.client.signedrequest(msg)
   ```

Consider the following when working with Open CTI and canvas apps:

- The Open CTI API script depends on the signed request and should be added after the call to `Sfdc.canvas.client.signedrequest()` has executed. We recommend that you load the scripts dynamically.
- To retrieve the entity ID of the record that is associated with the canvas sidebar component, do the following:

```
// Get signedRequest
var signedRequest = Sfdc.canvas.client.signedrequest();
var parsedRequest = JSON.parse(signedRequest);
// get the entity Id that is associated with this canvas sidebar
component.
var entityId =
parsedRequest.context.environment.parameters.entityId;
```

- To retrieve the `entityId` for OAuth, do the following:

```
var entityId = msg.payload.environment.parameters.entityId;
```

To see an example on how to retrieve `msg.payload`, see "Getting Context in Your Canvas App" in the *Force.com Canvas Developer's Guide*.

Best Practices

- Since many of the methods in Open CTI are asynchronous and return their results using a callback method, Salesforce.com recommends that you refer to the documentation for each method to understand the information for each response.
- Errors generated by Open CTI are typically emitted in a way that doesn't halt JavaScript processing. Therefore, Salesforce.com recommends you use a tool such as Firebug for Firefox to monitor the JavaScript console and to help you debug your code.
- For information on customizing, extending, or integrating the sidebars of the Salesforce console using Visualforce, see "Custom Console Components Overview" in the Salesforce online help.

Call Center Definition Files

A call center definition file specifies a set of fields and values that are used to define a call center in Salesforce for a particular SoftPhone. Salesforce uses call center definition files in order to support the integration of Salesforce CRM Call Center with multiple CTI system vendors.

A call center in Salesforce CRM Call Center must have a call center definition file that works specifically with a SoftPhone. If you build a custom SoftPhone with Open CTI, you must write a call center definition file to support it. The first instance of a call center for a particular

SoftPhone must be defined by importing the adapter's call center definition file into Salesforce. Subsequent call centers can be created by cloning the original call center that was created with the import.

If your organization modifies a SoftPhone or builds a new one, you must customize the SoftPhone's call center definition file so that it includes any additional call center information that is required. For example, if you are building a SoftPhone for a system that supports a backup server, your call center definition file should include fields for the backup server's IP address and port number. SoftPhones for systems that do not make use of a backup server do not need those fields in their associated call center definition files.

Use a text or XML editor to define a call center definition file according to the guidelines in the following topics.

Note: For more information on setting up Salesforce CRM Call Center or importing and cloning call definition files, see "Setting Up Salesforce CRM Call Center" and "Creating a Call Center" in the Salesforce online help.

Call Center Definition File XML Format

A call center definition file consists of three XML elements: `callCenter`, `section`, and `item`. The following list provides details about the properties and attributes of each element:

callCenter

This element represents a definition for a single call center phone system. At least one `<callCenter>` element must be included in every call center definition file. A `<callCenter>` element consists of one or more `<section>` elements.

section

This element represents a grouping of related data fields, such as server information or dialing prefixes. When a call center is edited in Salesforce, fields are organized by the section to which they are assigned. A `<section>` element belongs to a single `<callCenter>` element, and consists of one or more `<item>` elements.

Attributes:

Name	Type	Required?	Description
sortOrder	Positive Integer	Required	The order in which the section should appear when the call center is edited in Salesforce. For example, a section with

Name	Type	Required?	Description
			`sortOrder="1"` comes just before a section with `sortOrder="2"`.
			The values for `sortOrder` must be non-negative integers, and no numbers can be skipped within a single call center definition. For example, if there are three section elements in a call center definition file, one `<section>` element must have `sortOrder="0"`, one `<section>` element must have `sortOrder="1"`, and one `<section>` element must have `sortOrder="2"`.
`name`	String	Required	The internal name of the section as defined in the Salesforce database. You can use this value to refer to the section when writing custom adapter or SoftPhone code.
			Names must be composed of only alphanumeric characters with no white space or other punctuation. They are limited to 40 characters each.
			Names beginning with `req` are reserved for required Salesforce sections only (see "Required Call Center Elements and Attributes" in the Salesforce Help). Other reserved words that cannot be used for the `name` attribute include `label`, `sortOrder`, `internalNameLabel`, and `displayNameLabel`.
`label`	String	Optional	The name of the section when viewed in Salesforce. Labels can be composed of any string of UTF-8 characters. They are limited to 1000 characters each.

467

item

This element represents a single field in a call center definition, such as the IP address of a primary server or the dialing prefix for international calls. When call centers are edited in Salesforce, each `<item>` element is listed under the section to which it belongs. You can have multiple `<item>` elements in a `<section>` element.

Attributes:

Name	Type	Required?	Description
sortOrder	Positive Integer	Required	The order in which the item should appear when the call center is edited in Salesforce. For example, an item with `sortOrder="1"` comes just before an item with `sortOrder="2"`. The values for `sortOrder` must be non-negative integers, and no numbers can be skipped within a single call center definition. For example, if there are three item elements in a call center definition file, one `<item>` element must have `sortOrder="0"`, one `<item>` element must have `sortOrder="1"`, and one `<item>` element must have `sortOrder="2"`.
name	String	Required	The internal name of the item as defined in the Salesforce database. You can use this value to refer to the item when writing custom adapter or SoftPhone code. Names must be composed of only alphanumeric characters with no white space or other punctuation. They are limited to 40 characters each. Names beginning with `req` are reserved for required Salesforce sections only (see "Required Call Center Elements and Attributes" in the Salesforce Help). Other reserved words that cannot be used for the name attribute include `label`, `sortOrder`,

Name	Type	Required?	Description
			`internalNameLabel`, and `displayNameLabel`.
`label`	String	Optional	The name of the item when viewed in Salesforce. Labels can be composed of any string of UTF-8 characters. They are limited to 1,000 characters each.

Required Call Center Elements and Attributes

There must be one `<section>` that includes `<item>` elements with the following names in every call definition file:

`<item>` Name	Description
`reqInternalName`	Represents the unique identifier for the call center in the database. It must have a `sortOrder` value of 0, and its value must be specified in the call center definition. A value for `reqInternalName` must be composed of no more than 40 alphanumeric characters with no white space or other punctuation. It must start with an alphabetic character and must be unique from the `reqInternalName` of all other call centers defined in your organization.
`reqDisplayName`	Represents the name of the call center as displayed in Salesforce. It must have a `sortOrder` value of 1. A value for `reqDisplayName` has a maximum length of 1,000 UTF-8 characters.
`reqAdapterUrl`	Represents the location of where the CTI adapter or SoftPhone is hosted. For example, `http://localhost:11000`. Note that relative URLs are allowed for Visualforce pages, for example, : `/apex/softphone`. Also, if you add Force.com Canvas applications to Open CTI, those apps can trump `reqAdapterUrl` when specified.
`reqUseApi`	Represents that the call center is using Open CTI (`true`) or not (`false`).
`reqSoftphoneHeight`	Represents the height of the SoftPhone in pixels as displayed in Salesforce.

`<item>` Name	Description
`reqSoftphoneWidth`	Represents the width of the SoftPhone in pixels as displayed in Salesforce.
`reqCanvasNamespace`	Represents the namespace associated with any Force.com Canvas applications added to your call center. Required if you add canvas apps to Open CTI.
`reqCanvasApiName`	Represents the API name associated with any Force.com Canvas applications added to your call center. Required if you add canvas apps to Open CTI.

You can add additional `<item>` elements to this section if needed.

Optional Call Center Elements and Attributes

In addition to the required elements for a call definition file, you can add optional elements to configure a SoftPhone.

`<item>` Name	Description
reqStandbyUrl	Represents the location that hosts the secondary SoftPhone. The standby SoftPhone is used after the timeout period for the primary SoftPhone has elapsed and the `notifyInitializationComplete()` method hasn't been called within the required timeout period. When you specify a standby URL, you must also specify the `reqTimeout` field.
reqTimeout	Represents the time in milliseconds after which the standby URL is used to host the SoftPhone. Before the timeout period has elapsed, the SoftPhone displays a loading icon indicating that the SoftPhone is initializing. When you specify a required timeout, you must also specify the `reqStandbyUrl` field.
reqSoftphoneWidth	Represents the width of the SoftPhone in pixels as displayed in Salesforce.

Sample Call Center Definition File

The following XML code makes up a sample call center definition file:

```xml
<!--
    All sections and items whose name value begins with "req" are
    required in a valid call center definition file. The sortOrder
    and label attributes can be changed for all required sections
    and items except reqGeneralInfo, reqInternalName, and
    reqDisplayName, in which only the label attribute can be altered.


  Note that the value for the reqInternalName item is limited to
    40 alphanumeric characters and must start with an alphabetic
    character. reqInternalName must be unique for all call centers
    that you define.
-->
<callCenter>
   <section sortOrder="0" name="reqGeneralInfo" label="General
Information">
     <item sortOrder="0" name="reqInternalName"
label="InternalNameAAA">DemoAdapter</item>
     <item sortOrder="1" name="reqDisplayName" label="Display
Name">Demo Call Center Adapter</item>
     <item sortOrder="2" name="reqAdapterUrl" label="CTI Adapter
URL">https://c.force.com/softphone</item>
     <item sortOrder="3" name="reqUseApi" label="Use CTI
API">true</item>
     <item sortOrder="4" name="reqSoftphoneHeight" label="Softphone
Height">300</item>
     <item sortOrder="5" name="reqSoftphoneWidth" label="Softphone
Width">500</item>
     <item sortOrder="6" name="reqCanvasNamespace" label="Canvas
Namespace">mm</item>
     <item sortOrder="7" name="reqCanvasApiName" label="Canvas API
Name">Hello_World</item>
   </section>
   <section sortOrder="1" name="reqDialingOptions" label="Dialing
Options">
     <item sortOrder="0" name="reqOutsidePrefix" label="Outside
Prefix">9</item>
     <item sortOrder="1" name="reqLongDistPrefix" label="Long Distance
 Prefix">1</item>
     <item sortOrder="2" name="reqInternationalPrefix"
label="International Prefix">01</item>
   </section>
</callCenter>
```

Methods

Use these methods to customize your CTI experience in Salesforce.

This guide provides an overview of the methods available with Open CTI. See the *Open CTI Developer's Guide* for more information on the calls and responses.

Methods are available for:

- Salesforce Application Interaction
- Computer-Telephony Integration (CTI)

Methods for Salesforce Application Interaction

Open CTI lets your CTI system interact with the Salesforce application.

You can use the following methods to set interactions between a CTI system and Salesforce, or between elements on a Case Feed page:

CTI Methods	
Method	**Description**
getPageInfo()	Returns information about the current page as a JSON string.
isInConsole()	Indicates if the SoftPhone is in the Salesforce console. For more information, see "Salesforce Console Overview" in the Salesforce online help.
isVisible()	Returns true if the SoftPhone is visible or false if the SoftPhone is hidden.
notifyInitializationComplete()	Notifies Salesforce that the SoftPhone initialization is complete and that Salesforce should not switch to a standby URL. While the SoftPhone initializes, a loading icon displays in the SoftPhone area.
onFocus()	Registers a function to call when the browser focus changes. In the Salesforce console, the browser focus changes when a user navigates between primary tabs or the navigation tab.
refreshPage()	Returns true if page refresh is invoked, false otherwise. When this method is called within the Salesforce console, it refreshes the current active tab.
refreshRelatedList()	Returns true if the related list with the given listName is refreshed, false otherwise. When this method is called within the Salesforce console, only the related list with the given list name in the currently focused view will be refreshed.

CTI Methods	
runApex()	Executes an Apex method from an Apex class that's exposed in Salesforce.
saveLog()	Saves or updates an object in Salesforce.
screenPop()	Pops to a target URL, which must be relative.
searchAndGetScreenPopURL()	Searches objects specified in the SoftPhone layout for a given string. Returns search results and the relative URL to be screen popped. Note that this method does not perform an actual screen pop. This method respects screen pop settings defined in the SoftPhone layout. For more information, see "Designing a Custom SoftPhone Layout" in the Salesforce online help.
searchAndScreenPop()	Searches objects specified in the SoftPhone layout for a given string. Returns search results and screen pops any matching records. This method respects screen pop settings defined in the SoftPhone layout.
setVisible()	Shows or hides the SoftPhone in the Salesforce console. For more information, see "Salesforce Console Overview" in the Salesforce online help.
Case Feed Methods	
onObjectUpdate()	Registers a function to call when case fields, the case feed, or case-related list data has changed on a Case Feed page.
refreshObject()	Notifies the Case Feed page that case fields, the case feed, or case-related list data has changed, and forces an update of these on the page.

Methods for Computer-Telephony Integration (CTI)

Open CTI lets you integrate your CTI system with Salesforce. For more information about CTI, see "Call Center Overview" in the Salesforce online help.

Use the following methods to integrate a CTI system with Salesforce:

Method	Description
disableClickToDial()	Disables click-to-dial.

Method	Description
enableClickToDial()	Enables click-to-dial.
getCallCenterSettings()	Returns the call center settings in the call center definition file as a JSON string.
getSoftphoneLayout()	Returns the SoftPhone layout as a JSON string. For more information on SoftPhone layouts, see "Designing a Custom SoftPhone Layout" in the Salesforce online help.
onClickToDial()	Registers a function to call when a user clicks an enabled phone number.
setSoftphoneHeight()	Sets the SoftPhone height in pixels.
setSoftphoneWidth()	Sets the SoftPhone width in pixels for the Salesforce console. For more information, see "Salesforce Console Overview" in the Salesforce online help.

Resources

Search on the Salesforce Developer's Network at http://developer.salesforce.com/docs for the following resources on Open CTI.

- Open CTI Developer's Guide
- "Salesforce Open CTI Overview" in the Salesforce Help
- "SoftPhone Overview" in the Salesforce Help
- "Call Center Overview" in the Salesforce Help

Index

Notes

Notes

Notes